SOCIAL SKILLS IN THE CLASSROOM

SOCIAL SKILLS IN THE CLASSROOM

SECOND EDITION
REVISED AND EXPANDED

THOMAS M. STEPHENS

The Ohio State University
Columbus, Ohio

PAR Psychological Assessment Resources, Inc.
P. O. Box 998/Odessa, Florida 33556

Published in 1992 by Psychological Assessment Resources, Inc., Odessa, FL 33556 USA

Library of Congress Cataloging-in-Publication Data
Stephens, Thomas M.
      Social skills in the classroom / Thomas M. Stephens – 2nd ed.
           p.   cm.
      Includes index.
      ISBN 0-911907-04-1 (previously ISBN 0936-32604-2)
      1. Social skills –Study and teaching (Elementary).   2. Social interaction in
children.   3. Social values.   I. Title.
      HQ783.S69   1992
      372.83'044 – dc20   91-42494
                                                                                                             CIP

Published 1978. Second Edition 1992

Manufactured in the United States of America
96 95 94 93 92   1 2 3 4 5 6 7 8 9

ACKNOWLEDGMENTS

This book is dedicated to those many classroom teachers, school psychologists, counselors, and consultants who encouraged me to develop these social skills materials and to those children who made it possible.

The first edition of these materials was developed under my direction over the period from 1970 to 1977 by many graduate students who were employed on a number of projects of which I was the principal investigator.

Since the publication of the original materials in 1978 by Cedars Press, classroom teachers, counselors, and school psychologists who used them provided valuable suggestions to me. Many of these suggestions have resulted in changes in the current text.

I very much appreciate the able assistance and patience of Kathy Richards who typed this manuscript.

Thomas M. Stephens
College of Education
The Ohio State University
Columbus, Ohio
July 1991

TABLE OF CONTENTS

1

USER'S GUIDE

INTRODUCTION TO TEACHING CLASSROOM SOCIAL SKILLS

Children acquire social behaviors through learning. Often, however, their learning of social skills is haphazard as a result of experience. While experience can be a good teacher, it can also be cruel and nonsystematic, resulting in faulty learning. Thus, children learn maladaptive responses, have gaps in their social learning, and at times learn incorrect behaviors.

Children learn ways of behaving in different situations and with different people. Often they learn by imitating others—parents, peers, siblings, and teachers. It is also known that children learn to imitate vicariously through movies, television, and published stories. As new behaviors are tried, they are corrected by the environment, telling children which behaviors to continue and which ones to stop under certain conditions. Children who have failed to learn functional social behaviors appropriately often have not had opportunities to learn through imitation or have received insufficient or inappropriate encouragement.

This handbook contains suggestions for teaching social skills in ways that children are known to learn these behaviors in their natural environments. Suggested instruction includes providing models for them to imitate as well as correction following demonstration of the skills. Positive reinforcement is emphasized to encourage the continued use of appropriate social skills.

Teachers generally agree that the social behaviors they value and wish to develop in students are those which will help students learn academic skills and concepts. Results of a number of studies indicate that certain kinds of social behaviors, in particular those related to attending, persevering at tasks, volunteering answers, and communicating with teachers, are highly correlated with academic success. Critical skills, such as these, which are prerequisites for academic learning, should be as much a part of teaching as are the academic responses themselves.

These social skills can be approached as a separate curriculum to be inserted into daily or weekly teaching schedules, or they may be taught in isolation to meet the needs of individual students or groups of students in response to problem situations within the school. These materials are also appropriate for use by those who are consultants to teachers. After assisting teachers to identify needed social behaviors and/or target children, consultants can use these materials as suggestions for teaching these behaviors in classrooms. Regardless of the context or the persons who teach these skills, it is important to remember that teaching and maintaining social behaviors are ongoing processes. Maintenance of the behaviors will occur more often for those teachers who attend to appropriate behaviors and reinforce them when they are demonstrated.

Directive Teaching

Materials in this handbook were developed to be used within a Directive Teaching approach. *Directive Teaching* (Stephens, 1970, 1975, 1976) is skill training oriented within a diagnostic-prescriptive model of teaching. First, the behavior is defined and stated in observable terms, specifying both the movements which make up the behavior and the conditions under which the behavior is to occur. Second, the behavior is assessed, and the student's level of performance on a particular skill is determined. Third, teaching is designed to fit the student's needs as determined by assessment.

In *Directive Teaching*, social skills instruction may be of three types: social modeling, social reinforcement, and contingency management. The method of teaching to be used is chosen on the basis of assessment information. Progress is routinely evaluated, and teaching is changed to fit the student's level of performance. Figure 1 shows the Directive Teaching process.

Step 1. Define the Behaviors to Be Taught

The Social Skills List. These 136 social skills are grouped into four categories: behaviors related to the environment (ER), interpersonal behaviors (IP), self-related behaviors (SR), and task-related behaviors (TR). Within each major category is a series of subcategories and groups of sequentially ordered skills.

Skills were obtained from classroom observations, a review of relevant literature, and a content analysis of behavior rating instruments. A list of skills was submitted in questionnaire form to a group of special education and regular education teachers for consensual validation (Milburn, 1974). Responses of these 260 teachers revealed that they considered all of the skills to have some degree of importance for their own classes.

Teachers may find that some of the skills included here are not relevant for their classes, the age group of their students, or the cultural context within which they are teaching. These social skills are developed in such a way that teachers may freely use or not use a given group of skills, because, except for the sequencing within subcategories, the groups of skills can be treated as independent of each other. In addition, since the format of the assessment tasks and teaching strategies is easily learned, teachers may wish to apply these techniques to develop other social behaviors not included in this handbook.

If teachers choose to identify behaviors other than those shown in the Social Skills List, they should be certain to define the behaviors clearly and specifically. They should try to follow the style used in the skill list when developing additional social skills.

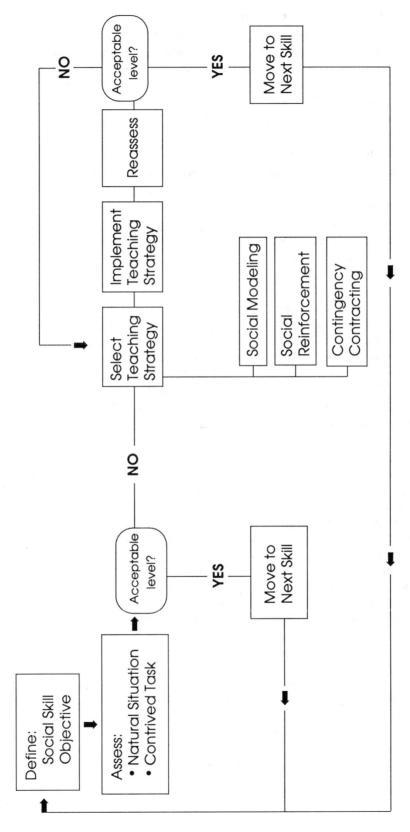

Figure 1. Flow chart of Social Skills Assessment and Teaching Procedures.

Step 2. Assess Target Behaviors

Target behaviors are best assessed through direct observations. The <u>Social Behavior Assessment Inventory</u> is designed for direct observations or as an interview schedule to be used with informed persons, such as, teachers, parents, siblings, and the target student. All 136 social skills are included in the inventory. Each behavior is rated on a scale from 0 to 3.

0   indicates the behavior was not observed or is not applicable for the student.

1   indicates the behavior was observed at an acceptable level.

2   indicates that the behavior was observed at a lower than acceptable level.

3   indicates that the behavior is not used by the student.

Information for using the <u>Social Behavior Assessment Inventory</u> is shown in the inventory manual.

From Assessment to Prescription. The rating scores provide direction to teachers and other users for selecting teaching strategies. Consider these procedures:

A rating of **0** indicates that the student has not been known to use that skill, or because of some barrier, e.g., handicapping condition, the behavior is not applicable for the student. If this particular behavior is needed by the student and if there is no barrier preventing the student from exhibiting the skill, the teacher may contrive a social situation that requires the student to exhibit the skill. The level of performance will determine the need for instruction.

A rating of **1** indicates that the student exhibits the skill at an acceptable level. Teachers need not spend time teaching this skill and may move to the next skill.

A rating of **2** indicates that the student exhibits the skill occasionally at a lower-than-acceptable level. The student has this behavior in his or her repertoire, but conditions in the environment do not provide sufficient incentives for the student to use these behaviors. It may also be that the student is getting some "payoff" for not engaging in desired behaviors and doing something undesirable instead. Reinforcement strategies—either Social Reinforcement or Contingency Contracting—are indicated for this student. Selection of reinforcement strategies should be made on the basis of the teacher's assessment of students' reward preferences. Do they respond to teacher praise and attention? Or, are these sufficient to increase the amount of desired behavior? If the latter is true, the teacher may need to use an explicit contract specifying behaviors and rewards, using tangible rewards if necessary.

A rating of **3** indicates that the student does not exhibit these skills. If it appears, on the basis of assessment through observation in the natural environment or on an assessment task, that the student never used the behaviors, it is safe to assume that the student may not know how. In this case, the teacher begins with a Social Modeling strategy to teach the behaviors. After the student exhibits behaviors in modeling and practice situations, the teacher needs to move to Social Reinforcement or Contingency Contracting strategies to maintain behaviors in the classroom environment as shown in Figure 2.

Step 3. Develop an Instructional Strategy

Each of the three kinds of instructional strategies follows a prescribed format that is intended to incorporate ideas developed through research in the area of behavior change. The strategies are written in programmed form, and the teacher is encouraged to use these strategies initially. Later, the teacher can develop strategies more appropriate for his or her own students. Some strategies are written for use with a group and some for individual target children. A teacher may adapt these strategies for use with one child, with a small group, or with a large class as the need arises.

Social Modeling Strategies. The format for social modeling strategies is designed to provide models for students to follow, with opportunities for them to make the responses themselves and to be reinforced for their efforts.

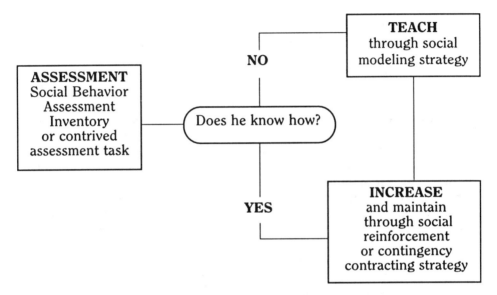

Figure 2. Select teaching strategy based on assessment.

1. The teacher sets the stage for modeling either through a discussion, a story, a film, or some other medium that will indicate to students the value of learning that skill. The teacher should encourage as much student discussion around the topic as possible. Behaviors should be related to events that are familiar to the students.
2. The teacher draws from the discussions specific steps which make up these behaviors and makes these steps explicit to the students, perhaps, when appropriate, outlining them on the chalkboard.
3. The teacher models the behaviors for the pupils. The teacher performs the behaviors and then has the students demonstrate, asking other students to observe and then to discuss their observations.
4. The teacher sets up situations in which each student has an opportunity to imitate the behaviors that were modeled and to practice them several times.

5. The teacher plans and implements reinforcement strategies so as to maintain the behaviors that pupils now have in their response repertoires.

6. For variations in the implementation of Social Modeling described in Steps 1 through 5, teachers should refer to the additional suggestions that are provided in each strategy.

At each step in the strategy, the teacher watches for appropriate responses and provides either reinforcement or corrective feedback, with an emphasis on *positive* responses for students' efforts. When students are first learning a behavior, it may not be performed perfectly. The teachers should reward efforts in the correct direction rather than only rewarding perfection. The teacher should also be alert for situations in which skills may need to be divided into smaller steps.

Social Reinforcement Strategies. Social reinforcement strategies stress utilizing various social reinforcers that teachers can readily use, including: looking at students, praising verbally, smiling, touching students, and attending to students in other ways. When using verbal praise, teachers are encouraged to use students' names, to tell students in specific terms why they are being praised and, when possible, to praise when other students can hear. In some instances, however, teacher praise is not rewarding when provided in the presence of students' peers. As with all reinforcement, it is necessary for teachers to identify those events that are rewarding to students and the conditions under which such events will be seen as rewarding. Strategies also include suggestions for providing cues and prompts to students by reinforcing other students or providing verbal, written, and other types of visual or auditory reminders. If cues, prompts, and social reinforcement do not bring about an increase in the desired behaviors, then teachers should consider accompanying social reinforcement with tokens, such as, points and stars to be exchanged later for something students value. This type of reward should be considered last, and teachers should then gradually decrease the use of tangible rewards while continuing social reinforcement for maintaining the behavior.

Contingency Management Strategies. Contingency management strategies are built around the idea of the contingency contract, e.g., if students perform desired behaviors, they will be rewarded according to specified terms. There are four steps in contingency management:

1. The teacher determines with students those behaviors that are desired, as in Step 2 of the Social Modeling Strategy. Ideally, this is carried out in a discussion with student participation.

2. The teacher, preferably together with students, identifies rewards for which students will work. Rewards can be almost anything that students value, ranging from activities to concrete objects, within the teacher's ability to provide. Teachers may also want to develop contracts in which rewards are delivered outside class or school by the building principal, parents, or other non-teaching personnel. An important consideration for rewards to be effective is that they must be available to students only as a result of performing desired behaviors.

3. The teacher sets up and makes explicit the terms of contracts, i.e., "When you do _____ you will receive _____." Contracts should

6

specify both the amount and quality of the behavior and the type and amount of the reward.

4. The teacher either watches for behaviors to occur naturally or sets up situations in which behaviors can occur. The teacher then rewards students for performing according to the terms of the contracts.

The following rules have been outlined by Homme et al. (1969) for carrying out contingency contracts:

- The payoff (reward) should be given immediately after performance of task.
- Initial contracts should require small amounts of behavior.
- Rewards should be frequent and in small amounts.
- Contracts should reward accomplishments rather than obedience.
- Performance should be rewarded *after* it occurs.
- Contracts must be fair.
- Terms must be clear.
- Contracts must be carried out honestly.
- Contracts must be positive.
- Contracting must be carried out systematically and consistently.

Step 4. Evaluate the Effectiveness of the Strategy

After carrying out teaching strategies, teachers need to evaluate the effectiveness of their teaching. Is the student who did not previously use the behavior now using the behavior some of the time? Is the student who exhibited the behavior only some of the time now using it at an acceptable level? If the answers to these questions are positive, teachers can believe that the interventions are appropriate. If the teacher is not satisfied with a student's level of performance, it may be necessary to make some instructional adjustments. Some of the following changes should be suggested to the teacher.

1. Change the instructional strategy.
2. Change the reward to a more powerful one, and make sure it is delivered immediately following desired behavior.
3. Examine the task to determine whether it should be broken down into smaller steps.
4. Determine if some prerequisite skills for performing the behavior are missing.
5. Look at the situation to see if rewards for inappropriate behaviors are occurring in the situation. Use extinction to eliminate competing rewards, or use punishment procedures to eliminate inappropriate behaviors. Punishment and extinction procedures should only be used, however, when appropriate behaviors are also being taught and reinforced.

TIPS FOR TEACHERS AND CONSULTANTS

Social skills instruction should be a regular part of a school program. At the lower grade levels, teachers may schedule "our psychology time." At the upper grade levels, the time may be designated as "personal improvement." Almost all people are interested in learning about their psychological selves. The teacher should begin such sessions by leading a group discussion about the students' concerns, interests, and so forth. The teacher should ask students such questions as:

What are some of the things that encourage you?

Why do we behave as we do?

Why are some people better liked than others?

What are some behaviors that you like to see in others?

What are some behaviors that irritate or annoy you?

Students sometimes are hesitant to role-play or rehearse behaviors. It is best not to insist that hesitant students perform. Instead; the teacher should begin with something they will do. For example, at first they may be observers while others perform, or they may be more comfortable playing a game, such as, "Charades." As the students become more involved, the teacher can often shift the focus from the limited responses typically required to more demanding roles.

Contingency Management

Contingency management has a substantial technical basis for its use. There are numerous professional books available on the subject. The following are some considerations when using contingency systems.

1. Contracting is useful after students have learned the behavior. If students rarely or never use the desired social behavior, the teacher should assume that they must be taught the behavior prior to contracting for its occurrence.

2. Tokens can be used to encourage the behaviors. Backup rewards should be available so students can purchase items or privileges with the tokens.

3. Rewards are events that increase the probability of the behavior occurring. Teachers should not expect all students to have the same reward preference. Nor should they expect individual students to always want the same rewards.

4. When possible, teachers should use rewards that are a natural part of the classroom or school environment. Such events as a special story time, shorter (or no) assignments, extra recess, special privileges, and educational games are closely related to school activities. When students view these as rewards, teachers should use them. Edibles, particularly sweets and other junk foods, should be avoided.

5. When tokens are first used, they should be issued frequently and in high quantity. As students become more responsive, the frequency of the tokens should be delayed, although the quantity may remain the same.

6. In situations where students take each other's tokens, teachers may need to use punch cards or a banking system. In a banking system,

tokens are credited to students, but the students do not actually possess the tokens. A public posting should show the amount credited to each student.

7. Teachers should arrange situations where target students may earn rewards for the entire class. Under such a system, the class is asked to identify a desired reward. If a target student also desires the reward, that student can be given an opportunity to earn the reward by using the desired social behavior when it is appropriate.

8. Social rewards are very powerful. Students appreciate being recognized for their efforts. Thoughtful teachers often provide social rewards through encouragement, special assistance, a kind remark or a good word or two.

Social Reinforcement

Thoughtful teachers provide social reinforcement as a natural part of their teaching. These may take the form of encouragement, special help, a kind remark, friendliness and various ways that show that students are supported in their efforts to learn.

Social rewards may be considered within five groups: positive proximity, positive physical expression, evaluation marks, recognition, and special privileges. Here are some suggestions for each.

Positive Proximity

Teacher eats with students.

Student has five minutes to discuss something with the teacher.

Teacher interacts with class at recess.

Principal serves as student's tutor.

Teacher sits near student.

Teacher sits within the students' group.

Teacher stands alongside the student.

Teacher combs student's hair.

Teacher dances with student.

Teacher gently raises student's chin.

Teacher shakes student's hand.

Teacher helps student with coat.

Teacher hugs student.

Teacher kisses student's hurt.

Teacher gently touches student.

Positive Physical Expression

Teacher says:

That is a good way to put it.

You are absolutely right!

I admire you when you _____.

I appreciate your attention.

I am glad you are here.

Splendid!

Terrific!

Thank you, _____.

That deserves my respect.

That was a wise choice.

That was very kind of you.

That's sweet of you.

Thinking!

You are doing just fine.

Teacher writes:

Beautiful work.

Bravo!

Brilliant!

Congratulations!

Cool!

Great!

Marvelous!

Fantastic!

For display.

Wow!

Evaluation Marks

A-1

Checkmarks

Stars

Happy face

Percentages

+

Letter grades

Rubber stamps with positive symbols

Recognition

Paper displayed on bulletin board.

Student's name in school (class) paper.

Student's name on board.

Student's name on honor roll.

Special Privileges

Special privileges permit students to engage in an activity and to use time in extraordinary ways. Any appropriate privilege may be used as rewards in either contingency management or social reinforcement. Here are some suggestions.

Choose seat for class.

Decorate desk.

Do homework in class.

Extra credit.

Extra recess.

Exempt a class exam.
Exempt an assignment.
Extra time for favorite subject.
Select a favorite book.
Borrow a book.
Lead discussion.
Have some privacy.
Write a letter.
Help another student.
Gardening.
Visit principal.
Visit another class.
Class snack break.
Dancing.
Table games.
Develop a mural.
Open discussion.
Choose an assignment.
Plan the day's schedule.
Present a skit or a play.
Puppet theater.
Outdoor lessons.
Field trips.
Extra visit to the library.

Social Modeling

Social modeling strategies are used to provide examples for students to follow. These may include vicarious modeling through the use of stories, or overt modeling, such as, role-playing or behavior rehearsing.

Vicarious modeling

Fictional and true accounts of desirable social behavior being rewarded can be used to teach social attitudes and behaviors. For young children and for others who do not read, stories can be read or told to them. Following are ten suggestions for teaching social behavior vicariously:

1. Discuss and post news items that portray people who engaged in socially desirable behavior. Select, in particular, those accounts that describe such behaviors being rewarded.
2. Show movies that display worthwhile social behavior.
3. Discuss scheduled television programs that you know depict desirable social behavior. Television magazines and news columns often describe programs in advance of their being shown. Encourage students to watch such programs and to discuss them the next day.
4. Call to students' attention books that depict behavior of a socially valuable nature.

5. Lead class discussions on topics of social importance. Encourage students to discuss ways that citizens can participate in such endeavors and what desirable consequences might occur.

6. Assign students to write short stories in which the characters perform worthwhile services for which they are rewarded.

7. Make socially acceptable behavior exciting to students. Point out how such behavior helps all people indirectly.

8. Take time to discuss with students, not lecture, socially beneficial events which occur or are scheduled to take place.

9. Use biographical accounts of noted individuals who contributed to the neighborhood's, the community's, the nation's or the world's well-being.

10. Lead students to recognize how mankind is dependent upon each of us to behave in socially responsible ways.

Overt modeling

It is important for students to observe models being rewarded for desirable behavior since social modeling occurs when students learn new behaviors by observing others. In this way, they learn those behaviors that have positive consequences.

Behaviors often consist of a string of responses that include both motor and verbal activities. Sometimes it is helpful to have one student verbalize responses, while another actually performs the behaviors.

Practicing social responses is another way to teach new behaviors. Behavior rehearsing is a technique where students are given instructions and sometimes models to imitate and are then assigned practice time to engage in the behavior.

Seven steps have been suggested for teachers to follow when implementing behavior rehearsing (Stephens, 1975):

1. Set up a sequence of responses for students to observe. It is important to make certain that the behaviors they will observe are the desired ones.

2. Instruct students in advance as to the responses to be noted by them.

3. Enact the behavior or have it performed by someone who will do it correctly.

4. Provide verbal descriptions for the behavior as it is occurring.

5. Reward those who are engaged in the activity as they are performing, making sure that the observers see or hear the reinforcement.

6. Have the student observers rehearse the activity while permitting the remaining students to provide verbal descriptions.

7. Repeat rehearsals as needed and have students engage in the actual behavior under authentic circumstances when possible.

Role-Playing. Students can learn social attitudes and behaviors by assuming roles that are not normally theirs. These are enacted in settings or with others not typically found in this situation. Role-playing has long been used in schools for teaching social values and decision making. Role-playing is often effective because it generates vivid, lifelike situations in a safe environment. It is important to role-play behaviors and attitudes that are desirable for students to learn.

Consultant Approaches

This book can be useful to consultants who are assisting teachers with classroom behavior problems. They can interview the classroom teacher as the informed person about a target student's behavior. The classroom teacher can be asked to complete the <u>Social Behavior Assessment Inventory</u>.

Materials in this book are organized in such a way that consultants can readily locate teaching strategies. When the behaviors to be improved are not among the 136 skills indexed here, many of these procedures and much of the content can be of assistance in identifying and improving other social skills.

Consider the following when assisting classroom teachers:

1. Ask the teacher to identify those students who are problematic in their behavior.
2. Ask the teacher to describe the problem behavior.
3. Ask the teacher to indicate the conditions under which the behavior is to be increased or, if undesirable, decreased.
4. Ask the teacher to rate (assess) the behavior as to its frequency and quality.
5. Create with the teacher a strategy to use in changing or improving the behavior.
6. Teach the behavior. Suggest to the teacher ways to continue to maintain or decrease the behavior.
7. Arrange a way for the teacher to report progress in that specific social behavior.
8. Plan a follow-up contact with the teacher.

Teachers who are not well prepared in behavioral application may use nonspecific and nondescriptive language in requesting help with students' behavior problems. Consultants should encourage teachers to be more specific and descriptive when discussing behavior problems by:

- Helping teachers to define or describe the problem behavior.
- Asking teachers to count the number of times the target student emits the inappropriate behavior.
- Asking teachers what the target student should be doing in place of the faulty behavior.
- Asking teachers to describe what the student does when a hypothetical construct is used to identify a problem, e.g., poor self-concept.
- Asking teachers to record for an entire day what the target student does that is inappropriate.

2

SOCIAL SKILLS

INDEXING AND CODING SYSTEM

Social Skills Categories and Subcategories

All social skills are listed in this handbook by four major categories with codes as follows:

ER: Environmental Behaviors
IP: Interpersonal Behaviors
SR: Self-Related Behaviors
TR: Task-Related Behaviors

Environmental Behaviors Subcategories

CE: Care for the Environment
DE: Dealing with Emergencies
LR: Lunchroom Behavior
MO: Movement around Environment

Interpersonal Behaviors Subcategories

AA: Accepting Authority
CC: Coping with Conflict
GA: Gaining Attention
GR: Greeting Others
HP: Helping Others
MC: Making Conversation
OP: Organized Play
PA: Positive Attitude toward Others
PL: Playing Informally
PR: Property: Own and Others'

Self-Related Behaviors Subcategories

AC: Accepting Consequences
EB: Ethical Behavior
EF: Expressing Feelings
PA: Positive Attitude towards Self
RB: Responsible Behavior
SC: Self-Care

Task-Related Behaviors Subcategories

AQ: Asking and Answering Questions
AT: Attending Behavior
CD: Classroom Discussion
CT: Completing Tasks
FD: Following Directions
GA: Group Activities
IW: Independent Work
OT: On-Task Behavior
PF: Performing before Others
QW: Quality of Work

Coding Systems

Each subcategory contains specific tasks to be used for teaching students' social behavior. A coding system is used to teach the skills, and each skill has been assigned a code number.

For example:

S-ER-DE-0004-L2-S

The above code is read as follows:

S: Indicates Social Skill. All codes in this handbook begin with the letter *S*.

ER: Refers to the major category. In this example the major category is **Environmental Behaviors**.

DE: Refers to the subcategory. In this example the subcategory is **Dealing with Emergencies**.

0004:   Refers to the skill number. In the example it is skill number 4 in the subcategory. Only even numbers are used to designate the skill number.

L2:   Refers to the level of skill. There are two levels: beginning (L1) and advanced (L2).

S: Indicates that a skill statement follows. The final letter or letters may be S, Im, Ir, or Ic, which have the following meanings:

    S: Skill statement

    Im: Instructional strategy: social modeling

    Ir: Instructional strategy: social reinforcement

    Ic: Instructional strategy: contingency management

Using the information above, you should practice reading these skill codes:

S-IP-GA-0010-L2-Im

S-SR-EB-0004-L1-Ic

S-TR-IW-0006-L2-Ir

SOCIAL SKILLS LIST

Environmental Behaviors (ER)

Care for the Environment (CE)

S-ER-CE-0002-L1-S	To dispose of trash in the proper container.
S-ER-CE-0004-L1-S	To drink properly from water fountain.
S-ER-CE-0006-L1-S	To clean up after breaking or spilling something.
S-ER-CE-0008-L2-S	To use classroom equipment and materials correctly.
S-ER-CE-0010-L2-S	To use playground equipment safely.

Dealing with Emergency

S-ER-DE-0002-L1-S	To follow rules for emergencies.
S-ER-DE-0004-L2-S	To identify accident or emergency situations which should be reported to the teacher.
S-ER-DE-0006-L2-S	To report accident or other emergency to teacher.

Lunchroom Behavior (LR)

S-ER-LR-0002-L1-S	To use eating utensils properly.
S-ER-LR-0004-L1-S	To handle and eat only one's own food.
S-ER-LR-0006-L1-S	To dispose of unwanted food properly.

Movement around Environment (MO)

S-ER-MO-0002-L1-S	To walk through the hall quietly at a reasonable pace.
S-ER-MO-0004-L1-S	To enter classroom and take seat without disturbing objects and other people.
S-ER-MO-0006-L1-S	To form and walk in a line.
S-ER-MO-0008-L1-S	To follow safety rules in crossing streets.

Interpersonal Behaviors (IP)

Accepting Authority (AA)

S-IP-AA-0002-L1-S	To comply with request of adult in position of authority.
S-IP-AA-0004-L1-S	To comply with request of peer in position of authority.
S-IP-AA-0006-L1-S	To know and follow classroom rules.
S-IP-AA-0008-L1-S	To follow classroom rules in the absence of the teacher.
S-IP-AA-0010-L2-S	To question rules which may be unjust.

Coping with Conflict (CC)

S-IP-CC-0002-L1-S	To respond to teasing or name-calling by ignoring, changing the subject, or using some other constructive means.
S-IP-CC-0004-L1-S	To respond to physical assault by leaving the situation, calling for help, or using some other constructive means.
S-IP-CC-0006-L1-S	To walk away from peer when angry to avoid hitting.
S-IP-CC-0008-L1-S	To politely refuse the request of another.
S-IP-CC-0010-L2-S	To express anger with nonaggressive words rather than physical action or aggressive words.
S-IP-CC-0012-L2-S	To constructively handle criticism or punishment perceived as undeserved.

Gaining Attention (GA)

S-IP-GA-0002-L1-S	To gain teacher's attention in class by raising hand.
S-IP-GA-0004-L1-S	To wait quietly for recognition before speaking out in class.
S-IP-GA-0006-L1-S	To use "please" and "thank you" when making requests of others.
S-IP-GA-0008-L2-S	To approach teacher and ask appropriately for help, explanation, instructions, etc.
S-IP-GA-0010-L2-S	To gain attention from peers in appropriate ways.
S-IP-GA-0012-L2-S	To ask a peer for help.

Greeting Others (GR)

S-IP-GR-0002-L1-S	To look others in the eye when greeting them.
S-IP-GR-0004-L1-S	To state one's name when asked.
S-IP-GR-0006-L1-S	To smile when encountering a friend or acquaintance.
S-IP-GR-0008-L1-S	To greet adults and peers by name.
S-IP-GR-0010-L1-S	To respond to an introduction by shaking hands and saying "how-do-you-do?"
S-IP-GR-0012-L2-S	To introduce oneself to another person.
S-IP-GR-0014-L2-S	To introduce two people to each other.

Helping Others (HP)

S-IP-HP-0002-L1-S	To help teacher when asked.
S-IP-HP-0004-L1-S	To help peer when asked.
S-IP-HP-0006-L1-S	To give simple directions to a peer.
S-IP-HP-0008-L2-S	To offer help to teacher.
S-IP-HP-0010-L2-S	To offer help to classmate.
S-IP-HP-0012-L2-S	To come to defense of peer in trouble.
S-IP-HP-0014-L2-S	To express sympathy to peer about problems or difficulties.

Making Conversation (MC)

S-IP-MC-0002-L1-S	To pay attention in a conversation to the person speaking.
S-IP-MC-0004-L1-S	To talk to others in a tone of voice appropriate to the situation.
S-IP-MC-0006-L1-S	To wait for pauses in a conversation before speaking.
S-IP-MC-0008-L1-S	To make relevant remarks in a conversation with peers.
S-IP-MC-0010-L1-S	To make relevant remarks in a conversation with adults.
S-IP-MC-0012-L2-S	To ignore interruptions of others in a conversation.
S-IP-MC-0014-L2-S	To initiate conversation with peers in an informal situation.
S-IP-MC-0016-L2-S	To initiate conversation with adults in an informal situation.

Organized Play (OP)

S-IP-OP-0002-L1-S	To follow rules when playing a game.
S-IP-OP-0004-L1-S	To wait for one's turn when playing a game.
S-IP-OP-0006-L1-S	To display effort to the best of one's ability in a competitive game.
S-IP-OP-0008-L2-S	To accept defeat and congratulate the winner in a competitive game.

Positive Attitude toward Others (PA)

S-IP-PA-0002-L1-S	To make positive statements about qualities and accomplishments of others.
S-IP-PA-0004-L1-S	To compliment another person.
S-IP-PA-0006-L2-S	To display tolerance for persons with characteristics different from one's own.

Playing Informally (PL)

S-IP-PL-0002-L1-S	To ask another student to play on the playground.
S-IP-PL-0004-L1-S	To ask to be included in a playground activity in progress.
S-IP-PL-0006-L1-S	To share toys and equipment in a play situation.
S-IP-PL-0008-L1-S	To give in to reasonable wishes of the group in a play situation.
S-IP-PL-0010-L2-S	To suggest an activity for the group on the playground.

Property: Own and Others' (PR)

S-IP-PR-0002-L1-S	To distinguish one's own property from the property of others.
S-IP-PR-0004-L1-S	To lend possessions to others when asked.
S-IP-PR-0006-L2-S	To use and return others' property without damaging it.
S-IP-PR-0008-L2-S	To ask permission to use another's property.

Self-Related Behaviors (SR)

Accepting Consequences (AC)

S-SR-AC-0002-L1-S   To report to the teacher when one has spilled or broken something.

S-SR-AC-0004-L1-S   To apologize when actions have injured or infringed on another.

S-SR-AC-0006-L2-S   To accept deserved consequences of wrong-doing.

Ethical Behavior (EB)

S-SR-EB-0002-L1-S   To distinguish truth from untruth.

S-SR-EB-0004-L1-S   To answer truthfully when asked about possible wrong-doing.

S-SR-EB-0006-L2-S   To identify consequences of behavior involving wrong-doing.

S-SR-EB-0008-L2-S   To avoid doing something wrong when encouraged by a peer.

Expressing Feelings (EF)

S-SR-EF-0002-L2-S   To describe one's own feelings or moods verbally.

S-SR-EF-0004-L2-S   To recognize and label moods of others.

Positive Attitude toward Self (PA)

S-SR-PA-0002-L1-S   To say "thank you" when complimented or praised.

S-SR-PA-0004-L1-S   To be willing to have one's work displayed.

S-SR-PA-0006-L1-S   To make positive statements when asked about oneself.

S-SR-PA-0008-L2-S   To undertake a new task with a positive attitude.

Responsible Behavior (RB)

S-SR-RB-0002-L1-S   To be regular in school attendance.

S-SR-RB-0004-L1-S   To arrive at school on time.

S-SR-RB-0006-L1-S   To hang up one's clothes in required place.

S-SR-RB-0008-L1-S   To keep one's desk in order.

S-SR-RB-0010-L1-S   To take care of one's own possessions.

S-SR-RB-0012-L2-S   To carry messages for the teacher.

S-SR-RB-0014-L2-S   To bring required materials to school.

Self-Care (SC)

S-SR-SC-0002-L1-S   To use toilet facilities properly.

S-SR-SC-0004-L1-S   To put on clothing without assistance.

S-SR-SC-0006-L1-S   To keep face and hands clean.

Task-Related Behaviors (TR)

Asking and Answering Questions (AQ)

S-TR-AQ-0002-L1-S   To answer or attempt to answer a question when called on by teacher.

S-TR-AQ-0004-L1-S   To acknowledge when one does not know the answer to a question.

S-TR-AQ-0006-L1-S   To volunteer an answer to teacher's question.

S-TR-AQ-0008-L2-S   To ask a question appropriate to the information needed.

Attending Behavior (AT)

S-TR-AT-0002-L1-S   To look at the teacher when a lesson is being presented.

S-TR-AT-0004-L1-S   To watch an audiovisual presentation quietly.

S-TR-AT-0006-L1-S   To listen to someone speaking to the class.

Classroom Discussion (CD)

S-TR-CD-0002-L1-S   To use tone of voice in classroom discussion appropriate to the situation.

S-TR-CD-0004-L2-S   To make relevant remarks in a classroom discussion.

S-TR-CD-0006-L2-S   To participate in a classroom discussion initiated by teacher.

S-TR-CD-0008-L2-S   To bring things to class which are relevant to classroom discussion.

S-TR-CD-0010-L2-S   To express opinion in classroom discussion even when contrary to opinions of others.

S-TR-CD-0012-L2-S   To provide reasons for opinions expressed in group discussion.

Completing Tasks (CT)

S-TR-CT-0002-L1-S   To complete assigned academic work.

S-TR-CT-0004-L1-S   To complete assigned academic work within the required time.

S-TR-CT-0006-L2-S   To continue working on a difficult task until it is completed.

S-TR-CT-0008-L2-S   To complete and return homework assignments.

Following Directions (FD)

S-TR-FD-0002-L1-S   To follow teacher's verbal directions.

S-TR-FD-0004-L2-S   To follow written directions.

S-TR-FD-0006-L2-S   To follow directions in taking a test.

Group Activities (GA)

S-TR-GA-0002-L1-S   To share materials with others in a work situation.

S-TR-GA-0004-L2-S   To work cooperatively on a task with a partner.

S-TR-GA-0006-L2-S   To carry out plans or decisions formulated by the group.

| S-TR-GA-0008-L2-S | To accept ideas presented in a group task situation which are different from one's own. |
| S-TR-GA-0010-L2-S | To initiate and help carry out a group activity. |

Independent Work (IW)

S-TR-IW-0002-L1-S	To attempt to solve a problem with school work before asking for help.
S-TR-IW-0004-L2-S	To find productive use of time while waiting for teacher assistance.
S-TR-IW-0006-L2-S	To find acceptable ways of using free time when work is completed.

On-Task Behavior (OT)

S-TR-OT-0002-L1-S	To sit straight at desk when required by teacher.
S-TR-OT-0004-L1-S	To do seatwork assignment quietly.
S-TR-OT-0006-L1-S	To work steadily for the required length of time.
S-TR-OT-0008-L1-S	To ignore distractions from peers when doing seatwork assignment.
S-TR-OT-0010-L1-S	To discuss academic material with peers when appropriate.
S-TR-OT-0012-L1-S	To change from one activity to another when required by the teacher.

Performing before Others (PF)

S-TR-PF-0002-L1-S	To participate in a role-playing activity.
S-TR-PF-0004-L1-S	To read aloud in a small group.
S-TR-PF-0006-L1-S	To read aloud before a large group or the entire class.
S-TR-PF-0008-L2-S	To make a report before a small group.
S-TR-PF-0010-L2-S	To make a report before a large group or the entire class.

Quality of Work (QW)

S-TR-QW-0002-L1-S	To turn in neat papers.
S-TR-QW-0004-L2-S	To accept correction of school work.
S-TR-QW-0006-L2-S	To make use of teacher's corrections to improve work.
S-TR-QW-0008-L2-S	To go back over work to check for errors.

SOCIAL SKILLS AND TEACHING OBJECTIVES

Environmental Behaviors

Care for the Environment

Skills	Objectives
To dispose of trash in proper containers.	Student identifies what should be discarded, carries it to the proper receptacle, and deposits it.
To drink properly from water fountain.	Student drinks from water fountain by turning water on, bending over in front of fountain, and drinking without splashing water.
To clean up after breaking or spilling something.	Student picks up or mops up the remains of what he or she has broken or spilled, leaving the area in the same condition it was in before the incident.
To use equipment and materials correctly.	Student demonstrates correct use of classroom equipment and materials (e.g., books, audiovisual equipment, computers, furniture, etc.) by using them carefully and according to the rules or directions.
To use playground equipment safely.	Student demonstrates safe use of play ground equipment by using swings, slides, balls, bats, jump ropes, or any other available equipment in such a way as to not endanger the safety of self or others.

Dealing with Emergencies

Skills	Objectives
To follow rules for emergencies.	Student, when confronted with a fire drill or actual emergency, will follow the established rules for the situation.
To identify accident or emergency situations that should be reported to the teacher.	When presented with emergency situations, real or simulated, the student will be able to say which should be reported to the teacher.
To report accident or other emergency to the teacher.	Student reports accidents and emergencies to the teacher by stating (a) what happened, (b) where it happened, and (c) when it happened.

Lunchroom Behavior

Skills	Objectives
To use eating utensils properly.	When appropriate, student uses eating utensils properly.
To handle and eat only one's own food.	Student refrains from touching or taking other students' food unless it is offered.
To dispose of unwanted food properly.	Unwanted food will be left to one side of the plate until discarded.

Movement around Environment

Skills	Objectives
To walk through the hallway quietly at a reasonable pace.	Student walks through the hall at a moderate pace (not running or dawdling), quietly, and directly to destination.
To enter classroom and be seated without disturbing objects and other people.	Upon entering the classroom, the student moves around objects and people without disturbing them and goes to own seat and sits down.
To form and walk in a line.	When asked, the student will line up behind another student and walk in formation following the teacher or other leader.
To follow safety rules when crossing streets.	When necessary, the student crosses the street according to safety rules, e.g. observing traffic signals, looking both ways before crossing, and obeying school crossing guards or monitors.

Interpersonal Behaviors

Accepting Authority

Skills	Objectives
To comply with requests of adult in position of authority.	Student complies with requests of adults, such as teachers, aides, principal, lunchroom attendant, who are in positions of authority.
To comply with peer in position of authority.	Student complies with the requests of peers put in a position of authority, such as class monitors, school crossing monitors, hall monitors.
To know and follow classroom rules.	Student will demonstrate knowledge of defined classroom rules by complying with these rules during class.

To follow classroom rules in the absence of the teacher.

To question rules that may be unjust.

Student follows classroom rules when the teacher is not present.

When presented with a rule that may be unjust, the student will question the teacher about the rule in an appropriate way, e.g., asking the teacher politely to explain reasons for the rule.

Coping with Conflict

Skills

To respond to teasing or name calling by ignoring, changing the subject, or using some other constructive means.

To respond to physical assault by leaving the situation, calling for help, or using some other constructive means.

To walk away from peer when angry to avoid hitting.

To refuse the requests of another politely.

To express anger with nonaggressive words rather than physical action or aggressive words.

To constructively handle criticism or punishment perceived as undeserved.

Objectives

Student responds to teasing or name calling by ignoring, changing the subject, or using some other constructive means appropriate to the situation.

Student responds to physical assault by leaving the situation, calling for help, or using some other constructive means appropriate to the situation.

When angry with a peer, the student will walk away or use some other constructive means to avoid hitting.

Student, when refusing someone's request, does so politely, giving a reason for the refusal.

When angry, the student expresses the anger with nonaggressive words rather than physical action or aggressive words.

When the student perceives that he or she is being criticized or punished undeservedly, he or she will ask the teacher for an explanation.

Gaining Attention

Skills

To gain teacher's attention in class by raising hand.

To wait quietly for recognition before speaking out in class.

To use "please" and "thank you" when making requests.

Objectives

Student raises hand and waits to be called on when wishing to speak.

Student waits quietly for teacher to recognize him or her before speaking out in class.

Student appropriately uses the phrase "please" when requesting something and "thank you" when the request is answered.

Skills (cont.)

To approach teacher and ask appropriately for help, explanation, instructions.

To gain attention from peers in appropriate ways.

To ask a peer for help.

Greeting Others
Skills

To look others in the eye when greeting them.

To state one's name when asked.

To smile when encountering a friend or acquaintance.

To greet adults and peers by name.

To respond to an introduction by shaking hands and saying, "How do you do?"

To introduce oneself to another person.

To introduce people to each other.

Helping Others
Skills

To help teacher when asked.

To help a peer when asked.

To give simple directions to a peer.

To offer help to teacher.

Objectives (cont.)

Student approaches the teacher and asks appropriately for help, explanation, instructions at an appropriate time as defined by the teacher.

Student gains attention from a peer by saying the peer's name in a volume appropriate to the setting, and telling what is wanted.

Student will ask a peer for help when it is appropriate to the situation.

Objectives

Student looks others in the eye when greeting them.

Student states own name when asked.

Student smiles when meeting a friend or acquaintance.

Student greets adults and peers by name.

Student responds to an introduction by shaking hands and saying, "How do you do?"

Student, when required, will introduce himself or herself to another by saying, "Hello, my name is _____," or the equivalent.

When in a situation where the student is with one person, meets another, and the two don't know each other, the student introduces them to each other.

Objectives

When teacher asks the student to help, the student complies.

Student will help a peer when asked.

Student gives simple directions to a peer upon request.

Student offers to help the teacher with a specific task when given the opportunity.

Skills (cont.)

To offer help to a classmate when given the opportunity.

To come to the defense of a peer in trouble.

To express sympathy to peer about problems or difficulties.

Objectives (cont.)

Student offers help to a classmate

When someone is unfairly maligning or assaulting a peer, the student will come to the peer's defense.

Student will express sympathy to a peer about problems or troubles by making a statement, such as, "I'm sorry."

Making Conversation

Skills

To pay attention in a conversation to the person speaking.

To talk to others in a tone of voice appropriate to the situation.

To wait for pauses in a conversation before speaking.

To make relevant remarks in conversation with peers.

To make relevant remarks in conversation with adults.

To ignore interruptions by another in a conversation.

To initiate a conversation with peers in an informal situation.

To initiate conversation with adults in an informal situation.

Objectives

During a conversation, the student will look at the person speaking and demonstrate that he or she has listened by repeating or paraphrasing what the person has said.

Student speaks to others in a tone of voice (volume) appropriate to the situation, e.g., low when speaking to one or two others, louder when addressing a group, low in the classroom, and louder on the playground.

Student waits for pauses in a conversation before speaking.

Student makes relevant remarks in conversation with peers.

In a conversation with adults, student makes remarks that are relevant to the topic and appropriate for discussion with an adult.

When interrupted in conversation, the student will pause, say, "Excuse me," or some equivalent phrase, and continue talking.

Student initiates conversation with peers in an appropriate informal situation by approaching a peer and being the first one to speak in conversation.

Student initiates conversation with adults in an appropriate informal situation by approaching the adult and being the first one to speak.

Organized Play

Skills	Objectives
To follow rules when playing a game.	When playing an organized game, the student follows the rules of the game.
To wait one's turn when playing a game.	When playing an organized game, the student patiently waits his or her turn.
To display effort to the best of one's ability in a competitive game.	Student displays effort in a competitive game situation by paying attention to the action of the game and by taking as active a part in the game as possible.
To accept defeat and congratulate the winner in a competitive game.	Student, when defeated in a competitive game, congratulates the winner without grumbling or engaging in other negative behavior.

Positive Attitude toward Others

Skills	Objectives
To make positive statements about qualities and accomplishments of others.	Student makes positive statements about qualities and accomplishments of others.
To compliment another person.	Student compliments others, e.g., makes positive statements to them.
To display tolerance for persons with characteristics different from one's own.	Student will display tolerance for an individual with characteristics different from his or her own by accepting that person without derogatory comments or actions.

Playing Informally

Skills	Objectives
To ask another student to play on the playground.	Student asks other students to play on the playground or during free-play activities.
To ask to be included in a playground activity in progress.	Student asks to be included in a playground activity already in progress, e.g., a ball game, by approaching the other students and asking to play.
To share toys and equipment in a play situation.	Student will share toys and equipment with other students in a play situation by willingly allowing another student to use toys and equipment in conjunction with one or two other students.

To give in to reasonable wishes of the group in a play situation.

To ask permission to use another's property.

Student will accede to reasonable majority wishes of the group with regard to what they will play, by what rules, and when and where.

Student asks permission to use another's property by saying, "May I please borrow _____?," or the equivalent.

Property: Own and Others
Skills

To distinguish one's own property from the property of others.

To lend possessions to others when asked.

To use and return others' property without damaging it.

To accept deserved consequences of wrong-doing.

Objectives

When asked to whom something belongs, the student will distinguish someone else's property from his or her own.

When asked, the student lends own possessions to other students or refuses politely.

When student borrows something, it is returned to the owner without damaging it.

When student does something wrong, the student will accept the adverse consequences of that act without excessive complaining.

Self-Related Behaviors

Accepting Consequences
Skills

To report to the teacher when one has spilled or broken something.

To apologize when actions have injured or infringed on another.

To suggest an activity for the group on the playground.

Objectives

When student spills or breaks something, he or she reports the occurrence to the teacher, telling what happened and where.

Student apologizes when his or her actions have injured or infringed on another.

When with a group on the playground, the student suggests an activity for the group.

Ethical Behavior

Skills	Objectives
To distinguish truth from untruth.	Student will distinguish his or her own true statements from untrue statements when asked.
To answer accurately when asked about possible wrong-doing.	When student is asked about possible wrong-doing, he or she answers accurately.
To identify consequences of behavior involving wrong-doing.	Student identifies possible consequences of own or others' behavior involving wrong-doing.
To avoid doing something wrong when encouraged by a peer.	When a peer encourages the student to do something questionable, the student will avoid the wrong-doing.

Expressing Feelings

Skills	Objectives
To describe one's own feelings or moods verbally.	Student, when asked how he or she feels, can give an adequate verbal description of his or her feelings or moods.
To recognize and label moods of others.	When presented with someone showing obvious signs of emotion or "mood," the student provides a word or words to describe the emotion or mood.

Positive Attitude toward Self

Skills	Objectives
To say "thank you" when complimented or praised.	Student says "thank you" when complimented or praised.
To be willing to have one's work displayed.	When the teacher asks to display the student's work, the student agrees readily.
To make positive statements when asked about oneself.	Student makes positive statements about himself or herself.
To undertake a new task with a positive attitude.	When required, student begins a new task willingly without complaining or hesitating.

Responsible Behavior

Skills	Objectives
To be regular in school attendance.	Student attends school daily, unless ill.

Skills (cont.)

To arrive at school on time.

To hang up one's clothes in required place.

To keep one's desk in order.

To take care of one's own possessions.

To carry messages for the teacher.

To bring required materials to school.

Objectives (cont.)

Student arrives at school on time.

After entering the room, student removes outer clothes, hangs coat or jacket properly, and leaves boots and umbrella in designated place.

Student keeps own desk in order, i.e., books, and papers organized inside the desk and the top of the desk clear to work on.

Student takes care of own possessions—keeps own books, clothing, and other possessions in reasonably good condition, and does not regularly lose books, clothing and other possessions.

Student carries messages for the teacher when asked by taking message from teacher, delivering it to the appropriate person, and returning directly to the classroom.

Student brings to school required materials from home, e.g., books, paper, pens, pencils.

Self-Care

Skills

To use toilet facilities properly.

To put on clothing without assistance.

To keep face and hands clean.

Objectives

Student uses toilet facilities when necessary, neatly putting paper in bowl, and remembering to flush the toilet.

Student puts on outer clothing without assistance.

Student washes face and hands as needed.

Task-Related Behaviors

Asking and Answering Questions

Skills

To answer a questions when called on by teacher.

To acknowledge when one does not know the answer to a question.

Objectives

Student answers or attempts to answer questions when called on by teacher.

When asked a question to which the student does not know the answer, the student will reply that he or she doesn't know.

Skills (cont.)

To volunteer an answer to teacher's question.

To ask a question appropriate to the information needed.

Attending Behavior
Skills

To look at the teacher when a lesson is being presented.

To watch an audiovisual presentation quietly.

To listen to someone speaking to the class.

Classroom Discussion
Skills

To use tone of voice in classroom discussion appropriate to the situation.

To make relevant remarks in a classroom discussion.

To participate in a classroom discussion initiated by the teacher.

To bring things to class that are relevant to classroom discussion.

To express opinion in classroom discussion even when contrary to opinions of others.

Objectives (cont.)

Student volunteers the answer to the teacher's question in a way appropriate to the situation.

Student asks a question appropriate to the information needed by using appropriate interrogative (who, what, why how, when) and phrasing sentence so needed information is asked for.

Objectives

Student looks at the teacher when he or she is presenting a lesson.

Student watches an audiovisual presentation, sitting relatively still and not speaking aloud.

Student demonstrates that he or she has listened to the speaker by repeat ing what the person said.

Objectives

Student, when speaking to the class in a classroom discussion, speaks with an appropriate volume loud enough to be heard by everyone in the class, and soft enough so as not to disturb those in other classrooms.

In a classroom discussion, the student makes remarks relevant to the topic of conversation.

When a classroom discussion is initiated by the teacher, the student participates by listening to what is said, raising hand and waiting to be recognized, and making remarks or asking questions relevant to the topic.

Student brings things to class that are relevant to the class discussion.

Student expresses his or her opinions during a classroom discussion even when contrary to opinions of others.

To provide reasons for opinions expressed in class discussions.

Student, when asked, will give reasons for opinions he or she has expressed in class discussion.

Completing Tasks

Skills

Objectives

To complete assigned academic work.

When assigned an academic task at mastery level, the student works on it until it is completed.

To complete assigned academic work within the required time.

When assigned an academic task to complete in a reasonable time period, the student finishes on time.

To continue working on a difficult task until it is completed.

When assigned a difficult task (below the student's mastery level), the student will continue working until it is completed, asking for help when necessary.

To complete and return homework assignments.

When assigned homework, the student completes and returns the assignment at the required time.

Following Directions

Skills

Objectives

To follow teacher's verbal directions.

Student follows the teacher's verbal directions.

To follow written directions.

Student follows written directions.

To follow directions in taking a test.

Student follows directions in taking a test when the directions are given orally by the teacher or when the directions are written on the test sheet itself.

Group Activities

Skills

Objectives

To share materials with others in a work situation.

Student shares materials willingly with others in a work situation by letting other students use materials and by using materials conjointly with others.

To work cooperatively on a task with a partner.

When given a task to work on with someone, the student will cooperate with that partner by exhibiting some of the following behaviors: sharing materials, dividing responsibilities and completing assigned responsibility, exchanging opinions and information, and accommodating his or her view point to that of the partner.

To carry out plans or decisions formulated by the group.

When the group of which the student is a member makes a reasonable plan or decision, the student will take action to help carry out the plan or decision.

To initiate and help carry out a group activity.

The student, when in a group situation, suggests an activity for the group.

Independent Work

Skills

Objectives

To attempt to resolve a problem with school work before asking for help.

When given an academic assignment, the student will attempt to resolve problems with the assignment alone before asking for help.

To find productive use of time while waiting for teacher assistance.

Student finds something productive to do, such as continuing with school work, while waiting for the teacher's assistance.

To find acceptable ways of using free time when work is completed.

During a period of time when nothing is scheduled for the student, he or she will find acceptable ways to use the unscheduled time.

On-Task Behavior

Skills

Objectives

To sit straight at desk when required by teacher.

When required to do so by teacher, the student sits on chair at desk upright and facing front, with chair legs on the floor, and with feet in front of him or her.

To do a seatwork assignment quietly.

When given an assignment to complete, the student works without speaking aloud.

To work steadily for the required length of time.

The student, when given an assignment to work on, will work steadily for the length of time required by the teacher.

Skills (cont.)	Objectives (cont.)
To ignore distractions from peers when doing a seatwork assignment.	When presented with potentially distracting actions or verbalizations from peers while doing a seatwork assignment, the student will ignore the distractions by not responding and by continuing his or her work.
To discuss academic material peers when appropriate.	The student talks about academic with material to peers when appropriate, i.e., when directed to do so by teacher or when such a discussion would facilitate school work.
To change from one activity to another when required by the teacher.	When required by the teacher, the student changes from one activity to another promptly, without excessive hesitation or complaining.

Performing before Others

Skills	Objectives
To participate in a role-playing activity.	Student will participate in a role-playing activity by pretending he or she is the person whose role he or she is playing and acting as that person might act.
To read aloud in a small group.	When required, the student will willingly read aloud in a small group of three or four students, without signs of excessive nervousness or fear.
To read aloud before a large group or the entire class.	When required, the student willingly reads aloud in a large group (seven or more) or before the entire class, without signs of excessive nervousness or fear.
To make a report before a small group.	Student makes a report before a small group of three or four classmates, without signs of excessive nervousness or fear.
To make a report before a large group or the entire class.	Student makes a report before a large group (seven or more) or the entire class, without signs of excessive nervousness or fear.

Quality of Work

Skills	Objectives
To turn in neat papers.	Student's work is generally neat, papers are uncrumpled, papers have few stray marks, and writing is unsmudged.
To accept correction of school work.	When receiving correction of school work, student will respond with verbal affirmation when it is appropriate and/or will respond without signs of anger or dejection.
To make use of teacher's corrections to improve work.	When the student receives a corrected piece of work from the teacher, he or she will redo the work incorporating the teacher's corrections.
To go back over work to check for errors.	Student looks over his or her work to check for errors before he or she hands it in.

3

ENVIRONMENTAL BEHAVIORS

CARE FOR ENVIRONMENT

S-ER-CE-0002-L1-S	To dispose of trash in the proper container.
S-ER-CE-0004-L1-S	To drink properly from water fountain.
S-ER-CE-0006-L1-S	To clean up after breaking or spilling something.
S-ER-CE-0008-L2-S	To use classroom equipment and materials correctly.
S-ER-CE-0010-L2-S	To use playground equipment safely.

Skill:	To dispose of trash in the proper container.
	S-ER-CE-0002-L1
Objective:	Student identifies what should be discarded, carries it to the proper receptacle, and deposits it.
Assessment:	Assess from previous knowledge of student or through direct observation using the <u>Social Behavior Assessment Inventory</u>.

Code: S-ER-CE-0002-L1-Im

TEACHING STRATEGY

Objective: Student identifies what should be discarded, carries it to the proper receptacle, and deposits it.

Social Modeling

1. **Discuss with the class why trash should be thrown in waste cans.** The discussion could cover definitions of what is trash to be thrown away, what kinds of things might be saved to be used again, and what happens if people are careless with trash and litter the classroom, the playground, and the environment around the school. Learning this skill could be built into a unit on ecology and preservation of the environment. Films and stories might be used if they are available. You might want to have students make posters describing the effects of littering on the environment or gather commonly encountered items of trash to make into collages demonstrating items which should be thrown away.

2. **Identify specific behaviors to be modeled.** When there is litter on the floor, playground, or somewhere else around the school, pick it up and place it in the trash can.

3. **Model the behavior.** Go around the room and pick up pieces of trash, placing them in the wastebasket. As you do so, describe why you regard the item as something to be discarded. Identify other items that you would keep or dispose of in some other way; for example, something to be kept for recycling. Repeat the procedure on the playground and in the cafeteria. Ask students to describe what you did and why you disposed of various materials as you did. Praise students who give good quality responses.

4. **Provide opportunities for practice.** After an art project, ask students to put the trash in the wastebasket. Take students to the playground and have them identify and discard litter. Have students identify trash to be discarded in the lunchroom. Have a regular clean-up period every day when trash is picked up and discarded in the wastecan. Reinforce those students who follow the cleanup procedures.

5. **Maintain the behavior through reinforcement.**

Code: S-ER-CE-0002-L1-Ir

TEACHING STRATEGY

Objective: Student identifies what should be discarded, carries it to the proper receptacle, and deposits it.

Social Reinforcement

1. **Use social reinforcement when the student is observed discarding materials that are no longer of use into the waste container.** Be specific in praising the student. For example, "Jose, I appreciate the way you cleaned your desk after art and discarded the scraps in the wastebasket;" "Ruby, thank you for picking up those papers on the playground and putting them in the trash can."

2. **Cues may need to be provided for the target student by praising other students who are appropriately picking up and discarding trash.** The teacher may at first need to point out the specific items that should be discarded and then praise the student after he or she puts them in the trash can. Depending on the level of the student, he or she may need help in determining what is to be thrown away and what is to be kept. If the school is engaged in saving materials for recycling, additional discriminations will be required of the students.

Code: S-ER-CE-0002-L1-Ic

TEACHING STRATEGY

Objective: Student identifies what should be discarded, carries it to the proper receptacle, and deposits it.

Contingency Management

1. **Present the task to the student in specific terms.** When you no longer have use for something or when there is material on the floor or ground that is no longer usable, such as paper, broken crayons, broken pencils, lunch bags, candy wrappers, etc., carry it over and discard it in the waste container. Be clear about what items are to be discarded and where they are to go.

2. **Plan reinforcement.**

3. **State the contingency.** If when the student is through with something or when there is paper or other unusable material on the floor, the student picks it up and discards it in the waste container, he or she will receive the agreed-upon reward. Specify the type and amount of reinforcement.

4. **Watch for the behavior to occur naturally or set up a situation in which the student has an opportunity to perform the behavior.** For example, have an art project in which the floor gets littered naturally. Ask students to clean up. If the target student identifies waste material and discards it into the waste container, he or she receives an agreed-upon reward.

5. **Example.** Ms. Winston's second grade class ate lunch in the school cafeteria. The lunch workers and the principal had pointed out to Ms. Winston that her class left the floor around their table littered with bags, straws, and wrappers.

   Ms. Winston discussed the problem with the class. She explained that she wanted all students to pick up bags, straws, and other litter around the lunch table before leaving the table. Because several other classes had a similar problem, a contingency contract was established in which the class which had the cleanest floor and table won the award for the day. "Winning the award" meant that the winning class could be first in the cafeteria the following day and, thus, be the first to be served lunch and to be finished with lunch. If several classes were judged to be even in the way they cleaned up their areas, representatives of each class drew lots to determine which class would go first.

Skill:	To drink properly from the water fountain.
	S-ER-CE-0004-L1
Objective:	Student drinks from water fountain by turning water on, bending over in front of fountain, and drinking without splashing water.
Assessment:	Assess from previous knowledge of student or through direct observation using the Social Behavior Assessment Inventory.

Code: S-ER-CE-0004-L1-Im

TEACHING STRATEGY

Objective: Student drinks from water fountain by turning water on, bending over in front of fountain, and drinking without splashing water.

Social Modeling

1. **Identify a need for the behavior through a classroom discussion of elements of behavior.** For example, discuss proper use of school equipment and public property, what happens if the water fountain is not used properly and water is spilled on the floor, and consideration for others in the use of the water fountain. Write key words on board.

2. **Identify specific behaviors to be modeled.**
   (a) Drinking from the water fountain at appropriate times (as defined by existing rules).
   (b) Drinking by turning on the fountain.
   (c) Bending over in front of the fountain.
   (d) Drinking without spilling water out of the fountain.

3. **Model drinking from the fountain for the class.** Ask students to identify elements of the modeled behavior. Praise students who make good responses.

4. **Have class practice drinking from the fountain, with each student given an opportunity to drink.**

5. **Praise those students who drink properly from the fountain.**

6. **Maintain proper drinking through reinforcement.**

Code: S-ER-CE-0004-L1-Ir

TEACHING STRATEGY

Objective: Student drinks from water fountain by turning water on, bending over in front of fountain, and drinking without splashing water.

Social Reinforcement

1. **Praise target student when he is seen drinking properly from the water fountain at an appropriate time.** Call attention to specific actions: "Hal, you drank without spilling. Very good!"

2. **Provide cues for the target student(s) by praising others who drink properly from the water fountain.** Be sure to praise the target student immediately if he or she drinks properly following the cue.

3. **If social reinforcement in the form of praise, smiles, attention, etc., is not sufficient to increase the desired behavior, accompany social with tangible reinforcement, e.g., stars, chips, tokens, etc., to be exchanged for something the student wants.**

Code: S-ER-CE-0004-L1-Ic

TEACHING STRATEGY

Objective: Student drinks from water fountain by turning water on, bending over in front of fountain, and drinking without splashing water.

Contingency Management

1. **State the task in specific terms to the student.**
   (a) The student gets a drink of water at an appropriate time (defined by classroom rules).
   (b) The student turns the fountain on.
   (c) The student bends over in front of the fountain.
   (d) The student drinks without spilling.

2. **Define a consequence valued by the student which will be given following the demonstration of acceptable behavior of drinking from the water fountain.** (Plan reinforcement strategy selected from reinforcement menu.)

3. **State contingency.** If student drinks properly from the water fountain, at an appropriate time, he will be reinforced. Specify the amount of reinforcement.

4. **Give students opportunities to get drinks of water at appropriate times.** Observe use of water fountain and reinforce those who use it correctly.

5. **Example.** Angel often played around the water fountain, squirting the water from the fountain at other students. Mr. Barbel took Angel aside and demonstrated to her the proper way to drink from the water fountain. He told her that if she could drink from the fountain properly every time she got a drink of water that day, she could receive five minutes of extra recess time. He also warned her that if she continued to play with water around the drinking fountain, she would lose the privilege of using the drinking fountain. Mr. Barbel posted rules over the fountain. Mr. Barbel observed Angel each time she went to the fountain. She followed the rules each time and received the bonus time. Mr. Barbel continued to monitor her use of the water fountain, praising her for using it appropriately and reminding her, when necessary, of the aversive consequence.

Skill:	To clean up after breaking or spilling something. **S-ER-CE-0006-L1**
Objective:	Student picks up or mops up the remains of what he or she has broken or spilled, leaving the area in the same condition it was in before the incident.
Assessment:	Assess from previous knowledge of student or through direct observation using the Social Behavior Assessment Inventory.

Code: S-ER-CE-0006-L1-Im

TEACHING STRATEGY

Objective: Student picks up or mops up the remains of what he or she has broken or spilled, leaving the area in the same condition it was in before the incident.

Social Modeling

1. **Identify a need for the behavior through a classroom discussion.** Discuss cleanliness, consideration for others, responsibility, etc. Have students

contribute ideas to the discussion. To initiate discussion, you may want to ask questions, such as "What would you do if you dropped your milk carton on the floor?" "What would happen if you just left it there?" Write key words on the board.

2. **Identify specific behaviors to be modeled.** If you have spilled or broken something:

   (a) Pick up the pieces and throw them away.

   (b) Mop up the remaining litter.

   (c) Leave the area in the same condition it was in before the incident.

3. **Model the behavior for the class.** Simulate having broken or spilled something. You may use bits of crumpled papers or something else as props representing the litter you need to clean up. Model cleaning up the area. Ask students to identify elements of the modeled behavior. Praise students who make good responses.

4. **Have the group practice the behavior using the same props the teacher used.** Give each student the opportunity to clean up the "mess." Students may be asked to evaluate how well the others have performed the task.

5. **Praise those students who clean up completely.**

6. **Maintain cleaning-up behavior through reinforcement.**

Code: S-ER-CE-0006-L1-Ir

TEACHING STRATEGY

Objective: Student picks up or mops up the remains of what he or she has broken or spilled, leaving the area in the same condition it was in before the incident.

Social Reinforcement

1. **Identify and praise by name, aloud, target student when observed picking up or mopping up something he or she has broken or spilled.** Call attention to specific actions; for example, "Donald, thank you for cleaning up the milk you spilled." "Darrell, I'm so glad you cleaned up the floor. Everyone feels better in a clean room."

2. **Cue appropriate cleaning up in target student by praising others who clean up after they have broken or spilled something.**

Code: S-ER-CE-0006-L1-Ic

TEACHING STRATEGY

Objective: Student picks up or mops up the remains of what he or she has broken or spilled, leaving the area in the same condition it was in before the incident.

Contingency Management

1. **Explain the desired behavior to the student.** Tell him or her that after he or she has broken or spilled something, he or she is responsible for picking

up or mopping up the mess, leaving the area as clean as it was before. Show him or her where to get equipment for cleaning up, and, if necessary, show him or her how to go about doing the cleaning and where to put the debris.

2. **Plan reinforcement.**

3. **State contingency.** The contingency must be stated negatively with a negative consequence in order to avoid reinforcing spilling or breaking behavior. For example, "If, after you have spilled or broken something, you do not clean it up adequately, you will lose a privilege." Specify type and amount of aversive consequence.

4. **Observe the student in naturally occurring situations.** If after breaking or spilling something, he or she does not clean up adequately, deliver the aversive consequence.

5. **Example.** Sidney often drops or spills things. He then walks away without cleaning up. Ms. Cox informs him that he is required to clean up any mess he makes, either accidentally or on purpose. She shows him where the mop and pail are kept and where the trash can is located. She tells him that on days when he drops or spills things and does not clean up, he may be required to miss recess. She also works with him to help him avoid spilling and breaking things. She sets up a chart and gives him a star for every day he has not had an accident involving breaking or spilling.

Skill:	To use classroom equipment and materials correctly. **S-ER-CE-0008-L2**
Objective:	Student demonstrates correct use of classroom equipment and materials (e.g., books, audio-visual equipment, computers, furniture, etc.) by using them carefully and according to rules or directions.
Assessment:	Assess from previous knowledge of student or through direct observation using the <u>Social Behavior Assessment Inventory</u>.

Code: S-ER-CE-0008-L2-Im

TEACHING STRATEGY

Objective: Student demonstrates correct use of classroom equipment and materials (e.g., books, audio-visual equipment, computers, furniture, etc.) by using them carefully and according to rules or directions.

Social Modeling

1. **Teach this skill on an "as needed" basis as students are introduced to specific equipment and materials in the classroom.** For example, before giving students access to the tape recorder for free time or for carrying out an assignment, talk about the importance of using the equipment the way it was intended to be used. Elicit from students suggestions as to why we should be careful in our use of the equipment in question, and what might happen if students were not careful. Have students describe what would constitute careful and careless use of the equipment being discussed.

2. **Identify the specific behaviors involved in careful and correct use of the piece of equipment.** For example, for a tape recorder the behaviors might involve instructions about plugging the machine in, inserting the tape or cassette, choosing correct buttons to push to stop, start, and rewind the machine. Post a list of the rules or instructions close to where the machine is being used.

3. **Model the desired behavior.** Have students watch as you use the piece of equipment correctly. Have them verbalize the steps you went through to load the machine, start it, stop it, unwind it, etc. In the case of complex equipment, break the behaviors down to small steps and have students describe your behavior at each step and then, finally, add the steps together.

4. **Have students practice the behavior by operating the machine or piece of equipment under supervision.** A student who has mastered the careful use of the equipment might supervise other students. Make sure each student is given an opportunity to demonstrate correct use of a piece of equipment before using it without supervision. Praise students for correct responses.

5. **After students have learned correct use of equipment and materials, maintain the behavior through praise when they continue to handle the material carefully.**

Code: S-ER-CE-0008-L2-Ir

TEACHING STRATEGY

Objective: Student demonstrates correct use of classroom equipment and materials (e.g., books, audio-visual equipment, computers, furniture, etc.) by using them carefully and according to rules or directions.

Social Reinforcement

1. **Identify by name and praise aloud, target students when observed using a piece of classroom equipment and materials correctly.** Call attention to specific actions, e.g., "Alice, you are doing a careful job with the scissors," "Heather, thank you for keeping the textbook in such good condition," "Marion, you really are an expert at using that tape recorder."

2. **Cue appropriate behavior in target students by praising others who exhibit proper use of equipment and materials in the presence of target students.**

Code: S-ER-CE-0008-L2-Ic

TEACHING STRATEGY

Objective: Student demonstrates correct use of classroom equipment and materials (e.g., books, audio-visual equipment, computers, furniture, etc.) by using them carefully and according to rules or directions.

Contingency Management

1. **State task in observable terms.** The student should use a particular piece of classroom equipment or classroom materials carefully and according to the rules or directions specific to that equipment or those materials. Post a list of the rules or instructions particular to a piece of equipment prominently near the place where the equipment is stored or used.

2. **Plan reinforcement strategy selected from reinforcement menu.**

3. **State the contingency.** If the student uses a specified piece of equipment properly, he or she will be rewarded according to the agreed-upon terms.

4. **Set the situation to necessitate the student's use of the specified equipment (i.e., provide a lesson which requires the student to use the equipment, ask him or her to demonstrate its use to someone else, etc.).** Observe the student's use of the equipment and reward him or her if used carefully and according to the rules.

5. **Example.** Timothy, Colby, and Sara all have problems replacing the library books on the shelves. They usually leave the books out somewhere around the room. Ms. Jacobs tells them that they must put the books on the shelf in an upright position with the binding facing outward. She states the contingency that if, after reading hour that day, they put the books they used back on the shelf properly, they will each receive five points toward a gold star on their behavior charts (something known to be reinforcing to all three). After reading hour that day, Timothy and Sara brought their books back and shelved them properly, each receiving their five points. Colby left his books out and was not rewarded. The next day, all three replaced their books and received the reward.

Skill:	To use playground equipment safely. **S-ER-CE-0010-L2**
Objective:	Student demonstrates safe use of playground equipment by using swings, slide, balls, bats, jump ropes, or any other available equipment in such a way as to not endanger the safety of self or others.
Assessment:	Assess from previous knowledge of student or through direct observation using the <u>Social Behavior Assessment Inventory</u>.

Code: S-ER-CE-0010-L2-Im

TEACHING STRATEGY

Objective: Student demonstrates safe use of playground equipment by using swings, slide, balls, bats, jump ropes, or any other available equipment in such a way as to not endanger the safety of self or others.

Social Modeling

1. **Identify the need for the behavior through a classroom discussion.** Have students contribute ideas to the discussion of what is necessary to use various pieces of playground equipment safely. Have students identify

ways of using equipment that could result in someone's being injured. Have students draw pictures of students using various playground equipment safely.

2. **Identify specific behaviors to be modeled.**

   (a) Sitting on swing facing forward and swinging back and forth.

   (b) Sitting down on top of slide and sliding only when sliding board is clear of other students.

   (c) Using the tetherball without hitting oneself or other students.

   (d) Playing ball, being careful not to hit other students (except in games such as "dodgeball," requiring contact with the ball).

   (e) Swinging the bat, making sure not to swing in the vicinity of another student; dropping rather than throwing the bat when finished batting.

   (f) Jumping rope, being careful not to hit other students with the rope.

   (g) Other behavior as appropriate to the class.

3. **Conduct the lesson on the playground.** Model behavior for the class, i.e., demonstrate the safe way to swing. Ask students to identify what you are doing to make swinging safe. Praise students who make appropriate responses.

4. **Have class practice the behavior, with each student given an opportunity to use playground equipment safely.**

5. **Praise those students who use playground equipment safely.**

6. **Maintain safe use of playground equipment through reinforcement.**

Code: S-ER-CE-0010-L2-Ir

TEACHING STRATEGY

Objective: Student demonstrates safe use of playground equipment by using swings, slide, balls, bats, jump ropes, or any other available equipment in such a way as to not endanger the safety of self or others.

Social Reinforcement

1. **Identify and praise by name, out loud, target student when observed using equipment properly.** Call attention to students' specific actions, e.g., "Matt, you remembered to put the bat down safely when you finished batting;" "Did everyone see how José waited until Manuel got off the slide before going down?"

2. **Cue appropriate use of playground equipment in target student by praising others who are exhibiting proper use of playground equipment within hearing distance of the target child.** When target child does exhibit safe use of equipment, be sure to reinforce him or her also with praise.

3. **It may be necessary at first to accompany social reinforcement with some tangible reinforcement.**

TEACHING STRATEGY

Objective: Student demonstrates safe use of playground equipment by using swings, slide, balls, bats, jump ropes, or any other available equipment in such a way as to not endanger the safety of self or others.

Contingency Management

1. **State the task in observable terms.**

   (a) Student will sit on swing facing front and make sure other students are not in the way of the swing.

   (b) Student will come down slide sitting up and facing front after the slide is clear of other students.

   (c) The student will use tetherball so as not to hit other students or himself with the ball.

   (d) Student will use balls so as not to hit other students unless specified in the game (e.g., dodgeball).

   (e) Student will use bats to hit balls when at a safe distance from other students. After batting, the student will take care to avoid hitting others when dropping the bat.

   (f) Student will use jump ropes so as to avoid hitting other students.

   If necessary, post a list of appropriate use of other available playground equipment.

2. **Plan reinforcement strategy selected from reinforcement menu.**

3. **State contingency.** If student uses playground equipment safely he or she will be rewarded. Specify amount and types of reinforcement to student. If necessary, break the task down to one or two pieces of equipment that are of particular concern.

4. **Set situation for using playground equipment.** For example, take students to the playground and have students use each piece of equipment. Observe the use of the equipment by each student and reward those who follow it correctly.

5. **Example.** Marvin was continually trying to walk up the slide during recess. This had resulted in Marvin's falling off the slide or colliding with students going down the slide. The teacher decided to contract with Marvin. She told Marvin that if he went through the entire recess using the slide correctly, he would get 10 points to be used for 10 minutes of time doing something he enjoyed. To maintain correct use of the slide over a longer period of time, the teacher made a chart with a check for every recess in which Marvin used the slide correctly. After Marvin earned a certain number of checks, he was given a special privilege.

DEALING WITH EMERGENCIES

S-ER-DE-0002-L1-S	To follow rules for emergencies.
S-ER-DE-0004-L2-S	To identify accident or emergency situations which should be reported to the teacher.
S-ER-DE-0006-L2-S	To report accident or other emergency to teacher.

Skill:	To follow rules for emergencies, i.e., fire drills, disasters. **S-ER-DE-0002-L1**
Objective:	Student, when confronted with a fire drill or actual emergency, will follow the established rules for the situation.
Assessment:	Assess from previous knowledge of student or through direct observation using the <u>Social Behavior Assessment Inventory</u>.

Code: S-ER-DE-0002-L1-Im

TEACHING STRATEGY

Objective: Student, when confronted with a fire drill or actual emergency, will follow the established rules for the situation.

Social Modeling

1. **Meet with the class to discuss the need to follow rules during drills or emergencies.** Stress safety in dangerous situations. Have students contribute ideas to the conversation. Conversation may be stimulated with stories, pictures, films, etc., where available. You may want to have a poster contest and have students draw posters about safety rules in fires, tornadoes, floods, and other emergencies; or you may want to have students look for pictures in magazines and newspapers to use for posters.
2. **Identify the specific behaviors to be modeled.** "When there is a fire drill or emergency, follow the rules the teacher has stated for this situation." List the rules. Write them on a permanent chart and review them periodically.
3. **Model the behavior.** Stage a fire drill and have two or three students model by following the rules established for the situation. Ask other students to describe their actions.
4. **Have the class practice the behavior during several rehearsal drills.** Reinforce those students who follow the established rules during the drills.
5. **Maintain the behavior through reinforcement.**

Code: S-ER-DE-0002-L1-Ir

TEACHING STRATEGY

Objective: Student, when confronted with a fire drill or actual emergency, will follow the established rules for the situation.

Social Reinforcement

1. **When there is a fire drill or some other similar kind of rehearsal, or an actual emergency situation, identify and praise students who are observed following established rules.** (Depending on the situation, verbal praise may have to be given after the situation is over, with smiles and nods given during the drill.) Praise specific actions. "Molly, that was good quiet walking," "Deke, I liked the way you waited quietly on the playground until the bell rang to go in."

2. **Provide cues for the target student.**
   (a) Post rules for drills and emergencies in a prominent place in the classroom.
   (b) Praise a student near the target student who is following rules in an emergency situation.
   (c) Verbally remind students of the rules at the onset of a drill or emergency.

3. **If necessary, give tangible reinforcers, along with praise for following specific rules.**

Code: S-ER-DE-0002-L1-Ic

TEACHING STRATEGY

Objective: Student, when confronted with a fire drill or actual emergency, will follow the established rules for the situation.

Contingency Management

1. **State the task to the student in behavioral terms.** "When the fire drill bell rings (or whatever other emergency situation might arise), you will follow these specific rules." At this point, go over and explain clearly the rules for emergencies which have been established. Post these rules prominently.

2. **Plan reinforcement.**

3. **Explain the contingency to the student.** "When we have a drill or emergency, if you follow the rules I have stated for that situation, you will receive a reward." Specify the type and amount of reward.

4. **If there are no regularly scheduled fire drills at the time in the school, stage several yourself for the class.** Observe the student during these drills and reward him if he follows the rules established for the situation.

5. **Example.** During a fire drill, Nancy ran out of line and called out to her friends in other classes. There were several other students who had similar problems taking the fire drill seriously and following the rules. Mr. Fielding discussed with Nancy and the other students the rules which were established in the school for drills. The rules included walking through the halls in a line, not speaking during the drill, lining up on the playground, and waiting quietly until the bell rang to go in. He told the students that if they followed the rules during fire drills, they would be allowed to spend 20 minutes at free play on the afternoon of the drill. Mr. Fielding staged three fire drills in the next two weeks to give Nancy and the other students an opportunity to practice. He reminded them of the rules and the contingency before practicing the fire drill.

Skill:	To identify accident or emergency situations that should be reported to the teacher.
	S-ER-DE-0004-L2
Objective:	When presented with emergency situations, real or simulated, the student will be able to say which should be reported to the teacher.
Assessment:	Assess from previous knowledge of student or through direct observation using the <u>Social Behavior Assessment Inventory</u>.

Code: S-ER-DE-0004-L2-Im

TEACHING STRATEGY

Objective: When presented with emergency situations, real or simulated, the student will be able to say which should be reported to the teacher.

Social Modeling

1. **Identify a need for the behavior through a classroom discussion.** Explain to students what an emergency is, being sure to differentiate between serious events and minor situations that would involve "tattling." Elicit ideas from students about what kinds of events should be reported to the teacher or another adult and what kinds of happenings are not considered emergencies. Use stories or films where available. Have students paint pictures of different emergencies to watch for and report.

2. **Identify specific behaviors to be modeled.**
   (a) Report an injury.
   (b) Report dangerous events, such as, fires, deep open holes, broken glass.
   (c) Report sudden illness.
   (d) Report someone in danger, such as hanging on a limb, being taken in a car, crossing the street against the light.

3. **Model behavior for the class.** For instance, role-play reporting an injury on the playground involving a student who has fallen from the parallel bars and cannot move. Ask students to identify why this was a true emergency and identify elements of the modeled behavior. Also present scenarios that would and would not require reporting to the teacher (for example, minor incidents, such as, a child chasing another child, a broken window, etc.) and have students role-play ways to handle these situations.

4. **Have class practice the behavior by playing "Spin the Bottle," using slips of paper with true emergency situations which are not true emergencies.** Student must role-play how he would handle the situation he drew from the bottle. The rest of the class can discuss and evaluate whether it was an emergency and why.

5. **Praise students who make good responses in the social modeling situation.**

Code: S-ER-DE-0004-L2-Ir

TEACHING STRATEGY

Objective: When presented with emergency situations, real or simulated, the student will be able to say which should be reported to the teacher.

Social Reinforcement

1. **Praise students who report an accident or emergency which is appropriate to bring to the attention of the teacher.** Make the praise specific. "Jason, thank you for telling me Jasmine had cut her leg. That was a real emergency," "Nellie, I'm glad you and Mary worked out the problem yourselves when Johnny pushed you. That was not really an emergency."

2. **Cue the desired behavior in target students by praising others who report accidents or emergencies appropriately and who are able to make discriminations between minor events and real emergencies.** Use specific incidents which occur on the playground or the classroom to provide clarification about what is or is not an emergency. Students who have a tendency to "tattle" about minor events will need to be praised when they refrain from reporting unimportant incidents.

Code: S-ER-DE-0004-L2-Ic

TEACHING STRATEGY

Objective: When presented with emergency situations, real or simulated, the student will be able to say which should be reported to the teacher.

Contingency Management

1. **Specify to the students the kinds of situations you would regard as genuine emergencies you would want reported to you,** e.g., when someone appears to be hurt, when there is a fire, when there is a situation in which someone could be hurt, etc.

2. **Establish a contingency.** In the case of this skill, which relates to chance or infrequent occurrences, a positive contingency involving rewards for reporting accidents or emergencies actually may not be appropriate. Instead, the teacher may wish to emphasize the possible negative consequences from failing to report accidents or emergencies.

3. **A positive contingency contract might be established in relation to role-playing situations involving reporting accidents or emergencies.** "If you can tell which situations should be reported and which ones are not real emergencies, you will receive the agreed-upon reward."

50

Skill:	To report accident or other emergency to the teacher. **S-ER-DE-0006-L2**
Objective:	Student reports accidents and emergencies to the teacher by stating (a) what happened, (b) where it happened, and (c) when it happened.
Assessment:	Assess from previous knowledge of student or through direct observation using the <u>Social Behavior Assessment Inventory</u>.

Code: S-ER-DE-0006-L2-Im

TEACHING STRATEGY

Objective: Student reports accidents and emergencies to the teacher by stating (a) what happened, (b) where it happened, and (c) when it happened.

Social Modeling

1. **Identify a need for the behavior through a classroom discussion after observing a short puppet show involving an emergency.** For example, the scenario could relate to a baseball game in which one player is hit and struck unconscious by the ball. Have students decide what reporting procedure to follow and what to report; then allow students to finish the puppet show using their ideas.

2. **From ideas drawn out of the puppet show, identify specific behaviors to be modeled.**
   (a) Tell what happened.
   (b) Tell where is happened.
   (c) Tell when it happened.

3. **Model behavior for the class.** For example, set up another puppet show scenario involving telephoning the fire department to report a fire and demonstrate the providing of details. Ask students to identify elements of the modeled behavior. Praise students who make good responses.

4. **Have class practice the behavior with puppets.** Provide a scene description for each student to enact; for example, reporting to the teacher when someone is hurt, reporting a storm warning heard on the radio, reporting a fire, or reporting an automobile accident, reporting some accident or emergency event which would be likely to occur in the classroom.

5. **Praise those students who report the appropriate information in the role-playing situation.**

6. **Reinforce the desired behavior related to reporting emergencies if emergencies should occur in the natural environment.**

Code: S-ER-DE-0006-L2-Ir

TEACHING STRATEGY

Objective: Student reports accidents and emergencies to the teacher by stating (a) what happened, (b) where it happened, and (c) when it happened.

51

Social Reinforcement

1. **If an emergency should occur, praise student when reporting the appropriate information.** Call attention to specific actions, e.g., "Panda, thank you for calling me when John fell and got hurt. You gave me the right kind of information." "Raquel, you were such a help in the emergency last night. You stayed calm and remembered all the important facts." "Elton, you reported the accident quickly and accurately."

Code: S-ER-DE-0006-L2-Ic

TEACHING STRATEGY

Objective: Student reports accidents and emergencies to the teacher by stating (a) what happened, (b) where it happened, and (c) when it happened.

Contingency Management

1. **Describe to the student the specific behaviors that are desired.** "When there is an accident or emergency, find a teacher or someone else in authority and tell them what happened, where it happened, and when it happened."

2. **Select a reinforcer.**

3. **Establish a contingency.** Since this skill relates to a situation that is likely to occur infrequently in the natural environment, a positive reinforcement contingency may best be carried out in a role-playing setting. For example, "If in the role-playing situation, you describe an accident or emergency by accurately telling what happened and when and where it happened, you will be rewarded."

4. **Set up a role-playing situation using hypothetical emergencies which students might be likely to encounter.** Such emergencies as fires, accidents, floods, tornadoes, etc. could be used, and reward students according to the contingency for making good responses.

LUNCHROOM BEHAVIOR

S-ER-LR-0002-L1-S   To use eating utensils properly.

S-ER-LR-0004-L1-S   To handle and eat only one's own food.

S-ER-LR-0006-L1-S   To dispose of unwanted food properly.

Skill:	To use eating utensils properly. **S-ER-LR-0002-L1**
Objective:	When appropriate, student uses eating utensils properly.
Assessment:	Assess from previous knowledge of student or through direct observation using the <u>Social Behavior Assessment Inventory</u>.

Code: S-ER-LR-0002-L1-Im

TEACHING STRATEGY

Objective: When appropriate, student uses eating utensils properly.

Social Modeling

1. **Meet with target student(s) and discuss when forks and spoons should be used for eating and how to use these utensils properly.** Most children who reach school age will know how to use forks and spoons and will be able to make discriminations among foods that require utensils and ones that can be eaten with fingers. However, some teaching will be necessary. List or show pictures of foods that can be eaten neatly with the hands and those foods to be eaten with a fork and/or spoon. Show why it is neater, healthier, and easier to eat some foods with utensils. Have students contribute ideas to the discussion; for example, "Why should you use a fork or spoon? What foods should you eat with a fork and/or a spoon? Can some foods be eaten with your hands? If so, why, and what foods?"

2. **Identify specific behaviors to be modeled.** When given food that cannot be eaten neatly with your hands, use a fork and/or spoon by placing food on the utensil, taking it directly to your mouth, putting the food into your mouth, and returning the fork and spoon directly to the plate. Identify specific examples of food to be eaten with a spoon, e.g., soup, jello, ice cream; with a fork, e.g., spaghetti, cooked vegetables, some kinds of meat; with fingers, e.g., raw vegetables, fruit, cookies, bread.

3. **Model the behavior.** Choose a time, such as, lunch or snack time when food is available. Sit with target student(s) and have the student(s) watch your use of utensils. Break the behavior into steps, i.e., putting food on utensil, raising it to mouth, putting food in mouth, chewing and swallowing, returning utensil to plate. Show one step at a time and have student(s) repeat the step after you; then add another step. Praise responses that approximate the behavior you have modeled.

4. **Provide opportunities for supervised practice with a number of different kinds of foods.** Discuss in advance which ones should be eaten with utensils. Praise students who correctly identify foods to be eaten with utensils and those who eat them properly with the utensils provided.

5. **Maintain the behavior through reinforcement.**

Code: S-ER-LR-0002-L1-Ir

TEACHING STRATEGY

Objective: When appropriate, student uses eating utensils properly.

Social Reinforcement

1. **Observe the student in the lunchroom setting.** Use social reinforcement when student is observed using eating utensils properly. Be specific in praising the student. For example, "Matt, I like the way you are eating with your fork. You are doing a very fine job." " Judy, you are eating very neatly with your fork."
2. **Provide cues for the target student.** Remind student how to use the utensils. Reinforce students who are using the utensils properly. Reinforce target students for correct use by responding to cues.
3. **When necessary, provide tangible reinforcement (e.g., coupons, chips, tokens, stars, etc.) along with social reinforcement (e.g., smiles, praise, attention, etc.).** Tangible reinforcement can be exchanged for desirable items and privileges.

Code: S-ER-LR-0002-L1-Ic

TEACHING STRATEGY

Objective: When appropriate, student uses eating utensils properly.

Contingency Management

1. **Present task to student in specific terms.** When given foods that cannot be eaten with your hands, use a fork and/or spoon. Demonstrate the proper use of fork and spoon and review those foods that should be eaten with utensils and those that can be eaten with fingers.
2. **Plan reinforcement.**
3. **State contingency.** If when given food that requires spoon or fork, the student uses the utensils provided properly, the student will receive the agreed-upon positive consequences. Specify the type and amount of reinforcement.
4. **Observe student when eating during lunch or snack time.**
5. **Example.** Matt's teacher, Ms. Scott, observed that he had difficulty in properly using his spoon and fork, and he did not seem to know when to use those utensils. When Matt was eating, food would eventually be on the table, on the floor, and on Matt. Instead of using a fork or spoon, he often picked up things from his lunch tray with his fingers.

    Ms. Scott spoke to Matt and explained that certain foods could be eaten with the hands, but that others should be eaten with fork or spoon. Matt and Ms. Scott listed foods that could be eaten with the hands. Then they listed foods which needed to be eaten with a spoon and/or fork. She invited

Matt to eat lunch with her in the room. She then showed him how to use the spoon and fork properly and had him practice his behavior.

After practicing the desired behavior, Ms. Scott stated a contingency to Matt. He was told that if, when eating, he properly used a spoon or fork when he could not eat the food reasonably neatly in his hands, he would receive additional check marks. Ms. Scott had a lunch system whereby students were given check marks for good lunch behavior. She asked an older student from an upper grade to give lunch points when she could not be there. On Friday, the two students in Ms. Scott's class who had earned the highest total of points for lunchroom behavior ate lunch in the classroom watching TV, and all students who earned a certain number of points got an extra treat for dessert. The check mark system was accompanied by praise for doing a good job–eating with fork and spoon.

Skill:	To handle and eat only one's own food. **S-ER-LR-0004-L1**
Objective:	Student refrains from touching or taking other students' food unless it is offered.
Assessment:	Assess from previous knowledge of student or through direct observation using the <u>Social Behavior Assessment Inventory</u>.

Code: S-ER-LR-0004-L1-Im

TEACHING STRATEGY

Objective: Student refrains from touching or taking other students' food unless it is offered.

Social Modeling

1. **Meet with student(s) to explain that while eating, one should touch one's own food and not touch or take other students' food unless it is offered.** By the time students reach elementary school age, most of them will be able to discriminate what is their own food and what is others' food and know that another's food should not be taken or touched. There may be some students who have not learned this behavior and need to be taught, or some students who use touching or taking other's food as a way of teasing and attracting attention.

   Elicit student contributions to the discussion. Bring out the fact that it is not polite to take other's food unless offered and that people do not like it when someone touches their food. Stress also the health reasons involved. Describe conditions under which one may take food that is not on one's own place; for example, when another person offers you some food or when there is food in a community dish for everyone. Related skills might be touched on, such as, politely asking another person to give you some of his left-over food or serving oneself from a community dish, leaving enough for the others.

Students should be able to give answers to questions such as: "Why during lunch should you keep your hands on your own food? Why should you not touch other's food? Under what conditions can you take food from another's plate?"

2. **Identify the specific behaviors to be modeled.** During lunch, keep your hands on your own food and do not touch or take other students' food unless it is offered.

3. **Model the behavior.** Sit with students in the lunchroom during a time when each has a lunch tray. Point out and have students repeat which tray belongs to each person. Model eating from your own tray. For contrast, by pre-arrangement with another student, demonstrate inappropriately touching and taking food as well as appropriate ways to ask to share what the student does not want. Ask the other students to identify the behaviors you have demonstrated and relate to a discussion of how a student feels when someone else has handled or taken his or her food without asking.

4. **Provide opportunity for practice.** Sit with the students during lunch and have them demonstrate eating their own food and appropriately refraining from taking or touching another's food. Praise good responses.

5. **Maintain the behavior through reinforcement of students during lunch time for eating correctly.**

Code: S-ER-LR-0004-L1-Ir

TEACHING STRATEGY

Objective: Students refrain from touching or taking other students' food unless it is offered.

Social Reinforcement

1. **When in the lunchroom observe students.** Use social reinforcement, praise, and smiles when student is eating his or her own food and not taking others' unless it is specifically offered. Be specific in praising; for example, "Charlie, that was very polite of you to wait until Carl offered the cookie to you;" "Felice, I like the way you are sitting, eating your own lunch, and keeping your hands on your own food."

2. **Provide cues for target student.** Before going to the lunchroom, remind the students of this lunchroom rule. At the table, praise other students who are eating their own food and not inappropriately taking or touching others' food. Reinforce target student for responding correctly to the cue.

3. **If necessary, provide tangible reinforcement,** such as tokens, chips, coupons, along with social reinforcement to increase the desired behavior.

Code: S-ER-LR-0004-L1-Ic

TEACHING STRATEGY

Objective: Students refrain from touching or taking other students' food unless it is offered.

Contingency Management

1. **Discuss with the students the desired behavior of eating one's own food and not taking or touching another's food unless offered.** Stress that taking another's food without being offered is not polite and that people do not like others to touch or take their food. Make sure students can discriminate between their own food and others' food. Discuss times when it would be appropriate to take food that is not on one's own plate; for example, when another person offers you food or when the food is in a common dish.

2. **Plan reinforcement.**

3. **State contingency.** If during lunch the student eats his or her own food and does not take or touch another's food unless it is offered, the student will receive a stated type and amount of reinforcement.

4. **Observe student in natural setting and reinforce him or her according to the contract for touching and eating only his or her own food.**

5. **Example.** Students were complaining to Mr. Oliver about Kenny's behavior. He was touching and taking their food. Mr. Oliver discussed this behavior with Kenny. He explained that students did not like it when Kenny touched or took their food and that it was an inconsiderate thing to do. Mr. Oliver worked out a contingency contract with Kenny. He was told that a timer would be set at various timed intervals. If when the timer rang it was reported by the other students that he had kept his hands on his own food during the interval and had not touched or taken other students' food unless it was offered to him, he could pick a 3 x 5 card from the grab bag. Some cards were blank, some had expressions written on them such as, "Keep up the good work, beautiful job, super star," a happy face; and others contained various activities; for example, five extra minutes of recess, run film strip projector, reduce the amount of homework, etc. These cards were used in the lunchroom to increase and reward desired behaviors. Along with being allowed to pick a card, Kenny was also praised when he was observed eating appropriately. If Kenny had not responded to a positive contract, Mr. Oliver was prepared to introduce a penalty for each time Kenny touched or took food that belonged to someone else.

Skill:	To dispose of unwanted food properly. **S-ER-LR-0006-L1**
Objective:	Unwanted food will be left to one side of the plate until discarded.
Assessment:	Assess from previous knowledge of student or through direct observation using the <u>Social Behavior Assessment Inventory</u>.

Code: S-ER-LR-0006-L1-Im

TEACHING STRATEGY

Objective: Unwanted food will be left to one side of the plate until discarded.

Social Modeling

1. **Discuss with the class that unwanted food should be pushed to one side of the tray, leaving it there until the student can dispose of it properly.** Explain that disposing of unwanted food in this manner helps keep the lunchroom clean and neat and that the students are helping by keeping the table and floor clean of unwanted food. Ask such questions as, "When you have food on your tray you do not want, what are some of the things you could do with it? What are the best things to do with it? Why should you dispose of unwanted food in the proper way? What would happen if unwanted food were thrown on the floor and table?"

2. **Identify specific behaviors to be modeled.** When there is food on your tray that you do not wish to eat, push the food to one side and keep it there undisturbed until you can dispose of your tray.

3. **Model the behavior.** Take students to the lunchroom during lunch time and use the available lunches or ask lunchroom aide for a lunch to be used in modeling situation. Demonstrate disposing of some of the food by pushing it to one side of the tray and keeping it there undisturbed until it is time to dispose of the tray.

4. **Provide opportunity for practice.** Take students to the lunchroom and give them each a tray. Have students role-play that there is undesired food on their plates and have them demonstrate pushing the food aside and keeping it there until dismissed. Provide practice for each student both in role-playing and actual lunch time situations.

5. **Maintain the behavior through reinforcement.**

Code: S-ER-LR-0006-L1-Ir

TEACHING STRATEGY

Objective: Unwanted food will be left to one side of the plate until discarded.

Social Reinforcement

1. **Observe students in the lunchroom.** Use social reinforcement when student properly disposes of unwanted food. Be specific in praising the student. For example, "Ken, I appreciated the way you disposed of your food in the waste container. Our table area looks very neat and clean. Thank you;" "Marsha, I noticed that you didn't eat some of your lunch, and you followed the rule about pushing it aside and then discarding it in the trash. I like the way you follow the lunchroom rules."

2. **Provide cues for the target student.** Remind students of lunchroom rules before going to lunch. You may post a list of lunchroom rules in the lunchroom. To cue the target students, praise another student who follows the rules. Reinforce target students when they respond correctly.

3. **For some students it may be necessary initially to provide a tangible reinforcer,** such as stars on a chart, points, tokens, along with recognition for following lunchroom rules.

TEACHING STRATEGY

Objective: Unwanted food will be left to one side of the plate until discarded.

Contingency Management

1. **Present task to student in specific terms.** "When there is food on your plate that you do not want, push the food to one side of your plate until you can dispose of it. If the unwanted food is in your lunch bag, leave it in the bag until you can discard the bag in the proper container."

2. **Plan reinforcement.**

3. **State contingency.** If, when the student has unwanted food, it is pushed to one side of the plate or kept in the lunch bag for discarding in the proper container, the student will receive the agreed-upon positive consequence. Specify type and amount of reinforcement.

4. **Observe student(s) in the lunchroom.** Reward according to the contingency established for properly disposing of unwanted food.

5. **Example.** When Jackie had food on her plate that she did not want, she sometimes played with the food until it ended up on the table and the floor. Mrs. Rodgers talked with Jackie about pushing the food she did not want to one side of her plate and waiting until dismissed to dispose of it properly. She explained that disposing of food in this manner helps keep the lunchroom clean and neat and that the cleaning people would appreciate this help from Jackie. Mrs. Rodgers set up a contract with Jackie. Jackie was told that if she had unwanted food on her tray and she pushed it aside, keeping it there undisturbed until dismissed, and then disposed of the food properly, she would receive two courtesy lunch cards. Jackie was to write her name on the cards. Jackie's cards would be placed in the lunchroom raffle box. On Friday, the principal would draw 20 names from the raffle box. Students whose names were selected would be able to choose among rewards, such as five minutes of extra recess, ten minutes of early dismissal, taking the school tour with the principal, watching a TV show, or various other activities. Along with giving the courtesy cards, Mrs. Rodgers recognized with praise and attention Jackie's efforts to comply.

Note: For students who use behaviors such as throwing unwanted food at each other as a way of teasing others and receiving attention for misbehavior, a penalty for such behavior may need to be built into the contingency contract along with a positive consequence for appropriate behavior.

MOVEMENT AROUND ENVIRONMENT

S-ER-MO-0002-L1-S	To walk through the hall quietly at a reasonable pace.
S-ER-MO-0004-L1-S	To enter classroom and take seat without disturbing objects and other people.
S-ER-MO-0006-L1-S	To form and walk in a line.
S-ER-MO-0008-L1-S	To follow safety rules in crossing streets.

Skill: To walk through the hall quietly at a reasonable pace. **S-ER-MO-0002-L1**

Objective: Student walks through the hall at a moderate pace (not running or dawdling), quietly, and directly to destination.

Assessment: Assess from previous knowledge of student or through direct observation using the <u>Social Behavior Assessment Inventory</u>.

Code: S-ER-MO-0002-L1-Im

TEACHING STRATEGY

Objective: Student walks through the hall at a moderate pace, not running or dawdling, quietly, and directly to destination.

Social Modeling

1. **Identify a need for the behavior through a classroom discussion.** Have students contribute ideas to the discussion about the reasons that appropriate behavior is important while in the school corridors. Identify the elements of good hall-walking behavior. Write key words on the board. Ask students what might help them remember these.

2. **Identify specific behaviors to be modeled.** For example:
   (a) Walk through the hall quietly.
   (b) Walk through the hall to specified destination and return in specific amount of time.
   (c) Walk through the hall without stopping or running.

3. **Model behavior for the class.** Have students watch you walk down the hall. Ask students to identify elements of the modeled behavior. Recognize students who contribute good responses and prompt other desired responses.

4. **Have class practice the behavior.** Give each student an opportunity to walk down the hall. When the class is moving through the hall as a group, prompt students by reminding them of the rules about walking down the hall.

5. **Praise those students who walk down the hall correctly.**

6. **Maintain proper hall-walking behavior through reinforcement.**

Code: S-ER-MO-0002-L1-Ir

TEACHING STRATEGY

Objective: Student walks through the hall at a moderate pace (not running or dawdling), quietly, and directly to destination.

Social Reinforcement

1. **Identify and recognize by name, aloud, target student when observed walking through the hall properly.** Call attention to specific actions, e.g., "Matt, I'm so glad you came right back to the room;" "Marsha, thank you for walking down the hall so quietly and safely."
2. **Cue appropriate hall-walking behavior in target student.** Do this by recognizing others who are walking in the hall appropriately in proximity of target child. Be sure to watch for the behavior in target child and reinforce when he or she is walking appropriately in the hall.

Code: S-ER-MO-0002-L1-Ic

TEACHING STRATEGY

Objective: Student walks through the hall at a moderate pace (not running or dawdling), quietly, and directly to destination.

Contingency Management

1. **State task in observable terms.**
   (a) Student will walk at a moderate pace through hall.
   (b) Student will walk through the hall without making loud noises that disturb others.
   (c) Student will go only where appropriate and come right back.

   If needed, post a list of appropriate hall-walking behaviors as reminders.
2. **Plan reinforcement strategy selected from reinforcement menu.**
3. **State contingency.** If student walks through the hall properly, he or she will be rewarded. Specify amount and type of reinforcement.
4. **Set situation to necessitate walking through the hall.** For example, send students on errand or to restroom. Observe students walking in the hall and reward those who follow the rules correctly.
5. **Example.** When Edwardo walked with another student, he half walked and half ran to get ahead. The teacher explained to Edwardo that she wanted him to walk rather than run in the hall and to stay with the other students. She also told him that she was going to make a chart for him, and each time he walked correctly in the hall he would get one point or star. After he received five stars, he would then get a chance to be a line leader. As his behavior improved, she gradually increased the number of stars or points required to be line leader to eight, ten, etc.

<table>
<tr><td>**Skill:**</td><td>To enter classroom and be seated without disturbing objects and other people.
S-ER-MO-0004-L1</td></tr>
<tr><td>**Objective:**</td><td>Upon entering the classroom, the student moves around objects and people without disturbing them and goes to own seat and sits.</td></tr>
<tr><td>**Assessment:**</td><td>Assess from previous knowledge of student or through direct observation using the <u>Social Behavior Assessment Inventory</u>.</td></tr>
</table>

Code: S-ER-MO-0004-L1-Im

TEACHING STRATEGY

Objective: Upon entering the classroom, the student moves around objects and people without disturbing them and goes to own seat and sits.

Social Modeling

1. **Talk to students about reasons for appropriate behavior when they come into the room and take their seats.** Ask students to suggest correct ways to come in and go to their seats, and also identify some behaviors which are not acceptable in the classroom. Ask students to think about what the class would be like if there were not some rules about the way students entered and sat down.

2. **With the help of the students, specify and write on the board the desired behaviors,** e.g., when the student comes into the room:
   (a) Puts outer clothing in the assigned place.
   (b) Walks between tables and chairs without touching them or what is on them.
   (c) Avoids touching other students.
   (d) Walks to own chair and sits quietly.

3. **Model the behavior.** Come in and sit as described or select several students to demonstrate the appropriate way of entering the room and sitting down. Ask other students to describe what they did.

4. **Have everyone demonstrate his understanding of the behavior in a practice session.** Have each person go out of the room and come back in appropriately. Have several additional practice sessions built around coming in the first thing in the morning, at recess, and at lunch. Recognize students who come in properly, and provide additional practice for those who do not.

5. **Maintain the behavior through reinforcement.**

Code: S-ER-MO-0004-L1-Ir

TEACHING STRATEGY

Objective: Upon entering the classroom the student moves around objects and people without disturbing them and goes to own seat and sits.

Social Reinforcement

1. **Reinforce the target child with recognition when he or she enters the room appropriately and sits without disturbing others.** Tell student specifically why he or she is being recognized. "Luis, good job! You really got to your seat nicely," "Ferris, I like the way you came in and sat down," "Chuck really knows how to come in and get ready to work."

2. **Provide cues for the target student by praising others who are sitting down appropriately.** For example, "Did you all see how John went to his seat?"

3. **If recognition alone is insufficient to motivate a student to come into the room and sit down in the desired way, you may use an additional approach.** Set up an arrangement whereby the student can earn points or tokens for appropriate behavior, later exchanging them for something desired.

Code: S-ER-MO-0004-L1-Ic

TEACHING STRATEGY

Objective: Upon entering the classroom, the student moves around objects and people without disturbing then and goes to own seat and sits.

Contingency Management

1. **State task in observable terms.**
   (a) Student will come into the room.
   (b) Put away outer clothing.
   (c) Walk between tables and chairs without touching them or what is on them.
   (d) Walk to own chair and be seated carefully.

   If necessary, post these steps somewhere in the room. Call students' attention to these behaviors.

2. **Plan reinforcement strategy selected from the reinforcement menu.**

3. **State contingency.** If the student comes in and sits without disturbing anything or anyone, he or she will be rewarded. Specify type and amount of reinforcement.

4. **Observe the student coming into the room in the morning and after recess or lunch.** If he or she comes in without disturbing anyone or anything and sits, reinforce according to the contract.

5. **Example.** Herbie generally comes in from the schoolyard very agitated. He storms into the room, arms swinging, knocking down everything in his path. The teacher tells Herbie that each time he comes into the room keeping his hands at his sides, walks to his seat, and sits without knocking things over, he will receive five points toward a movie ticket. She demonstrates to Herbie and has him practice coming in properly. The next day when Herbie comes in, he doesn't knock anything over; the teacher rewards him, saying, "Thank you for coming in so calmly, Herbie," as she hands him his point cards. She keeps the contingency in effect for several weeks, gradually decreasing the number of points earned for each time Herbie enters appropriately.

Code: S-ER-MO-0006-L1-Im

TEACHING STRATEGY

Objective: When asked, the student will line up behind another student and walk in formation following the teacher or other leader.

Social Modeling

1. **Identify a need for the behavior through classroom discussion.** Have students contribute ideas to the discussion of why and when it is a good idea to walk in a line when the whole class is going somewhere, and what constitutes proper behavior when walking in a line. Write key words on the board.

2. **Identify specific behaviors to be modeled.**
   (a) When lining up, stand one behind the other without pushing.
   (b) Stand in line facing front.
   (c) When walking in line, be sure to follow the leader and remain in line.
   (d) Be careful not to push other students or leave a big space between you and the person in front of you.

3. **Model behavior for class.** Ask student to come up and be leader. Get in line behind the leader. Ask students to identify elements of the modeled behavior. Recognize students who make good responses, and cue other desired responses from students.

4. **Have class practice the behavior.** Give each student an opportunity to get in a line and walk in line.

5. **Praise those students who line up and walk in a line properly.**

6. **Maintain proper lining-up and line-walking behavior through reinforcement.**

Code: S-ER-MO-0006-L1-Ir

TEACHING STRATEGY

Objective: When asked, the student will line up behind another student and walk in formation following the teacher or other leader.

Social Reinforcement

1. **Identify and recognize, aloud, target student when observed lining up and walking properly in line.** Call attention to specific actions, e.g.,

"Marsha, I like the way you are standing in line and facing front;" "Dan, you are doing a beautiful job of following the leader in line today."

2. **Cue appropriate lining up and walking in line in target student by recognizing others who are showing the desired behavior.** Watch for the desired behavior in the target child and be sure to reinforce it.

3. **If social reinforcement in the form of praise, attention, smiles, pats on back, etc., is not sufficient to increase the desired behavior, pair social reinforcement with tangible reinforcement, e.g., tokens, chips, coupons, stars, etc., to be exchanged for something the child wants.**

Code: S-ER-MO-0006-L1-Ic

TEACHING STRATEGY

Objective: When asked, the student will line up behind another student and walk in formation following the teacher or other leader.

Contingency Management

1. **State the task in observable terms.**
   (a) When asked to get in line, students will stand behind one another.
   (b) Students will walk in line following the student in front of them.
   (c) Students will keep up with the person in front of them in line.
   (d) Students will all follow the line leader (teacher or other student).

   If needed, post a list of appropriate line-walking behaviors as reminders.

2. **Plan reinforcement strategy selected from reinforcement menu.**

3. **State the contingency.** If student lines up, walks in line, and follows the leader, he or she will be rewarded. Be sure to specify amount and type of reinforcement.

4. **Watch for the behavior to occur naturally, and reward it when it occurs according to established contingency** or, set up a situation requiring walking in line, e.g., going to lunchroom, recess, or dismissal. Observe the lining-up and line-walking behavior and reward those who follow it correctly.

5. **Example.** Unless she can be the leader, Minnie always makes sure she gets at the end of the line when the class lines up to go anywhere. She then lags behind the line, walking very slowly and making various stops along the way. The teacher explains to Minnie that it is important that she keep up with the rest of the children in line. The teacher makes a contract with Minnie that she will earn a star each time she keeps up with the rest of the line when going anywhere. For every three stars, Minnie will have a chance to be line leader. As Minnie's behavior improves, the teacher increases the number of stars required to be line leader. As well as the stars, the teacher will also recognize Minnie for her improved line-walking behavior.

Skill:	To follow safety rules in crossing streets.
	S-ER-MO-0008-L1
Objective:	When necessary, the student crosses the street according to safety rules, e.g., observing traffic signals, looking both ways before crossing, and obeying school crossing guards or monitors.
Assessment:	Assess from previous knowledge of student or through direct observation using the <u>Social Behavior Assessment Inventory</u>.

Code: S-ER-MO-0008-L1-Im

TEACHING STRATEGY

Objective: When necessary, the student crosses the street according to safety rules, e.g., observing traffic signals, looking both ways before crossing, and obeying school crossing guards or monitors.

Social Modeling

1. **Identify a need for the behavior through a classroom discussion.** You may wish to structure the discussion by posing questions such as, "Why must we all know how to cross the street safely? What would happen to us if we didn't know about the rules and tried to cross any way we felt like?" It would be helpful at this point to show the children a film strip (or any available media) to help illustrate this point. Have students contribute ideas to the discussion of elements of good street-crossing behavior. Write key words on chart or bulletin board. Have students make safety posters. Give a sheet to color.

2. **Identify specific behaviors to be modeled.**
   (a) Student will approach a traffic signal, look at it, and wait for the green light before crossing.
   (b) Student will stop at a corner and look both ways before crossing.
   (c) Student will approach a school crossing where there is a guard and do as the guard directs.

3. **Model the behavior for the class.** Ask students to watch teacher as he or she pretends to cross a street or crosses a real street. Ask students to identify elements of the modeled behavior. Recognize students who make good responses.

4. **Have class practice the behavior.** Give each student an opportunity to cross the street without a signal, with a signal, and with a school guard. Teacher may use replicas of a stop sign and traffic light for practice.

5. **Recognize those students who cross the street correctly.**

6. **Maintain proper street-crossing behavior through reinforcement.**

Code: S-ER-MO-0008-L1-Ir

TEACHING STRATEGY

Objective: When necessary, the student crosses the street according to safety rules, e.g., observing traffic signals, looking both ways before crossing, and obeying school crossing guards or monitors.

Social Reinforcement

1. **Identify and recognize by name, aloud, target student when observed crossing the street properly.** Call attention to specific actions, e.g., "Matt, that was really a safe way you crossed the street. You stopped and looked both ways;" "Mary, I received a good report from the school guard about the way you followed his or her signals."

2. **Provide cues for appropriate street-crossing behavior.** Recognize students who are exhibiting proper street-crossing behavior close to the target child. Post rules as reminders. Before the class leaves for home in the afternoon, have students review the rules. Assign an older student to assist the crossing guard by standing at the curb and calling out reminders to students who show signs of forgetting the rules. Assign an older student to stand by the crossing and give out tokens to students who have followed the rule in crossing the street.

Code: S-ER-MO-0008-L1-Ic

TEACHING STRATEGY

Objective: When necessary, the student crosses the street according to safety rules, e.g., observing traffic signals, looking both ways before crossing, and obeying school crossing guards or monitors.

Contingency Management

1. **State task in observable terms.** When you want to cross the street, remember to:
   (a) Walk when the light has the walk signal.
   (b) Stop before crossing the street and look both ways.
   (c) Stop at the school crossing when guards signal you to do so.
   (d) Only cross when no cars are coming.

   Post a list of appropriate street-crossing behaviors as reminders.

2. **Plan reinforcement strategy selected from reinforcement menu.**

3. **State contingency.** If you follow all the safety rules about crossing the street, you will be rewarded. Specify amount and type of reinforcement.

4. **Observe student when crossing street on the way to or from school.** Arrange a situation to necessitate students' crossing the street. For example, take a nature walk around the school neighborhood. Observe the street-crossing procedure, and reward those who follow it correctly according to the established contingency.

5. **Example.** Hank was continually reported by the school guards for not paying any attention to signals for crossing the street in front of the school. The teacher discussed with Hank the importance of following rules and the meaning of the different traffic signals. The teacher took Hank out and walked back and forth across the street with him, having him identify what the different lights meant and demonstrate correct walking across the street. She or he then told Hank he would be given a point for each day he crossed properly. The school guard was asked by the teacher to report how well Hank obeyed the rules. After he received five points, Hank would be the leader when the class went on their next walk in the school neighborhood. He would also accumulate points to be a helper for the school crossing guard.

4

INTERPERSONAL BEHAVIORS

ACCEPTING AUTHORITY

S-IP-AA-0002-L1-S	To comply with request of adult in position of authority.
S-IP-AA-0004-L1-S	To comply with request of peer in position of authority.
S-IP-AA-0006-L1-S	To know and follow classroom rules .
S-IP-AA-0008-L1-S	To follow classroom rules in the absence of the teacher
S-IP-AA-0010-L2-S	To question rules which may be unjust.

Skill:	To comply with request of adult in position of authority. **S-IP-AA-0002-L1**
Objective:	Student complies with requests of adults, such as teachers, aides, principal, lunchroom attendant, who are in positions of authority.
Assessment:	Assess from previous knowledge of student or through direct observation using the <u>Social Behavior Assessment Inventory</u>.

Code: S-IP-AA-0002-L1-Im

TEACHING STRATEGY

Objective: Student complies with requests of adults, such as teachers, aides, principal, lunchroom attendant, who are in positions of authority.

Introduction: It is possible that the child who does not comply with adults' verbal requests has a hearing problem. If this has not been checked as a contributing factor to the child's problem, it should be checked. For the child who never complies with adults' requests, the social modeling strategy provided below may not be effective. This type of child may not attend adequately enough to learn from the social modeling strategy. For these extremely noncompliant children, a highly structured reinforcement system may need to be set up. Under such a system, compliance with adults' requests would be the only way for the child to earn reinforcers, e.g., food, drink, shelter, and attention. The system would also need to be designed using the principle of successive approximation.

The social modeling strategy presented below should be effective with those pupils who comply in a delayed fashion, in the classroom only, and by grumbling or showing anger in some other fashion. Those who comply with some requests from some adults will benefit from this social modeling strategy, also.

Social Modeling

1. **Set the stage.** When some of the target pupils belong to the Boy Scouts, a pee-wee football or baseball team, or participate in athletics at school, hold a discussion by asking the following questions:

   (a) What is the scoutmaster's (or coach's) job?

   (b) Does he or she ever make requests of you?

   (c) What do you do when he or she makes requests?

   If none of your pupils belong to an organized group with a specific leader, begin by asking the following question. "Who is the person that is in charge of a basketball (or football, whichever is most appropriate) team?" (Student response.) If student response is incorrect or no response occurs, give correct answer: the coach. Be sure to recognize participation in the discussion and correct responses.

   The questions listed below are provided as guidelines for continuing the discussion:

   (a) What does the coach do?

   (b) Does he or she ever make requests of the players?

   (c) What do the players do when he or she makes a request?

   After following one of the above procedures to begin discussion, you should move the discussion toward generalization by asking, "Who are some other adults (grown-ups) who make requests of other people?" (Answers include: policemen, judges, teachers, generals, parents, grandparents, etc.) "What do all these people have in common?" If children do not indicate that they all are in positions of authority, the teacher should explain this.

2. **Identify the specific steps.** Say, "When an adult in authority makes a request, there are three important steps to remember:

   (a) If you are not sure of what is being requested of you, ask questions of the adult to clarify the request.

   (b) Acknowledge that you heard the adult and intend to comply by saying, 'Yes, sir,' 'Yes, ma'am,' or 'Yes, Mr. (Ms.) _____ ,' or some equivalent phrase and stating what you will do.

   (c) Begin immediately to do what was requested, or tell the adult when you will do it.

3. **Model the behavior.** Arrange for a pupil to play the role of the school principal (or have the principal come to your class) before the class session when you plan to model the behavior. Say, "Now, I'm going to show you how to respond to a request made by an adult authority. Julius will be playing the role of the school principal, and I will be a student."

Role-play the following situation with the principal and student in the hallway: The pupil can be whistling or singing as the principal approaches. The following is a suggested script:

Principal: When you sing like that in the hallway you disturb others. Please walk more quietly through the halls.

Pupil: Yes, sir. I will walk quietly in the halls.

Principal: Thank you.

Pupil should then proceed to model walking quietly.

After the role-playing episode, discuss what happened. Ask, "What did you observe?" If pupils do not point out the steps described above, ask, "Did I acknowledge the principal's request? How? Did I do as I was requested?" Have a pupil from the class come to the front of the room and model the pupil behavior. Give recognition for appropriate behaviors.

4. **Practice the behavior.** Prepare a set of index cards. One of the following episodes should be written on each card:

   (a) Teacher asks child to let a smaller child have a turn with the calculator.
   (b) Lunch attendant asks child to pick up trash and put it in wastebasket.
   (c) Principal asks child to move more quietly through the hall.
   (d) Substitute teacher asks child to put game away.
   (e) Student teacher asks child to stop talking to friend and join the group activity.
   (f) Teacher asks child to go to his or her seat.
   (g) Teacher's aide asks child to get in line.

   Say, "Now that we know how to respond to an adult request, we need to practice. (Shuffle the index cards.) These cards have a role-playing episode on them. I'll call on you, and you will pick up one which we will then role-play. I will be the adult, and you will be the pupil. Remember, you will need to (a) ask questions if you don't understand the request, (b) acknowledge the request, and (c) begin to do as requested."

   When pupils respond, the teacher should be sure to recognize appropriate responses to the adult request; for example, "John, I like the way you said 'Yes, sir. I'll go to my seat right away,' and then did it."

5. **Additional suggestions.** An alternative for setting the stage is to tell a story about a student who was asked by the teacher to use both hands on the monkey bars. He did not listen because the playground teacher was not his teacher. He fell and chipped a tooth. What would have been the right things to do? Why?

Code: S-IP-AA-0002-L1-Ir

TEACHING STRATEGY

Objective: Student complies with requests of adults, such as teachers, aides, principal, lunchroom attendant, who are in positions of authority.

Social Reinforcement

1. **Cue appropriate behavior in target student by praising others who are exhibiting the desired behavior in complying with the requests of adults.**

2. **Identify and praise the target student by name when observed complying with the requests of adults in authority.** Call attention to specific actions, e.g., "Caroline, I'm glad that you came indoors when the principal asked you to;" "Andrew, thank you for helping the lunchroom attendant when she asked you to. I'm proud of you;" "Juan, you were very polite to the student teacher; you did everything she asked you to. That makes me happy!"

3. **If pupils have not responded favorably to the above procedures, institute the following:**
   (a) Observe the frequency of your requests and the frequency of compliance on three to five days for a selected one-hour time block.
   (b) Compute the percentage of daily compliance.
   (c) Inform the pupils of their levels of compliance and tell them that when their compliance has improved by at least 10 percent, they will earn a reinforcer (appropriate to your target pupils).
   (d) Reinforce as promised when the percentage of compliance rises by 10 percent.
   (e) Repeat steps (c), (d), and (e) until an acceptable level of compliance is reached; then, begin to compute percentage of compliance on an intermittent basis.

Code: S-IP-AA-0002-L1-Ic

TEACHING STRATEGY

Objective: Student complies with requests of adults, such as, teachers, aides, principal, lunchroom attendant, who are in positions of authority.

Contingency Management

1. **State the task in observable terms.** When an adult in authority asks you to do something,
   (a) Make sure you listen carefully so you understand the instructions, and
   (b) Do exactly what he or she asks you to.

2. **Plan reinforcement strategy selected from reinforcement menu.**

3. **State contingency.** If you follow the instructions of _____, or _____, (adults in authority), you will receive the agreed-upon positive consequence.

4. **When a teacher's aide, student teacher, or other adult in position of authority is in the room, observe students and reward those who comply appropriately with the requests of the adult.** To correct a problem related to a student's accepting directions from another adult outside the classroom, a "feedback" system might be established whereby the student is provided with a dittoed feedback form for the other adult to check. The other adult might be given some form of token to hand to the student who complies with a request; the token is then brought by the student to the classroom teacher for exchange.

5. **Example.** Brian was not really a behavior problem until Ms. Maiju, student teacher, was assigned to his class. Each time Ms. Maiju asked Brian to do something— get in line, join the circle, eat your lunch, sit down, come back into the room, etc.—Brian would throw a tantrum and yell at her, "I don't have to do what you say;" "You can't make me;" "I don't have to;" "I don't want to;" etc. Ms. Maiju was confused. She didn't know what to do to get Brian to listen to her, but Mr. Daniels (Brian's teacher) knew Brian, and he knew what to do. He told Ms. Maiju that Brian liked her, and he suspected that Brian might even have a crush on her. He said that Brian sometimes threw tantrums to get attention, and his strategy was working! Mr. Daniels suggested that Ms. Maiju try making a contract with Brian, making her attention contingent on his compliance with her requests. Ms. Maiju made a contract with him, as stated in the contingency. "Brian, when you do what I ask you to, without fussing, then you can sit with me at lunch and be my partner."

Skill:	To comply with request of peer in position of authority. **S-IP-AA-0004-L1**
Objective:	Student complies with requests of peers put in a position of authority, for example, class monitors, school crossing monitors, hall monitors.
Assessment:	Assess from previous knowledge of student or through direct observation using the <u>Social Behavior Assessment Inventory</u>.

Code: S-IP-AA-0004-L1-Im

TEACHING STRATEGY

Objective: Student complies with the requests of peers put in a position of authority; for example, class monitors, school crossing monitors, hall monitors.

Social Modeling

1. **Set the stage.** Two students will act out a short play before the class, dealing with a student complying with the requests of a peer put in a position of authority. Choose two students from your class who have mastered this skill to do the role-playing. If none of your students have mastered the skill, have two pupils from another class do the play.

    One student will play the part of the hall monitor, and another will play a regular student. The play will start out with the regular student running or skipping down the hall (an area in the front of the classroom), and the hall monitor walking down the hall from the other side. When the hall monitor sees the student running, he says, "Please stop running in the hall." The other student stops running and begins to walk, saying, "Sorry, I forgot."

    After the play, the teacher will begin a discussion by saying, "What happened in this play?" (Student response.) "That's very good, Jamie." (Paraphrase what the child has said.) "Who can tell us more about what happened?" (Student response.) "Exactly! Boy, you were alert." (Ask for further student discussion if needed to describe what happened fully.) "Bob knew how to obey Shirley who was in charge of monitoring (watching) the hall." "Why did this student listen to the hall monitor?" (Student responses.) "That's right. And (s)he was a respectful girl/boy to listen to the monitor the way (s)he did. When are some other times that students are put in charge?" (Student responses, e.g., classroom monitor, school safety patrol, and so on.) "Why should you obey these students when they tell you what to do?" (Student responses, e.g., "To keep order;" "Because these students represent adults and must be obeyed just as an adult would be obeyed;" "To help him or her keep order;" etc.) "Very good, everyone."

2. **Identify specific behaviors.** Ask, "How should you behave when a student in charge tells you what to do?" Refer to incidents in skit as students discuss specific behaviors. For instance, ask questions, such as, "What did the student in the skit do when the hall monitor gave him(her) orders?" (Reinforce specific responses about required behaviors as well as general responses.) List the steps for accomplishing the desired behavior on the blackboard. Four steps that should be included:

   (a) Listen to him or her.

   (b) Apologize for breaking the rule.

   (c) Thank him or her for reminding you.

   (d) Do what he or she says.

   "Great, you have all had some very good ideas!"

3. **Model the behaviors.** Draw a name. This student will be the "regular" student, and you will be a hall monitor, classroom monitor, safety patrol, or some other student in a position of authority.

   Choose an authority position that the class has already been taught. If you have not taught an authority position, e.g., classroom monitor, hall monitor, line leader, safety patrol, etc., it will first be necessary to teach the chosen authority position to the pupils so that they will know the responsibilities of the authority position. Do not assume the pupils understand what it means to be a hall monitor.

   The student in charge (teacher) will tell the other student to do something, and the other student will comply with the steps discussed. If the "regular" student exhibits the desirable behaviors, he or she may assume the authority position; and the teacher will then draw another name to play the "regular" student. After each role-play, students should describe the behavior of the "regular" student and decide if he or she has acted properly in complying with the other student's request. Give each student an opportunity to participate.

4. **Practice the behavior.** This practice activity can occur immediately after the above lesson or in a subsequent period of days. Appoint a teacher assistant in class and give him or her a list of instructions to give members of the class. Praise students who comply with the monitor's instructions and have them assume the assistant's role. Choose a student to be the recipient of the instruction each time.

74

5. **Suggested list of instructions.**
   (a) Hand in your math papers.
   (b) Open your reading books to page 107.
   (c) Margie, please close the door.
   (d) Would you please get me the globe from the back of the room?
   (e) Do the assignment on page 17 in your reading book.
   (f) Please pick up your waste paper and put it in the trash basket.
   (g) Please sit in your seat.

For additional practice, the teacher may appoint a student to be in charge for several occasions following this initial presentation. For instance, the teacher may assign different students to be "litter" monitors or "quiet" monitors for a day at a time. (Each of these monitoring jobs must be explained to the monitor and the class.)

Code: S-IP-AA-0004-L1-Ir

TEACHING STRATEGY

Objective: Student complies with the requests of peers put in a position of authority; for example, class monitors, school crossing monitors, hall monitors.

Social Reinforcement

1. **Maintenance.** Recognize students who comply with the requests of students in charge by giving specific descriptive praise. For example, "Kevin, you obeyed Scott when he told you not to run in the hall. That was very cooperative." "Polly, I'm happy that you followed the crossing guard's instructions when you crossed the street."

2. **Additional suggestions.**
   (a) Students who exhibit the desired behavior may be delegated positions of authority for a certain period of time as a reward.
   (b) Students in charge may have tickets to hand out to students who follow directions. These tickets may have pictures or sayings having to do with how well the student responded.
   (c) For the students who do not learn the behavior, teacher may wish to set up contingency contracts. By exhibiting a certain number of the desired behaviors (complying with the requests of a peer in authority), students will be able to earn certain activities or privileges.
   (d) If pupils have considerable difficulty with this skill, assess S-IP-AA-0002 for mastery.

Code: S-IP-AA-0004-L1-Ic

TEACHING STRATEGY

Objective: Student complies with the requests of peers put in a position of authority; for example, class monitors, school crossing monitors, hall monitors.

Contingency Management

1. **Explain the task to the student.** Tell him or her that when a peer is put "in charge," he or she should listen to that student and follow directions.
2. **Plan reinforcement.**
3. **State contingency.** "If you do what the student in charge tells you to do, you will receive a specified reward." Set up a situation for the behavior to occur.
4. **Assign a monitor to be in charge of the class while you are otherwise engaged.** Have the monitor direct the students in an activity, such as lining up, handing in papers, or collecting materials. Reward the student if he or she complies with the monitor's request. Observe in naturally occurring situations, and reward student if observed complying with requests of a peer in a position of authority.
5. **Example.** Richie never listens to the school crossing guards. Mr. Riley discussed this with Richie and explained to him why it is necessary for him to obey the crossing guards. He explained to Richie that starting that day, every time he obeys the crossing guard when crossing the street, he will receive one point. When he receives 25 points, he will be assigned as the assistant crossing guard to aid the crossing guard. Mr. Riley observed Richie every morning and afternoon crossing the street and rewarded him when he was seen crossing the street properly and following the directions of the crossing guard. Richie fulfilled the contract and received his appointment as an assistant to the crossing guard.

Skill:	To know and follow classroom skills. **S-IP-AA-0006-L1**
Objective:	Student will demonstrate knowledge of defined classroom rules by complying with these rules during class.
Assessment:	Assess from previous knowledge of student or through direct observation using the <u>Social Behavior Assessment Inventory</u>.

Code: S-IP-AA-0006-L1-Im

TEACHING STRATEGY

Objective: Student will demonstrate knowledge of defined classroom rules by complying with these rules during class.

Introduction: Rules are present in every classroom. It is usually a good idea to post the three or four major rules that the teacher wants to be in effect in his or her classroom. All rules should be stated positively in as brief a fashion as possible. When teaching children the rules for your classroom, teach only one new rule at a time. After one rule is mastered, you may then add another; however, four rules are suggested as the maximum number to be posted at any one time.

Social Modeling

1. **Set the stage.** Divide target pupils into groups of four or less. Have each group play a table game that all of the pupils know, e.g., "Candyland," "Chinese Checkers," "Pick-Up Sticks," "Old Maid," etc. Set the maximum time limit at 15 minutes.

2. **Identify the specific steps.** (This step should immediately follow "setting the stage.")

   (a) Have the children identify the various rules followed while playing the game. List these rules on the chalkboard; for example:

      (1) Take turns playing.

      (2) Draw straws or pick a number to decide who plays first.

   (b) Discuss the purpose of the rules. Ask: "Why does this game have these rules?" Be sure that the following major ideas are brought out in discussion.

   (c) Say, "To play the game, you need to do two things: (a) know the rules, and (b) follow the rules. When you were first learning to play this game, you did not know the rules, so how did you follow them?" (Student response.) "Right, George. You read them or had someone tell you the rules until you knew them."

   (d) Say, "Just as this game and all others have rules so that everyone knows what to do, things move along in an orderly way, and everyone plays the game the same way; we have rules in school and here in class for the same reasons. You don't know what the rules are until I post them for you to read or tell you. Once I tell you or post them, you are expected to follow the rules. There are two things for you to do:

      (1) Know the rules so that you can tell me when I ask.

      (2) Follow the rules, i.e., do what the rule says."

3. **Model the behavior.** The teacher should role-play situations that involve classroom rules. It is suggested that the teacher write the specific rules he or she wants to establish in his or her classroom on 4" x 6" strips of poster paper. These can then be shown one at a time and modeled by the teacher. The following is an example: "Walk down the hall." Take the class into the hall and demonstrate appropriate ways to walk down the hall. Ask students to describe your behavior, and praise accurate responses. Proceed in the same manner for one or two other rules.

4. **Practice the behavior.** Write each classroom rule on a 3 x 5 card. Play the following game: Each child chooses a card. (S)He reads it silently and demonstrates the rule. The other children guess what his or her rule is. The child who is correct can demonstrate the next rule. Recognize students who properly demonstrate rules. (Variation for children who cannot read: have the child choose a card and bring to you for you to whisper to him or her.)

5. **Additional suggestions.**

   (a) Provide cues for target student:

      (1) Write a list on chart, putting forth the class rules, and post it in a prominent place.

      (2) Praise another student near the target student for following the relevant rules. Immediately recognize target student when rules are followed.

(b) The "raffle" can be easily modified to an "auction" format. For some pupils the "auction" may be more effective.

(c) For children who are unable to read, draw cartoons or cut out pictures depicting the rule and post.

Code: S-IP-AA-0006-L1-Ir

TEACHING STRATEGY

Objective: Student will demonstrate knowledge of defined classroom rules by complying with these rules during class.

Social Reinforcement

1. **Identify by name and recognize aloud a student who is observed following the classroom rules.** Recognize specific behaviors, i.e., "Leila, thank you for closing the door when you came in;" "Maria, you remembered our rule about speaking in a soft voice while I took attendance."

2. **When recognition alone does not produce the desired behavior try the following procedure:**
   (a) Prepare a ditto master with eight copies of a visual representation of the rule.
   (b) Inform the pupils that you will be holding a raffle and that they may earn raffle tickets by following a classroom rule. (Specify the rule and any additional conditions necessary. For some rules it will be necessary to put time limits so that "raffle tickets" can be earned frequently.)
   (c) Award tickets at a very high rate (continuous schedule) of reinforcement for those behaviors where this is possible initially.
   (d) Conduct a raffle at end of school day initially. After three days, do it every other day. Gradually lengthen the time for the raffle to one week. Discontinue the raffle when praise will maintain the behaviors.
   (e) Select backup reinforcers to be raffled based on your assessment of the target pupils' reward preferences.

Code: S-IP-AA-0006-L1-Ic

TEACHING STRATEGY

Objective: Student will demonstrate knowledge of defined classroom rules by complying with these rules during class.

Contingency Management

1. **Present the task to the student in specific terms.** Tell the student what the relevant classroom rules are, and explain that he or she must follow these rules. Be sure the rules are stated so they are easily understood and not ambiguous. Rules should be stated in positive terms; for example, "Raise your hand," rather than, "Don't talk out."

2. **Plan reinforcement.**

3. **State contingency.** If the student follows the relevant classroom rules during class, he or she will receive the agreed-upon reward. Specify type and amount of reward.

4. **Observe the student in a rule-following situation.** If the rules in this situation are followed, reward him or her. If rule is "Close the door when you come in," reward when he or she comes in and closes the door. This last step may be altered for different rules.

5. **Example.** José did not follow Mr. Rich's rule about asking permission before leaving the room. Mr. Rich sat down with José before school and explained the rule to him. He told José that if he remembered all day to ask for permission before leaving the room, he would be allowed to spend 20 minutes at the end of the day reading in the school library–his favorite activity. Each time José forgot, five minutes would be deducted from the 20 minutes. This contingency seemed to work, as José began to ask permission before leaving the room. The contract was then stretched to two days for reward and gradually increased to one week. During this time it was necessary to explain to José that he must stay in the room when denied permission to leave. An extra stipulation was added to the contract, stating that he would lose his reward for that day if he left the room when denied permission. The contingency was kept in force for a month on the once-a-week reinforcement schedule. At this time, it was dropped in favor of social reinforcement.

Skill:	To follow classroom rules in the absence of the teacher. **S-IP-AA-0008-L1**
Objective:	Student follows classroom rules when the teacher is not present.
Assessment:	Assess from previous knowledge of student or through direct observation using the <u>Social Behavior Assessment Inventory</u>.

Code: S-IP-AA-0008-L1-Im

TEACHING STRATEGY

Objective: Student follows classroom rules when the teacher is not present.

Social Modeling

1. & 2. Set the stage and identify the specific steps.

(a) The pupils should have mastered S-IP-AA-0006-L1. Begin by asking the pupils to state the classroom rules verbally. Recognition shall be given to pupils who respond correctly. Recognize the class for following the rules when the teacher is present in the room.

(b) Following recognition, the teacher may say, "Now that all of you have mastered these rules in my presence, we are ready to learn to follow the rules all of the time regardless of whether I'm here or not. You should follow the rules all of the time. Why should you follow the rules when I'm not in the room?" (Student response.) Be sure that the following major ideas are brought out in discussion.

(1) Provides order.

(2) Sets same standard for everyone.

(3) Allows independence for each student.

(These are the same reasons for having and following rules when the teacher is present.) Give recognition for appropriate verbal responses.

(c) If the classroom rules are not posted, post the rules. A maximum of four rules should be posted at any given time. These rules should be ones that the pupils have mastered when you are present in the room.

3. **Model the behavior.** Tell the class to pretend you are a student and that the teacher has just left the class. Role-play each of your classroom rules, one at a time, in the teacher's absence. For example, remain in your seat, speak softly, do not leave the room without permission (use the actual behaviors required in the class). Ask students which of the rules you have followed and recognize accurate responses.

4. **Practice the behavior.** Provide opportunity for practice. Leave the room, and leave one or two trusted students in charge of observing the others. When you return, recognize students who were reported to have followed the class rules in your absence. Practice may be carried out by starting with a brief period of absence and gradually increasing the amount of time spent out of the room. In addition to making sure students understand the rules to be followed, the activities in which students are to be engaged should be specified. Do not leave the room without specifying activities to be completed while you are absent.

5. **Additional suggestions.**

(a) Prepare a wall chart on which all the pupils' names may be listed in the left column and the rules listed across the top. Each time you leave the room, inform the pupils that upon returning you will award one star for each rule that was observed in your absence. (A student monitor may be appointed to observe in your absence or when you return, you may choose to ask who followed the rules.)

(b) If necessary, tangible backup reinforcers may be attached to the stars on the wall chart described above.

(c) Select rules that will be easy to follow, e.g., remain in the classroom when teacher is out of the room. Then move to more difficult rules to follow in the absence of the teacher, e.g., remain silent.

Code: S-IP-AA-0008-L1-Ir

TEACHING STRATEGY

Objective: Student follows classroom rules when the teacher is not present.

Social Reinforcement

1. **Identify by name and recognize aloud a student who has been observed or was reported following classroom rules in the absence of the teacher.**

Recognize specific behaviors, i.e., "Laurie, the substitute told me you did a good job of remembering to raise your hand." "Madeline, you stayed in your seat while I was out in the hall with the principal. You follow our class rules very well."

2. **Cue appropriate behavior in target student by leaving a chart listing class rules prominently displayed in the room.**

Code: S-IP-AA-0008-L1-Ic

TEACHING STRATEGY

Objective: Student follows classroom rules when the teacher is not present.

Contingency Management

1. **Explain to the student that he or she must follow the classroom rules, as stated by the teacher, when the teacher is not in the room.** Review the rules you expect the student to follow.

2. **Plan reinforcement.**

3. **State contingency.** If the student follows the rules of the classroom, or a specific rule when the teacher is out of the room, the student will be rewarded. Specify type and amount of reward.

4. **Leave the room and make arrangements for the class to be observed in your absence.** A trusted student may be asked to do this, or an aide, if one is available. When you return, ascertain whether the student has followed the rules in your absence; if he or she has, reward the student according to the agreed-upon contingency.

5. **Example.** Tom did not stay in his seat when the teacher, Mr. Jiminez, left the room for short periods. Mr. Jiminez explained to Tom that the rule about staying in his seat during work periods applied when the teacher left the room. The teacher explained that if Tom followed this rule while he was out of class, he would receive five points toward a miniature model airplane in the class store (250 points).

   Mr. Jiminez assigned Jacob, another student, to watch Tom while he was out of the room. Jacob was instructed to mark down every time Tom got out of his seat and to remind Tom of the contract. When Mr. Jiminez returned, he checked Tom's record and rewarded him accordingly. At the beginning one point was deducted for each time Tom got out of his seat. The amount of penalty was gradually increased until Tom would lose all of the points for being out of his seat. Mr. Jiminez set up a chart so Tom could see his progress toward earning the model. Tom began to fulfill the contract and continued to fulfill it for six weeks until he earned the model. Mr. Jiminez did not set up a new contract but used social reinforcement to maintain the behavior.

Skill:	To question rules that may be unjust.
	S-IP-AA-0010-L2
Objective:	When presented with a rule that may be unjust, the student will question the teacher about the rule in an appropriate way; for example, asking the teacher politely to explain reasons for the rule.
Assessment:	Assess from previous knowledge of student or through direct observation using the <u>Social Behavior Assessment Inventory</u>.

Code: S-IP-AA-0010-L2-Im

TEACHING STRATEGY

Objective: When presented with a rule that may be unjust, the student will question the teacher about the rule in an appropriate way; for example, asking the teacher politely to explain reasons for the rule.

Introduction: This skill should be taught to all pupils who have mastered S-IP-AA-0008. After all, we must recognize that sometimes we may make a rule or decision that is or at least seems unfair, and that the pupils are justified and should raise questions about it. It is far more preferable for a pupil to learn that it is acceptable to question a rule and take action to change it than to simply disregard it or to grumble and complain but do nothing about it.

Social Modeling

1. **Set the stage.** Tell the target students the following story:

MRS. J'S NEW RULE

Mrs. J. was a _____ grade teacher. She enjoyed teaching and wanted her pupils to do well in school. Mrs. J. decided that one way to help her pupils improve their academic performance was to make a rule that only those pupils who came to school one-half hour early could earn an "A" or "B" in her class.

Mrs. J. announced her new rule to the class and informed them that the rule would go into effect on Monday. During the lunch recess, Norma and Bill were discussing the rule. Bill said that he thought the rule was unfair. Norma agreed. Bill suggested that they should tell their parents about the rule and have them call Mrs. J. to make her change it. Norma told Bill that his idea was good, but she thought they should try another approach first. Norma suggested that they make a list of various reasons why the rule was unfair and that they then go to talk with Mrs. J. about the rule. Bill agreed.

Norma and Bill met after school and made their list of reasons why the rule was unfair. Included on their list were the following:

(a) Some pupils ride the bus.
(b) Some pupils work before school to earn spending money.
(c) Some pupils help their parents at home in the morning before coming to school.
(d) Before school is the only time some pupils have during the day to visit with friends.

The next morning, Norma and Bill went to see Mrs. J. They told her that they had come to talk about the new rule requiring everyone to be at school one-half hour early in order to earn an "A" or "B." They asked if she had time to discuss it. She indicated that she was very busy now but could talk with them at lunch time. They agreed to see her at lunch.

At lunch time, Norma and Bill met with Mrs. J. They first asked her to tell them the reasons she made the new rule. They told Mrs. J. that they were glad she wanted them to do well in school. They then explained that the rule seemed unfair, and they listed their reasons. Mrs. J. listened carefully and then said, "I'm very glad you told me these things. I really didn't think about those problems. I'll announce to the class tomorrow that I have dropped this rule because it would be unfair. Why don't we form a committee to develop a rule that would be fair and would allow me to spend more time giving help to you and the others?" Norma and Bill thought that was an excellent idea and agreed to help.

After telling the story, ask the following questions:

(a) Was Mrs. J's. new rule fair?

(b) Why not?

(c) What did Norma and Bill do first?

(d) After they made their list of reasons why the rule was unfair, what did they do?

(e) What was the first thing they asked when they met with Mrs. J. at lunch time?

(f) What did they say then?

(g) What happened?

After the discussion questions, say, "This story shows how rules that students believe are unfair may be changed. Whenever you believe a rule is unfair, I recommend that you use a similar approach. Remember, however, that what seems fair to one person may not seem fair to another and that compromises are sometimes necessary. This means that you won't always get exactly what you want even though you use the proper method to bring it about."

2. **Identify the specific steps.** When a rule or decision is perceived as unjust, several steps may be taken:

(a) Go to the teacher and politely ask the reasons for a rule he or she has made.

(b) If the rule is a school-wide issue, ask the teacher to find out from the principal or school authority the reasons for the rule, or go to see the principal by yourself or with a committee of other students to ask about the reasons for the rule.

(c) State your evaluation of the reasons for the rule.

(d) Explain why you believe the rule to be unfair.

(e) Offer to work with the teacher to develop a rule that will be fair and meet the needs of the teacher or principal which prompted the unfair rule.

(f) If the teacher and principal do not change the rule and you are not satisfied that their reasons justify the rule, consult with an adult—your parents, the school counselor, another teacher, the school psychologist, the superintendent, etc.

3. **Model the behavior.** Set up a role-playing situation in which you (playing a student) go to the teacher (played by a student) and model appropriate methods of questioning a classroom rule. An example follows:

Pupil (played by teacher):   Mrs. Potts, do you have a few minutes to talk about 'Open School Day'?

Teacher (played by pupil): Yes.

Pupil: Why did you make the rule that we had to bring our parents in during the day in order to have cake and ice cream at our Valentine party?

Teacher: Well, I want to meet and talk with all of your parents, and I know you will work hard to get them to come if your cake and ice cream depend on it.

Pupil: That is a good reason, but I think the rule is unfair because some of us have mothers who work, and we cannot bring them during the day. Here is a list of names of students whose mothers work.

Teacher: Well, I never thought about that.

Pupil: I'll be glad to help you work out some way for you to talk with all of our parents that will be fair to everyone.

Teacher: Why don't we set up a committee and have them work it out?

Pupil: That's great. I'll be glad to be on it.

Ask students to describe the actions taken to question unjust rules or decisions and attempt to change them. Recognize accurate responses.

4. **Practice the behavior.** Set up role-playing situations similar to the one above and have students take turns playing the questioning student. Make a list of unfair rules that can be used in the role-playing episodes. Some possibilities are listed below:

(a) Only girls may go to recess.
(b) All homework must be typewritten.
(c) No questions will be answered after 8:30 A.M.
(d) Only boys are required to do homework.

Have pupils role-play these episodes one at a time with the others observing. Coach the pupils as necessary. Ask the observing pupils to identify the appropriate behaviors of the role-playing pupil.

5. **Additional suggestions.**

(a) Provide general cues to the class with a discussion of fairness and its application to everyone, including teachers, principals, and school authorities. You may also find it helpful to have a bulletin board established on which would be placed newspaper articles which the students have collected about unjust laws and how they might be changed.

(b) Discuss the need to question and try to change unjust or unfair rules. General concepts of fairness and justice and their meaning should be explained and discussed. You may draw on historical events such as the colonists' reaction to the English taxation policies, the abolitionists' opposition to slavery, pacifist objections to the Vietnam conflict, civil rights movements, etc. Point out that many injustices would never have been corrected if someone had not questioned the laws or rules that maintained them. Have students comment on these ideas and contribute other examples of unfair laws or rules, drawn from governmental laws, school or classroom rules.

Code: S-IP-AA-0010-L2-Ir

TEACHING STRATEGY

Objective: When presented with a rule that may be unjust, the student will question the teacher about the rule in an appropriate way; for example, asking the teacher politely to explain reasons for the rule.

Social Reinforcement

1. **Name and recognize a student who has politely and reasonably raised a question about the fairness of a rule or decision.** Recognize behavior in a specific way. "Sarah, that's a valid question. It may be that the school rule about not talking in the halls during lunch is unfair and unnecessary. I'll ask the principal about it." (It would be important in this case to carry through with talking to the principal and report the results to the student who raised the question.) The teacher must use his or her own judgment in ascertaining the reasonableness of the student's question. While praising a student for raising questions in an appropriate way, it may be necessary to place some controls on the behavior so it does not become a means for disruption. For example, "John, I had reasons for making the rule about not bringing toys to school. Come and see me during recess, and I'll explain my reasons to you. I'm glad you asked me in such a nice way why we had the rule."

Code: S-IP-AA-0010-L2-Ic

TEACHING STRATEGY

Objective: When presented with a rule that may be unjust, the student will question the teacher about the rule in an appropriate way; for example, asking the teacher politely to explain reasons for the rule.

Contingency Management

1. **Specify the desired behavior to the students.** When you feel that a school rule or a rule made by the teacher is not fair, ask the teacher politely to explain the reasons for the rule.
2. **Select reinforcer.**
3. **Establish a contingency.** In this skill, although there are implicit rewards provided through teacher responses and the ultimate possibility of having

the unjust rule changed, an explicit, positive contract may not be desirable, since it may serve to increase the amount of questioning of rules beyond what would be reasonable or desirable. Instead, you may want to introduce a role-playing activity and establish a contingency, such as, "If you are able to ask the teacher politely in a role-playing situation to explain the reasons for an unfair rule, you will be rewarded."

4. **Arrange a role-playing activity.** Present students with a list of obviously unfair classroom rules. Give each student an opportunity to select a rule and ask the teacher politely to explain the rule, and then to thank the teacher for the answer. The role-playing may be done in small groups, with each group having the responsibility for formulating some plan of action for getting the rule changed. Reward students for good responses according to the contingency that was established.

COPING WITH CONFLICT

S-IP-CC-0002-L1-S	To respond to teasing or name-calling by ignoring, changing the subject, or using some other constructive means.
S-IP-CC-0004-L1-S	To respond to physical assault by leaving the situation, calling for help, or using some other constructive means.
S-IP-CC-0006-L1-S	To walk away from peer when angry to avoid hitting.
S-IP-CC-0008-L1-S	To refuse the request of another politely.
S-IP-CC-0010-L2-S	To express anger with nonaggressive words rather than physical action or aggressive words.
S-IP-CC-0012-L2-S	To constructively handle criticism or punishment perceived as undeserved.

Skill:	To respond to teasing or name calling by ignoring, changing the subject, or using some other constructive means. **S-IP-CC-0002-L1**
Objective:	Student responds to teasing or name calling by ignoring, changing the subject or by using some other constructive means appropriate to the situation.
Assessment:	Assess from previous knowledge of student or through direct observation using the Social Behavior Assessment Inventory.

Code: S-IP-CC-0002-L1-Im

TEACHING STRATEGY

Objective: Student responds to teasing or name calling by ignoring, changing the subject, or using some other constructive means appropriate to the situation.

Introduction: Local norms may conflict with this skill, i.e., the expected behavior on the part of the peer group and parents may be name-calling or physical assault in response to being called a derogatory name. When such is the case, the teacher is unlikely to change behaviors or attitudes solely through discussion of the appropriate behavior. It is recommended that the discussion approach include the teacher's expectation while students are at school. Of course, it is critical that the teacher also exhibit the appropriate behavior.

Social Modeling

1. **Set the stage.** The teacher should begin by telling this short story:

MARVIN, THE PROBLEM SOLVER

Everybody at _____ School liked Marvin. It was easy to see why. Marvin was kind to everyone and was very smart about staying out of trouble. In fact, Marvin was so smart about staying out of trouble that he was asked to be the "Problem Solving Super" of the whole school. Marvin had his own office with carpeting, a big desk, and his own secretary! Anyone in the school could go to Marvin's office to talk about a problem, and Marvin was always helpful.

One day José came running into Marvin's office with tears in his eyes. "Marvin," said José, "that big bully, Billy, just called me a name on the playground, and I feel bad!"

"What did you do when Billy called you a name?" asked Marvin.

"Why, I started to cry and then came to your office," replied José.

"You were very smart not to say anything back, José. Listen very carefully, and I will tell you my secret that helps people stay out of trouble:

> If ever you are called a name
> Just keep this in mind—
> Ignore that name and walk away
> Or say something that is kind."

José thought about this poem for quite a while, then left Marvin's office to go back to the playground. There stood big bully Billy and when he saw José he called him another name. José remembered the poem:

> If ever you are called a name
> Just keep this in mind—
> Ignore that name and walk away
> Or say something that is kind.

Instead of crying, José said to Billy, "Billy, you are a good baseball player; would you like to show me how you bat so well?" Billy was so pleased with José's nice comment that he said, "Sure, pal, let's go out to the baseball field."

2. **Identify the specific steps.**
   (a) Teach children the poem; write it on the board.
   (b) Discuss appropriate ways of responding to teasing. Prompt such responses as: one could ignore the teasing; one could walk away from the person doing the teasing; one could try to change the subject by talking about something else; one could show concern by saying something like, "Oh, I'm sorry you feel that way;" one could say something nice to the person.

   You may decide to teach the target pupils to respond in a specific way rather than giving them alternatives from which to choose. For example, you could teach the target pupils to respond to name calling by walking away and ignoring the name calling. This approach of selecting one specific response to teach is recommended for young children and for older children who have already developed an aggressive response to name calling.

   (c) Identify the components of responding to teasing.
      (1) Choose an appropriate, acceptable way of responding.
      (2) Do what you have chosen.

3. **Model the behavior.** This is a difficult skill to model in class. Any role-playing situation in which you would have one student demonstrating the

improper behavior of name calling is to be avoided. It is suggested that the teacher tell the pupils that they are to pretend someone teased them. The teacher should then model the appropriate behavior, without specifically focusing on the name calling itself.

4. **Practice the behavior.**

   (a) Have children memorize the poem and teach it to others.

   (b) Have each pupil select a specific way to respond to name calling. Inform the target pupils that you want them to now practice the response they have selected as you call their name. Call each pupil by name and say to the selected pupil, "Pretend that I just called you _____ (insert various names); respond in an acceptable way."

5. **Additional suggestions.**

   (a) This skill focuses on an avoidance response to certain antagonistic behaviors of others. In addition to teaching students to ignore name calling, it is advisable to teach the name callers a more desirable behavior. Thus, you may choose to stress the skill of complimenting others to reduce the undesirable behavior of name calling. You may wish to focus on "The Art of Complimenting" in your class discussions. Also, you could initiate a "Good Citizen of the Day" program in which speaking kindly to others would be one target behavior on which to focus. Also, you could set up a side bulletin board with each student's name listed. When a student is found complimenting another student, he or she could be instructed to put a happy face (made with construction paper and magic marker) next to his or her name.

   (b) An individual student may have a difficult time ignoring derogatory comments if he or she feels or fears them to be true. If that seems to be the case, you should help the student by emphasizing his or her strong points.

If there is any basis in reality for the teasing, the teacher can be honest with the student once a relationship between student and teacher has been established. By accepting the student and simultaneously helping him or her in problem areas, the teacher may eliminate the cause for teasing.

Code: S-IP-CC-0002-L1-Ir

TEACHING STRATEGY

Objective: Student responds to teasing or name calling by ignoring, changing the subject, or using some other constructive means appropriate to the situation.

Social Reinforcement

1. **Identify and recognize child by name when he or she is observed responding to teasing or name calling in some constructive way.** Call attention to the specific action; for example, "Theresa, I liked the way you walked away from Robert when he teased you and pulled your hair;" "Arthur, you did the right thing by walking away from Dujuan when he called you a name;" "Terry, I'm glad that you moved your desk close to mine when Kevin pushed you and knocked your things on the floor."

2. **Cue appropriate responses to teasing or name calling in the target student by recognizing others who respond constructively.**
3. **Soon after an incident of teasing occurs in which the student exhibited acceptable avoidance behavior, recognize him or her.** Explain to the class why you are pleased with that student's behavior.

Code: S-IP-CC-0002-L1-Ic

TEACHING STRATEGY

Objective: Student responds to teasing or name calling by ignoring, changing the subject, or using some other constructive means appropriate to the situation.

Contingency Management

1. **State the skill in observable terms.** When someone teases you or calls you a name, ignore him or her and, when possible, walk away. If you can't walk away, change the subject and try to make him or her start thinking about something else.
2. **Plan reinforcement strategy selected from reinforcement menu.**
3. **Inform target student that you are aware of the teasing and abusive name calling he or she received from the other student(s).** State the contingency that if the student will react to teasing and name calling by ignoring or walking away, he or she will be rewarded. Specify type and amount of reinforcement.
4. **Observe the target student and reward him or her each time he or she responds to teasing and name calling in a constructive manner.**
5. **Example.** During lunch period, Dujuan teases Doug by doing such things as throwing food at him, throwing paper wrappers and plastic forks into his lunch, kicking him under the table, and taking food from his tray. Eventually, Doug responds likewise with aggressive actions toward Dujuan, and a fight ensues. The teacher contracts with Doug: If he responds to Dujuan's teasing by gathering up his things and moving out of Dujuan's range, he will get to be Line Leader and wear the Line Leader Badge. (This is reinforcing to Doug.) Doug is made Line leader each day he responds accordingly. After keeping this contingency in force for a week, the teacher contracts with both Doug and Dujuan that if they can go through the entire lunch period with no teasing, aggression, and counter aggression, they will earn time to work on the jigsaw puzzle that is available at the back of the room. They must both cooperate in order to receive the reward.

Skill:	To respond to physical assault by leaving the situation, calling for help, or using some other constructive means. **S-IP-CC-0004-L1**
Objective:	Student responds to physical assault by leaving the situation, calling for help, or using some other constructive means appropriate to the situation.
Assessment:	Assess from previous knowledge of student or through direct observation using the <u>Social Behavior Assessment Inventory</u>.

Code: S-IP-CC-0004-L1-Im

TEACHING STRATEGY

Objective: Student responds to physical assault by leaving the situation, calling for help, or using some other constructive means appropriate to the situation.

Introduction: This is a difficult skill to teach because norms vary in the community and family. Some children are encouraged to fight when challenged to fight or physically assaulted. Additionally, children are exposed to innumerable situations on TV (cartoons and other programs) wherein violence is countered with violence. Thus, the best approach to dealing with fighting in school is usually to take preventive measures before the undesirable behavior reaches problem proportions.

It is very important to establish class and/or school rules to the effect that fighting in school is simply not allowed. It may be difficult to convince some students that fighting in school is improper. Despite these difficulties, students can realize that agree or not, fighting will not be tolerated. Teachers must then be consistent in upholding this rule. Next, students should be taught procedures for responding to physical assault. If they are to inform an adult, then some action must be taken by that adult. Often students do tell the teacher only to be frustrated when the teacher does nothing to deter the aggressor. For most effective results, teachers should establish rules and procedures early in the school year. These can then be used to reinforce established procedures if fighting becomes a significant problem. Teachers should be sure to emphasize the proper response, and not focus on the improper behavior of initiating a fight.

Social Modeling

1. **Set the stage.** State the rule that fighting is not allowed in school and explain why this rule has been established, e.g., there are many students here, we need to avoid possible injuries, and fighting is not a constructive way to solve problems. Define fighting in specific terms, e.g., fighting is any physical contact between two or more pupils where mutual consent is not present. Be sure the pupils can verbalize the definition in their own words. Discussion is not advisable for every group. Determine whether discussion in class will be beneficial. Some pupils might get carried away discussing how they would handle themselves in a fight. This can easily get the group worked up to a free-for-all emotional discussion of how to fight back. If you

believe a discussion may get out of control, do not initiate it; simply state the rule, give a rationale, and offer students alternative procedures to avoid fighting.

2. **Identify the specific steps.** Teacher says, "When someone challenges you to a fight, threatens to hit you, or does hit you, you should respond by telling the person you will not fight him or her because it is against school rules, and you know that you would both be punished for fighting. After saying you will not fight, leave the situation; walk away. If he or she persists, following you and calling you names or shoving, go to the adult on duty and tell him or her what has happened." This procedure gives the pupils in your class a specific way of behaving that should be expected from them at all times. Each teacher may have a particular set of behaviors that he or she may prefer to this particular approach. Alternatives may be substituted, but maintain specificity. Be sure each student can state the procedures to follow when attacked or challenged. It may be good to list and/or illustrate the components on the board or on a poster.

3. **Model the behavior.** It is suggested that the teacher model the response to aggression. You should begin by saying, "If someone wanted to start a fight on the playground, I would..." You should <u>not</u> role-play the improper behavior of intending to fight.

4. **Practice the behavior.** Ask students to demonstrate the three steps to be used to avoid physical fighting. Say, "John, show me what to do when someone tries to bother you." Recognize the student after proper demonstration, and reinforce and restate the desired behavior to the class. Follow the same procedure for the other target pupils.

5. **Additional suggestions.**

   (a) As a reinforcing strategy, you could prepare a large graph on which to record daily the number of "fights" that were avoided in school involving members of your class. You may assign tangible reinforcers to the graph by indicating the number of fights avoided to earn a reinforcer.

   (b) Provide cues for the target student(s) by recognizing others who handle conflict situations constructively.

Code: S-IP-CC-0004-L1-Ir

TEACHING STRATEGY

Objective: Student responds to physical assault by leaving the situation, calling for help, or using some other constructive means appropriate.

Social Reinforcement

1. **It is essential that you be alert and recognize students who demonstrate the appropriate behavior as soon as it occurs.** Be specific with your recognition; for example, "Darrell, you avoided a fight by walking away from LaMarr when he hit you. You did the right thing;" "Benny, I'm glad you came to me for help when Joe pushed you. I'm glad you didn't push him back;" "Pamela, thank you for picking up that eraser and bringing it to me instead of throwing it back when Robert threw it at you." If an individual

has a particularly difficult time avoiding fights, you may want to chart his or her behavior. He or she could make a check or receive a star each time he or she follows procedures for avoidng a fight. If necessary or desired, he or she may receive a predetermined reinforcer or privilege when a specified number of checks is accumulated. (See Contingency Management Strategy.)

2. **If fighting is a group problem, you may give the specified group or the entire class one point for every half day that no fighting occurs.** When the class has earned _____ points (optional number of points to be filled in; it is recommended that you start by requiring two or three points for a reward and gradually increase the number required) the class may see a movie, have outdoor recess, or engage in some other appropriate activity.

Code: S-IP-CC-0004-L1-Ic

TEACHING STRATEGY

Objective: Student responds to physical assault by leaving the situation, calling for help, or using some other constructive means appropriate.

Contingency Management

1. **State task in observable terms.** When someone hits you or threatens to hit you, walk away or call someone to help you. (Add other alternatives as appropriate.)

2. **Define a consequence valued by the student that will be given following demonstration of appropriate response to physical assault.** A group consequence is often useful for the behavior, i.e., rewarding the whole class if target students are able to avoid fights.

3. **State contingency.** If student responds to physical assault constructively, by leaving situations, by walking away from them, reward the student as stated in the contingency.

4. **Watch for the behavior to occur naturally.** If target child is able to avoid provocative situations by walking away from them, reward the student as stated in the contingency.

5. **Example.** During movement activity, Keith frequently bumps into Doug, trips him, pushes him, or falls on him. Doug usually responds with a hit or a push or a kick. Teacher contracts with Doug prior to movement activity, i.e., "If during movement activity, you move away from Keith when he pushes you instead of hitting him back, you can be in charge of the appropriate assignment (records and record players) for the rest of the day." The teacher watches Doug and rewards his attempt to avoid Keith with praise as well as the privilege. The teacher also sets contracts with the two boys that if they can avoid conflict with each other, they will earn points toward a reward for the whole class.

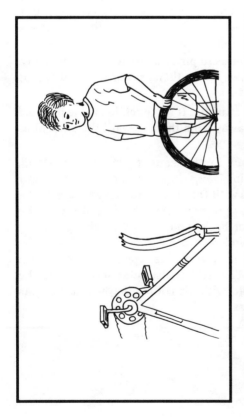

Figure 3. Four Panel Cartoon

94

<table>
<tr><td>**Skill:**</td><td>To walk away from peer when angry to avoid hitting.
S-IP-CC-0006-L1</td></tr>
<tr><td>**Objective:**</td><td>When angry with a peer, the student will walk away or use some other constructive means to avoid hitting.</td></tr>
<tr><td>**Assessment:**</td><td>Assess from previous knowledge of student or through direct observation using the <u>Social Behavior Assessment Inventory</u>.</td></tr>
</table>

Code: S-IP-CC-0006-L1-Im

TEACHING STRATEGY

Objective: When angry with a peer, the student will walk away or use some other constructive means to avoid hitting.

Social Modeling

1. **Set the stage.** In Figure 3, a short story is told through the use of cartoon characters. This should be available for the class to view. A transparency may be made of the page for projection. Show the cartoon strip to the class and ask the following questions:

   (a) "Did the boy in this story get angry?"

   (b) "What did he do?"

   (c) "How did he feel then?"

   (d) "What should he have done when he got angry?"

   Give praise for appropriate responses to these questions. After answers are taken for the last question and recognition is given, say, "Sometimes we behave like the boy in the story when we get angry. Today we're going to learn some different ways to behave when angry so that we can avoid hitting."

2. **Identify the specific behaviors.** You should say, "Beginning today, you will avoid hitting another person by walking away from the person with whom you are angry and/or by going to an adult to tell the adult what is happening to make you angry."

3. **Model the behavior.** You might demonstrate a series of situations in which he or she, playing the role of student, is angry with another student. Following are some sample situations:

   (a) Peer throws student's paper in the waste container.

   (b) Peer breaks the student's crayons.

   (c) Peer pushes student.

   Demonstrate the behaviors described in number 2. Give a verbal description of the peer behavior that precipitated the anger, rather than model the inappropriate behaviors.

4. **Practice the behavior.** Provide opportunity for practice. Follow the same procedures as in the modeling situation. Following are other sample situations for role-playing could include:

   (a) Peer gets into student's lunch and eats the cookies.

   (b) Peer throws student's books to the floor.

Reward students in the practice situation for finding satisfactory alternatives to hitting.

5. Additional suggestions.

(a) Provide cues for target students before going to the playground. Discuss with the class ways in which they can avoid hitting when they are angry; for example, walking away, changing the subject, or asking for adult intervention. Reinforcing students who display these behaviors provides cues for other students.

Note: In schools where there is a student mediator program, students should be instructed on the procedures to follow if they wish to have the dispute mediated by a peer.

(b) If cues and social reinforcement alone are not sufficient to help a student develop alternatives to fighting, recognition should be accompanied by a tangible reward for engaging in a constructive alternative when the student becomes angry. You could pair the assigning of jobs from the job board with praise for walking away from a peer when angry; for example, "John, I observed that you walked away from Larry after he threw your paper in the wastebasket. That took a lot of self-control. I'd like you to be teacher assistant this morning."

(c) See S-IP-CC-0010 for additional ways of handling anger.

Code: S-IP-CC-0006-L1-Ir

TEACHING STRATEGY

Objective: When angry with a peer, the student will walk away or use some other constructive means to avoid hitting.

Social Reinforcement

1. **Use social reinforcement when the student is observed walking away from a peer or using some means other than hitting when he or she is angry.** Be specific when reinforcing. For example, "Mickey, you showed your cool when Charlie grabbed the ball from you and you walked away from him;" "Jean, by changing the conversation you avoided an argument."

Code: S-IP-CC-0006-L1-Ic

TEACHING STRATEGY

Objective: When angry with a peer, the student will walk away or use some other constructive means to avoid hitting.

Contingency Management

1. **Present task to student in specific terms.** When you are angry with someone else, do not hit him or her. Instead, walk away, tell the person you are angry, or get an adult to intervene.

Note: There are occasions when "hitting back" may be the most constructive means for a student to handle aggression. You will need to use judgment in defining desirable alternatives based on the cultural context and the situation. This particular skill is aimed at the student's expression of his or her own anger rather than the handling of anger from others.

2. **Plan reinforcement.**

3. **State contingency.** If the student, when angry with a peer, walks away, talks about it rather than hitting, or uses some other constructive means to avoid hitting, the student receives the agreed-upon positive consequences. Specify type and amount of reinforcement.

4. **Watch for situations in the classroom or on the playground when a student who is angry avoids hurting another student and chooses some constructive alternative.** Reward the student according to the contingency that was established.

5. **Example.** Albert tended to be easily irritated by things that other children did. When he became angry, he yelled, pushed, and hit and was, therefore, frequently involved in fights. Albert's teacher, Mr. Simpson, worked on the problem from several angles. He talked with Albert about other ways in which he might express his anger without hurting others, e.g., getting out of the situation, telling the person that he was angry and asking why, and finding the teacher and telling why he was angry. Mr. Simpson also arranged with the gym that when Albert avoided hitting someone when he was angry, he could go into the gym and engage in an activity of his choosing.

Mr. Simpson felt that Albert's anger often arose out of misperceiving or misinterpreting someone else's actions and that he had some irrational ideas. For that reason, he also arranged for Albert to talk to the school counselor about those things that made Albert angry. Mr. Simpson established a contingency with Albert and the whole class. He set up a drawing of a thermometer in the class and gave marks on the thermometer for every day in which Albert was not involved in a fight. He also praised Albert's efforts to avoid fights and the other students for helping him. When the marks on the thermometer reached the top, the class had a pizza party.

Skill:	To politely refuse the request of another. **S-IP-CC-0008-L1**
Objective:	Student, when refusing someone's request, does so politely, giving a reason for the refusal.
Assessment:	Assess from previous knowledge of student or through direct observation using the <u>Social Behavior Assessment Inventory</u>.

Code: S-IP-CC-0008-L1-Im

TEACHING STRATEGY

Objective: Student, when refusing someone's request, does so politely, giving a reason for the refusal.

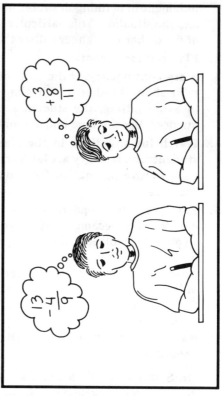

Figure 4. Four Panel Cartoon

Social Modeling

1. & 2. Set the stage and identify specific steps.

(a) Project the cartoon story depicted in Figure 4 and read the captions for the pupils. The projection can be done using this page with an opaque projector or by making a transparency from this page for projection. Say, "Look at this short story."

(b) Ask, "What happened in the story?" If the responses are not specific, ask specific questions, e.g., "What did Mike say to Chris?"

(c) Ask, "Was Chris polite?" (Student respose).

(d) Say, "Today, we are going to learn ways to say 'no' politely to someone's request, the way Chris did."

(e) Say, "Whenever someone asks you to do something and you do not want to do what he or she has asked, refuse politely. You do this by first saying, 'I'm sorry,' and then by giving the reason."

3. Model the behavior. You should ask a student to pretend that he or she wants to borrow something from you—the cassette player, for example. You will refuse the student's request politely and explain the reason for refusing to grant his request: "Billy, I know you like to listen to the cassette. I'm sorry, but you cannot use it now. I promised it to John for the next 15 minutes." Ask students to identify the elements of the modeled behavior. Recognize students who make good responses.

4. Practice the behavior. Create role-playing situations that enable each student to practice the behavior:

(a) Student asking another to be his or her partner.

(b) Student asking another to come to his or her house after school to play.

(c) Student asking to borrow another's paint set.

(d) Student asking to join game already in progress.

(e) Student asking another to have lunch with him or her.

These role-playing episodes can be put on 3 x 5 cards and drawn by pupils, then role-played for the class. The pupil drawing the card will be the pupil to refuse the request and will select a classmate to come to the front and make the request. Each pupil should be given an opportunity to practice.

5. Additional suggestions. For practice you may prepare cartoon stories like the one used in this strategy but leave the polite refusal frame blank for pupils to complete.

Code: S-IP-CC-0008-L1-Ir

TEACHING STRATEGY

Objective: Student, when refusing someone's request, does so politely, giving a reason for the refusal.

Social Reinforcement

1. Identify and recognize by name target student when observed refusing request politely. Call attention to specific actions; for example, "Darrell, I know you were using your crayons when Clement asked you to borrow them, and you remembered to be polite to him;" "Eric, you were very polite when you told Regis that you couldn't be his partner. That makes me happy;" "Theresa, I'm glad that you were so polite to Anthony when you told him that he couldn't borrow your paints. I'm very proud of you."

2. **Cue appropriate polite behavior in target student by recognizing others who are exhibiting proper behavior.**

3. **Make "Good Citizen" buttons for the class with ribbons so that little "merit" bars of contact paper can be added.** Award the button contingent upon politely refusing the request of a peer. "Bars" can be awarded in the same fashion.

Code: S-IP-CC-0008-L1-Ic

TEACHING STRATEGY

Objective: Student, when refusing someone's request, does so politely, giving a reason for the refusal.

Contingency Management

1. **State the task in observable terms.** When someone asks you for something and you do not want to comply, you should say, "No, I'm sorry," and then give your reason.

2. **Plan a reinforcement strategy selected from reinforcement menu.**

3. **State contingency.** When someone asks you for something and you want to refuse, if you say no politely and give a reason why you have to say no, you will receive the agreed-upon reward.

4. **Watch for behavior to occur naturally.** Reward it according to the terms of the contingency contract or set situation to necessitate student's asking something of another, and other student's having to refuse. For example, set up a practice activity in the form of a game. Give each child a number. Put slips of paper with a number written on each one in a box. Have students take turns drawing a number and making a request of the student whose number was drawn. The student whose number is drawn is to refuse the request politely and give a reason. Observe the procedure, and reward those who follow the rules for refusing politely.

5. **Example.** The children in Ms. Stinson's class go to the library, to recess, and to lunch in pairs. They are usually directed to choose a partner. When Pamela is selected by another student, she usually says rudely, "I don't want a partner." A contract is made with Pamela as stated in the contingency. When asked to do something, if she refuses politely and states her reason for refusing, then she may walk with the teacher to the lunchroom. (This is a "special privilege" that is reinforcing to Pamela.)

Skill:	To express anger with nonaggressive words rather than physical action or aggressive words. **S-IP-CC-0010-L2**
Objective:	When angry, the student expresses the anger with nonaggressive words rather than physical action or aggressive words.
Assessment:	Assess from previous knowledge of student or through direct observation using the <u>Social Behavior Assessment Inventory</u>.

Code: S-IP-CC-0010-L2-Im

TEACHING STRATEGY

Objective: When angry, the student expresses the anger with nonagressive words rather than physical action or aggressive words.

Social Modeling

1. **Set the stage.** Read the following story to the target pupils.

ENGLEBERT'S COOKIES

One morning, Englebert brought 24 oatmeal cookies, his favorite kind, to school for his birthday treat. He put the cookies in the file cabinet as the teacher had told him to do. As he was about to return to his seat, he noticed a classmate, Corky, leaving the room. Englebert knew that Corky would try to eat all of the oatmeal cookies, so he hid them in the file cabinet. Engelbert then left the room to go to the playground. When he left, Corky came back to the room and sniffed out the cookies. By the time Engelbert came back, Corky had eaten all 24 oatmeal cookies!

Needless to say, Engelbert was very angry! But Engelbert knew how to handle his anger; he knew that hitting or calling Corky names would not get his cookies back and would get him in trouble with the teacher. So he said to Corky, "Because you ate my oatmeal cookies, Corky, I have no dessert to serve for my birthday treat. This makes me angry."

Then Corky felt very bad that he had eaten the oatmeal cookies. He said, "I'm sorry, Engelbert. It was very selfish of me." Corky felt so bad that he went to the cafeteria and bought 24 cookies to give to Engelbert!

Begin a discussion with students asking, "How did Engelbert express his anger?" (Student response.) "Good, everyone!" Continue the discussion with questions such as the following:

(a) Why do you think Engelbert's way of expressing anger was the best way?

(b) What are some of the things that make us angry?

(c) Sometimes when we get angry, we have to stop a minute and think clearly about the right way to express our anger. Why should we stop to think about the right way to handle our anger?

2. **Identify specific steps.** Identify the steps composing the skill by saying, "When angry, the appropriate way to express your anger is to tell the

person how you feel, what he has done and how what he has done affects you. Is this what Engelbert did in the story?" (Student response.) "What did Engelbert say?" Help the pupils reconstruct what Engelbert said in the story. Recognition should be given to the pupils for appropriate verbal responses, e.g., "Juan, that was an excellent summary of what Engelbert said in the story."

3. **Model the behavior.** Pretend you are angry at students. Show how you might express anger by saying you are angry and then explaining why, relating it to the actions of the child, i.e., "When you are noisy, I get angry because I know that everyone cannot hear what I say," rather than, "You are so bad!" Ask students to identify elements of the modeled behavior. Recognize students who make good responses. Avoid pinpointing a particular student in front of the group.

4. **Practice the behavior.** Set role-playing situations to permit students to practice the appropriate behavior. Write each of the following (include those appropriate for your target group) on index cards and have pupils draw one card which the teacher reads to the pupil:

    (a) Student discovers that another has taken his or her crayons without asking.

    (b) Student is interrupted by another during discussion.

    (c) Student discovers that another student has lost his paint set.

    (d) Student accidently knocks another over during movement activity.

    (e) Student sticks his foot into the aisle to trip another as he walks by.

    (f) Student steals another's lunch money.

    (g) Student cuts in line in front of another.

    (h) Student takes a toy from another who had been playing with it.

    (i) Student throws food at another during lunch.

    Give each student an opportunity to participate. Have students observe the modeling and identify the desired behaviors by repeating what the role-playing pupil has stated in response to the situation.

    Note: This practice activity is deliberately structured to avoid having pupils role-play inappropriate behavior.

5. **Additional suggestions.**

    (a) Have those children who do not learn the behavior write about the situations that make them angry in a notebook or on index cards. You can then role-play each situation; the teacher will be assuming the student's role so that he or she may demonstrate the way anger could have been handled in each situation. Students should then assume their own role to practice expressing anger.

    (b) This skill would fit in well with a unit on feelings or emotions. It may be necessary with younger children to note that anger as a feeling is not "bad," but certain ways of expressing it may not be socially acceptable.

    (c) The use of self-recording may be useful as a device to help the student having difficulty with this skill. This would entail having the student use an index card or some other recording device to tally the frequency of appropriate and inappropriate expressions of anger.

TEACHING STRATEGY

Objective: When angry, the student expresses the anger with nonaggressive words rather than physical action or aggressive words.

Social Reinforcement

1. **Identify and recognize by name target student when observed expressing anger with nonaggressive words rather than physical action or aggressive words.** Call attention to specific actions. "Andy, you were angry, and you told John why you were angry with him. You did the right thing." "Gale, I'm glad that you told Gary why you were angry. You have a right to be angry, and it pleases me that you told him what made you angry." "Brian, you were angry with me, and you told me in a good way. It's good to tell someone why you're angry. That helps me to avoid the behavior that made you angry."

2. **Cue appropriate behavior in target student by praising others who are exhibiting proper behavior.**

TEACHING STRATEGY

Objective: When angry, the student expresses the anger with nonaggressive words rather than physical action or aggressive words.

Contingency Management

1. **State task in observable terms.** Here are two things to do when you feel angry:
   (a) Express your anger with words that will not make other people angry.
   (b) Avoid words or actions that will hurt another person or make another person angry also.

2. **Plan reinforcement strategy selected from reinforcement menu.**

3. **State contingency.** If student follows the rules for expressing anger by saying he or she is angry and telling why rather than by physical action or aggressive words, he or she will be rewarded.

4. **Observe the student in interaction with others.** When observed expressing anger by saying he or she is angry and telling why or by using some other appropriate means that avoids physical action or aggressive words, provide the agreed-upon reward.

5. **Example.** When Robert got angry with classmates or teacher, he expressed his anger by shouting names or kicking and hitting his teacher and classmates. Teacher contracted with Robert, as stated in the contingency. "When you are angry and you can tell us why you are angry without kicking, hitting, or calling names, you may remain in the group. When you fail to do so, you will go to the time-out room for the duration of the activity." Participating with the group was reinforcing to Robert. Each time Robert expressed his anger appropriately, he was rewarded verbally and allowed to remain with the group. To avoid the possibilities of increasing

Robert's expression of anger, the teacher was careful also to praise Robert for periods when he was in a "good mood" and did not express anger at all.

Skill:	To constructively handle criticism or punishment perceived as undeserved. **S-IP-CC-0012-L2**
Objective:	When the student perceives that he or she is being criticized or punished undeservedly, he or she will ask the teacher for an explanation.
Assessment:	Assess from previous knowledge of student or through direct observation using the <u>Social Behavior Assessment Inventory</u>.

Code: S-IP-CC-0012-L2-Im

TEACHING STRATEGY

Objective: When the student perceives that he or she is being criticized or punished undeservedly, he or she will ask the teacher for an explanation.

Introduction: In order not to encourage students to use this skill as a way of avoiding punishment for wrong-doing, stress that one should have good reasons for feeling that the blame or criticism is unjust and that explanations should only be offered if they are true and will help to clear up a misunderstanding. S-SR-AC-0006-L2 should be mastered as a prerequisite skill.

Social Modeling

1. & 2. Set the stage and identify the specific steps. Select a time when everything has gone well for your class and everyone is in a good mood. Open a discussion related to this skill by asking the following questions: "Have you ever been blamed, criticized, or punished for something you did not do?" (Caution: Avoid exchanging anecdotes by asking and/or listening to specific examples.)

"At one time or another just about everyone has been. Usually, the first thing we do is to deny our involvement. Sometimes this does not work, i.e., people do not believe us. If this happens, it is best not to argue with the person at the time, because the person will get angry, and it may make things worse. Here are three things to do when you have been punished or blamed, and you don't feel that you deserve to be punished or blamed:

(a) Wait until you feel fairly calm.

(b) Go to the teacher and ask why you are being punished.

(c) Explain why you do not deserve the punishment or blame."

3. Model the behavior. Explain to the class that you are going to model this behavior for them. Tell them that you are pretending that Ms. M., the principal, had earlier in the day criticized you for leaving the art room in a mess the night before and that she would not listen when you tried to explain what happened. Tell them to pretend that a selected pupil is the principal and you are in her office. Have a pupil sit at your desk and play the role of principal. (Talk and play with the pupil beforehand about the role.)

Teacher: Ms. M., may I talk with you for a few minutes?

Principal: Yes, Mr. Z., come in.

Teacher: This morning you told me that my class could no longer use the art room. Why?

Principal: Because the room was left in a mess after you used it yesterday.

Teacher: I understand how you feel about that messy room, but our class should not be punished. We have not used that art room in more than two weeks.

Principal: According to the schedule, your class used the room the last period of the day yesterday.

Teacher: I know that the schedule shows we used the art room the last period on Tuesday, but we made a special arrangement to use it for several consecutive days beginning next week. Here is a copy of the memo I sent you.

Principal: You are right, Mr. M., your class should not be punished. I forgot about this. Please accept my apology.

Teacher: Yes, I will. Thank you for listening.

Encourage the students to identify the specific elements of the modeled behavior. Recognize those who respond correctly.

4. **Practice the behavior.** Provide opportunity to practice. In pairs or small groups, direct children to role-play situations involving reacting to underserved punishment. Write a number of situations on 3 x 5 cards. Have pupils draw a card and role-play the situation on the card. You should play the role of the party who has criticized, blamed, or punished the pupil. Here are some possible examples:

(a) One student accuses another of taking his book.

(b) One student accuses another of cheating and says he or she can't play with the group anymore.

(c) One student accuses another of talking about him or her "behind his or her back."

(d) One student stops talking to another because he or she thinks the student "tattled" on him or her.

(e) One student tells another that he or she can't play on the team because the student doesn't "try hard enough."

Observe the simulations and praise those who make good responses, demonstrating asking calmly why they are being blamed and offering an explanation to clear up the misunderstanding. You may want to provide the students an opportunity to create their own situations and present them to the class.

5. **Additional suggestions.**

   (a) Provide cues for target student. If he or she is upset about criticism or punishment and indicates he or she does not feel it was deserved, provide an opportunity for him or her to explain why. The student must be allowed to clear up misunderstandings by giving explanations, but you must exercise judgment in distinguishing legitimate explanations from made-up excuses or alibis, and avoid reinforcing the latter.

   (b) The teacher may want to take advantage of a situation in which a student has felt unjustly criticized or punished and has reacted strongly. The teacher may want to talk to the target student privately, when he or she is calm enough to discuss the occurrence, suggesting some alternative ways to handle the problem.

Code: S-IP-CC-0012-L2-Ir

TEACHING STRATEGY

Objective: When the student perceives that he or she is being criticized or punished undeservedly, he or she will ask the teacher for an explanation.

Social Reinforcement

1. **When appropriate, identify by name and recognize student when observed reacting in a constructive way to criticism or punishment that is perceived as undeserved.** Be sure the recognition is specific so that the student knows what he or she did right. "I'm glad you told me that you had your homework, Jackie. Now we can erase this X;" "I'm sorry for punishing you for coming late, Terry. Thank you for explaining."

Code: S-IP-CC-0012-L2-Ic

TEACHING STRATEGY

Objective: When the student perceives that he or she is being criticized or punished undeservedly, he or she will ask the teacher for an explanation.

Contingency Management

1. **Explain.** Tell the student that when he or she feels punished, blamed, or criticized for something he or she didn't do, he or she should explain calmly and politely to the teacher why the student does not deserve the punishment or blame, and ask the teacher why he or she is being punished, blamed, or criticized.

2. **Plan reinforcement.**

3. **Tell the student that each time he or she comes to the teacher and asks politely for justification of possibly unfair criticism or punishment and explains why it is unfair, he or she will receive a reward.** Also, explain that he or she will not be rewarded unless he or she can provide good reasons why he or she feels the criticism is unjust. Specify the type and amount of reinforcement.

4. **Deliver to the student the agreed-upon reward if he or she reacts appropriately to criticism or punishment that is seen as unfair,** calmly and politely explaining to the teacher why it was unjust and asking for further explanation of why he or she received the criticism or punishment.

5. **Example.** When Simone is punished or criticized, she often sulks and mutters complaints under her breath. Ms. Eagen explains to her that the proper thing to do when one feels she is criticized unfairly is to ask the teacher calmly and politely why she is being criticized and explain why she feels she should not be criticized. Ms. Eagen tells Simone that each time she does this instead of being angry or sulking, she will receive five minutes at the Interest Center of her choice, and that each time she sulks and complains she will lose five minutes of Interest Center time.

During the first week Simone reacts appropriately twice to criticism and inappropriately once, gaining a total of five minutes "reward" time. The next week she reacts appropriately twice and has no inappropriate responses, gaining ten minutes. The contingency is kept for six weeks, five weeks of which Simone shows no inappropriate responses. The contingency is then dropped, and social reinforcement is used to maintain the behavior.

GAINING ATTENTION

S-IP-GA-0002-L1-S	To gain teacher's attention in class by raising hand.
S-IP-GA-0004-L1-S	To wait quietly for recognition before speaking out in class.
S-IP-GA-0006-L1-S	To use "please" and "thank you" when making requests of others.
S-IP-GA-0008-L2-S	To approach teacher and ask appropriately for help, explanation, instructions, etc.
S-IP-GA-0010-L2-S	To gain attention from peers in appropriate ways.
S-IP-GA-0012-L2-S	To ask a peer for help.

Skill:	To gain teacher's attention in class by raising hand. **S-IP-GA-0002-L1**
Objective:	Student raises hand and waits to be called on when wishing to speak.
Assessment:	Assess from previous knowledge of student or through direct observation using the <u>Social Behavior Assessment Inventory</u>.

Code: S-IP-GA-0002-L1-Im

TEACHING STRATEGY

Objective: Student raises hand and waits to be called on when wishing to speak.

Social Modeling

1. **Identify a need for the behavior through classroom discussion.** Ask questions so that students can contribute ideas to the discussion. For example, "What would happen if all students yelled out their questions or answers? What would be a better thing to do? What should you do after you raise your hand?"

2. **Identify specific behaviors to be modeled.** Raise your hand and wait to be called on when you want to say something in class.

3. **Model the behavior.** Ask a student to play teacher and conduct a simple lesson, such as giving spelling words for a practice test. The teacher can model a student, sitting in the student's desk, demonstrating how to raise hand and wait to be called on.

4. **Provide opportunities for practice.** Cue students before a lesson that you want them to practice raising their hands before they speak out. The lesson might require, for example, that students raise their hand when they are finished with a seat work assignment, and wait to get it checked.

5. **Maintain the behavior through reinforcement.** Remember that providing attention by calling on a student to speak is reinforcing. Be careful not to call on a student or provide attention and recognition if the student has called out.

Code: S-IP-GA-0002-L1-Ir

TEACHING STRATEGY

Objective: Student raises hand and waits to be called on when wishing to speak.

Social Reinforcement

1. **Reinforce with smiles and praise when the student is observed raising hand and waiting to be called on by the teacher.** Use recognition that described the student's behavior. For example, "Marsha, thank you for raising your hand and waiting so patiently;""Charlie, I appreciated your raising your hand and waiting for me to call on you. Thank you."
2. **Provide cues for the target student.** Praise another student who is demonstrating the behavior. Reinforce the target student for responding to the cue.
3. **If social reinforcement in the form of praise, smiles, pats on the back, etc. is not sufficient to increase the desired behavior, it may be necessary to accompany social reinforcement with tangible reinforcement in the form of tokens, chips, points.** Tangible reinforcement can be exchanged for items desired by the students.

Code: S-IP-GA-0002-L1-Ic

TEACHING STRATEGY

Objective: Student raises hand and waits to be called on when wishing to speak.

Contingency Management

1. **Discuss with the student the desired behavior of raising hand and waiting to be called on before speaking out in class.**
2. **Plan reinforcement.**
3. **State contingency.** If the student, when wanting to say something in class, raises hand and waits to be called on, then he or she will receive the agreed-upon consequence. Specify type and amount of reinforcement.
4. **Watch for the behavior to occur naturally, or set up a situation in which the behavior can occur.** Give the student an independent task to do on a skill that has been mastered. Tell the student to inform you when the task is completed by raising hand and waiting to be called on. If the student demonstrates the behavior, reinforce according to the contingency that was established.
5. **Example.** Whenever Donna wanted the teacher's attention, she would call out her teacher's name, "Ms. Roberts, come here!" Ms. Roberts observed that Donna seldom raised her hand and waited to be called on. Ms. Roberts spoke with Donna one morning before school started. She told Donna that she wanted her to raise her hand and wait to be called on before speaking. She had Donna practice sitting at her desk, raising her hand, and waiting to be called on by Ms. Roberts before speaking.

Ms. Roberts set up the following contingency with Donna: If she could decrease the number of times she called out without raising her hand and waiting to be called on, she would receive free time to play a game with a friend. Ms. Roberts counted Donna's talking-out behavior before she set up the contract and established what Donna's rate per minute for talk-outs was during work periods. She made a graph of talk-outs, and for every talk-out that Donna eliminated, she would receive three minutes of free time. For example, if Donna's **baseline average** (the average of her talking-out behavior **before** contracting) of four talk-outs per minute was decreased to one, Donna would receive nine minutes of free time. Ms. Roberts also praised Donna when she remembered to raise her hand.

Skill: To wait quietly for recognition before speaking out in class.
S-IP-GA-0004-L1

Objective: The student waits quietly for teacher to recognize him or her before speaking out in class.

Assessment: Assess from previous knowledge of student or through direct observation using the Social Behavior Assessment Inventory.

Code: S-IP-GA-0004-L1-Im

TEACHING STRATEGY

Objective: Student waits quietly for teacher to recognize him or her before speaking out in class.

Social Modeling

1. **Identify a need for the behavior through a classroom discussion.** You may want to structure discussion by asking such questions as, "What can you do to let us know in a polite way that you have something to say? When we're having a discussion and you want to talk, what should you do? Why can't you talk out anytime you want to? What happens if everyone talks at once?" Ask students for ideas.

2. **Identify specific behaviors to be modeled.** When you want to speak in class:

   (a) Raise your hand.

   (b) Wait quietly for the teacher to call on you.

   (c) Speak out only after the teacher has called on you.

   Write key words on board or chart.

3. **Model the behavior for the class.** For example, form a discussion circle. Take the role of a student, and select a student to play the part of teacher. Take a seat in the circle and pretend that you want to speak. Raise your hand and wait quietly, without interrupting anyone or bothering anyone, to be recognized by the teacher. Ask students to identify elements of the modeled behavior. Praise students who make good responses.

4. **Have the class practice waiting to be recognized before speaking.** Give children an opportunity to demonstrate in a group discussion how they can

raise their hands, wait to be recognized, and then speak after the teacher calls on them.

5. **Recognize those students who wait to be called upon before speaking in the role-playing situation.** Maintain the behavior in the classroom by praising students who remember to raise their hands and wait for recognition before speaking out.

Code: S-IP-GA-0004-L1-Ir

TEACHING STRATEGY

Objective: Student waits quietly for teacher to recognize him or her before speaking out in class.

Social Reinforcement

1. **Praise target student when raising hand and waiting to be recognized before speaking out in class.** Call attention to specific actions; for example, "Kitty, you remembered to wait until I called on you before you spoke;" "August, you remembered to raise your hand;" "Gladys, you have been waiting so quietly. You remembered the classroom rule about waiting to be called on;" "I like the way Tom is raising his hand."

   Cue appropriate behavior in target student by recognizing others who raise their hands and wait to be called on before speaking.

2. **If social reinforcement is not sufficient to increase the desired behavior, it may be necessary to accompany social reinforcement with tangible reinforcement.**

Code: S-IP-GA-0004-L1-Ic

TEACHING STRATEGY

Objective: Student waits quietly for teacher to recognize him or her before speaking out in class.

Contingency Management

1. **State task in observable terms.**
   (a) Raise your hand.
   (b) Wait quietly until the teacher calls on you.
   (c) Speak out only after the teacher has called on you.

2. **Plan reinforcement strategy selected from reinforcement menu.**

3. **State contingency.** When you want to speak in class, if you raise your hand and wait quietly to be called on before you speak, you will be rewarded. Specify type and amount of reinforcement.

4. **Observe target child during a small group or class discussion.** Observe the behavior exhibited when he wants to speak. Reward him when he raises his hand and waits quietly to be recognized before speaking. Observe student throughout the school day and reward him according to the established contract for raising his hand and waiting to be recognized before speaking out.

111

5. **Example.** When Terry has something to tell the class or show the class during Group Circle time, she frequently blurts out without waiting for a turn. When she isn't talking, she often annoys the others around her (hits, kicks, pinches, whispers, falls out of her chair, etc.). A contract was made with Terry: "If you raise your hand when you have something to say and then sit quietly and wait your turn until I call on you before I start talking, I will give you a plastic brick." The teacher in this class used plastic bricks as tokens. Several times a day, the students added bricks they earned to a building the whole class was building and were praised for earning the bricks. When the entire building was completed, the class had story time.

Skill:	To use "please" and "thank you" when making requests. **S-IP-GA-0006-L1**
Objective:	Student appropriately uses the phrase "please" when requesting something and "thank you" when the request is answered.
Assessment:	Assess from previous knowledge of student or through direct observation using the <u>Social Behavior Assessment Inventory</u>.

Code: S-IP-GA-0006-L1-Im

TEACHING STRATEGY

Objective: Student appropriately uses the phrase "please" when requesting something and "thank you" when the request is answered.

Social Modeling

1. **Identify the need through a classroom discussion.** Have students contribute reasons for using the phrases "please" and "thank you." Have students identify situations when they would use "please" and "thank you." Make two lists of situations under the words "please" and "thank you" on the bulletin board.

2. **Identify specific behaviors to be modeled.**
   (a) The student will say "please" when asking someone for something.
   (b) The student will say "thank you" when someone gives him or her something.

3. **Model the behavior for the class.** Ask to borrow a piece of paper by saying, "Please, may I have a piece of paper?" Then say, "Thank you for giving me a sheet of paper." Ask students to identify elements of the modeled behavior. Praise students who make good responses.

4. **Have class practice the behavior.** Give each student an opportunity to use the terms "please" and "thank you" when giving something to and receiving something from another class member.

5. **Recognize those students who say "please" and "thank you" when appropriate.**

6. **Maintain proper use of "please" and "thank you" through reinforcement.**

Code: S-IP-GA-0006-L1-Ir

TEACHING STRATEGY

Objective: Student appropriately uses the phrase "please" when requesting something and "thank you" when the request is answered.

Social Reinforcement

1. **Identify and recognize by name, aloud, target student when observed saying "please" when requesting something, and "thank you" when the request is answered.** Call attention to specific actions, e.g., "Bob, that was nice of you to say 'please' when you wanted to borrow a piece of paper;" "Hal, that was really polite of you to thank Mary when she gave you a piece of candy."

2. **Cue appropriate uses of the term "please" when requesting something and "thank you" when the request is answered, by recognizing others near the target child who are exhibiting this behavior.** Watch for the desired behavior in target child and be sure to reinforce it.

3. **Use a tangible reinforcer along with social reinforcement if necessary.**

Code: S-IP-GA-0006-L1-Ic

TEACHING STRATEGY

Objective: Student appropriately uses the phrase "please" when requesting something and "thank you" when the request is answered.

Contingency Management

1. **State task in observable terms.**
   (a) Student will say "please" when he or she asks someone else to do something.
   (b) Student will say "thank you" when another person gives him or her something or does something for him or her.
   (c) Students will write these words on a card and tape them to their desks as reminders.

2. **Plan reinforcement strategy selected from reinforcement menu.**

3. **State contingency.** If student uses phrases "please" and "thank you" properly, he or she will be rewarded. Specify amount and type of reinforcement.

4. **Set situation to necessitate classmates borrowing from each other,** e.g., art project where half the class has paint brushes and the other half has scissors, and all the students need to use both. Observe the use of "please" and "thank you," and reward those who use them properly.

5. **Example.** The teacher noticed that students in her class had not been using "please" and "thank you" when asking for or receiving things from one another. She discussed the reasons for using "please" and "thank you" and then set up a contingency with the students. Each student would receive a point each time she heard him or her use "please" and "thank you." When the teacher needed someone to run an errand, she would choose the

student with the most points. At first, these points were kept each day for morning and afternoon separately, so everyone would receive an opportunity for reward. The teacher also praised those students receiving the award for their use of the words "please" and "thank you."

Skill:	To approach teacher and ask appropriately for help, explanation, instruction, etc. **S-IP-GA-0008-L2**
Objective:	Student approaches the teacher and asks appropriately for help, explanation, or instructions at an appropriate time as defined by the teacher.
Assessment:	Assess from previous knowledge of student or through direct observation using the <u>Social Behavior Assessment Inventory</u>.

Code: S-IP-GA-0008-L2-Im

TEACHING STRATEGY

Objective: Student approaches the teacher and asks appropriately for help, explanation, or instructions at an appropriate time as defined by the teacher.

Social Modeling

1. **Identify a need for the behavior through a classroom discussion.** To structure the discussion, you may want to ask questions, such as, "Can you think of some reasons why you might need to talk to me during the day? When do you think a good time to talk to me might be? When you need to talk to me, how can you let me know? What are some things to say in asking for help or explanation?" Involve students in the discussion by asking them for ideas and suggestions. Write on the board the key elements of their suggestions for the appropriate way to approach the teacher.

2. **Identify specific behaviors to be modeled.** When you want to speak to the teacher or ask for help, ask a question, or ask for instructions, you should approach the teacher at appropriate times. (It is important for the teacher to specify how he or she defines appropriate conditions since teachers will vary in their definition of what are proper times and conditions for seeking help.) In asking the teacher for help or instructions, address the teacher by name, use please and thank you, and try to tell the teacher specifically what you need help with.

3. **Model behavior for the children.** Select a student to play teacher while you play the role of student, approaching the teacher for help under several different conditions; for example, teacher writing on the board, teacher sitting alone at desk, teacher at desk conferring with another student, teacher sitting with reading group. Demonstrate right and wrong times to approach the teacher and right and wrong ways to go about asking for help or explanations. Have students point out which were correct and

114

which were incorrect, and tell why. Recognize students who make quality contributions.

Note: Many children have difficulties with academic work because they are not comfortable seeking help from the teacher. This skill is a complex one involving a number of prerequisite skills, such as using the teacher's name, using please and thank you, following classroom rules, and asking a question appropriate to the information needed. You will need to be available to students and establish the conditions under which students can approach for help. At the same time, in order for this behavior to stay within reasonable limits, you will need to reinforce students for the skills involving listening to assignment directions, attempting to solve a problem themselves before asking for help, and finding productive uses of time while waiting for teacher assistance.

Code: S-IP-GA-0008-L2-Ir

TEACHING STRATEGY

Objective: Student approaches the teacher and asks appropriately for help, explanation, or instructions at an appropriate time as defined by the teacher.

Social Reinforcement

1. **Identify and recognize by name, target students when oberved approaching you and asking for help, explanation or instructions appropriately.** Call attention to specific actions: "Timothy, I'm glad that you waited until I was finished talking to Arthur before you asked your question. You are very polite;" "George, thank you for waiting for me to finish passing out the papers before asking me for the instructions;" "Darrell, it makes me happy when you remember to wait until I'm finished talking before you ask me for help. I'm proud of you;" "Mary, you asked me for help very politely. You remembered to use my name and say please."

2. **Cue appropriate behavior in target students by recognizing others who ask for assistance at appropriate times and in appropriate ways.**

3. **Specific classroom conditions can be set up to assist with this behavior,** such as providing numbers when several students have to wait for help or to have papers checked, or by setting up a "waiting" chair or bench near the teacher's desk.

Note: Social reinforcement for this skill can be accompanied by a tangible reinforcer if necessary. However, reinforcement should be used selectively and provided especially for those students who need to be encouraged to ask for help more often or those who need to learn to discriminate between appropriate and inappropriate ways and times to ask for help.

TEACHING STRATEGY

Objective: Student approaches the teacher and asks appropriately for help, explanation, or instructions at an appropriate time as defined by the teacher.

Contingency Management

1. **State task in specific terms.** When you want to ask the teacher for help, you:

   (a) Wait until he or she is not busy.

   (b) Then walk up to him or her and ask your question.

   If needed, provide a list of appropriate asking-for-help behaviors as reminders. For example, address the teacher by name, use please and thank you, ask the question clearly.

2. **Plan reinforcement.**

3. **State contingency.** When the student wants to ask the teacher for help or instruction, if he or she waits until the teacher is through talking or working and then asks the questions, he or she will receive the specified reward.

4. **Watch for the behavior to occur naturally.** Reinforce it when it occurs according to established contingency, or set up situation which necessitates asking for explanation and instructions. For example, you may hand materials or worksheets to students giving an explanation for only part of the worksheet. Students would be required to come to your desk and ask for instructions for completing the worksheet. Students who approach the teacher appropriately, waiting their turn and asking for help clearly and politely, would receive the specified positive consequence.

5. **Example.** When given an assignment, Robert frequently interrupted the teacher's explanation with such questions and comments as, "I can't do this...I don't understand this...Teacher, come here and help me... What am I supposed to do with this?" He seldom waited to learn the instructions. A contract was made with Robert that if he listened and waited until the teacher had completed her instructions before asking a question, then he could pass out and collect all papers for the day.

   Christie, in the same class, had a different problem. She often did not understand the instructions, but instead of asking for help, she sat quietly in her seat and did not work. The teacher demonstrated to Christie how she would like her to go about asking for help, either by raising her hand and waiting until the teacher came or by going to the teacher's desk when the teacher was free and telling the teacher or showing her what she did not understand. The contract established for Christie was based on worksheets completed, rather than on asking questions, in order to avoid reinforcing unnecessary asking for help. Christie liked to draw with magic markers. For every worksheet completed, Christie earned free time later in the day to draw with the teacher's magic markers.

Skill:	To gain attention from peers in appropriate ways.
	S-IP-GA-0010-L2
Objective:	Student gains attention from a peer by saying the peer's name in a volume appropriate to the setting, and telling what is wanted.
Assessment:	Assess from previous knowledge of student or through direct observation using the <u>Social Behavior Assessment Inventory</u>.

Code: S-IP-GA-0010-L2-Im

TEACHING STRATEGY

Objective: Student gains attention from a peer by saying the peer's name in a volume appropriate to the setting, and telling what is wanted.

Social Modeling

1. **Identify a need for the behavior through a classroom discussion.** Teacher may begin by posing questions, such as, "If you need to talk to one of your classmates, how could you do so without disturbing anybody else? Why do you think we should have a rule about yelling across the room? When someone wants to talk to you, would you rather be called by name, or do you think it is all right for people to call out 'Hey you'?" Discuss other ways to get attention which are **not** appropriate, such as doing something silly or aggressive, like teasing the other person. Bring out attention-seeking behaviors that present problems in the class. It may be brought out that everyone likes attention, admiration, and liking from others but that some ways of seeking attention make one disliked rather than liked. Ask students to contribute ideas, and write key elements of appropriate attention-getting on the board.

2. **Identify specific behaviors to be modeled.** When you want to get attention of a classmate:

   (a) Call him or her by name in an appropriate tone of voice.

   (b) Tell him or her what you want.

3. **Model the behavior for the class.** You may first demonstrate the incorrect way to gain attention of the person to whom you want to speak:

   (a) Teacher may address student by snapping fingers and saying, "Hey you, come here, I want to borrow your pencil."

   (b) Teacher whistles and gestures with hand to student, "Come over here, you."

   (c) Teacher yells loudly across room, "Ida, let me see your book."

   Next, explain to students that all three of these ways of getting attention are inconsiderate and disturbing. Call on students individually to demonstrate a better way of:

   (1) Borrowing pencil.

   (2) Asking student to come to desk.

   (3) Looking at book.

Other kinds of inappropriate attention-getting behavior that are problems in the particular class may also be used as examples. Ask students to identify elements of the modeled behavior. Recognize students who make good quality responses.

4. **Allow each child to practice the behavior.** Set up situations for each child to properly gain a classmate's attention:

   (a) Student asks another to walk home from school with him.
   (b) Student asks another to help him with math problems.
   (c) Student asks another if she has an eraser he can borrow.
   (d) Student asks another if he needs help with his homework.
   (e) Student asks another to eat lunch with him.
   (f) Student asks another to play with her at recess.
   (g) Student asks another to repeat her question.
   (h) Student asks another to explain his answer again.
   (i) Student asks another if she could see the items she brought for "show and tell."
   (j) Student wants another to watch how well she can jump rope.

5. **Recognize those students who demonstrate appropriate behavior in role-playing.**

6. **Maintain appropriate gaining attention from peers through social reinforcement.**

   Note: For those students for whom peer attention is highly reinforcing and who resort to inappropriate means of seeking it, in addition to being taught appropriate ways to gain attention by addressing other students, it may be necessary to provide opportunities for legitimately obtaining peer attention. For example, such a student can be taught a skill to demonstrate to the class or can be called on to perform something he or she does well.

Code: S-IP-GA-0010-L2-Ir

TEACHING STRATEGY

Objective: Student gains attention from a peer by saying the peer's name in a volume appropriate to the setting, and telling what is wanted.

Social Reinforcement

1. **Identify and recognize by name target student when observed gaining attention from a peer by saying the peer's name in a volume appropriate to the situation.** Call attention to specific actions, e.g., "Pamela, I'm glad that you walked to Terry's desk and asked her quietly to borrow her crayons. I like that. You didn't disturb anyone else." "Brian, I'm proud of you—you called Derrell by his name when you talked to him." "Penny, you are very polite, you remembered to talk to Barry quietly at his desk. I like it when you observe the rules in the classroom." Cue appropriate behavior in target student by recognizing others who are gaining peer's attention appropriately.

Note: If social reinforcement is insufficient, it may be necessary to accompany social reinforcement with tangible reinforcement.

Code: S-IP-GA-0010-L2-Ic

TEACHING STRATEGY

Objective: Student gains attention from a peer by saying the peer's name in a volume appropriate to the setting, and telling what he or she wants.

Contingency Management

1. **State task in observable terms.** When you want attention from one of your classmates:

    (a) Say that person's name quietly rather than yelling or shouting.

    (b) Tell him or her what you want.

    (c) Make sure you are not interrupting or bothering others when you are seeking his or her attention.

    If necessary, display these "classroom rules" on bulletin board or chart.

2. **Plain reinforcement strategy selected from reinforcement menu.**

3. **State contingency.** When you want attention from one of your classmates, if you wait until an appropriate time, remember to say that person's name quietly, and then tell him or her what you want, you will be rewarded. Specify amount of reinforcement.

    Because inappropriately seeking peer attention is often a classroom problem, you may also want to set up an aversive contingency. For example, "If you try to get attention from a classmate at inappropriate times, (e.g., during a work period) or in inappropriate ways (e.g., yelling, teasing), you will receive _____ (an aversive consequence)." You may also want to handle problem behaviors in this area by teaching other students S-IP-CC-0002 (responding to teasing or name calling by ignoring, etc.).

4. **During times when students are together on the playground or in the classroom, observe the student(s) for appropriately seeking classmates' attention.** Reward (or punish) according to the contingency which was established.

5. **Example.** Allan was a rather obese boy who was not well liked by classmates. He very much wanted peer attention and found that if he made silly remarks and teased other students, he could generally create considerable attention to himself. He was, consequently, very disruptive in the classroom. The teacher, Ms. Evans, took him aside one day and talked to him about his behavior, letting him know that she understood how important it was to him to have other children pay attention to him, but that there were better ways to get peer attention. She reviewed with him the inappropriate things he did as well as how he could appropriately gain a peer's attention by having a legitimate reason, waiting until an appropriate time, addressing the peer by name, and stating in a polite way what he wanted. Ms. Evans knew that Allan liked to do magic tricks and had a number of routines he could do very well. She established a contingency with Allan that if he could decrease inappropriate efforts to get peer

attention, she would set up opportunities for him to do magic shows for his own class and for other classes as well. Ms. Evans set up a point system in which Allan would have to earn 50 points to put on a magic show. She gave him 12 points to start each day and subtracted a point for each time he did one of the things she had defined as inappropriate. If he could go all day without having any points subtracted, he earned three bonus points.

Skill:	To ask a peer for help. **S-IP-GA-0012-L2**
Objective:	Student will ask a peer for help when it is appropriate to the situation.
Assessment:	Assess from previous knowledge of student or through direct observation using the <u>Social Behavior Assessment Inventory</u>.

Code: S-IP-GA-0012-L2-Im

TEACHING STRATEGY

Objective: Student will ask a peer for help when it is appropriate to the situation.

Social Modeling

1. **To introduce this skill, you may want to structure a class discussion around the theme of "Helping Others" or "Sharing," using films, stories, or other available media.** Encourage the students to contribute their own ideas in developing reasons for asking for **and** giving help to others. Involve students in identifying times when they might want to ask a peer for help and times when it might not be appropriate. For example, it would not be appropriate to ask another student for help on a test or if the teacher specified that the work was to be done alone. It would be appropriate if the teacher suggested that students could help each other.

2. **Identify the specific behavior to be modeled.** When you need help with your school work, you may:

    (a) Go to one of your classmates when he or she is not busy.

    (b) Tell him or her what you are having trouble with.

    (c) Ask politely if he or she has time to help you.

3. **Model the behavior.** Choose two students who are willing to role-play and ask one to demonstrate how he would go about asking the other for help with a seatwork paper, learning spelling words, understanding an assignment, etc. Try to make a distinction between receiving help that enables one to complete the work itself and asking someone else to do the work for you. Ask students to identify the desired behaviors. This skill could be extended to asking for help on the playground, help fastening clothing, help with a cleaning-up task, etc.

4. **Provide opportunity for practice.** Have students role-play in pairs, with either simulated or actual school work, how to ask someone to help with such problems as understanding directions, understanding a word or two

in a reading assignment, giving spelling words or sight words for drill, etc. Observe students, and reinforce for good responses in the role-playing.

5. **Establish conditions in the class under which it is appropriate to ask a peer for help.** Maintain the behavior through reinforcement.

Code: S-IP-GA-0012-L2-Ir

TEACHING STRATEGY

Objective: Student will ask peer for help when it is appropriate to the situation.

Social Reinforcement

1. **Recognize by name student observed correctly asking another for help.** Reinforce with verbal recognition that is specific to the behavior. "Jeff, I'm glad to see that you asked Shawn to help you with your math problems;" "Patrick, I noticed that you asked Scott to look at your English paper before you handed it in. That makes me happy;" "Good, Lucy, I like the way you asked Nancy to help you on with your boots." (Also recognize students who do the helping.)

2. **Provide cues for target student.** Remind the student, if necessary, that he or she may ask classmates for help with school work, and remember to reinforce others who do ask for help appropriately. If the target student does respond to your cue, reinforce immediately.

3. **If social reinforcement does not produce a change in behavior, it may be necessary to add a more tangible reward.** A student who needs particular encouragement to approach other students may be given a token or some other tangible reinforcer along with recognition.

Code: S-IP-GA-0012-L2-Ic

TEACHING STRATEGY

Objective: Student will ask a peer for help when it is appropriate to the situation.

Contingency Management

1. **State the task to the student in specific, observable terms.** Discuss with him or her, if necessary, setting up the conditions for asking for help. For example, when you are having trouble with your school work, before coming to me for help:

   (a) Go to a classmate.
   (b) Ask him or her is he or she is busy.
   (c) Tell him or her your problem.
   (d) Ask him or her if he or she has time to help you.

   If you still need help, then you may come to me.

2. **Plan reinforcement.**

3. **State the contingency.** When you need help with your school work, if you appropriately ask a classmate to help you, then you will be rewarded.

4. **During independent work sessions, observe the interaction among the students.** Reward those who approach their peers quietly and at the appropriate time to ask for help. You could structure specific situations for helping each other; for example, peer tutoring or "buddy" systems.

5. **Example.** Becky loved to spend time alone with Ms. Ericson and constantly sought personal attention. Often before attempting a difficult math problem she would ask Ms. Ericson for help. It was not at all unusual for Becky to visit Ms. Ericson's desk nine or ten times during a 30-minute independent work session. Ms. Ericson realized that her attention was reinforcing to Becky and decided to make that attention contingent on Becky's asking her classmates for help first before coming to her. Ms. Ericson explained to Becky that Mary, Carole, Rita, and Gale were all working on the same math problems as she, and that any one of them would be glad to help her if she would only ask. Further, she told Becky that if she asked a peer for help during a study period and visited the teacher's desk only at the end of the period to have her paper checked, she could sit with Ms. Ericson to help grade the papers and record the marks in the grade book. In carrying out this contingency, the teacher made sure that Becky understood the work and that the other girls knew how to help her without doing the problems for her.

GREETING OTHERS

S-IP-GR-0002-L1-S	To look others in the eye when greeting them.
S-IP-GR-0004-L1-S	To state one's name when asked.
S-IP-GR-0006-L1-S	To smile when encountering a friend or acquaintance.
S-IP-GR-0008-L1-S	To greet adults and peers by name.
S-IP-GR-0010-L1-S	To respond to an introduction by shaking hands and saying "how-do-you-do?"
S-IP-GR-0012-L2-S	To introduce oneself to another person.
S-IP-GR-0014-L2-S	To introduce two people to each other.

Skill:	To look others in the eye when greeting them. **S-IP-GR-0002-L1**
Objective:	Student looks others in the eyes when greeting them.
Assessment:	Assess from previous knowledge of student or through direct observation using the <u>Social Behavior Assessment Inventory</u>.

Code: S-IP-GR-0002-L1-Im

TEACHING STRATEGY

Objective: Student looks others in the eyes when greeting them.

Social Modeling

1. **Identify a need for the behavior through a classroom discussion.** To structure the discussion, you may want to raise questions, such as, "Do you like it when a person looks right at you when speaking to you? How do you feel when that person looks at the floor or looks the other way instead of looking at you? Why is it better to look at the person you are talking to?" Encourage the students to contribute their own ideas to the discussion.

2. **Identify specific behaviors to be modeled.**
   (a) Walk up to the person you want to speak to.
   (b) Look directly into his or her eyes.
   (c) Greet him or her.

3. **Model the behavior for the class.** Walk around the classroom and greet the students in various ways, making eye contact with some and not making eye contact with others. Ask the students to identify the elements of the modeled behavior. Recognize those who make good responses.

4. **Allow the children to practice the behavior with each other.** Call on one student to move about the room and greet three other children. The third (or last) person greeted then gets up and repeats the procedure. Continue until each child has had an opportunity to practice.

5. **Recognize those students who maintain eye contact when greeting another in the modeling situation.**

6. **Maintain the behavior in the classroom by noticing and reinforcing students who display the desired behavior.**

Code: S-IP-GR-0002-L1-Ir

TEACHING STRATEGY

Objective: Student looks others in the eyes when greeting them.

Social Reinforcement

1. **Identify and recognize by name target student when observed making eye contact in greeting another person.** Call attention to specific actions, e.g., "Derrell, I like the way you look right at me when you say hello;" "Fred, I'm glad you look right at me when you talk to me. That way I know you are talking to me;" "Dujuan, I'm so happy that you remembered to look at my eyes when you spoke to me."

2. **Cue appropriate behavior in target student by recognizing others who are maintaining eye contact when greeting another.**

3. **You may need to pair a tangible reinforcer with the social reinforcers, if the recognition, smiles, attention, etc., do not increase the desired behavior.**

Code: S-IP-GR-0002-L1-Ic

TEACHING STRATEGY

Objective: Student looks others in the eyes when greeting them.

Contingency Management

1. **State task in observable terms.** When you want to greet someone:
   (a) Walk up to him or her.
   (b) Look him or her in the eyes.
   (c) Greet him or her.

2. **Plan reinforcement strategy selected from reinforcement menu.**

3. **State contingency.** If you remember to look right into the eyes of the person you are greeting, you will receive the agreed-upon positive consequence.

4. **During the course of the day, observe those students who greet you and greet their peers. Reward those who maintain eye contact.**

5. **Example.** Donald is very shy. When he comes into the classroom in the morning, he remembers to greet Ms. Mort, his teacher, but he has very poor eye contact. When talking to her, he may sneak in a glance or two, but he usually keeps his eyes glued to the floor. Ms. Mort made a contract with Donald. "Donald, when you speak to me, if you will look at me rather than at the floor or somewhere else, I will give you a square of red construction paper. When you earn 20 of these, you may borrow on of your favorite games to take home overnight." Ms. Mort gradually increased the number of squares required to earn the privilege, and when Donald became more comfortable looking at other people when he talked to them, she maintained the behavior by recognizing him.

124

Skill:	To state one's name when asked.
	S-IP-GR-0004-L1
Objective:	Student states own name when asked.
Assessment:	Assess from previous knowledge of student or through direct observation using the <u>Social Behavior Assessment Inventory</u>.

Code: S-IP-GR-0004-L1-Im

TEACHING STRATEGY

Objective: Student states own name when asked.

Social Modeling

1. **Most children will have learned to tell their names before they reach school age.** In the case of very young, immature, or handicapped children, some teaching of this skill may be necessary. (Teaching procedures outlined here assume there are no hearing problems and that the student is able to imitate verbal sounds.) If a child does not respond with own name when asked because he or she does not know his or her name, it is necessary initially to provide a model for imitation, i.e., teacher (pointing), "Your name is 'John'. Say 'John'. Good. What is your name?...John." Repeat in numerous ways and many times under many conditions, first providing the whole name for the child to imitate and then fading out part of the name with just the beginning sound as a prompt, gradually eliminating that. Vary cues. For example, "What is your name?...Tell me your name...Who are you?" After the first name is mastered, add the last name and practice until student can respond with his or her entire name.

2. **If more than one student is involved, after individual practice, have students sit in a circle and take turns asking everyone in the circle, "What is your name?"** Reinforce students who respond correctly. Reinforcement may also be given for articulating the name clearly and looking directly at the person who is asking, rather than looking down or away.

Code: S-IP-GR-0004-L1-Ir

TEACHING STRATEGY

Objective: Student states own name when asked.

Social Reinforcement

1. **Identify and recognize by name target student for responding correctly when asked own name.** Call attention to student's specific action, e.g., "Good, Marty. I liked the way you told me your name when I asked you;" "Mary, you told the principal your name very well."

2. **Provide cues by recognizing children who are able to respond clearly when asked to state their names.** Cue the target child by asking and having others ask, "What is your name?" If necessary, provide a tangible reinforcer along with recognition when he clearly states his name.

Code: S-IP-GR-0004-L1-Ic

TEACHING STRATEGY

Objective: Student states own name when asked.

Contingency Management

1. **Present task to student in specific terms.** When asked own name, the student will state his or her name.
2. **Define a consequence valued by the student which will be given following demonstration of stating own name when asked.** (Plan reinforcement strategy selected from reinforcement menu.)
3. **State contingency.** If student states own name when asked, he or she will receive the agreed-upon positive consequence.
4. **Watch for the behavior to occur naturally, and reward it when it occurs according to established contingency,** or, set up a situation for the behavior to occur. For example, ask a fellow teacher to come into your room to observe the class for a brief interval. The teacher is to ask the target student his or her name. If he or she states own name clearly, the student will receive the agreed-upon positive consequence.
5. **Example.** Robin knew her name but seldom stated her own name when she was asked. She would smile and then would look away without replying, or would mumble her name so it could not be understood. The teacher stated to Robin the conditions of the contingency. "Sometime during the day I am going to ask you what your name is. If you can look at me and tell me your whole name loudly and clearly, I will give you one of these happy-face cards." The teacher rehearsed with Robin the kind of response which would earn the happy-face card. Robin was able to exchange the happy-face cards for extra cookies at snack time to share with the other students.

Skill:	To smile when encountering a friend or acquaintance. **S-IP-GR-0006-L1**
Objective:	Student smiles when meeting a friend or acquaintance.
Assessment:	Assess from previous knowledge of student or through direct observation using the <u>Social Behavior Assessment Inventory</u>.

Code: S-IP-GR-0006-L1-Im

TEACHING STRATEGY

Objective: Student smiles when meeting a friend or acquaintance.

Social Modeling

1. **Meet with the class and discuss the behavior of smiling when greeting a friend or acquaintance.** If available, use films, film strips, pictures, or stories which demonstrate the behavior. Have students contribute ideas to the discussion. For example, "How do you feel when a friend smiles when he greets you?" "How should we greet a friend?" "Why should we smile

when we see someone we know?" Put reminder words and pictures around the classroom.

2. **Define the behavior to be modeled.** Smile when greeting a friend or acquaintance.

3. **Model the behavior for the class.** Select two students to demonstrate the behavior of smiling when greeting a friend or acquaintance. Ask students to identify elements of the modeled behavior. Reinforce those students who make appropriate responses.

4. **Have class practice the behavior.** Have each student take a turn smiling and saying hello to various members of the class.

   Note: Practicing this behavior may make some students feel self-conscious and silly. Ignore inappropriate grimaces or silly behavior and reinforce any effort to smile appropriately.

Code: S-IP-GR-0006-L1-Ir

TEACHING STRATEGY

Objective: Student smiles when meeting a friend or acquaintance.

Social Reinforcement

1. **Recognize target student when observed smiling when greeting a friend.** Be specific in recognizing the student. For example, "Marsha, what a nice smile!" "Tom, I liked the way you smiled when you said hello."

2. **Provide cues for target students.** Recognize other students who smile frequently. Watch for the behavior in the target student and reinforce it.

   Note: If needed, accompany social reinforcement with tangible reinforcement (tokens, stars, chips). Arrange so that tokens can be exchanged for desirable items.

Code: S-IP-GR-0006-L1-Ic

TEACHING STRATEGY

Objective: Student smiles when greeting a friend or acquaintance.

Contingency Management

1. **State task to student in specific terms.** When you see someone you know, smile at him or her and say hello. If needed, display pictures of smiling faces and reminder signs.

2. **Plan reinforcement.**

3. **State contingency.** If student smiles when greeting a friend or acquaintance, he or she will receive the agreed-upon positive consequence.

4. **Watch for the behavior to occur naturally, and reinforce it when it occurs according to established contingency,** or, set a situation for the behavior to occur. Ask several students to greet target student upon arriving in the classroom. Observe target student. If target student smiles when greeting other students, he or she will receive the agreed-upon reward.

5. **Example.** Jackie typically wore a sad expression and seldom smiled when she greeted friends. The teacher desired to increase Jackie's smiling behavior. The teacher observed Jackie in 12 situations and recorded that Jackie smiled three times when greeting a friend. The teacher discussed with Jackie why it is good to smile when you see someone you know. The teacher and Jackie practiced the behavior. A contract was agreed on by Jackie and the teacher. Each time Jackie smiled when greeting the teacher or a friend, she could color a bar on the wall chart, "A Trip to the Happy Face." When Jackie reached the Happy Face she would select two movies for the class. The teacher helped Jackie earn her reward, frequently prompting her by smiling and saying, "Hello, Jackie."

Skill:	To greet adults and peers by name.
	S-IP-GR-0008-L1
Objective:	Student greets adults and peers by name.
Assessment:	Assess from previous knowledge of student or through direct observation using the <u>Social Behavior Assessment Inventory</u>.

Code: S-IP-GR-0008-L1-Im

TEACHING STRATEGY

Objective: Student greets adults and peers by name.

Social Modeling

1. **Have a class discussion on the behavior to be modeled, greeting peers and adults by name.** Use films, stories, film strips, or other aids where available. Have students contribute to the discussion. For example, "Why should we use someone's name when we say hello to them?" "How should we greet peers and adults?"
2. **Define behaviors to be modeled.** For example, when greeting a peer or an adult, call him or her by name.
3. **Demonstrate the behavior to the class.** Greet a student, calling him or her by name. Call on students to identify elements of the modeled behavior, and reinforce appropriate responses.
4. **Give each student an opportunity to greet a peer, calling him or her by name.** Create different situations to be role-played, e.g., meeting a friend on the playground, seeking a friend in the hallway, going to the door of a friend's house, seeing the principal on the walkway. Reinforce appropriate responses.
5. **Maintain the behavior in the classroom through reinforcement.**

Code: S-IP-GR-0008-L1-Ir

TEACHING STRATEGY

Objective: Student greets adults and peers by name.

Social Reinforcement

1. **Reinforce target student with praise, smiles, and nods when observed greeting adults and peers by name.** Tell the child what he or she is doing right. For example, "John, I liked the way you used my name when you said hello to me." "Mary, you remembered to greet the principal by name. That was good!"

2. **Provide cues for target student.** For example, recognize others who greet people by name. Then watch for the behavior in the target child and reinforce it.

3. **Tangible reinforcers (tokens, chips, trading stamps) may be presented with social reinforcers (recognition, smiles, nods).** Tangible reinforcers can be exchanged for items desired by the student.

Code: S-IP-GR-0008-L1-Ic

TEACHING STRATEGY

Objective: Student greets adults and peers by name.

Contingency Management

1. **State task in specific terms.** When greeting an adult or peer, call him or her by name.

2. **Plan reinforcement.**

3. **State contingency.** If student greets adults and peers by name, he or she will receive the agreed-upon reward.

4. **Watch for the behavior to occur naturally, and reinforce it when it occurs according to the established contingency,** or, set a situation for the behavior to occur. Ask several students or other adults to greet target student when he or she arrives at school. Observe target student. If he or she greets peers by name, he or she will receive the agreed-upon positive consequences.

5. **Example.** Freddy lacked social skills. For example, he seldom, if ever, used another person's name. The teacher discussed the behavior of greeting a friend by name with Freddy. Freddy and the teacher practiced the behavior. Then, the teacher and Freddy agreed on a contract. The teacher would observe in the morning, before school and recess, the number of times Freddy greeted another person by name. The number recorded would equal the number of minutes at the art center. Freddy would eventually record his own behavior. The teacher provided additional opportunities by greeting Freddy herself and having other adults greet Freddy to elicit greetings from him.

Skill:	To respond to an introduction by shaking hands and saying, "How do you do?" **S-IP-GR-0010-L1**
Objective:	Student responds to an introduction by shaking hands and saying, "How do you do?"
Assessment:	Assess from previous knowledge of student or through direct observation using the <u>Social Behavior Assessment Inventory</u>.

Code: S-IP-GR-0010-L1-Im

TEACHING STRATEGY

Objective: Student responds to an introduction by shaking hands and saying, "How do you do?"

Social Modeling

1. **Meet with the class and discuss how to respond to an introduction.** Ask the students questions. For example, "How should we respond when being introduced? When do we shake hands and say, 'How do you do,' during an introduction? When is it appropriate to shake hands and when not? Which hand do we use in shaking hands?" Help students remember which hand to use by tying a ribbon around their wrists, if necessary. Remind them also to say the name of the person after saying, "How do you do." Write key words on the board.

2. **Identify specific behavior to be modeled.** When being introduced, shake hands and say, "How do you do?"

3. **Model the behavior.** Select two students. Introduce the students to each other and have students demonstrate the desired behavior. Ask students to identify the elements of the modeled behavior. Reinforce appropriate responses.

4. **Provide opportunity for practice.** Give each student an opportunity to be introduced to another student and demonstrate shaking hands and saying, "How do you do?" Reinforce correct responses.

5. **Maintain the behavior through reinforcement.**

Code: S-IP-GR-0010-L1-Ir

TEACHING STRATEGY

Objective: Student responds to an introduction by shaking hands and saying, "How do you do?"

Social Reinforcement

1. **Use social reinforcers, smiles, nods, or recognition when target student is observed appropriately shaking hands and saying, "How do you do?" when being introduced.** Tell the student what he or she is doing right, e.g., "Tim, I liked the way you shook hands and said, 'How do you do?' to Mr. Jones. You are very polite."

130

2. **Provide cues for target students.** For example, recognize another student who demonstrates the behavior. Elicit the behavior by reaching out your hand and saying, "How do you do?" Introduce someone to the target student and recognize student for responding appropriately.

Code: S-IP-GR-0010-L1-Ic

TEACHING STRATEGY

Objective: Student responds to an introduction by shaking hands and saying, "How do you do?"

Contingency Management

1. **Tell student the behavior in specific terms.** When being introduced, shake hands and say, "How do you do?"
2. **Plan reinforcement.**
3. **State contingency.** If student responds to an introduction by shaking hands and saying, "How do you do?," he or she will receive the agreed-upon reward.
4. **Watch for behavior to occur naturally and reinforce it when it occurs according to established contingency,** or, set a situation for the behavior to occur. Introduce the student to another student. Observe the student. If appropriate behavior is demonstrated, then he or she will receive the agreed-upon reinforcement. Have someone new visit the class, and introduce him or her to the student. Ask the principal to come and help students practice the behavior by being introduced to them one-by-one.
5. **Example.** Ms. Grey's class was made up of rather boisterous students who lacked appropriate behaviors in relating to other students and adults. Among the skills Ms. Grey wanted them to learn was how to acknowledge an introduction when meeting someone new. Ms. Grey divided them into teams to practice greeting skills. She set up a team contingency, i.e., when new people came to the class and were introduced, one person from each team would be chosen to shake hands and say, "How do you do?" using the person's name. The teams would earn points, and the team with the most points would gain the privilege of eating lunch in the room and watching television on Friday. Ms. Grey arranged for several new people to come to the class during the week and called on group members in rotation to be greeters. The class as a whole voted on which teams should receive points.

Code: S-IP-GR-0012-L2-Im

TEACHING STRATEGY

Objective: Student, when required, will introduce himself or herself to another by saying, "Hello, my name is _____," or the equivalent.

Social Modeling

1. **Discuss the behavior of introducing oneself to another student.** Ask questions about the behavior; for example, "How should one introduce oneself?" "Why should on state his or her name when introducing oneself?"
2. **Identify specific behaviors to be modeled.** When introducing yourself to another, say, "Hello, my name is _____."
3. **Model the behavior for the class.** Introduce yourself to another student. Ask students to identify elements of the modeled behavior.
4. **Provide opportunity for practice.** Have student introduce himself or herself to another student saying, "Hello, my name is _____." If portable videotape equipment is available, videotape the role-playing and allow student to evaluate his or her own behavior.

Code: S-IP-GR-0012-L2-Ir

TEACHING STRATEGY

Objective: Student, when required, will introduce himself or herself to another by saying, "Hello, my name is _____," or the equivalent.

Social Reinforcement

1. **Use social reinforcement when the student introduces himself or herself appropriately.** Be specific when reinforcing; for example, "Martha, you were quite mature in the way you introduced yourself by giving your name to our visitors."
2. **Provide cues for target students.** For example, use cartoon character pictures demonstrating an appropriate behavior for introducing oneself. Recognize other students who introduce themselves.

Code: S-IP-GR-0012-L2-Ic

TEACHING STRATEGY

Objective: Student, when required, will introduce himself or herself to another by saying, "Hello, my name is _____," or the equivalent.

Contingency Management

1. **Discuss with student how to introduce himself or herself to another student.**

2. **Plan reinforcement.**

3. **State contingency.** If student introduces himself or herself to another student, stating his or her name, the student will receive the agreed-upon reward.

4. **Watch for the behavior to occur naturally, and reinforce it when it occurs according to the established contingency,** or, set up a situation for the behavior to occur. For example, ask target student to introduce himself or herself to another student. If the desired behavior is demonstrated, the student will receive the agreed-upon reward.

5. **Example.** A new student, Jennifer, was expected in Ms. Todd's room. Ms. Todd wanted to use the opportunity to teach greeting skills. She had the class practice how they would introduce themselves by saying, "Hi (or hello), my name is _____." Ms. Todd set up a contingency that each student who appropriately introduced himself or herself would be allowed an extra five minutes of recess.

Skill:	To introduce two people to each other. **S-IP-GR-0014-L2**
Objective:	When in a situation where the student is with one person, meets another, and the two people do not know each other, the student introduces them to each other.
Assessment:	Assess from previous knowledge of student or through direct observation using the <u>Social Behavior Assessment Inventory</u>.

Code: S-IP-GR-0014-L2-Im

TEACHING STRATEGY

Objective: When in a situation where the student is with one person, meets another, and the two people do not know each other, the student introduces them to each other.

Social Modeling

1. **Discuss with the class the appropriate way to introduce two people who do not know each other.** Ask questions; for example, "When do we introduce people to each other? How should we introduce people to each other? What should you do if you are with a friend and you meet another friend and the two do now know each other?"

2. **Identify specific behaviors to be modeled.** Introduce two people who do not know each other by saying, "Mark, this is Karen; Karen, this is Mark." Discuss rules for which person to introduce first, e.g., men to women, younger people to older people. Review related skills involving acknowledging an introduction.

3. **Model the behavior.** Select two students to serve as models with the teacher. The teacher will introduce the two students to each other. Ask students to identify the modeled behavior.

4. **Provide opportunity for practice.** Have each student introduce two students to each other demonstrating the appropriate behavior. Reinforce correct responses.

5. **Maintain the behavior through reinforcement.**

Code: S-IP-GR-0014-L2-Ir

TEACHING STRATEGY

Objective: When in a situation where the student is with one person, meets another, and the two people do not know each other, the student introduces them to each other.

Social Reinforcement

1. **Use social reinforcement when target student is observed introducing two people who do not know each other.** Be specific in praising the student, e.g., "Jim, I like the way you introduced Sam to Rhonda." "Debbie, you did a good job of introducing Sue to Linda."

2. **Provide cues for target students.** Provide signs or cartoons of characters exhibiting the appropriate behavior of introducing people to each other. Reward student for correctly responding to the cue.

Code: S-IP-GR-0014-L2-Ic

TEACHING STRATEGY

Objective: When in a situation where the student is with one person, meets another, and the two people do not know each other, the student introduces them to each other.

Contingency Management

1. **Present task to student in specific terms.** When you are with a friend and you meet another friend and the two do not know each other, introduce them to each other by saying, for example, "Tony, this is Bill; Bill this is Tony."

2. **Plan reinforcement.**

3. **State contingency.** If student exhibits the appropriate behavior of introducing two people to each other, he or she will be rewarded according to the specified contingency.

4. **Watch for the behavior to occur naturally, and reinforce it when it occurs according to the established contingency,** or, set up a situation for the

behavior. Ask target student to role-play introducing two friends who do not know each other. If the student demonstrates the appropriate behavior he would receive the agreed-upon reward.

5. **Example.** Ms. Gibson's class was chosen to be the "hosts" and "hostesses" for a PTA social hour. Ms. Gibson wished to use the occasion as an opportunity to teach social behaviors. She modeled the behavior of making introductions and had the class practice. She established the contingency that each student was to bring his or her parents to her and introduce them properly. If a student's parents were not at the meeting, he or she was to introduce himself or herself properly to another student's parents. Ms. Gibson kept track of introductions and provided each child with recognition for an acceptable attempt at an introduction.

HELPING OTHERS

S-IP-HP-0002-L1-S	To help teacher when asked.
S-IP-HP-0004-L1-S	To help a peer when asked.
S-IP-HP-0006-L1-S	To give simple directions to a peer.
S-IP-HP-0008-L2-S	To offer help to teacher.
S-IP-HP-0010-L2-S	To offer help to a classmate.
S-IP-HP-0012-L2-S	To come to defense of peer in trouble.
S-IP-HP-0014-L2-S	To express sympathy to peer about problems or difficulties.

Skill:	To help teacher when asked. **S-IP-HP-0002-L1**
Objective:	When teacher asks the student to help, the student complies.
Assessment:	Assess from previous knowledge of student or through direct observation using the <u>Social Behavior Assessment Inventory</u>.

Code: S-IP-HP-0002-L1-Im

TEACHING STRATEGY

Objective: When teacher asks student to help, the student complies.

Social Modeling

1. **A need for this behavior may be identified through a classroom discussion.** Ideas about the importance of complying with the teacher's request should be generated by the students. To initiate and structure the discussion, you may wish to raise questions, such as, "Do you think it is necessary and important to be helpful? Do you think it's important to help your teacher? What are some ways students can help teachers?" If appropriate, make a list of student suggestions on the board.

2. **Identify specific behaviors to be modeled.** When the teacher asks you for help:
   (a) Do exactly what you were asked to do.
   (b) Ask him or her to repeat the directions if you don't know what you are supposed to do.

3. **Model the behavior.** Choose a student to play the role of the teacher, and direct him or her to ask you to help. Then proceed to carry out the request. You may also want to demonstrate how to ask for clarification. Call on students to identify the specific elements of the modeled behavior, and recognize those who make good responses.

4. **For practice, divide the class into small groups and direct them to alternate playing the role of teacher and student.** Some suggested situations are:
   (a) Teacher asks student to collect lunch money from students and check off names of those who pay on a form.

136

(b) Teacher asks student to help grade test papers.

(c) Teacher asks student to be in charge of the class while he or she leaves the room.

(d) Teacher asks student to help demonstrate a science experiment.

(e) Teacher asks student to write an assignment on the board.

(f) Teacher asks student to deliver a message, wait for a reply, and return with the reply.

(g) Teacher asks student to help sort papers into piles.

(h) Others appropriate to the class and age level.

Allow each student to have an opportunity to play both teacher and student.

5. **Recognize those who comply with the requests exactly as stated.**

6. **Be sure to reward this skill consistently to maintain the behavior of helping the teacher when asked.**

Code: S-IP-HP-0002-L1-Ir

TEACHING STRATEGY

Objective: When teacher asks the student to help, the student complies.

Social Reinforcement

1. **When target student complies with the requests of the teacher for help, identify the student by name and recognize the student.** Call attention to specific actions. "Robert, thank you for leading the class to the lunchroom. You did just as I asked." "Ken, you remembered to close all the windows during the fire drill. I'm so proud of you." "Lynwood, you did a good job of cleaning up our classroom. It's so nice to have a helper like you."

2. **Cue the appropriate behavior in the target student by verbally recognizing others who comply with the requests of the teacher for help.**

3. **If social praise is insufficient to increase the desired behavior, pair a token or some other tangible item with the verbal praise.**

Code: S-IP-HP-0002-L1-Ic

TEACHING STRATEGY

Objective: When teacher asks the student to help, the student complies.

Contingency Management

1. **Discuss with the student the desired behavior.** When asked to help the teacher, you will agree.

2. **Plan reinforcement.**

3. **State contingency.** If the student agrees to help the teacher when asked, the student will receive the agreed-upon reward.

4. **Set up a situation in which the behavior can occur by asking the student at various times to help.**

5. **Example.** Most children in the class were willing and even eager to be helpful to the teacher, but not Charlie. When asked to help, he always had an excuse for not helping. He had something to do, his foot hurt, or he did not seem to understand what was being asked of him. The teacher discussed "helping" with him and how important it was for everyone in the class to help each other and the teacher too. She set up a contingency that she would make Charlie the "No. 1 Helper" for a day. If he agreed to help when she asked, at the end of the day she would send a note home telling Charlie's mother how helpful he had been. The teacher made a "Helper" sign for Charlie to wear, because he liked attention. She was careful to make requests for help reasonable and to make sure Charlie understood. She arranged with Charlie's mother to recognize him when he brought the note home. The teacher repeated the contingency on several occasions and was able after that to maintain Charlie's being helpful by praise and using the term "No. 1 Helper" as a cue.

Skill:	To help peer when asked.
	S-IP-HP-0004-L1
Objective:	Student will help a peer when asked.
Assessment:	Assess from previous knowledge of student or through direct observation using the <u>Social Behavior Assessment Inventory</u>.

Code: S-IP-HP-0004-L1-Im

TEACHING STRATEGY

Objective: Student will help peer when asked.

Social Modeling

1. **Meet with the class and discuss being helpful to classmates.** Use stories, films, film strips, or other aids having to do with helping others. Ask questions, such as, "Why should you help classmates? When should you help a friend? Are there some times you might not want to help someone else?" Have students present their ideas.

2. **Identify specific behaviors to be modeled.** When a student asks you for help, you will agree to help.

3. **Model the behavior.** Teacher selects a student to role-play. Student will ask for help with a task, and the teacher will demonstrate helping. Repeat, choosing different students to play both roles.

4. **Provide opportunity for practice.** Set up a "Help Others" week. Make a list of ways to help other students and post it. At the end of each day, have a feedback session in which students tell who was willing to help them when they asked for help. Add to the list of ways to help, and provide verbal reinforcement to students both for being helpers and for providing names of others who helped them.

5. **Maintain the behavior through reinforcement.**

138

Code: S-IP-HP-0004-L1-Ir

TEACHING STRATEGY

Objective: Student will help a peer when asked.

Social Reinforcement

1. **Identify and recognize student when observed helping a peer.** Call attention to specific actions. For example, "Jerry, that was very kind of you to help Jim." "Marsha, I am pleased to see that you helped Carol when she asked you."
2. **Provide cues for target students.** Design a bulletin board on helping others. Provide pictures of helping others. Reinforce other students who help others.
3. **It may be necessary, at first, to provide tangible reinforcers, such as chips, tokens, coupons, along with social reinforcers.**

Code: S-IP-HP-0004-L1-Ic

TEACHING STRATEGY

Objective: Student will help a peer when asked.

Contingency Management

1. **Discuss with the student the desired behavior.** When a classmate asks you to help, you will agree to help (provided the request for help is a reasonable one).
2. **Plan reinforcement.**
3. **State contingency.** If student helps a peer when asked, the student will receive the agreed-upon reward.
4. **Watch for the behavior to occur naturally, and reinforce it when it occurs according to the established contingency,** or set up a situation in which the behavior can occur. Ask the student to help another student, or cue another student to ask the target student for help. If the target student follows through, the student receives the agreed-upon reinforcement.
5. **Example.** Joey was unwilling to help other students when asked. He would tell them he was too busy or make up some other excuse. At the same time, Joey expected other students to help him. The teacher talked to Joey about helping others and some of the benefits of being helpful along with situations in which Joey could agree to help other students. A contingency was then started. If Joey helped another student when asked, he would receive a card with a number on it. The cards would be numbered one through eight. When Joey received all eight cards he would see that they spelled out an activity (e.g., painting) on the back. He could then have time to engage in the activity he earned.

<table>
<tr><td>Skill:</td><td>To give simple directions to a peer.
S-IP-HP-0006-L1</td></tr>
<tr><td>Objective:</td><td>Student gives simple directions to a peer upon request.</td></tr>
<tr><td>Assessment:</td><td>Assess from previous knowledge of student or through direct observation using the <u>Social Behavior Assessment Inventory</u>.</td></tr>
</table>

Code: S-IP-HP-0006-L1-Im

TEACHING STRATEGY

Objective: Student gives simple directions to a peer upon request.

Social Modeling

1. **Set the stage for discussion by asking the class how you would get to some location within the school building** (e.g., the gym, the school cafeteria, the school office, etc.). Call on students and have them give directions to you. Write the main aspects of their directions on the board. Discuss the students' responses. Point out the characteristics of the students' responses that are desirable. Ask students for their ideas, also. Explain that giving directions covers any situation where someone is asked for an explanation of how to do a task. Give examples: "How do you play checkers?" "How do you work this math problem?"

2. **Identify the specific behaviors to be modeled.** For example, when asked for directions, you respond immediately by giving the person the specific information requested. It is important to make the directions short, easy to understand, and specific to the question asked. Write the key words and/ or phrases on the board.

3. **Model the behavior.** Have students ask you questions from a list you provide. The questions should require you to give simple directions. Do two or three from the list and ask the class to describe your responses. For contrast, respond to one or two questions inappropriately. Have students identify what you did incorrectly. Have several students (one at a time) take your place in the role-playing. Ask the class to identify the appropriate behaviors that are modeled. Recognize correct responses.

4. **Provide an opportunity for everyone to practice the skill.** Divide the class into triads. Have each student in the triad take turns asking for directions, giving directions, and observing. Explain that after each turn, the observer and the student who asked for directions should provide feedback to the direction giver. Circulate around the room and praise appropriate behaviors.

5. **Maintain behavior through reinforcement.**

   Note: Students sometimes believe that they should not indicate when they do not know directions to a place or site. They should be informed that it is better to say, "Sorry, I don't know," than to misinform. A discussion about why misinforming knowingly is unethical can encourage students to be thoughtful in making social decisions.

Code: S-IP-HP-0006-L1-Ir

TEACHING STRATEGY

Objective: Student gives simple directions to a peer upon request.

Social Reinforcement

1. **When you observe the target student giving directions to a peer upon request, praise the student.** Be descriptive with your praise. For example, "Theo, when Aldo asked you for directions on how to work his math, you responded immediately. That's wonderful;" "Shawna, you gave directions to Maribeth when she asked how to get to Mrs. Holister's room. That was very helpful of you."
2. **Cue the target student.**
   (a) Place a small sign on his or her desk that reads, "Give directions when asked." For nonreaders, make a pictorial representation of a student giving directions.
   (b) Verbally remind the student before each seatwork period to give directions when asked.
   (c) Praise another student for exhibiting the desired behavior so that the target student can hear. When the target student responds correctly, reinforce the behavior.
3. **Sometimes social reinforcement in the form of praise, smiles, pats, etc., is not sufficient to increase the desired behavior.** In such instances, a tangible reward or activity reinforcer, e.g., happy faces or five minutes extra recess, can be paired with the social reinforcer. The tangible reinforcement should be phased out as quickly as possible.

Code: S-IP-HP-0006-L1-Ic

TEACHING STRATEGY

Contingency Management

1. **Meet with the student to discuss the desired behavior.** Ask questions. For example, "If a classmate asks you for directions about how to do a task, how would you respond?" Explain to the student what an appropriate response includes. Be specific. For example, "When asked for directions by a peer, you respond with a short, easy-to-understand answer that is only about the question asked."
2. **Plan reinforcement.**
3. **State contingency.** When you give simple directions to a peer upon request, you will earn the agreed-upon reward. Specify amount and type of reinforcer.
4. **Watch for the behavior to occur naturally,** or, set up a situation in which the behavior is required. For example, ask another student to request directions from the target student. If the target student responds by giving directions, recognize and reward the student.

5. **Example.** After Ms. Williams had used the "social modeling strategy" for teaching students to give simple directions to a peer when requested, she observed that the class was exhibiting this behavior regularly, with the exception of Samantha. Ms. Williams decided to develop a contingency contract with Samantha in order to have her develop the desired behavior. From her observations of Samantha, Ms. Williams had noted that Samantha worked with the modeling clay during "free time," if she had enough points to buy it.

Ms. Williams met with Samantha and discussed with her the importance of giving directions to a peer when asked. Ms. Williams role-played a student asking Samantha for directions, and Samantha practiced giving directions. The following contingency contract was then developed: "Each time that you give directions to a fellow student after it is requested, you will earn two points that may be used for buying an activity during free time."

Ms. Williams observed Samantha in class and reinforced her according to the stated contingency. She was always sure to pair the awarding of points with social reinforcers, e.g., praise, smiles, pats, etc. Within three weeks, Samantha was giving directions upon request consistently. Ms. Williams then told Samantha that she would continue to award two points to Samantha for every third time she was observed giving directions to a peer. Eventually, Ms. Williams phased the points out completely and maintained the behavior with intermittent social reinforcement.

Skill:	To offer help to teacher. **S-IP-HP-0008-L2**
Objective:	Student offers to help the teacher with a specific task when given the opportunity.
Assessment:	Assess from previous knowledge of student or through direct observation using the <u>Social Behavior Assessment Inventory</u>.

Code: S-IP-HP-0008-L2-Im

TEACHING STRATEGY

Objective: Student offers to help the teacher with a specific task when given the opportunity.

Social Modeling

1. **Discuss the behavior with the class.** When available, use stories, films, or film strips about helping others. Have students contribute ideas to the discussion. "Why should we help the teacher or help other people in general? Can you name situations in which you might offer help to the teacher?" A list of helpful behaviors might be generated and put on the chalkboard.

   Note: This is a more complex behavior than S-IP-HP-0004 and requires the student to recognize opportunities for helping rather than to wait to be asked before helping.

142

2. **Identify specific behaviors to be modeled.** When in a situation in which the teacher needs help, the student offers to help the teacher.

3. **Model the behavior.** Take the role of student and have student play teacher. Role-play situations in which the student offers to help the teacher. For example, opening doors, hanging papers, carrying messages, correcting spelling papers, cleaning chalkboards, carrying books.

4. **Provide opportunity for practice so that each student can model the behavior of offering to help the teacher.** Reinforce correct responses.

5. **Maintain the behavior through reinforcement.**

Code: S-IP-HP-0008-L2-Ir

TEACHING STRATEGY

Objective: Student offers to help the teacher with a specific task when given the opportunity.

Social Reinforcement

1. **Reinforce with smiles and recognition when student offers to help the teacher with a specific task.** Use descriptive praise. For example, "Colin, I appreciate your helping me carry these books. It was very kind of you to offer." "Marcie, you are very thoughtful to hold the door open for me. Thank you."

2. **Provide cues for target student.** Recognize another student who is exhibiting the desired behavior. When the target student responds correctly, reinforce the student.

3. **If social reinforcement in the form of recognition, smiles, attention, etc., is not sufficient to increase the desired behavior, it may be necessary to accompany social reinforcement with tangible reinforcement** (i.e., chips, coupons, tokens, etc., to be exchanged for something the child wants).

Code: S-IP-HP-0008-L2-Ic

TEACHING STRATEGY

Objective: Student offers to help the teacher with a specific task when given the opportunity.

Contingency Management

1. **Discuss with the student in specific terms the desired behavior.** When the teacher is doing a task, such as carrying books, cleaning boards, handing papers, in which the teacher could use help, offer to help. Discuss what the student might say when offering help.

2. **Plan reinforcement.**

3. **State contingency.** If the student offers to help the teacher when assistance is needed by the teacher, he or she will receive the agreed-upon reward.

4. **Watch for the behavior to occur naturally, and reinforce it,** or, set up a situation in which the behavior can occur. For example, ask the student to

go with you to the art room to get supplies. If the student offers to help carry the supplies or hold the door for you, reinforce the student.

5. **Example.** Freddy lacked many social skills, among them being helpful to other people. The teacher discussed with Freddy how she would appreciate his help when needed. Freddy could offer to help, for example, carrying books, cleaning boards, hanging papers, carrying the record player or films and holding doors. A contingency was then started. If Freddy offered to help the teacher when needed, he would receive a raffle ticket. Raffle tickets were drawn on Friday morning and exchanged for various activities. The teacher also praised Freddy for helping and gradually discontinued the raffle.

Skill:	To offer help to a classmate.
	S-IP-HP-0010-L2
Objective:	Student offers help to a classmate when given the opportunity.
Assessment:	Assess from previous knowledge of student or through direct observation using the <u>Social Behavior Assessment Inventory</u>.

Code: S-IP-HP-0010-L2-Im

TEACHING STRATEGY

Objective: Student offers help to a classmate when given the opportunity.

Social Modeling

1. **Meet with the class and discuss helping other students.** When available, use stories, films, film strips, and other material about helping others. Have students contribute ideas. For example, "What are some situations in which you might offer to help a classmate? Why do we offer to help others?"

   Note: The emphasis in this skill is on the student's recognizing opportunities to help others and offering without being directly asked to help. It is more complex behavior than helping when asked (S-IP-HP-0006).

2. **Identify specific behaviors to be modeled.** When the opportunity arises, offer to help a friend or classmate.

3. **Model the behavior.** Use puppets to demonstrate the behavior, or role-play several situations in which the teacher takes the role of a student offering to help another student with carrying objects, moving a desk, or working on school work.

4. **Provide opportunity for practice.** Divide the class into pairs. Select a pair to role-play a situation. One student will offer to help the student who is performing the task. Students reverse roles. Select another pair. Situations for role-playing might include carrying books, carrying gym equipment, moving desks, cleaning up, putting away materials, practicing school work.

5. **Maintain the behavior through reinforcement.**

144

Code: S-IP-HP-0010-L2-Ir

TEACHING STRATEGY

Objective: Student offers help to a classmate when given the opportunity.

Social Reinforcement

1. **Use social reinforcement when student is observed offering to help a classmate.** Be specific in recognizing the student. For example, "Sam, that was kind of you to offer to help Mary practice her spelling words." "Jill, I appreciate the way you offered to help Debbie move her desk. Thank you."

2. **Provide cues for target student.**
   (a) Recognize children who offer to help others.
   (b) Put up reminder signs or pictures of children helping other children.

3. **Provide tangible reinforcement (stars, chips, tokens, etc.), if necessary, along with social reinforcement (smiles, praise, attention).** Tangible reinforcement may be exchanged for desired items by the student.

Code: S-IP-HP-0010-L2-Ic

TEACHING STRATEGY

Objective: Student offers help to a classmate when given the opportunity.

Contingency Management

1. **Present task to student in specific terms.** For example, if another student needs help, offer to help. Specify helping activities.

2. **Plan reinforcement.**

3. **State contingency.** If the student offers to help another student when needed, the student will be reinforced.

4. **Watch for the behavior to occur naturally,** or, set up a situation in which it could occur. For example, ask for volunteers to help another student learn sight words with flash cards. If the target student offers to help, the student receives the agreed-upon consequence.

5. **Example.** Jamie was a shy student who seldom initiated any activity involving another student. Ms. Rieth felt that learning to be helpful to other students might help Jamie develop some social relationships. Ms. Rieth and Jamie discussed why and how he might offer to help another student. They also discussed situations in which Jamie might offer to help. Situations discussed were holding the door, moving a desk, carrying books, carrying gym equipment, and helping others with school work. Jamie was a good student academically.

   A contingency was then stated. If Jamie offered to help another student when needed, he would receive a piece to his puzzle card. Ms. Rieth had written various activities on 5 x 7 cards. Each card was then cut into pieces to form a puzzle. The pieces were placed in an envelope. Each student had his own envelope to draw from. When Jamie had his puzzle card constructed, he would receive time to do the activity written on the card.

Ms. Rieth verbally reinforced Jamie and continued with verbal reinforcement after the contingency was completed.

Skill:	To come to defense of a peer in trouble.
	S-IP-HP-0012-L2
Objective:	When someone is unfairly maligning or assaulting a peer, the student will come to the peer's defense.
Assessment:	Assess from previous knowledge of student or through direct observation using the <u>Social Behavior Assessment Inventory</u>.

Code: S-IP-HP-0012-L2-Im

TEACHING STRATEGY

Objective: When someone is unfairly maligning or assaulting a peer, the student will come to the peer's defense.

Social Modeling

1. **Discuss with the class situations in which they should come to the aid of a classmate.** For example, when another student is being called unkind names, being bullied, being kept out of games, or not being allowed to use playground equipment. Explain how the student can aid a fellow student by disagreeing with a student who is name calling, walking away with the classmate from the situation, or getting an adult to help. Ask for ideas from the class. For example, "What would you do in the following situations?"

   (a) A friend is being called unkind names.

   (b) A classmate is not allowed by others to use the slide.

   (c) A boy who is larger and older is pushing and punching a friend.

   (d) A new student is being kept out of a game on the playground.

   Stress that there are many ways to come to the aid of another classmate and that they will vary according to the situation. Emphasize that the students have a responsibility to recognize injustices to others and to try to intervene rather than to ignore or to join in the injustice.

2. **Identify specific behaviors to be modeled.** When another classmate is being treated unfairly, intervene verbally, get an adult, leave the situation with the classmate, or find some other constructive way of helping.

3. **Model the behavior.** Select two students to role-play the situation with you. One student will call the student names and verbally attack the other student. The teacher will come to the aid of the student by intervening verbally and then getting the student to walk away with him or her. Ask students to identify elements of the modeled behavior and suggest other things you could have done. Reinforce correct responses.

4. **Provide opportunity for practice.** Divide class into groups of three. One student will come to the defense of the student who is being treated unfairly by the third student. Then rotate students so that each student in the group can demonstrate the desired behavior. Have the rest of the class observe

and evaluate, suggesting other things which could be done in the situation. Provide situations for role-playing which are typical of the class and age group. Some suggested situations might include:

(a) A student makes unkind remarks about another student's family or friends.

(b) A student makes fun of the way another student is dressed.

(c) An older student pushes a younger student down.

(d) A group of students call a student names, pointing and laughing.

Reward good role-playing responses and good contributions from the rest of the class. Provide opportunity for each group of three to role-play. Reinforce correct responses.

Code: S-IP-HP-0012-L2-Ir

TEACHING STRATEGY

Objective: When someone is unfairly maligning or assaulting a peer, the student will come to the peer's defense.

Social Reinforcement

1. **Use social reinforcement when the student is observed demonstrating the appropriate behavior.** Call attention to specific actions. For example, "Mark, that was quick thinking. I liked the way you helped Harold by coming to get me." "Sammy, I liked the way you stuck up for Joan when the others were teasing her." "Mary, that was responsible of you to tell Shirley she was wrong when she called Linda a name."

2. **Provide cues for the target student.** List ways in which a student can come to the defense of a peer; for example, helping the student leave the situation, verbally intervening by telling the others they are wrong, and getting help from a teacher, playground aide, or principal. Adapt the cues to the particular situation.

3. **If needed, provide tangible reinforcement (stars, tokens, chips) with social reinforcement (smiles, praise, attention, etc.).** Tangible reinforcement can be exchanged for desired items by the student.

Code: S-IP-HP-0012-L2-Ic

TEACHING STRATEGY

Objective: When someone is unfairly maligning or assaulting a peer, the student will come to the peer's defense.

Contingency Management

1. **Meet with the class to explain situations in which a student may come to the defense of a peer.** For example, when an individual is being called names, being teased, being discriminated against, or being physically hurt, present to the class various ways of helping the peer, for example, verbal intervention, helping the peer leave the scene, and getting help from an

adult. Suggest interventions that are appropriate to the particular class and age group. If needed, display a list of possible ways to help someone else.

2. **Plan reinforcement.**

3. **State contingency.** If the student comes to the aid of a peer who is being teased or assaulted, he or she will receive the agreed-upon reinforcement.

4. **Watch for the behavior to occur and reward it according to the established contingency,** or, set up a situation in which the behavior can occur. For example, have three students role-play a situation in which the target student can come to the defense of a classmate. If the student demonstrates in the role-playing situation how he or she might help the classmate, the student will be reinforced according to the established contingency.

5. **Example.** Mr. Schroeder's second-grade class had recess with third- and fourth-grade classes. Mr. Schroeder had one child in his class, Eddie, who walked with a brace on his leg. Some other students teased Eddie, bumped into him, took things away from him, and tormented him in various ways. Some of the second-grade students thought it was funny and laughed at what the older students were doing. Mr. Schroeder talked to the class about their responsibility to help Eddie as a member of their class and someone who could not fend for himself as well as they. Mr. Schroeder set up a contingency that if another student started bothering Eddie, his classmates were to first help Eddie move away to another area of the playground and stay with him, ignoring the other student(s). If the other student(s) kept bothering Eddie, the class members were to report the incident to the teacher in charge of the playground with specific names of students who were doing the teasing. If the class could help Eddie in this way and there were fewer playground incidents involving Eddie, Mr. Schroeder promised to bring in his popcorn popper for a special party. At the same time Mr. Schroeder discussed the matter with the teachers of the other classes who also set up a contingency to discourage the older students from picking on Eddie.

Note: In this example, the teacher should also arrange conditions so that Eddie can demonstrate competencies in his areas of strength.

Skill:	To express sympathy to peer about problems or difficulties. **S-IP-HP-0014-L2**
Objective:	Student will express sympathy to a peer about problems or troubles by making a statement such as, "I'm sorry."
Assessment:	Assess from previous knowledge of student or through direct observation using the <u>Social Behavior Assessment Inventory</u>.

Code: S-IP-HP-0014-L2-Im

TEACHING STRATEGY

Objective: Student will express sympathy to a peer about problems or troubles by making a statement such as, "I'm sorry."

Social Modeling

1. **Discuss with the class situations in which they might express sympathy to a peer and how to go about expressing sympathy.** Examples might include: a family member is ill, a bike has been stolen, a dog or cat has died, a peer cannot go to the movies, a peer did not make the team, a peer did not win the class election, a peer was injured on the playground. Have students contribute ideas to the discussion. Ask questions, such as "Why do we express sympathy to a friend? What can we say to a friend who has

   (a) Lost a pet.

   (b) Lost a class election.

   (c) Lost his or her final report.

   (d) Did not make the team?

   When are some other times we might tell someone we are sorry?"

2. **Identify specific behaviors to be modeled.** For example, discuss specific ways to go about telling someone you are sorry.

3. **Model the behavior.** Select a student to model the behavior with the teacher. Provide the student with a problem to tell about; for example, not being chosen for the team. Teacher will tell the student he or she is sorry that the peer did not make the team. Repeat with other examples.

4. **Provide an opportunity for practice.** Select two students to role-play a situation in which one student will tell another about a problem, and the other student will demonstrate the appropriate behavior of saying, "I am sorry." Have students reverse roles. Give opportunity for each student to demonstrate the behavior. Reinforce correct responses.

   Note: This skill requires the ability to empathize, placing oneself in another's position. Discussion and activities that help students to be empathetic toward others and animals may be necessary before students will go beyond the mechanical verbal statements.

Code: S-IP-HP-0014-L2-Ir

TEACHING STRATEGY

Objective: Student will express sympathy to a peer about problems or troubles by making a statement, such as "I'm sorry."

Social Reinforcement

1. **Use social reinforcement when student is observed expressing sympathy to a peer.** Be specific in praising the student. For example, "Marsha, that was very kind of you to tell Robin you were sorry about the death of her dog;" "Carl, you were very thoughtful to tell Matt you were sorry to hear that his brother is ill."

2. **Provide cues for target student.** Be a model for students by expressing sympathy to someone who has a problem. When appropriate, the attention of the class could be called to situations that warrant sympathy; for example, "Class, Mary is out today because her mother is very ill. When she comes back it would be nice of you to tell her you are sorry to hear about her mother's illness."

TEACHING STRATEGY

Objective: Student will express sympathy to a peer about problems or troubles by making a statement such as "I'm sorry."

Contingency Management

1. **Talk with the student about the specific behaviors that are desired.** For example, "When you see or hear that a person is having a problem, tell the person you are sorry about his or her problem." Provide the student with examples of problem situations where this behavior would be appropriate.

2. **Identify reinforcers which would be meaningful to the student.**

3. **State the contingency.** If, when you see or hear that someone is having (or has had) a problem, you say that you are sorry to hear about his or her problem, you will be rewarded.

4. **Watch for situations in the classroom or on the playground where students express sympathy to another student for a problem.** Reward the behavior according to the terms which have been established. (The teacher may need to evaluate the behavior to determine that it is sincere and appropriate.)

5. **Example.** Ms. Harris felt that members of her class needed to develop skills related to understanding feelings of others and appropriately expressing sympathy when others were having problems about which they felt unhappy. After having a discussion about expressing sympathy, she set up a role-playing situation, first asking each student to think of something bad that had happened to him or her in the past or something imaginary about which he or she would like someone to express sympathy. The teacher then had each student draw another student's name, and students in pairs demonstrated telling what the problem was and responding by saying, "I'm sorry." The teacher gave five points to each student who demonstrated the behavior satisfactorily. Students who did not receive five points received corrective feedback and another opportunity to try out the behavior. The points were added to other points the students were earning toward free time.

MAKING CONVERSATION

S-IP-MC-0002-L1-S	To pay attention in a conversation to the person speaking.
S-IP-MC-0004-L1-S	To talk to others in a tone of voice appropriate to the situation.
S-IP-MC-0006-L1-S	To wait for pauses in a conversation before speaking.
S-IP-MC-0008-L1-S	To make relevant remarks in a conversation with peers.
S-IP-MC-0010-L1-S	To make relevant remarks in a conversation with adults.
S-IP-MC-0012-L2-S	To ignore interruptions of others in a conversation.
S-IP-MC-0014-L2-S	To initiate conversation with peers in an informal situation.
S-IP-MC-0016-L2-S	To initiate conversation with adults in an informal situation.

Skill:	To pay attention in a conversation to the person speaking. **S-IP-MC-0002-L1**
Objective:	During a conversation, the student will look at the person speaking and demonstrate he or she has listened by being able to repeating or paraphrasing what the other person has said.
Assessment:	Assess from previous knowledge of student or through direct observation using the <u>Social Behavior Assessment Inventory</u>.

Code: S-IP-MC-0002-L1-Im

TEACHING STRATEGY

Objective: During a conversation, the student will look at the person speaking and demonstrate he or she has listened by repeating or paraphrasing what the other person has said.

Social Modeling

1. **A need for the behavior may be identified through a classroom discussion or through the use of any media available to the teacher.** You may want to raise the questions of how to show you are listening, how it feels to talk when people aren't listening, and why it is important to listen, both to be polite and to learn what the other person has to say. Encourage the children to participate, and write their ideas on the board. Two lists might be formed–one a list of "don'ts," i.e., distracting things people do; and one being a list of "do's," i.e., ways to be a good listener.

2. **Identify specific behaviors to be modeled.** For example, when someone else is talking, you should:

    (a) Look right at the person talking.

    (b) Be able to show that you have been listening by being able to repeat what was said.

3. **Model the behavior for the class during sharing or "show and tell" time.** Tell the class at the beginning that you are going to practice being a "good listener," and you want them to watch what you do to be a good listener. Proceed by paying close attention to what each child is saying, look right at the speaker, ask questions, and make comments. Then, interrupt the session to ask the children to identify specifically the elements of your behavior. Praise correct responses. You may also want to demonstrate improper behavior for contrast and ask the children the same types of questions.

4. **Give each child an opportunity to practice the proper behavior.** Build practice into any class activity where students are required to listen to the teacher or a peer. Remind students at the beginning that you are watching for good listeners. Call on the children to demonstrate that they have been listening by answering a question or restating what has been said.

5. **Verbally praise those who demonstrate they have listened by looking at the person speaking and being able to repeat some of what was said.**

6. **Maintain a good listening behavior with reinforcement.**

Code: S-IP-MC-0002-L1-Ir

TEACHING STRATEGY

Objective: During a conversation, the student will look at the person speaking and demonstrate he or she has listened by repeating or paraphrasing what the other person has said.

Social Reinforcement

1. **When target student is observed attending to the person speaking, identify and recognize aloud.** Call attention to specific actions. "Audrey, you're listening so quietly; I like that." "Jed, I like the way you look at me when I'm talking. You are a good listener." "Ken, you showed us all that you were listening. I'm proud of you!"

2. **Cue the target student's attending behavior by praising others, aloud, who are attending to the conversation.**

3. **Pair tangible reinforcement with the social reinforcement, if the positive reinforcement is not sufficient to develop good listening behavior.** For example, provide a token, a coupon, or a check mark when a student has given the appearance of listening.

Code: S-IP-MC-0002-L1-Ic

TEACHING STRATEGY

Objective: During a conversation, the student will look at the person speaking, and demonstrate he or she has listened by repeating or paraphrasing what the other person has said.

Contingency Management

1. **State task in observable terms.** When someone is talking, you should:

152

(a) Look right at him or her.

(b) Be able to show that you have been listening by telling what was said. It might be helpful to post a list of reminders, or incorporate the idea of listening into a bulletin board theme, stressing eyes and ears.

2. **Plan reinforcement.**

3. **State contingency.** When someone is talking, if you look right at that person, listen very carefully, and show us that you have been listening by telling us what was said, you will receive a specific reward.

4. **During a normal activity in which conversation takes place, watch target child for the appearance of listening, and then ask a question about the context of the conversation.** Initially reward for having eyes on the speaker even if the listener cannot repeat the conversation. Then require the student to answer a simple question or repeat some part of the conversation in order to receive the reward.

5. **Example.** Mr. Husseini starts each morning with "Group Circle" time where each child has an opportunity to share thoughts with the others. Carole loves to talk and always has something to share. However, she is so anxious to have her turn that she seldom pays attention to the other students. Her lack of attention is often distracting. Mr. Husseini makes a contract with Carole. He tells her that when she settles down and pays attention to the others and proves to him that she is listening, she will have a turn to speak too. Otherwise she will not have a turn that day. He told her she would have to watch the speaker, and when each speaker is finished, he will ask her to tell something the speaker said. In addition to Carole talking contingent on her listening to others, Mr. Husseini reminds her by recognizing other students who had their eyes on the speaker and by recognizing her when she gives the appearance of listening.

Skill:	To talk to others in a tone of voice appropriate to the situation. **S-IP-MC-0004-L1**
Objective:	Student speaks to others in a tone of voice (volume) appropriate to the situation; for example, low when speaking to one or two others, louder when addressing a group, low in the classroom, and louder on the playground.
Assessment:	Assess from previous knowledge of student or through direct observation using the <u>Social Behavior Assessment Inventory</u>.

Code: S-IP-MC-0004-L1-Im

TEACHING STRATEGY

Objective: Student speaks to others in a tone of voice (volume) appropriate to the situation; for example, low when speaking to one or two others, louder when addressing a group, low in the classroom, and louder on the playground.

Social Modeling

1. **A classroom discussion may be helpful in identifying a need for the behavior.** You may want to structure the discussion by raising such questions as, "Do we always talk in the same tone of voice? Why is it necessary to talk loudly sometimes and softer sometimes? Can you think of some times when we might want to talk more softly?" Generate ideas from the students.

2. **Identify the specific behavior to be modeled.** When talking to others, always remember to use the right tone of voice:

   (a) Speak softly in the classroom.

   (b) Speak louder on the playground, if necessary.

   (c) Speak softly when talking in a small group.

   (d) Speak louder when talking to the whole class.

3. **Model the behavior for the class.** Demonstrate several tones of voice, and ask students to identify the appropriate times and places for each. Praise those who respond correctly. Talk to the students in various tones of voice, and ask them to raise their hands when your tone is appropriate and to lower them when you voice gets too loud or too soft.

4. **Provide an opportunity to practice the behavior.** Call on students to demonstrate tones of voice to use in the classroom when speaking privately to someone and when giving a talk to a group or the whole class. It will probably not be necessary to practice voice tones appropriate for the playground.

5. **Praise students who demonstrate appropriate tones of voice.**

6. **Maintain good speaking habits through consistent reinforcement.**

Code: S-IP-MC-0004-L1-Ir

TEACHING STRATEGY

Objective: Student speaks to others in a tone of voice (volume) appropriate to the situation; for example, low when speaking to one or two others, louder when addressing a group, low in the classroom, and louder on the playground.

Social Reinforcement

1. **When target student is observed speaking to others in a tone that is appropriate to the situation, identify by name and praise aloud.** Be specific. For example, "Judy, I'm glad that you remembered to lower your voice when you came back from the playground;" "Gale, when you were working with Bud and Lynn, you kept your voice down and didn't disturb anyone. I'm proud of you;" "Shasta, we are all interested in what you have to say. Thank you for speaking up so we could all hear you."

2. **Recognizing others who are speaking in the proper tone of voice may be helpful in cuing the target student.**

3. **Remember that social reinforcements alone may not increase the desired behavior initially.** It may be necessary to pair a more tangible reinforcer,

154

such as a token or a coupon, with the social reinforcement until the behavior becomes firmly established.

Code: S-IP-MC-0004-L1-Ic

TEACHING STRATEGY

Objective: Student speaks to others in a tone of voice (volume) appropriate to the situation; for example, low when speaking to one or two others, louder when addressing a group, low in the classroom, and louder on the playground.

Contingency Management

1. **State task in observable terms.** When talking to others, remember to use the right tone of voice:

    (a) Speak softly in the classroom and more loud on the playground.

    (b) Speak softly when talking to one person or a small group, and more loudly when talking to a big group.

    Demonstrate different tones of voice that would be appropriate under each condition.

2. **Identify privileges from the reinforcement menu.**

3. **State the contingency.** When you remember to use the right tone of voice, you will be rewarded. (Specify the amount and kind of reinforcer.)

4. **Observe the children throughout the day in their normal activities.** Reward those who remember to adjust their voice to fit the situation.

5. **Example.** Eric likes to work with his friends, Regis and Steve. The boys work well together, but Eric frequently gets loud and has to be reminded to quiet down, as he disturbs the others who are trying to work too. On the other hand, when Eric is called on to speak before the group or share in "Sharing Time," he mumbles in a tone that is barely audible. Ms. Maki, Eric's teacher, reminds him to speak up or watch his noise level, more times than she can count. Ms. Maki contracted with Eric. She told him that when he speaks to the group loud enough for everyone to hear and also remembers to keep his voice down when working with his friends **without being reminded,** he will receive a star on his "Personal Chart." If he receives five start by the end of the day, he may select a privilege from the reinforcement menu.

Skill:	To wait for pauses in a conversation before speaking.
	S-IP-MC-0006-L1
Objective:	Student waits for pauses in conversation before speaking.
Assessment:	Assess from previous knowledge of student or through direct observation using the <u>Social Behavior Assessment Inventory</u>.

Code: S-IP-MC-0006-L1-Im

TEACHING STRATEGY

Objective: Student waits for pauses in conversation before speaking.

Social Modeling

1. **Discuss with the class the reasons why it is important to wait for pauses in a conversation before speaking out.** Depending on the ages of the students involved, the teacher may wish to structure the discussion by raising such questions as, "What would happen if we all talked whenever we felt like it? How do you feel when someone interrupts you when you're talking? When someone else is talking, what should you do if you have something to say, too?" Encourage students to suggest reasons for waiting for pauses before speaking.

2. **Identify the behaviors to be modeled.** When someone else is talking, wait until that person stops talking before you begin to talk.

3. **Model the behavior.** After the behavior has been adequately described, the teacher may want to demonstrate both the incorrect and correct behaviors for the class, for clarity. Model the appropriate behavior in role-playing situations. Have two students talk to each other with the teacher demonstrating when it is appropriate to break into the conversation. Have students role-play the teacher talking to another student at his desk, with the teacher showing appropriate ways to enter the conversation. Encourage the students to identify and describe the correct and incorrect behaviors. Be sure to recognize those students who respond correctly.

4. **Provide opportunity for practice.** Divide the class into small groups and set up a group discussion activity. Give each group a familiar topic to discuss. Watch for those who remember to wait for an appropriate time before speaking. Reinforce, through praise, those students who demonstrate the correct behavior. Practice could also be provided by continuing the role-playing with the teacher carrying on a discussion, giving each student an opportunity to practice breaking into the teacher's conversation appropriately.

5. **Maintain the behavior through reinforcement.** Consistent reinforcement should help maintain the behavior.

156

Code: S-IP-MC-0006-L1-Ir

TEACHING STRATEGY

Objective: Student waits for pauses in a conversation before speaking.

Social Reinforcement

1. **Reinforce verbally, by name, target student when he or she remembers to wait for a pause in the conversation before speaking.** Be specific: "Audrey, thank you for waiting for Ken to finish talking before you told us about your new kitten." "George, I'm so glad that you remembered to wait for Gale and me to finish our conversation before you asked your question." "Sandy, I really like the way you always wait your turn to talk."

2. **Provide cues for the target student.** Recognize other students who remember to wait for their turn to speak so that the target student is constantly reminded of what is expected. When the student does speak out of turn, call attention to the error briefly with a glance, a gesture, a shake of the head, or, if necessary, say "Wait until he or she finishes talking." If the student responds to the cue and waits until the appropriate time to speak, provide verbal reinforcement.

3. **Initially, if social reinforcement does not produce a change in behavior, the addition of a more tangible reinforcer should help to increase the desired behavior.**

Code: S-IP-MC-0006-L1-Ic

TEACHING STRATEGY

Objective: Student waits for pauses in a conversation before speaking.

Contingency Management

1. **Meet with the student(s) to explain the desired behavior.** For example, when you have something to say, wait until no one else is talking before you start talking.

2. **Plan reinforcement.**

3. **State contingency.** When you remember to wait until no one else is talking before you start talking, you will be rewarded. Specify kind and amount of reward.

4. **During class discussions and informal conversations, observe the students' behavior.** Reward those who wait for pauses in conversation before speaking.

5. **Example.** Gladys is a very friendly, outgoing child in Ms. Ericson's class. Gladys loves to talk, so much so that she forgets to wait for others to stop talking, interrupts, blurts out thoughts whenever they come into her head. Ms. Ericson is constantly reminding Gladys to be polite, to wait her turn to talk, not to interrupt others. Finally, Ms. Ericson carefully explains to Gladys that she enjoys her ideas and is pleased that she enjoyed talking, but she needs to learn to wait her turn before talking. She sets up a contract that allows Gladys to earn points by talking only when no one else is talking.

Ms. Ericson observed her behavior in three different situations and kept a tally of her behavior. Together she and Gladys made a chart with the three headings–Classroom Discussion, Group Circle Time, Work Group–and decided that Gladys would receive one point every time she contributed to the conversation in the specified way. She would also lose points for interrupting. If Gladys accumulated 36 points (nine points daily), she would be allowed to "lead" Group Circle on Friday. A public posting of the chart served as a reminder (cue) for Gladys.

Skill:	To make relevant remarks in conversation with peers. **S-IP-MC-0008-L1**
Objective:	Student makes relevant remarks in conversation with peers.
Assessment:	Assess from previous knowledge of student or through direct observation using the <u>Social Behavior Assessment Inventory</u>.

Code: S-IP-MC-0008-L1-Im

TEACHING STRATEGY

Objective: Student makes relevant remarks in conversation with peers.

Social Modeling

1. **Structure a discussion with the class using questions,** such as, "How do you feel when you are talking and someone makes remarks that have nothing to do with what you are saying? Do you feel as though the other person isn't listening to you? Do you feel as though the other person doesn't care about what you are saying?" Ask for ideas from the class about the best ways to carry on a conversation. Look for stories which provide conversations and use these as examples of relevant remarks. It might be helpful also to discuss ways to behave if the conversation involves an unfamiliar topic; for example, asking a question to find out more about it or just nodding and listening.

2. **Identify specific behaviors to be modeled.** When you are talking with your friends, remember to:

   (a) Listen carefully to what the others are saying.

   (b) Make comments that have something to do with what they are talking about.

3. **Model the behavior.** To demonstrate the difference between making relevant and irrelevant remarks in a conversation, set up a role-playing situation involving a small group of students who can converse easily. Suggest a topic of conversation that all the students are interested in, and then advise the rest of the class to pay attention to your behavior. Ask the group to begin a discussion, and join in. Make both relevant and irrelevant comments. Stop the discussion periodically to point out which comments were relevant and which were not, and why. Continue the role-playing, asking students to raise their hands when they hear a relevant comment.

4. **Provide opportunity for practice.** Repeat the above procedure, providing each student with an opportunity to participate in the role-playing group. Have other students evaluate the contributions to the conversation and tell why they think they are relevant or not relevant.

5. **Maintain the behavior through reinforcement.**

Code: S-IP-MC-0008-L1-Ir

TEACHING STRATEGY

Objective: Student makes relevant remarks in a conversation with peers.

Social Reinforcement

1. **Use social reinforcement, such as verbal recognition, smiles, touching, when the target student is observed exhibiting the desired behavior.** Recognize the student by name and call attention to the specific behavior: "Judy, you've shown me that you have really been paying attention to the conversation. Keep up the good work." "Bobbie, that was an interesting thought. Thank you for sharing it with us." "Sandy, I really like the way you talked to the new student today."

2. **Provide cues for target student.** Recognize students who demonstrate the skill. Have students define a list of topics which they enjoy talking to each other about, and post the list.

3. **If social reinforcement does not increase the desired behavior, it may be necessary to pair a token, check mark, star, etc., with the verbal reinforcement.**

Code: S-IP-MC-0008-L1-Ic

TEACHING STRATEGY

Objective: Student makes relevant remarks in a conversation with peers.

Contingency Management

1. **Present the task to the students in specific, observable terms.** When you are talking with your friends, remember to:

   (a) Listen carefully.

   (b) Say things that have something to do with the topic being discussed.

2. **Plan reinforcement.**

3. **State the contingency.** When talking with your friends, if you make comments or ask questions that are appropriate to the topic, you will be rewarded.

4. **Peer conversations are not always observable by the teacher.** As an alternative, you might want to set up discussion groups and direct a student monitor to keep a record of relevant questions and comments made by the group members. A group discussion could be tape recorded and played for the whole class with the class to evaluate and give points to students who make relevant comments.

5. **Example.** Rita is a real talker! She takes advantage of every opportunity to visit and chat with her friends. Rita is a good student but gets off task easily when working with a group. Invariably she will bring up irrelevant matters that distract the group. Ms. Maki decides to make a contract with Rita. She explains to Rita in private that when she could make more relevant than irrelevant comments in any work period, she will be rewarded with extra free time. Next (with Rita present), Ms. Maki explains the contract to the group members. The teacher directs the leader of Rita's work group to keep a chart of Rita's relevant and irrelevant comments. At the end of the work period, the chart is presented to the teacher. If Rita makes more relevant comments than irrelevant comments she is rewarded with extra free time and a star is placed on her chart.

Skill:	To make relevant remarks in conversation with adults. **S-IP-MC-0010-L1**
Objective:	Student makes relevant remarks in conversation with adults that address the topic and are appropriate for discussion with an adult.
Assessment:	Assess from previous knowledge of student or through direct observation using the <u>Social Behavior Assessment Inventory</u>.

Code: S-IP-MC-0010-L1-Im

TEACHING STRATEGY

Objective: Student makes relevant remarks in conversation with adults that address the topic and are appropriate for discussion with an adult.

Social Modeling

1. **Discuss with the class the general area of conversational skills.** Talk about the need to look at the person who is talking, to listen to what is said, and to think about what is being said so one can respond to what the other person is saying. Review also the skill involving waiting for pauses in the conversation before speaking. If there is a film or a story available that illustrates a good conversation, it might be used to bolster the discussion. Have students contribute ideas about "do's" and "don'ts" when having a conversation with their teacher, parent, or some other adult.

2. **Identify the specific behaviors to be modeled.** For example, when talking to an adult, look at the speaker, listen to what is said, wait until the speaker stops speaking before you speak, think about what has been said, and try to say something that fits with what is being said. Make a list of appropriate conversational behaviors.

3. **Model the behavior.** Sit in front of the class with another adult or with an older student who has good conversational skills. Carry on a conversation about a topic of general interest. Ask students to watch what each person does and identify the behaviors they have engaged in. Reinforce students who make good contributions.

4. **Provide opportunity for practice.** Have each student take a turn sitting with the adult and continuing the discussion. Have the rest of the class watch and evaluate. Reinforce good responses.

5. **Maintain the behavior through reinforcement.**

Code: S-IP-MC-0010-L1-Ir

TEACHING STRATEGY

Objective: Student makes remarks in a conversation with adults that address the topic and are appropriate for discussion with an adult.

Social Reinforcement

1. **Use social reinforcement, such as smiles, recognition, and attention, when the student is observed demonstrating the behavior.** Be specific in recognizing the child. For example, "Boyd, your conversation with Mr. McNalty was very good;" "William, thank you for your comment. It added to our conversation;" "Mary, you are good at carrying on a conversation with grown-ups."

2. **Provide cues for the target student.** Recognize another student who is demonstrating the appropriate behavior.

3. **If social reinforcement in the form of praise, smiles, etc., is not sufficient to increase the desired behavior, it may be necessary to accompany social reinforcement with tangible reinforcement (i.e., coupons, chips, tokens, etc.) to be exchanged for something the child wants.** For example, if you wish to increase the amount of conversation a student carries on with you, consider handing the student a token or coupon when the student makes an appropriate remark to you.

Code: S-IP-MC-0010-L1-Ic

TEACHING STRATEGY

Objective: Student makes remarks in a conversation with adults that address the topic and are appropriate for discussion with an adult.

Contingency Management

1. **Present task to student in specific terms.** When talking to an adult, listen to what the adult is saying and make replies that have something to do with the conversation.

2. **Plan reinforcement.**

3. **State the contingency.** When talking to an adult, if the student makes comments that are appropriate and are related to the topic being discussed, he or she will receive the agreed-upon consequence.

4. **Watch for the behavior to occur naturally,** or, set up a situation in which the behavior can occur. For example, set up a conversation between the student and yourself. Other adults could be included also. If the student makes comments which are appropriate to the topic, he or she receives positive reinforcement. Such situations could include having lunch with

the teacher, a conference with the teacher, a meeting between the parents and the teacher that includes the child, or a casual conversation on the playground.

5. **Example.** Jeff had few language skills and was very shy around adults. There were several other students in the class who similarly found it hard to talk when they were with adults. Ms. Johnson, Jeff's teacher, set up a weekly lunch time conversation group involving herself, Jeff, and the other students. She made a contract with the students that she would give a token for each relevant comment or answer to a question. The teacher initiated the discussions with topics the student were familiar with and kept the conversation going with questions to different students. At the end of the conversation period, students marked down on a card the number of tokens they earned. The tokens were exchanged later for time in the library for looking at books or videos or listening to recordings. The teacher occasionally asked other teachers to join the conversation group and later added tokens for good responses in conversations with adults outside the lunch period.

Skill:	To ignore interruptions of others in a conversation. **S-IP-MC-0012-L2**
Objective:	When interrupted in a conversation, the student will pause, say, "Excuse me," or some equivalent phrase, and continue talking. (Other means of dealing with interruptions may also be regarded as acceptable if they are appropriate to the situation in which they occur.)
Assessment:	Assess from previous knowledge of student or through direct observation using the <u>Social Behavior Assessment Inventory</u>.

Code: S-IP-MC-0012-L2-Im

TEACHING STRATEGY

Objective: When interrupted in a conversation, the student will pause, say, "Excuse me," or some equivalent phrase, and continue talking. (Other means of dealing with interruptions may also be regarded as acceptable if they are appropriate to the situation in which they occur.)

Social Modeling

1. **Identify a need for the behavior through a classroom discussion.** This skill might be combined with other skills dealing with carrying on a conversation. Ask questions about the behavior. For example, "How should you respond to someone who interrupts your conversation? What can you say and do?" Have students contribute ideas.

2. **Identify specific behavior to be modeled.** When having a conversation and you are interrupted by another, say, "Excuse me," and continue talking.

3. **Model the behavior.** Have a conversation with a student, and have another student come up and interrupt the conversation. Demonstrate how you would handle the interruption.

162

4. **Provide opportunity for practice.** Divide students into groups of three. Two students will have a conversation and a third student will interrupt. Students having conversation will say, "Excuse me," and continue talking. Rotate roles so that each student can demonstrate the appropriate behavior. Reinforce correct responses.

5. **Maintain the behavior through reinforcement.**

Code: S-IP-MC-0012-L2-Ir

TEACHING STRATEGY

Objective: When interrupted in a conversation, the student will pause, say, "Excuse me," or some equivalent phrase, and continue talking. (Other means of dealing with interruptions may also be regarded as acceptable if they are appropriate to the situation in which they occur.)

Social Reinforcement

1. **Reinforce with smiles, recognition, etc., when student is observed demonstrating the behavior.** Use descriptive praise. For example, "Carolynn, I liked the way you ignored Mike's interruptions, said, 'Excuse me,' and continued talking;" "Paul, you handled the situation beautifully. Instead of getting made at John, you ignored his interruption and went on talking."

2. **Provide cues for target student.** If talking and another student interrupts, give a gesture or tell the student to continue. Provide a model for handling students who interrupt you.

3. **If needed, provide tangible reinforcement (coupons, stars, checks, etc.) with social reinforcement (smiles, praise, pats on the back, etc.).** Tangible reinforcement can be exchanged for desirable items.

Code: S-IP-MC-0012-L2-Ic

TEACHING STRATEGY

Objective: When interrupted in a conversation, the student will pause, say, "Excuse me," or some equivalent phrase, and continue talking. (Other means of dealing with interruptions may also be regarded as acceptable if they are appropriate to the situation in which they occur.)

Contingency Management

1. **Discuss with student how to handle interruptions by saying, "Excuse me," and continuing to talk.**

2. **Plan reinforcement.**

3. **State the contingency.** If the student, when interrupted in a conversation, says, "Excuse me," and continues talking, he or she receives the agreed-upon reinforcement.

4. **Watch for the behavior to occur naturally.** Watch for occasions when the target student(s) handles interruptions constructively, and provide the reward.

5. **Example.** Kevin tended to be quarrelsome and easily irritated by actions of other students. If someone interrupted him when he was talking, for example, he would push the other student and say, "Shut up, I'm talking." Mr. Anderson called Kevin aside one morning and discussed his behavior with him. He told Kevin that when another student interrupted their conversation he was to ignore the interruption, say "Excuse me," and then continue the conversation. Mr. Anderson called another student so that Kevin could practice the behavior. A contingency was set up with Kevin by Mr. Anderson. If Kevin demonstrated the behavior as practiced, he would mark up one point on the chart. Kevin was asked to record his own behavior and report to the teacher how he handled each incident for which he gave himself a point. Kevin was able to exchange the points for time at the listening center.

Skill:	To initiate a conversation with peers in an informal situation. **S-IP-MC-0014-L2**
Objective:	Student initiates conversation with peers in an appropriate information situation by approaching a peer and being the first one to speak in conversation.
Assessment:	Assess from previous knowledge of student or through direct observation using the <u>Social Behavior Assessment Inventory</u>.

Code: S-IP-MC-0014-L2-Im

TEACHING STRATEGY

Objective: Student initiates conversation with peers in an appropriate information situation by approaching a peer and being the first one to speak in conversation.

Social Modeling

1. **Talk with students about the art of "making conversation," and about being the one to start the conversation.** (This skill might be combined with MC-0016, initiating conversation with adults.) The discussion of the skill might cover both the behaviors involved in starting a conversation and those involved in keeping a conversation going, i.e., topics of conversation. You may want to stress the value of being able to converse with another person as the best way to get to know him or her and develop a friendship. Students may be able to contribute ideas and answer questions related to why it is good to be able to walk up to someone and start a conversation, what would happen if nobody did, what are some topics about which one could talk to a classmate in an informal situation. You may also want to discuss appropriate and inappropriate times for conversations. By the time this skill is taught, other skills related to conversation should have been mastered, and the teacher might review the skills of greeting others, looking at them, speaking in an appropriate tone, and making relevant remarks.

2. **Identify the specific behaviors to be modeled.** When in an appropriate situation, the student will walk over to a peer and begin a conversation. Specific phrases to be used might be identified also. For example, "Hi, Mary, what are you doing?" "Hello. Bob. How are you feeling today?"

3. **Model the behavior.** Set up a situation where you role-play a student walking over and starting a conversation with another student.

4. **Provide opportunity for practice.** Have students help develop a set of opening phrases, such as, "Hello, how are you?" "Hi, what are you doing?" "Where are you going?" "How do you like this weather?" Divide students into two facing rows. Give each student in one of the rows a slip of paper with a phrase on it. The student is to initiate a conversation with the opposite student. The students are to converse until a timer rings at the end of two minutes. When the timer rings, students rotate partners and slips of paper. Continue reversing roles until everyone has had a chance to initiate a conversation. Repeat the practice without the prompting slips of paper.

5. **Maintain the behavior by reinforcing it when it occurs in the classroom or on the playground under appropriate circumstances.**

Code: S-IP-MC-0014-L2-Ir

TEACHING STRATEGY

Objective: Student initiates conversation with peers in an appropriate informal situation by approaching a peer and being the first one to speak in conversation.

Social Reinforcement

1. **When students are observed initiating conversation with other students, recognize them in specific terms.** For example, "Alec, I was happy to see that you went over and talked with John;" "Peggy, that was very friendly of you to walk over and start talking with Karen." (Note: Praise especially the shy student who makes an effort to start a conversation or a student who talks to a new student or someone else he or she does not know well.)

2. **Provide cues for target student by recognizing another student who has initiated a conversation.**

3. **A student may be encouraged to start conversation if he or she receives a tangible reward along with the praise.**

Code: S-IP-MC-0014-L2-Ic

TEACHING STRATEGY

Contingency Management

1. **Discuss with student(s) the behaviors involved in initiating a conversation, i.e., approaching a peer and being the first to speak.** Suggest ways to begin a conversation with a peer. For example, "Did you understand the homework assignment?" "Did you see the movie last night on TV?" "You have on a pretty dress. Did your mom make it?" "You play a good ball game.

165

Could you give me some ideas on improving my batting?"

2. **Plan reinforcement.**

3. **State contingency.** If the student initiates a given number of conversations with peers under appropriate conditions, he or she will receive the agreed-upon reward. Specify the type and amount of reinforcement.

4. **Watch for the behavior to occur naturally and reinforce it.** It may be difficult to monitor student interactions, so a feedback system involving other students or a self-monitoring system might be set up. For example, the student might keep a chart and record each time he or she approached another student and initiated a conversation, noting the date and the name of the other student on the chart.

5. **Example.** Lucille had an eye condition that was recently discovered and corrected with glasses. Because she was shy, and her eye condition had made it hard for her to recognize other children, she had a reputation of being unfriendly. She actually wanted very much to talk with other students, but they did not approach her, and she was afraid to approach them. Ms. Ramsey set up a group with Lucille and some other withdrawn students to practice social behaviors. She had them practice smiling and looking at the other person, saying "hello," using the other person's name, and making a brief comment or question which could develop into a conversation. She set up a point system in the group to reward these specific behaviors. The group could exchange the points for a variety of special activities. After practicing initiating conversations, Ms. Ramsey extended the requirements to the classroom and playground and had Lucille and the other members of the group report back on times they had spoken first to other students.

Skill:	To initiate conversation with adults in an informal situation. **S-IP-MC-0016-L2**
Objective:	Student initiates conversation with adults in an appropriate informal situation by approaching the adult and being the first one to speak.
Assessment:	Assess from previous knowledge of student or through direct observation using the <u>Social Behavior Assessment Inventory</u>.

Code: S-IP-MC-0016-L2-Im

TEACHING STRATEGY

Objective: Student initiates conversation with adults in an appropriate informal situation by approaching the adult and being the first one to speak.

Social Modeling

1. **The skill of initiating conversation with an adult is fairly sophisticated behavior requiring the student to master a number of prerequisite skills related to making conversation.** Although the student can learn appropriate ways to initiate conversations with adults, whether he or she will

continue to display the behavior will depend on the conditions established by adults: whether adults are receptive to his or her efforts, will make the time available, and are willing to listen.

2. **Establishing a need for this skill with students can be an extension of other activities related to making conversation.** You may want to talk with students about whether they like to talk to adults, what kinds of things they talk about to adults, what times and places seem to be best for being able to have conversations with adults. It may be helpful to students to identify times when adults may not want to engage in conversation, and you should enable them to recognize that some adults may not feel comfortable talking to children. For children (or anyone) to be able to carry on a conversation, it is necessary that the other person be willing to make responses that keep the conversation going. The discussion might also cover ways to leave a situation where it appears that the adult is not interested in having a conversation.

3. **Model the behavior.** Ask a student to role-play a teacher standing on the playground at recess, while the teacher, role-playing a student, approaches and initiates a conversation. Demonstrate greeting the teacher by name and opening the conversation with a remark, such as, "Ms. _____ , I'd like to show you a picture of my new baby sister," or "Mr. _____ , I brought my rock collection to school today," or "Ms. _____ , Mary and I have a problem we want to tell you about." Vary the situations showing a student approaching two teachers who are talking with each other, and a situation where the teacher is busy and does not want to talk. Ask student to describe your behavior and what you did in the different situations to initiate a conversation.

4. **Provide opportunities for practice.** Continue the role-playing described in Step 3 above, letting each student have an opportunity to play the role of student approaching an adult to initiate a conversation. Have each student think of two or three remarks he or she might use to open the conversation. Reinforce students for good attempts.

5. **Maintain the behavior through reinforcement.** Be sure to make opportunities available to students to approach you and initiate a conversation.

   Note: One way to help reluctant initiators is by teaching them to ask age-appropriate questions, i.e., favorite story, TV program, etc.

Code: S-IP-MC-0016-L2-Ir

TEACHING STRATEGY

Objective: Student initiates conversation with adults in an appropriate informal situation by approaching the adult and being the first one to speak.

Social Reinforcement

1. **Use social reinforcement when the student is observed beginning a conversation with an adult in an appropriate way and at an appropriate time.** Be specific in praising the student. For example, "Lucy, Mr. Carlton told me that you saw him at the mall last night. I am pleased to hear that you went over and spoke to him." "Robert, thank you for coming up and telling me about the new baby at your house."

2. **Provide cues for the target students.** Before an informal situation in which adults will be present, remind students how to greet and talk to them. Set up a time when you will be available to students for them to initiate a conversation with you about things they would like to tell you.

Code: S-IP-MC-0016-L2-Ic

TEACHING STRATEGY

Objective: Student initiates conversation with adults in an appropriate informal situation by approaching the adult and being the first one to speak.

Contingency Management

1. **Outline to student the steps involved in initiating a conversation with adults, suggesting appropriate conditions (for example, when the student would be interrupting or interfering with the adult's activity).** Help the student think of phrases for beginning a conversation.

2. **Plan reinforcement.**

3. **State the contingency.** If the student, at an appropriate time and place, walks over and starts a conversation with an adult, he or she will be reinforced. Specify type and amount of reinforcement.

4. **Watch for times when student initiates a conversation with an adult.** Reward according to the contingency that has been established, or set up a situation that makes it possible for the behavior to occur. For example, set up a time when you will be available to the student for conversation, possibly during a free-time period or recess. Reinforce if the student takes the initiative, i.e., beginning a conversation with you.

5. **Example.** Ken was part of a small group of immature students in Mr. Carl's room who were having special training sessions on conversation skills. They learned to look at people, greet them, make relevant remarks, and finally, to initiate a conversation with peers and then with adults. In the group, the students discussed and modeled appropriate times and places to start conversations with adults, some possible things to say, and what to do if the adult was busy and did not wish to talk with them. After the practice, Mr. Carl set up a contingency. Each student was to initiate at least two conversations per day with an adult—the teacher, the crossing guard, the librarian, the principal, etc.—and graph the results on a chart. Even if the adult did not respond, the students were to give themselves a point on the chart for making the effort. Students reported on their efforts and compared charts in the meetings of the group. At the end of 10 weeks, Mr. Carl rewarded students who had maintained their charts at a level of two or more conversations a day initiated with an adult by having a special lunch with them in the room. The principal was invited to come and provide additional recognition for mastering conversational skills.

ORGANIZED PLAY

S-IP-OP-0002-L1-S	To follow rules when playing a game.
S-IP-OP-0004-L1-S	To wait for one's turn when playing a game.
S-IP-OP-0006-L1-S	To display effort to the best of one's ability in a competitive game.
S-IP-OP-0008-L2-S	To accept defeat and congratulate the winner in a competitive game.

Skill:	To follow rules when playing a game. **S-IP-OP-0002-L1**
Objective:	When playing an organized game, the student follows the rules of the game.
Assessment:	Assess from previous knowledge of student or through direct observation using the <u>Social Behavior Assessment Inventory</u>.

Code: S-IP-OP-0002-L1-Im

TEACHING STRATEGY

Objective: When playing an organized game, the student follows the rules of the game.

Social Modeling

1. **Identify a need for the behavior through a classroom discussion.** Discuss fairness and cooperation. Ask why students think that we have rules for games; what would happen if no one followed the rules? Have the students contribute ideas to the conversation.

2. **Identify specific behaviors to be modeled.**

    (a) Learn the rules of the game.

    (b) Follow the rules when you play.

    It may be helpful here to discuss a few specific games while the students play, write the rules of the game on the board, and discuss how to follow them. Make sure students are in agreement about the rules which have been specified.

3. **Model rule following for the class.** Choose a game you can easily play, write the rules on the board, and model following them. For example, choose a board game which you can play with a group of students. As you play, describe the rules and what each is doing to follow the rules. Repeat the process on the playground with a more active game.

4. **Have student practice following the rules to an organized game.** Organize a game, write the rules on the board, and have the students play the game.

5. **Recognize those students who are observed following the posted rules for the game.**

6. **Maintain rule-following with social reinforcement.**

TEACHING STRATEGY

Objective: When playing an organized game, the student follows the rules of the game.

Social Reinforcement

1. **Name and recognize a student observed following the game's rules when playing an organized game.** Praise specific behaviors; for example, "Jamey, you took your turn when you were supposed to;" "Marsha, you remembered to move your checkers according to the rules."

2. **Cue rule-following in the target student by recognizing a student near him or her who is following the rules of the organized game in which they are involved.** Provide cues by posting game rules and reviewing rules before the game is started.

3. **It may be necessary at first to pair tangible reinforcement with social reinforcement to increase behavior; for example, giving points to students who follow specified rules, along with praise.**

TEACHING STRATEGY

Objective: When playing an organized game, the student follows the rules of the game.

Contingency Management

1. **State task in specific terms for the student.** When playing an organized game, the student will follow the rules of the game accurately when these rules are known to the student.

2. **Plan reinforcement strategy from reinforcement menu.** Identify a reward valued by the student that will be given following demonstration of acceptable organized game playing.

3. **State the contingency.** If the student follows the rules in playing an organized game, he will be reinforced. Specify amount and type of reinforcement.

4. **Watch for the behavior to occur naturally, and reinforce it when it occurs according to established contingency,** or, set up a situation giving the student an opportunity to play a specified game, according to the rules. Go over the rules of that game beforehand until you are reasonably sure he or she knows and understands them, e.g., until he or she can repeat them and tell what they mean. Then watch the student play the game and observe whether the rules discussed are followed. If so, reward the student.

5. **Example.** Jody doesn't follow the rules for baseball. He throws the bat and doesn't run in the base lines. Mr. Carr explains the rules until he is sure Jody understands them. He then contracts with him that if he follows all the rules of the game for one day, he can be co-captain of a team the next day. Jody follows the rules and becomes co-captain. He follows them for one week. Mr. Carr then explains that others want their turn at co-captain, but if he

follows the rules all week, he can be co-captain again on Friday. Mr. Carr kept this contingency in effect for several weeks, periodically giving Jody the privilege of being co-captain in exchange for remembering the rules.

Skill:	To wait one's turn when playing a game. **S-IP-OP-0004-L1**
Objective:	When playing an organized game, the student patiently waits his or her turn.
Assessment:	Assess from previous knowledge of student or through direct observation using the <u>Social Behavior Assessment Inventory</u>.

Code: S-IP-OP-0004-L1-Im

TEACHING STRATEGY

Objective: When playing an organized game, the student patiently waits his or her turn.

Social Modeling

1. **Identify a need for waiting turns through a classroom discussion.** Introduce ideas, such as what a game might be like if no one waited his or her turn, ideas of fairness in letting everyone get a turn, etc. Have students contribute ideas to this discussion.
2. **Identify specific turn-taking behaviors to be modeled.**
   (a) Wait in the specified place with others who are waiting their turn.
   (b) Stand or sit patiently watching the game while waiting.
   (c) Wait without interrupting others who are playing.

   Write specific behaviors on board.
3. **Model taking turns while playing.** Choose a game the students play often and have them play with you as a participant. Ask them in advance to watch how you take turns. After the game (or shortly after you have demonstrated taking turns), ask the students to describe how you waited your turn. Recognize students for good responses or descriptions.
4. **Organize a game and have students practice taking turns during the game.**
5. **Praise those students who patiently wait their turn to act during the course of the game.**
6. **Maintain turn-taking behaviors with social reinforcement.**

Code: S-IP-OP-0004-L1-Ir

TEACHING STRATEGY

Objective: When playing an organized game, the student patiently waits his or her turn.

Social Reinforcement

1. **Name and recognize the target student when seen patiently waiting for his or her turn in an organized game.** "Alice, you are waiting patiently." "I like the way John is sitting quietly waiting for his turn."

2. **Cue target child by recognizing aloud a student nearby who is patiently waiting his or her turn.** Recognize target student immediately if he or she follows the cue.

3. **It may be necessary to pair a tangible reinforcer with social reinforcement at first to provide a more powerful reward for waiting patiently.**

Code: S-IP-OP-0004-L1-Ic

TEACHING STRATEGY

Objective: When playing an organized game, the student patiently waits his or her turn.

Contingency Management

1. **State the task in behavioral terms.** When involved in playing a specified organized game, the student waits his turn to act, without showing signs or impatience, anger, annoyance, etc.

2. **Plan reinforcement from reinforcement menu.**

3. **State the contingency.** If the student, during a specified game, will wait his or her turn patiently, the student will receive a reward. Specify type and amount of reward.

4. **Organize an opportunity to play the specified game.** Observe the target student, and reinforce upon completion of the game if the student patiently waits. At first it may be necessary to reinforce after every phase of the game (e.g., innings in baseball, or punchball).

5. **Example.** Franklin had problems taking turns at bat. Mr. Benson wanted to increase Franklin's turn-taking behavior. He discussed it with the student, including how and why we take turns during games. He set up a contingency in which Franklin played two innings of baseball, waiting patiently on the bench for his turn to bat in order to earn a chance to play the next two innings. Franklin kept the contract and earned the right to play in the rest of the game. The next day the contract was increased to three innings, and so on, until Franklin could play an entire ball game waiting his turn. The contract was then dropped in favor of social reinforcement.

Skill:	To display effort to the best of one's ability in a competitive game. **S-IP-OP-0006-L1**
Objective:	Student displays effort in a competitive game situation by paying attention to the action of the game and by taking as active a part in the game as possible.
Assessment:	Assess from previous knowledge of student or through direct observation using the <u>Social Behavior Assessment Inventory</u>.

Code: S-IP-OP-0006-L1-Im

TEACHING STRATEGY

Objective: Student displays effort in a competitive game situation by paying attention to the action of the game, and by taking as active a part in the game as possible.

Social Modeling

1. **Discuss in class the concept of competition.** Discuss how it works in a game, how competition increases the excitement of a game, how a member of a team owes it to teammates to do the best. Stress that not everyone is equally good at playing every game, but that paying attention and trying hard helps one to improve. To stimulate discussion and interest, have students contribute ideas to the discussion. Use stories or other media about the excitement of competition and the importance of doing one's best.

2. **Identify specific behaviors to be modeled.** First discuss and list general guidelines for displaying effort:

   (a) Pay attention to the action of a game.

   (b) Take as active a part as you are able in the action of the game.

   Then discuss specific games played by the class and what specific actions in that game are needed to show effort. For example, when playing checkers, watch your opponent's moves, try to plan ahead, try to get your checker crowned, try to jump over as many of your opponent's checkers as you can.

3. **Model displaying effort in one of the games discussed for the class by playing the game with the class.** Ask the students to describe the things you did which displayed effort, and recognize those students who give accurate descriptions.

4. **Have the class practice by organizing one of the discussed games and having each class member participate.**

5. **Recognize those students who seem to display effort in the organized game.** It may be necessary to use a "shaping" procedure, i.e., recognizing some students for small amounts of effort in the right direction. Remember to recognize interest and effort in the game rather than skill.

Code: S-IP-OP-0006-L1-Ir

TEACHING STRATEGY

Objective: Student displays effort in a competitive game situation by paying attention to the action of the game, and by taking as active a part in the game as possible.

Social Reinforcement

1. **Identify by name and recognize aloud a student who is displaying effort in a game situation by paying attention to the action of the game and by taking as active a part in the action of the game as possible.** Recognize specific actions. "Walter, I like the way you are watching the checker game so carefully. You are doing a good job;" "Janet, you try hard at tetherball. That's really good."

2. **Cue displaying effort in a competitive situation in the target student by recognizing a student who is within hearing distance of the target student and who is paying attention and taking an active part in the game.** Immediately recognize target student when he or she displays effort in a competitive game.

3. **It may be necessary to begin by pairing a tangible reinforcement with social reinforcement to elicit displaying effort in a game.** For example, you might want to give the student points or tokens for paying attention to the game and making an effort to meet the demands of the game. It should be stressed that effort rather than skill at playing the game is being valued and rewarded.

Code: S-IP-OP-0006-L1-Ic

TEACHING STRATEGY

Objective: Student displays effort in a competitive game situation by paying attention to the action of the game and by taking as active a part in the game as possible.

Contingency Management

1. **State the task in observable terms.** When playing in a competitive game, the student will display effort to the best of his or her ability by:

    (a) Paying attention to the action of the game.
    (b) Taking as active a part in the action of the game as possible.

    Specify the desired behaviors that are appropriate to the game being played. For example, try to swing at the ball; run as fast as you can; kick hard when the ball comes to you; throw the ball to your teammate as fast as you can.

2. **Plan reinforcement from reinforcement menu.**

3. **State the contingency.** If the student displays effort in the course of a competitive game, he or she will receive a reward. Specify to the student the type and amount of reinforcement as planned in Step 2.

174

4. **Place the student in a competitive game situation.** If effort is shown by paying attention and taking an active part in the action, reward as stated in the contingency.

5. **Example.** Harvey and Walter, two friends, are both fearful and hesitant in playing competitive games. They are afraid of the ball and sometimes have problems because their attention wanders from the game. Ms. Johnson starts with dodgeball as a game in which they have problems. She reviews the rules with them and has them practice dodging the ball when it comes at them. She reinforces them with praise for making an effort in the practice situation. She sets up a contingency that each time they successfully dodge the ball they will earn two points. They will earn one point if, when the ball comes at them, they are looking and make an attempt to dodge it, even if they are not successful. The points are to be accumulated and spent at the end of the week for time to go together to the learning center. Points for dodgeball are gradually faded out and the contingency applied to other competitive games.

Skill:	To accept defeat and congratulate the winner in a competitive game. **S-IP-OP-0008-L2**
Objective:	Student, when defeated in a competitive game, congratulates the winner without grumbling or engaging in other negative behavior.
Assessment:	Assess from previous knowledge of student or through direct observation using the <u>Social Behavior Assessment Inventory</u>.

Code: S-IP-OP-0008-L2-Im

TEACHING STRATEGY

Objective: Student, when defeated in a competitive game, congratulates the winner without grumbling or engaging in other negative behavior.

Social Modeling

1. **Discuss the need for accepting defeat in a competitive game.** Include discussion of what it feels like to lose, why we do not like to play with a "sore loser," etc. It may be helpful to role-play a situation involving a student reacting poorly to being defeated, and follow up with questions, such as "How does the loser feel? How does the winner feel? Do you think the winner will want to play with the poor loser again? Why?" Stories and media may also be used to illustrate these ideas. Have students contribute ideas to the discussion. Call students' attention to sportsperson-like behaviors shown by well-known athletes on televised games, etc.

2. **Identify specific behaviors which go into sportsperson-like losing.**

    (a) Congratulating the winner of the game with words, hand shakes, etc.

    (b) Not making excuses for having lost.

(c) Not getting angry or despondent upon losing.

Write key words on board.

3. **Role-play a situation which involves losing a competitive game.** Model appropriate losing behavior, and ask the students to describe your actions. Recognize good descriptions and responses.

4. **Have class practice.** Set up a series of tournaments for pairs of students (e.g., checkers) or small teams (e.g., relay races). Rehearse with students before the game appropriate ways for losers to respond to the winners.

5. **Observe the defeated players, and reward those who accept defeat graciously and congratulate the winner of the game.**

6. **Maintain accepting defeat in a competitive game by recognizing students who display sportsperson-like behaviors when they or their team loses a game.**

Code: S-IP-OP-0008-L2-Ir

TEACHING STRATEGY

Objective: Student, when defeated in a competitive game, congratulates the winner without grumbling or engaging in other negative behavior.

Social Reinforcement

1. **Recognize the student when observed accepting defeat and congratulating the winner in a competitive game.** Point out specific behaviors, e.g., "Carla, it was very sportsperson-like of you to congratulate Jason when he beat you at checkers. I like that." "Bobby, I like the way you acted when Deena won your tetherball game. You smiled and congratulated her. Very nice."

2. **Cue the desired sportsperson-like behavior by recognizing other students who accept defeat well.** Immediately praise the target student when observed accepting defeat graciously or congratulating the winner of the game.

3. **It may be necessary to pair tangible reinforcement at first with social reinforcement.**

Code: S-IP-OP-0008-L2-Ic

TEACHING STRATEGY

Objective: Student, when defeated in a competitive game, congratulates the winner without grumbling or engaging in other negative behaviors.

Contingency Management

1. **State task in observable terms.** The student, when defeated in a competitive game, will congratulate the winner without grumbling or engaging in other negative behaviors.

2. **Plain reinforcement schedule from reinforcement menu.**

3. **State the contingency.** If, when the student or team loses a game, he or she congratulates the winner(s) and avoids negative behavior, he or she will receive a reward. Specify type and amount of reward.

4. **Set up a series of competitive games involving the target student as a participant.** Observe the student when defeated. If he or she reacts by congratulating the winner without excessive outward signs of anger, despondency, frustration, etc., reward according to the contract.

5. **Example.** Mr. Stachs observed that David was a sore-loser at checkers. He discussed with David the importance of losing graciously, explaining how no one likes to play with someone who whines, complains, or becomes angry when he loses. Mr. Stachs and David agreed upon a contract whereby if David lost a game of checkers and congratulated the winner, smiled and did not complain, he would be able to choose the next game activity from the game board, a privilege having high prestige and reinforcement strength in that particular classroom. Since winning was so important to David, this contract seemed unlikely to evoke the negative reaction of losing purposely to manipulate the contingency. Mr. Stachs then set up a checkers game between David and Timothy, who was a slightly better player than David and likely to beat him. David lost the game and congratulated Timothy, thereby fulfilling the contract and receiving the reward. This contract was kept in force for six game sessions, four of which David lost. He complied with the contract on all four occasions. The contract was changed to require a greater number of occasions for the reward and was eventually dropped in favor of social reinforcement.

POSITIVE ATTITUDE TOWARD OTHERS

S-IP-PA-0002-L1-S   To make positive statements about qualities and accomplishments of others.

S-IP-PA-0004-L1 S   To compliment another person.

S-IP-PA-0006-L2-S   To display tolerance for persons with characteristics
different from one's own.

Skill:	To make positive statements about qualities and accomplishments of others. **S-IP-PA-0002-L1**
Objective:	Student makes positive statements about qualities and accomplishments of others.
Assessment:	Assess from previous knowledge of student or through direct observation using the <u>Social Behavior Assessment Inventory</u>.

Code: S-IP-PA-0002-L1-Im

TEACHING STRATEGY

Objective: Student makes positive statements about qualities and accomplishments of others.

Social Modeling

1. **Meet with the class and discuss the behavior of making positive statements about the qualities and accomplishments of others.** Bring out in the discussion how everyone has both good and bad qualities and that everyone has some things that they can do well. Talk about why it is better to be aware of a person's good qualities. For example, it is easier to be friends with people and get along well with them if we can think of the things we like about them. It makes other people happy if they know we are aware of their good qualities. When available, use stories, films, videos, or other aids to stimulate the discussion. Have students contribute ideas to the discussion. Stress that one does not have to be perfect or have outstanding accomplishments to get recognition. We can praise and give recognition to people who make an effort and try to do a good job. Ask students to contribute ideas about qualities they like in other people. Make a list on the board.

2. **Identify specific behaviors to be modeled.** For example, when an individual has qualities that you like or has performed a task very well, say something good about that person and what he has done.

3. **Model the behavior.** Make a positive statement about each member of the class. If possible, make statements specific rather than general (i.e., "Mary has neat handwriting," rather than "Mary is a nice girl") and about something observable. Try to find a wide variety of positive things to say. Ask students to listen to what you are saying and reflect back what you said that was positive.

4. **Provide opportunities for practice.** Make a list of positive qualities on the board; for example, nice smile, tries hard, neat dresser, neat desk, good handwriting, good runner, always on time, sits up straight, speaks clearly, catches the ball well, helps other people, talks nicely to other people, is kind to animals, etc.

   Make the list as long as possible and have the class contribute to it. Practice by having students think of someone who has one of the qualities listed, or match one of the qualities to someone in the room. Make sure everyone is given recognition as having one or more of the positive qualities.

5. **Maintain the behavior through reinforcement.**

   Note: You serve as a model by watching for and recognizing the qualities and efforts of students.

Code: S-IP-PA-0002-L1-Ir

TEACHING STRATEGY

Objective: Student makes positive statements about qualities and accomplishments of others.

Social Reinforcement

1. **Use social reinforcement when student is observed making positive statements about another.** Use praise that describes the desired behavior. For example, "Neil, I liked your statement that Mark is a good artist. I agree with you;" "Tina, your comment about Ruth was very nice. Ruth certainly is good in math."

2. **Provide cues for target student.** Show the target student the desired behavior by telling him or her about some good qualities he or she possesses, e.g., "Mark, you sure are a good listener. I like people who listen." Next, try to elicit the desired behavior by telling the child some positive thing you would like him to say to you, e.g., "Ms. Miller, you sure are a good teacher." When Mark makes such a statement, thank him for doing so.

3. **If needed, provide tangible reinforcement, e.g., stars, coupons, tokens, etc., with social reinforcement, e.g., smiles, praise, attention, etc.** These can be exchanged for desirable items by students. Gradually reduce the tangible reinforcement until only social reinforcement need be used.

Code: S-IP-PA-0002-L1-Ic

TEACHING STRATEGY

Objective: Student makes positive statements about qualities and accomplishments of others.

Contingency Management

1. **Discuss with the student how people have both good and bad qualities.** Explain that sometimes if feels good to hear someone tell us about the good things we do. We usually don't like to hear about the bad things. Tell the

179

student that sometimes we forget that people have good qualities and if we try, we can find out about these good qualities and tell people about them.

2. **Plan reinforcement.**

3. **State the contingency.** If the student makes positive comments about qualities and accomplishments of others, the student will receive the agreed-upon consequences. Specify type and amount of reinforcement.

4. **Watch for the behavior to occur naturally, or set up a situation for the behavior to occur.** For example, announce that it is "Be Positive" week, and that you will be calling on people all week to think of something good to say about another person. You might give assignments, such as, "On Monday, we will think of positive things to say about classmates; Tuesday, about teachers; Wednesday, about members of our family, etc."

5. **Example.** Ms. Braum observed that students in her class seldom made comments which were positive about others' accomplishments or qualities and instead tended to find fault and criticize others. The class and Ms. Braum discussed this behavior. The class composed a list of people they all knew; for example, janitor, principal, gym teacher, librarian, patrol guard at the crossing, a favorite sports figure, etc. The class had a practice session in which they made positive comments about these people.

After the practice session Ms. Braum stated to the class that each student would draw a name from the bowl, 10 minutes before recess. If the student made a comment that was positive about the qualities or the accomplishments of that person the class would go to recess five minutes early. Ms. Braum used the list that the students had compiled. After one week Ms. Braum changed the names in the bowl to those of the students in the class. The contingency remained the same. Ms. Braum gradually phased out the contingency. When she felt the class needed to be reminded about being positive, she reinstituted the contingency.

Skill:	To compliment another person. **S-IP-PA-0004-L1**
Objective:	Student compliments others, i.e., makes positive statements to them.
Assessment:	Assess from previous knowledge of student or through direct observation using the <u>Social Behavior Assessment Inventory</u>.

Code: S-IP-PA-0004-L1-Im

TEACHING STRATEGY

Objective: Student compliments others, e.g., makes positive statements to them.

Social Modeling

1. **Talk with students about the need to learn how to say nice things to other people.** Ask students how they feel when someone praises or compliments them. You might prompt discussion by paying compliments to some

students and having them tell how they feel. Have students think of examples of complimentary things people have said to them or which they have said to others. The students might help generate a list of positive things that they could say to their peers, their teacher, their parents.

2. **State the behaviors which are to be modeled.**
    (a) Think of something specific that you like about a person or about something he or she is doing or has done.
    (b) Tell the person what it is you like about him or her or that person's actions.

    Model the desired behavior for the class. Compliment a student on some quality or accomplishment. Be specific rather than general. For example, use phrases such as, "I like the blue in your dress, Mary," rather than "Mary, you always have pretty clothes." Ask students to describe how you went about saying something positive or paying a compliment.

4. **Have the class practice complimenting others.** Have students draw names and then give that person a specific compliment. Have each student think of a compliment he or she could give to a parent.

5. **Recognize students who make efforts to compliment others in the practice situation.**

6. **Maintain the behavior through reinforcement.** Continue to be a model for the students by finding positive things to say to them.

Code: S-IP-PA-0004-L1-Ir

TEACHING STRATEGY

Objective: Student makes positive statements, i.e., compliments others.

Social Reinforcement

1. **Recognize students who make complimentary remarks to other people.** Describe the specific behaviors you want to increase. For example, "Cynthia, you gave Penrod a nice compliment when you said he look very neat today;" "Christopher, I'm glad you went up to Jonathan and told him he made a great catch;" "Martha is good at saying nice things to other people;" "Thank you for the compliment, Agnes."

2. **Provide cues by being a model for students.** Look for opportunities to recognize specific behaviors and accomplishments of students. Remember to be specific rather than general in giving compliments.

3. **If models and social reinforcement alone are not enough to encourage students to make positive remarks to other people, this behavior may be increased by accompanying social reinforcement with some tangible reinforcer when the student makes an attempt to compliment another.** You may also have to reward for approximations at first rather than wait for "polished"-sounding compliments.

TEACHING STRATEGY

Objective: Student makes positive statements, e.g., compliments others.

Contingency Management

1. **State the task in observable terms.**
   (a) Think of something specific that you like about another person or about something he or she has done.
   (b) Tell the person what it is that you like about him or her or that person's actions.

2. **Plan reinforcement strategy selected from reinforcement menu.**

3. **State the contingency.** If the student says a given number of positive statements to someone else within a given time period, he or she will be rewarded. The teacher should indicate the number of statements required and the time period, as well as the type and amount of reinforcement.

4. **Watch for the situation to occur naturally, or create a situation in which classmates can give compliments to each other.** For example, ask students to correct each other's work papers and find something positive to write on the paper. You could generate with the students a list of positive comments, such as, good paper, good work, very neat, you tried hard, good effort.

5. **Example.** Ms. Lemke wants to increase the number of positive things that members of her class say to each other. She discusses with them how to look for things they can compliment in other people and how to go about paying specific compliments. She put a list on the board of positive things to say to people. She set up a contingency with the class. When a student has finished his work and earned time in the free-time corner, he must choose a partner who has also finished his work. Before the two students go to the free-time corner, they have to demonstrate to the teacher how they can make a positive statement to each other. At first the students can rely on the statements written on the board. After they feel comfortable with these statements, the teacher requires them to make up compliments of their own.

Skill:	To display tolerance for persons with characteristics different from one's own.
	S-IP-PA-0006-L2
Objective:	Student will display tolerance for an individual with characteristics different from his or her own by accepting the person without derogatory comments or actions.
Assessment:	Assess from previous knowledge of student or through direct observation using the <u>Social Behavior Assessment Inventory</u>.

Code: S-IP-PA-0006-L2-Im

TEACHING STRATEGY

Objective: Student will display tolerance for an individual with characteristics different from his or her own by accepting the person without derogatory comments or actions.

Social Modeling

1. **Discuss the need to display tolerance for people different from oneself.** Use stories, film, and other available media to stimulate conversation on the subject. Human relations materials dealing with tolerance, religious or racial discrimination, or similar problems would be appropriate. Ask questions such as, "Have you ever been in a situation where you were different from other people? Were people nice to you? Are people sometimes unkind to people who look different, talk differently, do different things? What are some problems which people who are different sometimes have? Why do you think people are sometimes unkind or discriminate against people with differences? Are these good reasons?" Have students make notebooks or design bulletin boards devoted to the theme of racial or religious tolerance or the accomplishments of people with physical handicaps.

2. **Identify specific behaviors to be modeled.** When you are with someone who is different from yourself, treat him or her as you would treat anyone else, without making unkind comments or behaving in an unkind way:

    (a) Approach him or her in a friendly manner.

    (b) Greet him or her in friendly terms.

    (c) Include him or her in your activities.

    (d) Listen to ideas he or she may have that are different from your own.

    Write key words on the board.

3. **Model the behavior for the class through several role-playing situations. For example:**

    "A foreign exchange student from Taiwan comes to our class. She speaks very poor English and dresses a little strangely." Role-play greeting her and introducing her to others.

    "A young boy comes to the class. He has a speech defect that makes him lisp." Model a student approaching him for the first time on the playground.

The student has difficulty understanding him, but he makes the effort and invites him to play baseball.

"An Arab Muslim boy enrolls in class. He will not eat the food the cafeteria serves." Model a student dealing with this difference on first meeting and in the cafeteria.

Ask students to describe what you (or each of the participants in the role-playing) are doing and how each participant might feel. Recognize responses that provide good descriptions of actions and feelings.

4. **Have the class practice the behavior using role-playing situations similar to those above.** Students should be divided into groups of three or four. Each group may enact several of the role-playing situations, preferably having students take turns playing the "different" member. Sample situations follow:

   (a) A black student is transferred to an all-white class. Two of the students in the class meet him in the hall outside the class. Have these students approach and greet him. This can be repeated with a white student transferring to an all-black class.

   (b) A student who comes into class has a prosthesis in place of his right arm and hand. The other students are curious and a bit repulsed by his mechanical arm. Have students enact a free-play period and how they might invite him to play with them.

   Develop other scenarios and use situations that may have happened or are likely to happen to members of your class, given the area and circumstances of their environment. Have students describe what they were trying to do in the role-playing situation, and discuss how they felt or might have felt. Reinforce students who behave appropriately, i.e., in a tolerant, accepting fashion in the role-playing situations.

5. **Maintain the desired behavior through reinforcement.**

Code: S-IP-PA-0006-L2-Ir

TEACHING STRATEGY

Objective: Student will display tolerance for an individual with characteristics different from his or her own by accepting the person without derogatory comments or actions.

Social Reinforcement

1. **Identify and praise target student when observed interacting in a positive way with individuals of other races, ages, or physical characteristics.** Call attention to specific behaviors you wish to increase, e.g., "Russell, I'm glad to see you're trying to make Yoko feel at home;" "Dean was having an interesting talk with our new student about life in Alaska, his home state; it's good to learn about new customs;" "Conrad, I was happy to see you go up to our exchange student from Mexico and introduce yourself;" "Mary, I saw you pick up a package the lady dropped. That was a kind thing to do."

2. **Cue appropriate interactions with others in target student by recognizing another who demonstrates the specific behavior of interacting**

positively with people who are different from himself or herself. Be sure to reinforce the target child when he or she exhibits the same behavior.

3. **Provide cues using bulletin boards that stress life in other cultures or the accomplishments of people from different subcultures, people with handicaps, etc.**

Code: S-IP-PA-0006-L2-Ic

TEACHING STRATEGY

Objective: Student will display tolerance for an individual with characteristics different from his or her own by accepting the person without derogatory comments or actions.

Contingency Management

1. **State the task in specific, observable terms.** When you meet another person who is different from you, for example, someone who is either younger or older, is of a different race, or who has a special handicap, you should:
   (a) Not draw extra attention to the difference.
   (b) Keep from making any kind of negative comment or action toward him or her.
   (c) Be as nice to him or her as you would to any of your friends.

2. **Plan reinforcement.**

3. **State the contingency.** When you treat the children who are different from you with kindness, without behaving in a negative way or making an issue of the difference, you will be rewarded. State terms of the contract.

4. **If there is a child in your class who is noticeably "different" from the others (racially, ethnically, physically, etc.), observe the way the students relate to that child.** Reward those who treat him or her with acceptance, courtesy, and kindness. It may be necessary to identify a particular student or group of students who have a problem with tolerance and take them aside to establish a contingency. The teacher may also need to find ways to enhance the image of the 'different' child, identifying and making the class aware of his or her positive qualities and finding ways to help him or her overcome or compensate for the handicaps. For example, a child with a different ethnic background might be willing to share artifacts from his or her culture if reinforced for doing so, or one of his or her parents might be invited to make a contribution to the class. If you serve as a model in displaying a tolerant attitude toward students with differences and handicaps, the other students are more likely to follow suit.

5. **Example.** Billy was a new child in Ms. Mill's class. He was being treated for "emotional problems" and was taking medication for hyperactivity. Billy did not like to be teased. When teased or provoked he would not fight; rather he would turn red, shake, hit himself, and sometimes throw himself against the wall. Most of the children in Ms. Mill's class accepted and liked Billy and willingly included him in activities. Jack, however, deliberately antagonized Billy to get such a reaction out of him, and when he succeeded,

he laughed at him. Ms. Mill usually was able to keep the boys apart, but frequently at lunch, Jack would throw things in Billy's lunch, knock his milk over, push his sandwich on the floor, and steal his cookies. Billy reacted strongly each time. Finally, Ms. Mill decided to make a contract with Jack. The contract was twofold. First, she decided it was necessary to exclude Jack from the lunch table. She explained to him that when he was "ready" to eat lunch without disturbing Billy, he could return; and until then he was to eat at a different time with a different group of students he did not know. Ms. Mill kept him apart for a week and then told him he would be allowed to eat with his own class provided he left Billy alone. If he 'minded his own business' and did not bother Billy or other students, he would be allowed to stay and could lead the class back to the room. If he teased Billy again, he would have to return to the different lunch hour. At the same time, Ms. Mill also worked with Billy on learning to ignore children like Jack who like to tease.

Playing Informally

S-IP-PL-0002-L1-S	To ask another student to play on the playground.
S-IP-PL-0004-L1-S	To ask to be included in a playground activity in progress.
S-IP-PL-0006-L1-S	To share toys and equipment in a play situation.
S-IP-PL-0008-L1-S	To give in to reasonable wishes of the group in a play situation.
S-IP-PL-0010-L2-S	To suggest an activity for the group on the playground.

Skill:	To ask another student to play on the playground. **S-IP-PL-0002-L1**
Objective:	Student asks other students to play on the playground or during free-play activities.
Assessment:	Assess from previous knowledge of student or through direct observation using the <u>Social Behavior Assessment Inventory</u>.

Code: S-IP-PL-0002-L1-Im

TEACHING STRATEGY

Objective: Student asks other students to play on the playground or during free-play activities.

Social Modeling

1. **Discuss a need for appropriately asking others to play with you.** Stimulate conversation with questions, such as, "Is it sometimes more fun to play with someone else than alone? How does it feel to be left out when others are playing?" Have students suggest ways to go about approaching others to play and what to do if the others refuse. (Note: Teaching the skill involved in approaching others to play should not be construed to mean that solitary play is necessarily undesirable.) Books and films may also be used to establish reasons for asking others to play.

2. **Discuss specific actions that go into asking someone to play.**

    (a) Walk over to the person.

    (b) Address him or her by name if you know it.

    (c) Ask him or her politely if he or she would like to play with you.

    (d) If you wish, specify what you would like to play.

3. **Model the behavior for the class.** Role-play a situation where one student is standing alone on the playground or during free play. Approach the student and ask him or her to play with you according to the above guidelines. Ask the class to describe your actions, and praise those students who give adequate responses. It may also be useful to role-play the situation in which the other student says he or she does not care to play.

4. **Have students role-play this same situation in pairs, with each student taking a turn in different roles.**

5. **Reward those students who ask other students to play with them according to the above guidelines.**

6. **Maintain the behavior by observing the students on the playground and recognizing students who ask others to play with them.**

Code: S-IP-PL-0002-L1-Ir

TEACHING STRATEGY

Objective: Student asks other students to play on the playground or during free-play activities.

Social Reinforcement

1. **Recognize a student by name when observed asking another student to play on the playground or during free play.** Recognize specific behaviors, e.g., "Mike, I'm so pleased you asked Betty to play with you at recess;" "John, it was very friendly of you to include Steven in your game of marbles during free play."

2. **Cue asking students to play on the playground by recognizing aloud a student within hearing distance of the target student, for asking another student to play.** Be sure to recognize the target student immediately when observed asking another student to play.

3. **It may, at first, be necessary to pair a tangible reinforcement with social reinforcement to teach students to ask others to play.** Fade the tangible reinforcer as soon as possible, however.

Code: S-IP-PL-0002-L1-Ic

TEACHING STRATEGY

Objective: Student asks other students to play on the playground or during free-play activities.

Contingency Management

1. **State the task in behavioral terms.** When the student observes another student who is alone on the playground or during free play, he or she will ask that student to play with him or her. (Make clear that this is an invitation and not a demand. The other student may not want to play, in which case target student should leave the student alone.)

2. **Plan reinforcement from reinforcement menu.**

3. **State the contingency.** If the target student asks another student who is alone on the playground or at free play, to play, the target student will be rewarded according to the agreed-upon terms. Specify type and amount of reward.

4. **Observe students on the playground or in the classroom during free-play activities.** Reward the target student when seen asking another student to play.

5. **Example.** James complained often to the teacher that no one like him and he had no one to play with. He tended to stay apart from other children.

Mr. Sachs explained to James that to be friendly, we cannot always wait for someone to approach us to play but must ask someone to play with us. He and James discussed specific ways James could ask another student to play with him, describing how to approach another and what phrases to use. He made it clear to James that others may not always want to play; and if this is the case, he should leave the other person alone. Mr. Sachs set up a contract so that James would be rewarded for asking a student to play with him in an appropriate fashion. He was allowed to take a new library book home with him that night, something very rewarding to James that he could not otherwise earn. Mr. Sachs observed James on the playground to see if he complied with the conditions of the contract. After five days in which James made successful attempts to approach other children, the reinforcement of playing with another student seemed sufficient alone to maintain the behavior; and the contract was dropped.

Skill:	To ask to be included in a playground activity in progress. **S-IP-PL-0004-L1**
Objective:	Student asks to be included in a playground activity already in progress, for example, a ball game, by approaching the other students and asking to play.
Assessment:	Assess from previous knowledge of student or through direct observation using the <u>Social Behavior Assessment Inventory</u>.

Code: S-IP-PL-0004-L1-Im

TEACHING STRATEGY

Objective: Student asks to be included in a playground activity already in progress, for example, a ball game, by approaching the other students and asking to play.

Social Modeling

1. **Discuss why one might want to ask to be included in a playground activity already in progress.** Include ideas, such as the enjoyment of participation, how it feels to be left out, and the fact that other people might be happy to include you in the game if they knew you wanted to play. Discuss various ways one might go about asking to be included. Conversation may be stimulated through use of related stories or films or discussion of actual situations that have occurred on the playground. Encourage students to contribute ideas to the discussion. Some discussion of appropriate and inappropriate times to ask to be included might also be held, along with discussion of what to do if one asks to play and is turned down.
2. **Describe specific behavior involved in asking to be included in an activity in progress.**
   (a) Approach the other students at a time that does not interrupt the game.
   (b) Politely ask if you may play.

(c) Accept the group's decision as to whether you may play and the conditions (e.g., if they say you must play outfield, do not argue).

You may wish to add things specific to activities of the particular class.

3. **Model the behavior for the class.** Set up a role-playing situation with a group of students who are playing something. Demonstrate approaching and asking to be included in the activity. Ask students to describe your actions in the role-playing situation. Recognize those students who make good responses.

4. **Have class practice asking to be included in playground activity through role-playing.** Have the group engage in a play activity and ask each student in turn to play the part of someone who asks to be included in that activity.

5. **Recognize students who approach the situation using the guidelines discussed in Step 2 of this strategy.**

6. **Maintain the behavior by recognizing students when they are observed asking appropriately to play with others.**

Code: S-IP-PL-0004-L1-Ir

TEACHING STRATEGY

Objective: Student asks to be included in a playground activity already in progress, for example, a ballgame, by approaching the other students and asking to play.

Social Reinforcement

1. **Praise aloud a student who is observed asking to be included in a playground activity already in progress.** Praise specific behaviors: "Lisa, it was great the way you went up to the children playing ball and asked if you could be an outfielder."

2. **Cue asking to be included in a playground or recess activity already in progress by praising another student for doing so within the target student's hearing.** Be sure to praise target student immediately for performing the desired behavior. It might be necessary to prompt a shy child by leading the child to the activity and telling him or her how, when, and whom to approach.

Note: At first you may need to pair tangible reinforcement with social reinforcement to get the desired response.

Code: S-IP-PL-0004-L1-Ic

TEACHING STRATEGY

Objective: Student asks to be included in a playground activity already in progress, for example, a ball game, by approaching the other students and asking to play.

Contingency Management

1. **State the task in observable terms.** The student will approach a group of children already playing, either on the playground or during a free-play period, and politely ask to be included in the play activity.

2. **Plan reinforcement schedule from reinforcement menu.**

3. **State the contingency.** If the student approaches other students and asks to participate in a playground activity already in progress, he or she will receive a reward.

4. **Assess in the naturally occurring playground situation or set up situation by holding target student back a few minutes at the beginning of recess to let activities begin on the playground.** Observe whether student approaches the other students and asks to be included in play.

5. **Example.** Marcy is very shy and usually gets left out of the group activities. She is so quiet that no one notices her. She usually goes off and plays by herself, but she has told her mother that she wishes she could play with the others. After a talk with her mother, the teacher, Ms. Jackson, discusses this with Marcy and explains that she cannot always wait for an invitation to play, but must sometimes make known that she would like to play. They discuss the proper way to ask to be included in play, being polite and not demanding, watching for a good time to ask someone. Ms. Jackson has Marcy role-play the behavior with her. They then decide to set up a contingency such that if Marcy asks the group to include her, she will receive extra library time for free reading, a very reinforcing activity for Marcy. Ms. Jackson observes Marcy for several days on the playground, during which time Marcy complies with the contingency and is rewarded. After several days, Marcy seems more comfortable with the behavior, and the reinforcement of playing with the others seems strong enough to sustain the behavior of asking to play, so the contingency is dropped.

Skill:	To share toys and equipment in a play situation. **S-IP-PL-0006-L1**
Objective:	Student will share toys and equipment with another student in a play situation by willingly allowing the other student to use toys and equipment previously used or by using toys and equipment in conjunction with one or two other students.
Assessment:	Assess from previous knowledge of student or through direct observation using the <u>Social Behavior Assessment Inventory</u>.

Code: S-IP-PL-0006-L1-Im

TEACHING STRATEGY

Objective: Student will share toys and equipment with another student in a play situation by willingly allowing the other student to use toys and equipment previously used or by using toys and equipment in conjunction with one or two other students.

Social Modeling

1. **Discuss why we need to share toys and other things with others when we play.** Have class members give their ideas. Include ideas such as how some games are more fun to play with others, ideas of fairness in sharing, and how the student who does not have toys feels when another student has refused to share with him. Describe ways in which adults share with each other; for example, teachers sharing materials and equipment in the school.

2. **Discuss specific behaviors to be modeled.**
   (a) Allow another student to come over and play with the toys and/or equipment you are using.
   (b) Play with another student where you are both using the same toys or equipment.

   Write key words on the board.

3. **Model the behavior for the class.** Role-play a situation in which you share toys and/or equipment with a student. Use different pieces of equipment or toys available in the class and call on different students to come up and ask to share them; then continue using them together with the student.

   Ask students to discuss your behavior in the role-playing situation. Praise students who make reasonable comments in this discussion.

4. **Have students practice sharing by providing toys for the class and pairing students in groups of two or three to share the toys.** Explain that this is a practice-sharing exercise.

5. **Move around the class and observe students in the practice activity.** Recognize students who share the toys adequately and play with them in conjunction with others.

6. **Maintain the behavior through reinforcement.**

Code: S-IP-PL-0006-L1-Ir

TEACHING STRATEGY

Objective: Student will share toys and equipment with another student in a play situation by willingly allowing the other student to use toys and equipment previously used or by using toys and equipment in conjunction with one or two other students.

Social Reinforcement

1. **Identify by name and recognize aloud a student observed sharing toys and equipment with other students.** Call attention to specific behaviors that relate to the skill, e.g., "Joshua, thank you for letting Amy play with the blocks you were playing with;" "Patsy, it was very nice of you to play with the trucks with Marie;" "Carlotta, you shared your crayons with Magda very nicely."

2. **Cue sharing behavior in the target student by recognizing another student who is sharing toys and/or equipment with someone else.** Be sure to recognize the target student immediately if she begins to share her toys with another student.

3. It may be necessary at first to pair tangible reinforcement with social reinforcement to increase sharing behaviors.

Code: S-IP-PL-0006-L1-Ic

TEACHING STRATEGY

Objective: Student will share toys and equipment with another student in a play situation by willingly allowing the other student to use toys and equipment previously used or by using toys and equipment in conjunction with one or two other students.

Contingency Management

1. **State the task to the student in observable terms.** For example, the student will share toys and equipment with other students in a play situation by willingly allowing another student to use toys and equipment previously used alone or by using toys or equipment together with other students.

2. **Plan reinforcement schedule from reinforcement menu.**

3. **State the contingency.** If the student will share toys or equipment with another student during play periods or recess, he or she will receive a particular reward. Specify type and amount of reinforcement.

4. **Set up play period such that there are toys and/or equipment for the students to use.** Observe target student during play period. If he or she is seen sharing toys or equipment with other students, reward the student at the end of the play period according to the agreed-upon contingency.

5. **Example.** Fred, a first grader, does not share toys with others. Mr. Murray, his teacher, talked with him about sharing, why we need to share, and how to do it. He set up a contingency with Fred stating that if Fred shares toys or equipment for at least 10 minutes (one-third of the free-play-period time) with another student, he will be line monitor on the way to lunch directly after free play. The first day Fred shares some blocks with Harvey for 12 minutes and receives his reward. This contingency is kept and met for three days and then increased to 20 minutes. After six days of meeting this contingency, the contract is dropped in favor of social reinforcement. In order to give Fred some freedom to play as he wishes, e.g., in ways where there is no opportunity for sharing, the contingency does not extend to all 30 minutes of free play.

Skill:	To give in to reasonable wishes of the group in a play situation. **S-IP-PL-0008-L1**
Objective:	Student will accede to reasonable majority wishes of the group with regard to what they will play, by what rules, and when and where.
Assessment:	Assess from previous knowledge of student or through direct observation using the <u>Social Behavior Assessment Inventory</u>.

Code: S-IP-PL-0008-L1-Im

TEACHING STRATEGY

Objective: Student will accede to reasonable majority wishes of the group with regard to what they will play, by what rules, and when and where.

Social Modeling

1. **Identify and discuss a need for acceding to the wishes of the majority with regard to questions about a game or activity.** Discuss the need for cooperation in play activities. Bring up such questions as, "What happens if no one can agree on what to play, and everyone insists on his own way? What do we mean by majority, if we say that people should give in to the wishes of the majority? Are there times when we would **not** want to let the majority decide? What would we want to do then?" Have students contribute ideas to this discussion. Videos and stories may also be used to stimulate discussion.

2. **Identify specific behaviors to be modeled.** For example, when most of the members of the group want to do something and you do not want to do it:

   (a) You may try to talk them into doing it your way by pointing out the benefits and asking them to reconsider.

   (b) If the majority still disagrees with your wishes, you may either go along with their decision without complaining or withdraw from the activity quietly and without interrupting the continuation of the activity.

   Point out the benefits of each of these approaches. Basically, it is up to the student to decide in each case whether to play according to the group wishes or whether to play alone, and this should be explained and discussed. Write key words on the board.

3. **Model the behavior for the class in a role-playing situation with a number of students.** Following is a sample scenario:

   Teacher role-plays a student who wants to play softball. The students play a group who want to play dodgeball. The teacher first tries to convince the others to play softball with him or her, and they continue to refuse. He or she gives in and plays with them. Teacher should verbalize his or her decision to play and why he or she made that decision.

   Ask the students to discuss your actions in the role-playing situation. Recognize students who make adequate responses.

4. **Have class practice the behavior by role-playing situations such as those used in the teacher-modeling exercise.** For example, one student wants to be the pitcher in the softball game. The others want the student who regularly pitches to do it. Use situations which come up frequently with the class. Reinforce appropriate responses in the role-playing situation.

5. **Maintain the behavior with social reinforcement.**

Code: S-IP-PL-0008-L1-Ir

TEACHING STRATEGY

Objective: Student will accede to reasonable majority wishes of the group with regard to what they will play, by what rules, and when and where.

Social Reinforcement

1. **Recognize a student who has been observed acceding to majority wishes in a play situation (when such wishes are reasonable and not objectionable).** Recognize him or her by name and for specific actions, i.e., "Julie, you played tetherball with the others even though you wanted to play soccer. That was very cooperative of you. I'm proud of you;" "Maggie, I liked the way you gave in to the group's decision on whether your ball was fair or foul. That was very sportsperson-like."

2. **Cue the desired cooperative behavior in the target student by praising a student near him who is exhibiting this behavior.** If this situation does not occur, it may be appropriate to cue the behavior by making a general statement about the concept of "majority rules," to the target student when necessary. Be sure to recognize immediately when he or she appropriately accedes to the majority's wishes.

   Note: It may be necessary to pair social reinforcement with tangible reinforcement to increase this behavior at first. The tangible reinforcers should be faded out upon attaining an adequate level of the behavior.

Code: S-IP-PL-0008-L1-Ic

TEACHING STRATEGY

Objective: Student will accede to reasonable majority wishes of the group with regard to what they will play, by what rules, and when and where.

Contingency Management

1. **Explain the skill to the student in terms of actions and observable behavior.** For example, when the target student disagrees with the majority of the other students about what to play, how, when or where to play, the student will give in to the group's wishes, provided the group's wishes are reasonable. If the student does not wish to give in, he or she may try to convince the group of the benefits of his or her point of view or may leave the situation.

2. **Using reinforcement menu, plan reinforcement schedule for the student.**

3. **State the contingencies of the contract to the student.** If the student gives in to the reasonable wishes of the majority during game or play period with regard to what the group will play, by what rules, when and where, etc., he or she will be rewarded. Specify type and amount of reward.

4. **Observe the student during periods of informal group play.** Reward the student for going along with the majority wishes when he or she disagrees. The student may (and should be encouraged to) try to sway the wishes of the group by verbally defending or espousing his or her own ideas and wishes. The student should also be allowed to withdraw from the game. This may seem less cooperative and sportsperson-like, but it should remain the child's prerogative. He or she should only be penalized if upon disagreement he or she actively interferes with the continuation of the activity by the others.

5. **Example.** Abbie always demanded to have her own way in group play activities, and the other children told the teacher they were getting "sick and tired" of being bossed around by her. Ms. Kaye, the teacher, discussed this with Abbie, explaining how the other students felt and why. She suggested alternative ways Abbie could express her desires and different ways she could act when the group made a decision contrary to her wishes. She explained to Abbie that she had the alternative of giving in to the group's wishes or leaving the game, but that pushing her wishes onto the group by interfering with the game or yelling and complaining would not be allowed. She explained that if Abbie did react to the group's contrary decisions by interfering with the game, she would be taken out of the group activity and not be allowed to participate in play period for the rest of that day and the next. On the other hand, if she got through an entire play period without demanding her own way over the reasonable wishes of the group as a whole, she would be rewarded by being allowed to pick the story to be read to the class at story time directly following play period.

This contingency was put in force, and after the first two times Abbie was removed from the play situation, she seemed more willing to be cooperative. After a week of receiving a reward, the contract was changed to two days without complaint to receive reinforcement. After another successful week, the contract was dropped in favor of social reinforcement.

Skill:	To suggest an activity for the group on the playground. **S-IP-PL-0010-L2**
Objective:	When with a group on the playground, the student suggests an activity for the group.
Assessment:	Assess from previous knowledge of student or through direct observation using the Social Behavior Assessment Inventory.

Code: S-IP-PL-0010-L2-Im

TEACHING STRATEGY

Objective: When with a group on the playground, the student suggests an activity for the group.

Social Modeling

1. **Discuss the need for each member of the group to contribute ideas regarding the group's activities.** Talk about how a group works better and everyone has a better time when all members make suggestions. Discuss how members of a group feel when one or two of them make all the suggestions and decisions. Ask members of the class how they feel about this, and try to stimulate a conversation around this point.

2. **Identify specific behaviors to be modeled.**
   (a) When to make a suggestion. For example, when the group has nothing to do, when someone else has suggested something and it has been rejected by the others, or when you do not want to do it.
   (b) How to make a suggestion. Uses phrases such as "How about _____?" "Why don't we play _____?" "Would anyone like to play _____?"

   Explain that a suggestion may be accepted or rejected. The student must be prepared to deal with the rejection of his suggestion without anger or dejection.

3. **Model the behavior for the class.** Role-play a common playground situation in which you make suggestions to the group as to what things they might do. Ask the students to describe how you make your suggestions, and reinforce relevant responses.

4. **Divide the class into small groups and send them to the playground to practice the activity.** Provide instructions that they are to decide among themselves what they will play. Visit each group and observe their decision making. Reinforce those students who contribute suggestions to this process.

Code: S-IP-PL-0010-L2-Ir

TEACHING STRATEGY

Objective: When with a group on the playground, the student suggests an activity for the group.

Social Reinforcement

1. **Use praise, smiles, nods, etc., to reinforce target student for making an appropriate suggestion to the group regarding an activity.** Tell the student what he or she is being reinforced for and use his or her name when praising. Examples: "Bonnie, thank you for suggesting we play dodgeball. Isn't that a good idea, class?" "Bill, that is a good suggestion! Class would the rest of you like to go over and play on the swings for a while?"

2. **Cue appropriate behavior in the target student.**
   (a) Ask to suggest an activity for the group.
   (b) Ask the class in general for suggestions as to activities on the playground or in the class.
   (c) Recognize another student who has made a suggestion to the group.

3. **Immediately reinforce any acceptable suggestions that the target student makes.** Unacceptable suggestions (inappropriate to the situation) may be handled by thanking the student for the suggestion but pointing out the

unacceptability (e.g., "Thank you, Bob, I like you contributing ideas, but we have no football field or equipment."). Antisocial suggestions should be ignored.

Note: It may sometimes be necessary to use a more tangible incentive to increase suggestions. These should be used only when absolutely necessary and always paired with social reinforcers.

Code: S-IP-PL-0010-L2-Ic

TEACHING STRATEGY

Objective: When with a group on the playground, the student suggests an activity for the group.

Contingency Management

1. **Discuss the skill with the student, outlining what actions you expect him or her to take.** For example, "I want you to suggest something for the group to do when you are on the playground with them." You may also spell this out in more detail if necessary, e.g., "If the group is looking for something to do, and you have an idea, say something like, 'How about playing baseball,' or whatever your idea is."

2. **Plan reinforcement.**

3. **Explain the contingency to the student.** Explain that the student will be reinforced for suggestions made. Specify type, amount, and schedule of reinforcement.

4. **Observe the students on the playground, and watch for the target student to make suggestions to the group as to a play activity.** Reward the student when a suggestion is made. It is not necessary for other students to accept the suggestion.

5. **Example.** Boris is very passive on the playground, and Mr. Bond would like to encourage him to have more initiative. He discusses this with Boris. "Boris, I would like to see you give some suggestions to the rest of the class when we go out to the school yard to play. Think of something you would like us to play, and when we go out today, suggest it to the others. Playing with a group is more fun when everyone contributes ideas about what to play."

   "If you suggest at least one thing, I will let you be line monitor after recess." (This reinforcement was chosen because Boris had previously expressed a desire for this position). Mr. Bond gives Boris an extra prompt by letting him choose a piece of play equipment, e.g., a bat and ball, around which to structure a suggested activity. Boris complies with this request and is reinforced. The contingency is put in force on an every-other-day basis for two weeks and then once a week for a month. It is soon phased out in favor of social reinforcement.

PROPERTY: OWN AND OTHERS

S-IP-PR-0002-L1-S   To distinguish one's own property from the property of others.

S-IP-PR-0004-L1-S   To lend possessions to others when asked.

S-IP-PR-0006-L2-S   To use and return others' property without damaging it.

S-IP-PR-0008-L2-S   To ask permission to use another's property.

Skill:	To distinguish one's own property from the property of others. **S-IP-PR-0002-L1**
Objective:	When asked to whom something belongs, the student will distinguish someone else's property from his or her own.
Assessment:	Assess from previous knowledge of student or through direct observation using the <u>Social Behavior Assessment Inventory</u>.

Code: S-IP-PR-0002-L1-Im

TEACHING STRATEGY

Objective: When asked to whom something belongs, the student will distinguish someone else's property from his or her own.

Social Modeling

1. **Being able to tell whether property is one's own or belongs to someone else is an essential prerequisite to any other behaviors related to respect for property rights.** Most children by elementary school age, will have a sense of property ownership. For those students who do not, however, discuss the fact that each of them has personal belongings. Enumerate what belongs to each child, and have him or her repeat after you what is his or hers and what belongs to another student, as well as what things belong to the teacher or the school. Mark the student's belongings with his or her name, initials, or a symbol to provide cues.

2. **Identify specific behaviors to be modeled.** Say whether something belongs to you or to someone else. If possible, tell who else it belongs to.

3. **Model the behavior for the class by walking around the room, pointing to objects, and telling who they belong to.** To stimulate interest, you may have students point to items for you to label. Ask students to describe your behavior and praise correct answers.

4. **Have class practice the behavior by calling on a student, pointing to an object, and asking who it belongs to.** Reinforce students for correct answers. If desired, this could be done in the form of a game, in which students cover their eyes and are led to an object. When they open their eyes, they tell who the object belongs to.

Code: S-IP-PR-0002-L1-Ir

TEACHING STRATEGY

Objective: When asked to whom something belongs, the student will distinguish someone else's property from his or her own.

Social Reinforcement

1. **In a situation where the student is required to distinguish what is his or her own property from what belongs to someone else, provide praise when he or she correctly makes this distinction.** "That's good, Bob. That book belongs to Helen;" "Right, Jan. This is your coat;" "Yes, Tara, these crayons are yours, and those belong to Kathy. You are smart to know that."
2. **Provide cues for the target student.**
   (a) Post a general question, such as, "Do you know what things in our classroom belong to you?" or by asking this question verbally.
   (b) Have the student label those items which belong to him or her with his or her own name.
3. **Reinforce the target student immediately when the student accurately labels an item as belonging to him or her or to someone else.**

Code: S-IP-PR-0002-L1-Ic

TEACHING STRATEGY

Objective: When asked to whom something belongs, the student will distinguish someone else's property from his or her own.

Contingency Management

1. **A contingency contract might be set up as part of an effort to provide practice for students in distinguishing their own property from that of others or as a reminder for students who have problems in this area.** Begin by specifying that when students are asked who something belongs to, they are able to say that it is theirs or someone else's.
2. **Plan reinforcement.**
3. **State the contingency.** When I ask to whom something belongs, if you tell me correctly whether it belongs to you or someone else, I will reward you. Specify type and amount of reinforcement.
4. **In the case of a student who has difficulty distinguishing his or her property from that of others, when he or she is seen handling or using something, ask to whom the item belongs.** If the student tells you accurately, reward him or her with the promised reward.
5. **Example.** Zelda helps herself freely to other people's belongings, sometimes grabbing and saying, "This is mine," which creates unhappiness on the part of the other students. Ms. Coda, her teacher, tells Zelda specifically which things belong to her and which belong to others. She has Zelda repeat this after her several times until she feels that Zelda understands. She then sets up a contract with Zelda that she will sometimes ask her to whom something belongs. If Zelda tells her correctly, she will give her a

play-money coin. Zelda is able to exchange the play-money coins for a privilege, or she can keep the coins.

Skill:	To lend possessions to others when asked.
	S-IP-PR-0004-L1
Objective:	When asked, the student lends own possessions to other students or refuses politely.
Assessment:	Assess from previous knowledge of student or through direct observation using the <u>Social Behavior Assessment Inventory</u>.

Code: S-IP-PR-0004-L1-Im

TEACHING STRATEGY

Objective: When asked, the student lends own possessions to other students or refuses politely.

Social Modeling

1. **In establishing the need for this behavior, teach it along with Skills IP-PR-0006 and 0008, related to appropriate borrowing behaviors.** In a discussion, stress the value of sharing (IP-PL-0006) and that one way to share is to lend things temporarily to someone who will return them in good condition. Students might discuss their experiences with lending and borrowing, times they have lent possessions and not had them returned in good condition, times they have borrowed things, and how they feel people should treat the things they borrow. Emphasize that it is always the owner's right to refuse to lend something, but he or she should do so in a polite and considerate manner.

2. **Identify specific behaviors to be modeled.** When asked to lend something:
   (a) Decide if you want to lend it (you might need to use it yourself, or you might be afraid to lend it for fear something would happen to it).
   (b) Say, "Yes," and give it to the person.
   (c) Say, "No, I'm sorry," in a polite way, and give the reason for not lending the item.

3. **Model the behavior for the class.** Have a student ask to borrow a pencil or some other articles. Respond appropriately, showing both how you would go about agreeing to lend and refusing to lend. Ask students to identify elements of modeled behavior. Praise students who make good responses.

4. **Have class practice the behavior, with each student given an opportunity to respond to a request to lend something to another class member.** Have students role-play responding to students who ask to borrow items they have in their desks; or have an art lesson requiring glue, scissors, and crayons, and pass out only a limited number of each so students are forced to consider lending items to other students.

5. **Recognize those students who respond appropriately to requests to borrow their possessions.**

6. Maintain proper lending behavior through reinforcement.

Code: S-IP-PR-0004-L1-Ir

TEACHING STRATEGY

Objective: When asked, the student lends own possessions to other students or refuses politely.

Social Reinforcement

1. **Recognize target student when observed lending an object to someone else.** Call attention to specific actions. "Aloysus, it was good of you to say yes to Jose when he asked to borrow your eraser;" "Zoe, thank you for lending your crayons to Zachariah;" "Jeremy, I can understand why you would not want to lend your camera to Dennis. You told him in a very polite way."

2. **Cue target student in lending behavior by praising others who lend their possessions (or who refuse to lend possessions in a polite way).**

Code: S-IP-PR-0004-L1-Ic

TEACHING STRATEGY

Objective: The student, when asked, lends own possessions to other students or refuses politely.

Contingency Management

1. **State the task in observable terms.** When someone asks to borrow one of your things:
   (a) Decide if you want to lend the object or not.
   (b) Say, "Yes," and give it to the person.
   (c) Say, "No, I'm sorry," in a polite way, and give the reason for not lending the item.
   (d) If you decide to lend the item and you need it back at a specific time, tell the person who borrows it when you want it back.

2. **Plan reinforcement strategy selected from reinforcement menu.**

3. **State the contingency.** If student lends something properly, he or she will be rewarded. Specify amount of reinforcement.

4. **Reward the behavior as it occurs naturally, or set up a situation such as a project where materials or books need to be shared to necessitate classmates' lending things to each other.** Observe the lending procedure, and reward those who follow it correctly.

5. **Example.** Ms. Hartman has one student who very rudely refuses to lend things, even when he does not need them. She talks to him about the need to share with others and about the need at least to be polite about refusing. She sets up a contract with him as follows: If you agree to lend things the way we talked about, David, or at least politely say, "No, I'm sorry," you will receive a star for your "Good Behavior" chart. ("Good Behavior" chart stars are exchanged for minutes of free-play time each day before the students

go home.) Ms. Hartman then observes David and reinforces him with verbal praise and a star for each proper lending behavior. When David is lending or refusing to lend things appropriately 90% of the time or better, Ms. Hartman begins reinforcing him less often with stars but keeps up verbal praise to maintain the behavior.

Skill:	To use and return other's property without damaging it. **S-IP-PR-0006-L2**
Objective:	When student has borrowed something, it is returned to the owner without damaging it.
Assessment:	Assess from previous knowledge of student or through direct observation using the <u>Social Behavior Assessment Inventory</u>.

Code: S-IP-PR-0006-L2-Im

TEACHING STRATEGY

Objective: When student has borrowed something, it is returned to the owner without damaging it.

Social Modeling

1. **Discuss with the class the need to return borrowed items in good condition after use.** Discuss the idea that when you borrow something, you are responsible for it. Ask such questions as, "How would you feel if someone borrowed something from you and didn't return it or broke it? Would you lend anything else to someone who did this?" Have students answer questions and contribute ideas to the conversation.

2. **Identify specific behaviors to be modeled.** When you have borrowed something:
   (a) Use it and return it as quickly as possible.
   (b) Be careful using a borrowed item so you do not damage it.
   (c) Return it in good condition.

3. **Model the behavior for the class by borrowing something from a student, using the item, and returning it in good condition.** For example, ask to borrow a crayon and return it. For contrast, you might model using the pencil carelessly, breaking the lead, chewing on it, and failing to return it. Ask class members to describe your actions, and recognize those answers that incorporate the important aspects of good borrowing behavior.

4. **Have students practice the behavior by assigning an activity that needs materials, such as scissors, tape, crayons, stapler, etc., for completion.** Distribute a limited number of these items, assigning each to one student, to necessitate the borrowing of these items for completion of the assignment. Reward those students who borrow the item, use it carefully, and return it quickly.

5. **Maintain the behavior with reinforcement.**

Code: S-IP-PR-0006-L2-Ir

TEACHING STRATEGY

Objective: When student borrows something, it is returned to the owner without damaging it.

Social Reinforcement

1. **Recognize target student, loudly enough for others to hear, when observed borrowing, using, and returning an object properly.** Call attention to specific actions, "Dawn, I see you remembered to return Duane's book as soon as you were finished with it;" "Gwen, you were very careful with Carole's paste, and you returned it to her just as clean as when you got it;" "JoAnne, I was glad to see that you were careful with Gale's book and returned it after you had finished with it."

2. **Provide cues for the target child by recognizing others who are careful with borrowed items.**

Code: S-IP-PR-0006-L2-Ic

TEACHING STRATEGY

Objective: When student borrows something, it is returned to the owner without damaging it.

Contingency Management

1. **State the task to the student in terms of specific behaviors.**
   (a) Don't borrow things unless it is absolutely necessary.
   (b) Use the borrowed item as carefully as you can.
   (c) Return the item as quickly as you can when you are finished with it.

2. **Plan reinforcement strategy selected from reinforcement menu.**

3. **State the contingency.** If the student borrows a necessary item, uses it, and returns it in good condition, he or she will be rewarded. Specify kind and amount of reinforcement.

4. **Watch for situations in the classroom in which students borrow from other students, or set up a situation in which classmates will have to borrow from each other.** For example, pass out one set of materials to half the class and another set to the other half for a project which requires both kinds of materials. Observe the borrowing, using, and caring of the items. Reward those who meet the criteria for good borrowing behavior.

5. **Example.** Ms. Luckey had a group of students in her first-grade class who were careless with each other's possessions. She discussed good borrowing and lending behavior with them and made a list of appropriate behaviors related to borrowing and lending possessions. Rather than set up a positive contingency, such as rewards for good borrowing behavior, Ms. Luckey set up a negative contingency for misusing another's property or failing to return it promptly. She was afraid that a positive contingency might encourage unnecessary borrowing. The terms she established were the following: If a student felt that the person to whom he or she had loaned

an item had not followed good borrowing rules as established by the teacher, he or she was asked to report the details. The teacher then discussed the situation with the negligent students and reviewed the rules. He or she was asked to demonstrate to the teacher and the student from whom he or she had borrowed the item, how he or she would use and return the item more carefully if borrowed again. In order to control "tattling" over trivial matters, Ms. Luckey made sure that the complaint against the negligent student was justified before she asked him or her to demonstrate more desirable behavior.

Skill:	To ask permission to use another's property. **S-IP-PR-0008-L2**
Objective:	Student asks permission to use another's property by saying, "May I please borrow your _____?" or the equivalent.
Assessment:	Assess from previous knowledge of student or through direct observation using the <u>**Social Behavior Assessment Inventory**</u>.

Code: S-IP-PR-0008-L2-Im

TEACHING STRATEGY

Objective: Student asks permission to use another's property by saying, "May I please borrow your _____?" or the equivalent.

Social Modeling

1. **Identify a need for the behavior through a role-playing situation.** Ask the class to watch you carefully while you demonstrate something. Then go up to several students and take one of their possessions without asking. Have students contribute ideas to a discussion of how they felt when someone took their possessions, why one should ask to use another's possessions, and how one should ask to use another's possessions. Write key words on board.

2. **Identify specific behaviors to be modeled.** For example, when you want to borrow something from someone:

   (a) Ask if you may please borrow it.

   (b) Wait for his or her reply before you take it.

   (c) Do not use it if he or she says, "No."

3. **Model the behavior for the class.** Go to several students and ask to borrow items from them. Ask students to identify elements of the modeled behavior. Recognize students who make good responses.

4. **Have class practice the behavior with each student given an opportunity to ask to borrow something from another class member.**

5. **Recognize those students who correctly ask to borrow others' property.**

6. **Maintain proper asking behavior through reinforcement.**

Code: S-IP-PR-0008-L2-Ir

TEACHING STRATEGY

Objective: Student asks permission to use another's property by saying, "May I please borrow your _____?" or the equivalent.

Social Reinforcement

1. **Identify and recognize target student when observed asking properly for permission to use another's property.** Call attention to specific actions, e.g., "Jerome, you remembered to say 'please;'" "Lee, I like the polite way you asked George for his compass;" "Ferris, you did a good job of remembering the rules about borrowing."

2. **Cue appropriate behavior in target student by praising students who remember to ask permission before using others' property.** Watch for the behavior in the target child, and be sure to reinforce it.

Code: S-IP-PR-0008-L2-Ic

TEACHING STRATEGY

Objective: Student asks permission to use another's property by saying, "May I please borrow your _____?" or the equivalent.

Contingency Management

1. **State task in observable terms.** When you want to borrow something from someone:
   (a) Ask if you may please borrow it.
   (b) Wait for his or her reply before you take it.
   (c) Do not use it if he or she says, "No."
2. **Plan reinforcement strategy from reinforcement menu.**
3. **State the contingency.** If student asks properly to borrow something, he or she will be rewarded. Specify amount of reinforcement.
4. **Set situation to necessitate classmates' borrowing from each other.** For example, pass out scissors to half the class and paste to the other half and then ask students to do something that requires both materials. Observe the asking behavior and reward those who follow it correctly.
5. **Example.** Ms. Lawlor has a boy Duncan, in her class, Duncan, who takes other students' property without asking. Other students are continually complaining to the teacher about Duncan. She sets up a contingency with Duncan and the class. If Duncan remembers to ask politely to use someone else's property and waits for the other person to say, "Yes," before taking it, he earns points toward a class party. Ms. Lawlor asks the class to report to her when Duncan has politely asked to borrow something, and she watches for this behavior also. When Duncan exhibits the proper behavior, he receives two points on a chart and praise from Ms. Lawlor. If he forgets and takes something without asking, he loses two points; and Ms. Lawlor requires him to go to the child whose property he has taken and ask to borrow it. If he can do this properly, he will earn one of the lost points back. When he has earned the specified number of points, the class will have a party.

206

5

SELF-RELATED BEHAVIORS

ACCEPTING CONSEQUENCES

S-SR-AC-0002-L1-S	To report to the teacher when one has spilled or broken something.
S-SR-AC-0004-L1-S	To apologize when actions have injured or infringed on another.
S-SR-AC-0006-L2-S	To accept deserved consequences of wrong-doing.

Skill:	To report to the teacher when one has spilled or broken something. **S-SR-AC-0002-L1**
Objective:	When student spills or breaks something, he or she reports the occurrence to the teacher, telling what happened and where.
Assessment:	Assess from previous knowledge of student or through direct observation using the Social Behavior Assessment Inventory.

Code: S-SR-AC-0002-L1-Im

TEACHING STRATEGY

Objective: When student spills or breaks something, he or she reports the occurrence to the teacher, telling what happened and where.

Social Modeling

1. **Identify a need for the behavior through a classroom discussion.** Make it clear that everyone at some time or other accidentally breaks or spills things and that a person does not usually get punished for accidents, particularly if he or she is sorry and does something to make amends. Ask questions, such as, "Why is it important to report accidents to the teacher? If you accidentally spill or break something, what should you do? Why do you think it is not a good idea to try to hide accidents from the teacher?" Have students contribute ideas to the discussion, perhaps telling about times they broke or spilled something and what happened.

2. **Identify specific behaviors to be modeled.** When you have spilled or broken something:

   (a) Report the accident to the teacher.

   (b) Tell what happened and where.

   (c) Say you are sorry.

3. **Model the behavior for the class.** Pretend that you have spilled, dropped, or broken something. You know that no one saw you do it and that you could "get away with it" if desired. Select a student to play the role of the teacher, and in the role of student you demonstrate how you would report the incident to the teacher, giving details and apologizing. Ask the students to identify what you did in the role-playing. Recognize students who make good responses.

4. **Allow each child to practice the behavior.** Direct each child to work with a partner, taking turns playing the role of "teacher" and the role of "student," to practice situations involving reporting accidents to teacher. Simulated situations could include:

   (a) Knocking over the wastebasket.

   (b) Dropping someone's lunch and breaking the thermos bottle.

   (c) Spilling the contents of the pencil sharpener.

   (d) Knocking books off the bookshelf.

   (e) Knocking a pile of papers off the teacher's desk onto the floor.

   (f) Spilling water on the floor (from the sink).

   (g) Spilling water on teacher's desk.

   (h) Knocking display over.

   (i) Knocking bulletin board down.

   (j) Spilling paint or water on someone's work.

   (k) Spilling contents of a game on the floor.

5. **Recognize those students who report accidents correctly in the role-playing.**

6. **Maintain the desired behavior through reinforcement of students who report appropriately when they have broken or spilled something.**

Code: S-SR-AC-0002-L1-Ir

TEACHING STRATEGY

Objective: When student spills or breaks something, he or she reports the occurrence to the teacher, telling what happened and where.

Social Reinforcement

1. **Identify and recognize by name target student when he or she reports to teacher that he or she has spilled or broken something.** Call attention to specific actions. "Andy, thank you for telling me quickly that you spilled the paint on the floor. That makes it easier to clean up." "Judy, you remembered our rule about reporting accidents to the teacher." "LaMar, I know you feel bad about breaking my vase of flowers. I'm glad you came to me and told me what happened."

2. **Cue appropriate behavior in target student by recognizing others who report instances of spilling and breaking.** Recognition for reporting the incident needs to be accompanied by expressions of regret that it happened, and, where possible, a requirement that the student participate in cleaning up. Some kind of aversive consequence may be necessary to offset the danger that breaking and spilling will be increased by the praise and attention for reporting it.

Code: S-SR-AC-0002-L1-Ic

TEACHING STRATEGY

Objective: When student spills or breaks something, he or she reports the occurrence to the teacher, telling what happened and where.

Contingency Management

1. **State task in observable terms.** When you have spilled or broken something:
   (a) Report the accident to the teacher.
   (b) Tell what happened and where it happened.
2. **Plan reinforcement strategy selected from reinforcement menu.**
3. **State the contingency.** When you accidentally spill or break something, if you tell what happened, you will be rewarded. Specify type and amount of reinforcement.
4. **Observe students in normal daily activities.** Observe those who report accidents properly. Reward those who do so. It is not useful to make reward contracts with target student (student who habitually drops and spills things and lies or denies the occurrence), because doing so may encourage student to deliberately create accidents so he or she can receive rewards for reporting them. A contingency involving a penalty should be more useful.
5. **Example.** Robert often spills milk all over the floor during lunch. Ms. Mort, the teacher, sees him do it, and so do all the other students, but Robert always blames another student and denies responsibility for the occurrence. Ms. Mort contracts with Robert. "Robert, when you spill milk on the floor and tell me what happened, we will help you clean up. If you fail to tell me, you will clean the floor by yourself, and you will also dispose of the entire classes' trash. If you can avoid spilling your milk at all, you will get a star on your 'Good Behavior' chart." Robert does not like to clean up spilled milk and gather and dispose of the trash. Therefore, this consequence is considered **aversive**. He can avoid the aversive consequence by complying with the rules of reporting accidents to the teacher. He can gain a positive consequence by avoiding the accident.

Code: S-SR-AC-0004-L1-Im

TEACHING STRATEGY

Objective: Student apologizes when his or her actions have injured or infringed on another.

Social Modeling

1. **Identify a need for the behavior through a classroom discussion.** When available, use stories, films, videos, or some other aid. Have students contribute ideas to the discussion. For example, "What is an apology?" "What kinds of situations require an apology?" "Why should we apologize when we accidentally injure another?" "What can we say when we want to apologize to someone else?"

2. **Identify specific behaviors to be modeled.** When your actions injure or create a hardship or inconvenience for someone else, apologize for your actions by saying, "I'm sorry," or some other appropriate phrase.

3. **Model the behavior.** Accidentally bump into a student and then apologize to the student.

4. **Provide opportunity for practice.** Role-play situations that require an apology, for example:

   (a) Student bumps into another student.
   (b) Student has his or her foot in the aisle, and another student trips over it.
   (c) Student drops something when handing it to someone else.
   (d) Student accidentally slams the door.
   (e) Student accidentally knocks another's coat on the floor.

   (Develop situations appropriate to the class and age of students.) Have each student practice the behavior. Reinforce correct responses.

5. **Maintain the behavior through reinforcement.**

Code: S-SR-AC-0004-L1-Ir

TEACHING STRATEGY

Objective: Student apologizes when his her actions have injured or infringed on another.

Social Reinforcement

1. **Use social reinforcement when student is observed apologizing for his or her actions.** Use praise that describes the student's behavior. For example, "Jack, I'm glad you told Mark you were sorry you ran into him." "Karen, you were very thoughtful to tell Jill you were sorry and that you did not know it was her turn."

2. **Provide cues for the target student.** Recognize other students when they make apologies under appropriate circumstances.

3. **It may be necessary to provide tangible reinforcement, such as coupons, stars, points, along with social reinforcement for appropriate behavior at first.**

Code: S-SR-AC-0004-L1-Ic

TEACHING STRATEGY

Objective: Student apologizes when his her actions have injured or infringed on another.

Contingency Management

1. **Present task to student in specific terms.** When your actions have infringed on or created some inconvenience for another student, apologize to that student for your actions.

2. **Plan reinforcement.**

3. **State the contingency.** If the student does not apologize when his or her actions have injured someone else, he or she will lose a privilege or receive some other mild punishment; for example, losing minutes of recess or being required to sit on the bench for a brief time instead of playing.

   Note: A positive contingency would be inappropriate for this skill. A positive contingency could have the effect of increasing the student's behavior of injuring someone else in order to apologize and receive the positive consequences.

4. **Watch for the behavior to occur naturally.** If the student apologizes appropriately, provide social reinforcement. If he or she fails to apologize when an apology is indicated, deliver the agreed-upon aversive consequence.

5. **Example.** Tim tended to play very aggressively and seldom apologized when he accidentally bumped into another student during a gym activity. Ms. Simms, the physical education teacher, discussed the behavior with Tim and the need for him to be more careful and to apologize when he played too roughly. Ms. Simms set up an agreement with Tim. For every gym period when Tim did not play too roughly (bumping into others, shoving them, hitting, or kicking them), he would earn five points toward two tickets to a professional ball game. Ms. Simms established the value of the tickets at 50 points each. For each time he exhibited behavior that Ms. Simms felt was too rough, he would lose two points. He could earn one point back, however, by apologizing to the person he had hurt. Ms. Simms provided feedback to Tim by blowing her whistle and stopping the game when Tim was too rough and by praising him when he played carefully.

<table>
<tr><td>**Skill:**</td><td>To accept deserved consequences of wrong-doing.
S-SR-AC-0006-L2</td></tr>
<tr><td>**Objective:**</td><td>When student does something wrong, the student will accept the adverse consequences of that act without excessive complaining.</td></tr>
<tr><td>**Assessment:**</td><td>Assess from previous knowledge of student or through direct observation using the <u>Social Behavior Assessment Inventory</u>.</td></tr>
</table>

Code: S-SR-AC-0006-L2-Im

TEACHING STRATEGY

Objective: When student does something wrong, the student will accept the adverse consequences of that act without excessive complaining.

Social Modeling

1. **Teach this skill in conjunction with SR-EB-0006 (i.e., identifying consequences of behavior involving wrong-doing).** In discussing possible consequence for wrong-doing, also bring up how one should act if one is punished for hurting someone or something or for doing some other wrong thing. Ask why there is such a thing as punishment, and talk about the value of punishment in helping us learn not to do things that are wrong. In the discussion, recognize that no one likes punishment (note: when "punishment" is pleasurable it is a reward), but becoming angry or complaining excessively may make the punishment worse. Have students suggest some appropriate ways to act when punished, possibly contrasted with inappropriate ways. Recognize good responses.

2. **Identify the specific behaviors to be modeled.** When you have done something wrong, for example, something that injures another or destroys property of another, accept the consequences for your actions without excessive complaining.

3. **Model the behavior.** Select a student to role-play with the teacher. Student (played by teacher) has broken a school window with a ball. Have the student role-play the principal giving out a punishment. In the role of student, demonstrate desirable and undesirable ways of responding to punishment. Have students identify the behaviors.

4. **Provide opportunity for practice.** Have each student role-play a situation where he or she is justly punished, demonstrating an appropriate way to respond. Sample situations:

   (a) Student is excluded from game for playing too roughly.
   (b) Student loses turn to talk in "Show and Tell" time because he or she has interrupted several times.
   (c) Student is required to pay for breaking a mirror in the washroom.
   (d) Student is required to stay after school for hitting another student.

   Add situations appropriate to the class involved. Recognize good responses in the practice situations.

5. **Maintain the behavior through reinforcement.**

Code: S-SR-AC-0006-L2-Ir

TEACHING STRATEGY

Objective: When student does something wrong, the student will accept the adverse consequences of that act without excessive complaining.

Social Reinforcement

1. **Identify and recognize when he or she is willing to accept adverse consequences of his or her behavior without excessive complaining.** Call attention to his or her specific actions. For example, "Shaun, you accepted the punishment for breaking the window without complaining. You acted very grown up;" "Don, I appreciated the way you acted when you were sent in from recess. You came in without complaining."

2. **Provide cues for target student.** Remind the student before giving the punishment that he or she must accept the consequences of what he or she did.

   Note: You can help lessen complaints or angry responses to deserved punishment by ignoring them, and by being careful not to reinforce them with attention or making complaints pay off with lessened punishment. Ideally, consequences should be established in advance and should be known to the student.

Code: S-SR-AC-0006-L2-Ic

TEACHING STRATEGY

Objective: When student does something wrong, the student will accept the adverse consequences of that act without excessive complaining.

Contingency Management

1. **State the task in observable terms.** When you have done something wrong, for example, something that has hurt someone or something, take the punishment you get without complaining.

2. **Define a consequence that is valued by the student that can be used as a reward for the desired behavior.**

3. **State the contingency.** If, when you have done something wrong for which you deserve punishment, you accept the punishment without complaining, you will be rewarded.

   Note: This behavior should not be taught in such a way as to emphasize compliance with unfair punishment. It should be clear that the student has committed an offense for which he or she deserves punishment, and the punishment should be fair. See Skill IP-CC-0012.

4. **Watch for the behavior to occur naturally, and reinforce it when it occurs, according to the contract.** You might also set up a situation where the behavior can occur. For this behavior, a role-playing situation would be most appropriate. See the Social Modeling strategy for examples of role-playing situations.

5. **Example.** Arthur was an aggressive student who got into trouble frequently. He was often the subject of some punishment inflicted by the

213

playground supervisor, the teacher, or the principal. Arthur reacted to attempts at discipline by arguing loudly and blaming someone else, even when he was clearly at fault. Arthur's teacher, after observing this behavior for a period, decided that Arthur's belligerent behavior served at times to get him into worse trouble. He talked to Arthur about accepting punishment and pointed out to Arthur some of the extra problems he created for himself by arguing and denying his responsibility when he was clearly at fault. He set up a contract with Arthur. If Arthur were willing to refrain from arguing and complaining when he (the teacher), the principal, the playground supervisor, or some other adult in authority established a punishment for something Arthur did wrong, he would attempt to see that the punishment would be less severe. If, on the other hand, Arthur continued to complain, he would see that an additional punishment was added. At the same time, the teacher set up a contract with Arthur for a daily reward based on the absence of any situation for which Arthur deserved punishment. The teacher established a thermometer and filled in a space for every day without an incident in the school involving Arthur. When the thermometer reached the top, Arthur was given the privilege of inviting friends to accompany him and the teacher to a nearby ice cream parlor after school.

ETHICAL BEHAVIOR

S-SR-EB-0002-L1-S	To distinguish truth from untruth.
S-SR-EB-0004-L1-S	To answer when asked about possible wrong-doing.
S-SR-EB-0006-L2-S	To identify consequences of behavior involving wrong-doing.
S-SR-EB-0008-L2-S	To avoid doing something wrong when encouraged by a peer.

Skill:	To distinguish truth from untruth. **S-SR-EB-0002-L1**
Objective:	Student will distinguish his or her own true statements from untrue statements when asked.
Assessment:	Assess from previous knowledge of student or through direct observation using the <u>Social Behavior Assessment Inventory</u>.

Code: S-SR-EB-0002-L1-Im

TEACHING STRATEGY

Objective: Student will distinguish his or her own true statements from untrue statements when asked.

Social Modeling

1. **Discuss the need to distinguish fact from fiction in one's own statements.** Explain that other people want and need to know whether what you are saying is true or not. Discuss honesty in general and how a person needs to tell the truth if he wants people to believe him. (The story of the boy who cried wolf may be useful here.) At the same time, it might be emphasized that being able to tell stories, to "make believe," to be able to imagine things, is fun and is a good thing to do, so long as one always is able to tell the difference between what is true and not true. Ask students to tell what makes something true or not true, and elicit examples from them of true and untrue statements and when it is all right to pretend. Use stories, television, or other media to provide opportunities to demonstrate what is real and what is make-believe.

2. **Identify specific behaviors to be modeled.**
   (a) Know when the statement you are making is a true fact.
   (b) Know when the statement you are making is made-up.
   (c) When asked, tell whether the statement is true or made-up.

3. **Model the behavior for the class.** Make a series of statements, some of which are true and some of which are false. You might make such statements as, "On the way to school this morning I was a blue giraffe;" "I woke up at 6:00;" "I swam for 200 miles in my bathtub;" "We are having hot dogs for lunch today." Direct the students to ask whether each statement is true or not. Answer with statements as to the truth or untruth of your original statements, explaining why they are true or not true.

215

4. **Have class practice the behavior by organizing a storytelling period in which each student is required to tell a story.** After each story ask the student whether the story was true or made-up. Reinforce the student if his or her answer seems accurate.

5. **Maintain the behavior through reinforcement.**

Code: S-SE-EB-0002-L1-Ir

TEACHING STRATEGY

Objective: Student will distinguish his or her own true statements from untrue statements when asked.

Social Reinforcement

1. **Use social reinforcement when the student accurately identifies a statement he or she has made as either true or untrue.** Use your own judgment about the accuracy of the identification and whether to call attention to the truth or untruth of a student's statements in front of other class members. In providing praise, be specific. "Liz, I'm glad you could tell that the story about your mother was just make-believe;" "John, thank you for telling me that you made up a story about what David did to you. You have a good imagination."

    Note: Stress to students that telling make-believe stories can be a valuable activity so long as they can tell the difference between those and what is factual.

2. **Provide cues for target student.**

    (a) When in doubt as to whether a student's statement is true or untrue, ask him or her in a nonthreatening way to tell you which it is. For example, "George, that was an interesting explanation of what happened to make you late this morning. Was that true or make-believe?"

    (b) Look for opportunities to provide reminders to students by labeling stories, events, etc., as true or untrue.

    (c) Remember that a student who knows the difference between a true and untrue statement, but who insists that a lie is the truth, is receiving some benefit from lying. Usually the "payoff" is the avoidance of punishment. Create an atmosphere in which students are rewarded for telling the truth, even though telling the truth may also result in some aversive consequences.

Code: S-SE-EB-0002-L1-Ic

TEACHING STRATEGY

Objective: Student will distinguish his or her own true statements from untrue statements when asked.

216

Contingency Management

1. **Discuss with the student the importance of knowing when he or she is telling the truth or making up a story.** Stress that making up stories is a good thing to do if one tells other people they are made up and not true.

2. **Plan reinforcement.**

3. **State the contingency.** If, when asked, you say accurately that a statement you have made is true or untrue, you will be rewarded. Specify type and amount of reinforcement.

4. **Arrange a storytelling period in which students must each tell two brief stories, one true and one make-believe.** After the target student has told his or her story, ask him or her to tell which story was true and which was not. If the student accurately labels the story, reward him or her. You may have to use your own judgment in ascertaining the accuracy of the students' labeling. Ask for students who have difficulty distinguishing fact from make-believe to tell you whether the statement was true or not, and reinforce answers that appear correct.

5. **Example.** Liz was a student in Ms. Fridell's class who often told elaborate stories about her family's great wealth and possessions and about the unusual things which had happened to her or members of her family. After talking with Liz's mother and learning more about the modest circumstances of the family, the teacher decided that Liz's made-up stories might involve some "wishful thinking" or might also be explained by the large amount of incredulous attention which Liz received from peers and adults as a result of her tales. Ms. Fridell talked to Liz privately and told her about talking to her mother and learning about her family. She told Liz that she could understand how she might wish some of the things she told about her family were true, but that she (Liz) could have friends and be liked without telling stories. She also told Liz that telling stories was not bad if she told people they were made up and did not insist they were true. She set up a contract with Liz that if she heard Liz telling a story or if someone told her about a story Liz told, she would ask Liz whether the story was true or not. If Liz told her accurately whether it was true or make-believe, she would give Liz a card with a star on it. When Liz earned a certain number of cards, she could exchange them for something in a "store" Ms. Fridell had which contained small toys and trinkets. In order not to focus too much attention on "storytelling," the teacher gave Liz an opportunity to earn cards for making true statements as well as for telling when one of her stories was made up.

<table>
<tr><td>**Skill:**</td><td>To answer accurately when asked about possible wrong-doing. **S-SR-EB-0004-L1**</td></tr>
<tr><td>**Objective:**</td><td>When student is asked about possible wrong-doing, he or she answers accurately.</td></tr>
<tr><td>**Assessment:**</td><td>Assess from previous knowledge of student or through direct observation using the <u>Social Behavior Assessment Inventory</u>.</td></tr>
</table>

Code: S-SR-EB-0004-L1-Im

TEACHING STRATEGY

Objective: Student will distinguish his or her own true statements from untrue statements when asked.

Social Modeling

1. **Discuss with students the need to answer truthfully when they are asked about possible wrong-doing.** Discuss general concepts of honesty and responsibility. Stimulate conversation by asking questions, such as, "Why should we admit it when we have done something wrong? How would you feel if you were accused wrongly of doing something bad because the person who did it would not admit to it?" Have students contribute ideas to the conversation about why it is better to admit wrong-doing than to lie about it. Stress that everyone at some time makes mistakes and does something for which he or she may need to be punished, but that punishment is often less severe if he or she is willing to admit the mistake.

2. **Identify specific behaviors to be modeled.** If the student has done something wrong, for example, has hurt someone or something, he or she will tell the truth about what he or she did.

3. **Model the behavior for the class with a role-playing situation using situations familiar to the class. For example:**

   (a) Student A has broken a window by throwing a rock through it. The teacher asks the students in the school yard who threw the rock. Student A steps forward and admits to it.

   (b) Student B throws Sally's books into a mud puddle. Sally tells the teacher, and the teacher confronts Student B. Students B tells the truth about what he or she did.

   (c) Student C is seen copying Harold's test answers during a spelling test. When the teacher confronts him or her with the cheating, Student C admits to it.

   (d) Student D takes a cupcake from Betty Lou's lunch. The teacher asks the class who took Betty Lou's cupcake. Student D raises his or her hand and confesses.

4. **Class is given opportunity to practice the behavior through similar role-playing situations.** Give each student an opportunity to role-play in a situation where he or she admits to wrong-doing. To be realistic, along with praise for admitting wrong-doing, the role-playing should include the suggestions of a punishment for the wrong-doing. This skill might be

combined with SR-AC-0004 (making apology) and AC-0006 (accepting deserved consequences of wrong-doing).

5. **Maintain the behavior through reinforcement of students who tell the truth when they have engaged in wrong-doing.**

Code: S-SR-EB-0004-L1-Ir

TEACHING STRATEGY

Objective: When student is asked about possible wrong-doing, he or she answers accurately.

Social Reinforcement

1. **Recognize the student when he or she tells the truth or provides accurate information about something he or she did that may have been wrong.** Praise for this behavior should most likely be done privately rather than publicly, and the student will need to understand that he or she is being praised for the behavior of telling the truth at the same time he or she may need to be punished for his or her wrong-doing.

2. **Be specific in praising.** "Richard, I'm sorry you lied to us before about stealing Danny's papers, but I'm really glad you finally told us the truth;" "John, I'm sorry you broke into the principal's office, but I'm very glad you told us what you did;" "Jane, it was not good to take Mary's lunch money, but you were honest to admit it."

3. **Provide cues to the student through general discussion of honesty.**

Code: S-SR-EB-0004-L1-Ic

TEACHING STRATEGY

Objective: When student is asked about possible wrong-doing, he or she answers accurately.

Contingency Management

1. **Discuss with student(s) the specific behavior that is desired.** If asked whether he or she is responsible for some specific wrong-doing, he or she is to tell the truth, even if it means punishment for the wrong-doing.

2. **Identify rewards that are meaningful to the student(s).**

3. **State the contingency.** If the student tells the truth when asked about something wrong for which he or she might have been responsible, he or she will be rewarded for telling the truth (even though he or she might also have to be punished for the wrong-doing).

4. **Watch for situations in the natural environment where student(s) must be asked whether they are responsible for hurting other children, damaging school property, etc.** Reward the student for answering truthfully according to the contingency that has been established. If punishment is required for the wrong-doing, the punishment might be made less severe as a result of the student's telling the truth.

5. **Example.** Eric was frequently involved in some sort of mischievous or aggressive escapade, either teasing or hitting others, throwing dirt or rocks at windows, etc. He usually denied all knowledge of the wrong-doing, often placing the blame on others. In addition to attempting to stop the undesirable behavior by punishment and setting up rewards for days with no such occurrences, Eric's teacher set up a contract with him. Ms. Jones told him that they both knew that he was responsible for doing some things which were wrong for which he needed to be punished. She told him that if he would tell the truth when he was asked about something he had done wrong, Ms. Jones would not report the wrong-doing to his parents, and he would only receive punishment at school. (The teacher knew that if she reported his behavior to the parents, he would also be punished at home.) Ms. Jones tried to make sure Eric was not accused of and punished for acts he did not do, and she particularly stressed praise and rewards for any day when there was no complaint about wrong-doing from Eric.

Note: A contract of this sort should be done with the parents' knowledge and consent. You should advise parents of the proposed terms of the contract and with their understanding and consent, negotiate the contract terms with the student who should, of course, be made aware of his or her parents' agreement.

Skill:	To identify consequences of behavior involving wrong-doing. **S-SR-EB-0006-L2**
Objective:	Student identifies possible consequences of own or others' behavior involving wrong-doing.
Assessment:	Assess from previous knowledge of student or through direct observation using the <u>Social Behavior Assessment Inventory</u>.

Code: S-SR-EB-0006-L2-Im

TEACHING STRATEGY

Objective: Student identifies possible consequences of own or others' behavior involving wrong-doing.

Social Modeling

1. **Involve the class in a discussion of the need to be able to identify the consequences of actions that involve wrong-doing.** Point out that although people sometimes are able to do something that is against the rules or against the law, there is usually some kind of unpleasant consequence for behavior that is wrong. Stress that before we do something wrong, we need to consider the consequences of what we do. If we decide to do it anyway, we have to be prepared to accept the consequences. Have class members contribute ideas to the discussion. Use stories, films, etc., where available, to stimulate conversation. Students might bring newspaper clippings to demonstrate adverse consequences that have occurred to people who have broken laws. Television programs may also provide

examples. Generate a list of aversive consequences that can occur in relation to some of the most frequent infractions of class rules, both for the person breaking the rules and for other people who might be hurt.

2. **Identify specific behaviors to be modeled.** When asked to, the student should tell the possible consequences of wrong actions, including effects they may have on others and what will happen as a result.

3. **Model the behavior for the class by presenting a situation involving wrong-doing.** The situations may be contrived or from stories in readers or other books. Have the class read the story, and then tell the consequences of the protagonist's actions. Sample stories:

   (a) Margie and Amy are on their way to school. Margie notices that a movie she wants to see is playing and decides to go to the movies instead of going to school. Amy goes on without her. The teacher outlines some possible consequences:

       (1) Margie will be made to stay after school for a week for skipping school.

       (2) Margie will miss the day's lesson and have to spend extra time making it up.

   (b) Ed leaves the classroom without permission during a class lesson. A possible consequence:

       (1) Ed will be punished for breaking the classroom rule.

4. **Have the class practice the behavior by presenting similar stories to them, and give each student an opportunity to identify the consequences of the actions of the people in the story.** Use examples that are realistic for the class involved. Reward students who respond correctly.

5. **Maintain the behavior with social reinforcement.**

Code: S-SR-EB-0006-L2-Ir

TEACHING STRATEGY

Objective: Student identifies possible consequences of own or others' behavior involving wrong-doing.

Social Reinforcement

1. **Recognize the student, if, during the class discussion or a personal conversation, he or she says something that gives evidence that he or she can identify possible consequences of own or another's behavior involving wrong-doing.** Praise the statement in specific terms. "Bob, I'm glad you understand that, because you fought with Jake on the playground this morning, you will have to stay late this afternoon. I hope you can avoid the punishment next time by following the rules." "Laurie, I'm glad you realize that your throwing snowballs on the driveway and steps could cause someone to slip on the snow and get hurt. Try to remember that next time you want to throw snowballs."

2. **Provide cues to the target student by asking the student, after an incident involving wrong-doing, what the consequences of the act are, how it could be avoided, and whether it should have been done.** Make sure the

students know the consequences of behavior in the classroom through knowledge of the classroom rules and the consequences of breaking them.

Code: S-SR-EB-0006-L2-Ic

TEACHING STRATEGY

Objective: Student identifies possible consequences of own or others' behavior involving wrong-doing.

Contingency Management

1. **Explain to the student that when asked by the teacher, he or she must be able to tell what the consequences are of own or another's behavior having to do with wrong-doing.**

2. **Plan reinforcement.**

3. **State the contingencies to the student.** When I present a situation to you involving wrong-doing, and ask you to describe the consequences of your own or another's behavior in the situation, if you identify the consequences, you will be rewarded. Specify type and amount of reward.

4. **In the course of naturally occurring activities, if the student or another is involved in wrong-doing, ask the student to identify the consequences of own or another student's actions.** If he or she can identify these consequences, deliver the promised reward. To facilitate this, be sure to go over the consequences of breaking the classroom rules when presenting them to the class.

5. **Example.** Richard is in frequent scrapes, and he does not seem to understand the consequences of this own wrong actions. The teacher, Ms. Ervin, talks with him about his behavior and reviews with him the rules and the consequences for breaking the rules. She also has him think about things he could do to avoid misbehaving. She contracts with him that if when asked by the teacher, he verbalizes the consequences on his own and tells what he should have done instead, he will receive five points toward participation in Friday afternoon movie time. During school hours when Richard is involved in some wrong-doing, Ms. Ervin asks him to tell her the consequences of his actions and how he might have avoided the wrong-doing. If he verbalizes them, he receives the reward. He also has to receive the aversive consequences that he has identified. Ms. Ervin is careful that positive benefits from verbally recognizing consequences do not outweigh the aversive consequences of the wrong-doing.

222

Skill:	To avoid doing something wrong when encouraged by a peer.
	S-SR-EB-0008-L2
Objective:	When a peer encourages the student to do something questionable, the student will avoid the wrong-doing.
Assessment:	Assess from previous knowledge of student or through direct observation using the <u>Social Behavior Assessment Inventory</u>.

Code: S-SR-EB-0008-L2-Im

TEACHING STRATEGY

Objective: When a peer encourages the student to do something questionable, the student will avoid the wrong-doing.

Social Modeling

1. **You may want to introduce this skill by presenting a film strip, a movie, or a story on the theme of avoiding pressure from others to misbehave.** Structure a discussion about knowing right from wrong, and choosing to do the right thing. Encourage the students to contribute ideas. Ask questions, such as, "What are some kinds of things that are wrong to do?" Stress and have students enumerate behaviors that would injury other people or property, or that violate laws or rules. "If someone tried to get you to do some of these wrong things, what might happen if you went along and helped them? What could you do instead? Why is it better to avoid doing wrong things?"

2. **Identify specific behaviors to be modeled.** If other students ask you to do something that you know is wrong:

   (a) Tell them that it would be wrong, and that you will not do it.

   (b) Get away from the other students as soon as you can.

3. **Model the behavior.** Ask one or two of the students to help you model how to refuse to do something wrong.

   Example: Pretend that the two students want you to help play a mean trick on another child. Demonstrate telling the students that you think that would be wrong, why you think it would be wrong, and that you will not do something wrong. Show how you would get out of the situation as soon as you could. Ask the children to identify what you did. Recognize good responses.

4. **Provide opportunity for practice.** Suggest some situations for role-playing, such as:

   (a) Group planning to let air out of teacher's tires.

   (b) Group deciding to exclude new girl from group interactions.

   (c) Group planning to hurt or tease animal.

   (d) Group planning to play a mean trick or joke on another.

   (e) Group planning to tear up or otherwise destroy teacher's papers.

Allow the children to create their own practice situations and present them to the class. Give each student an opportunity to play the role of student refusing to participate in wrong-doing. Recognize correct responses.

Note: Do not role-play inappropriate behavior.

5. **Maintain the behavior through reinforcement.**

Code: S-SR-EB-0008-L2-Ir

TEACHING STRATEGY

Objective: When a peer encourages the student to do something questionable, the student will avoid the wrong-doing.

Social Reinforcement

1. **If a student is seen resisting the encouragement of another student or students to engage in wrong-doing, take the student aside and praise him or her.** (Determine in this instance whether it is preferable to praise a student privately rather than publicly.) Recognize specific behaviors: "John, I'm glad you didn't lie about the broken window when Richie told you to. I'm glad to see you have a mind of your own." "Patrick, I'm very glad you didn't give Bob the answers to the test when he asked you to. You are very honest. I'm proud of you." "Erica, I'm very proud of you. You know better than to tease others the way Susan wanted you to." "Faye, I'm glad that you waited your turn for the swing instead of grabbing it as Mary suggested. You did the right thing."

2. **Provide cues for the target student through discussions about right and wrong behaviors and doing what is right even when others want you to do something wrong.** Recognize other students who do the right thing, even when encouraged to do otherwise by peers. Recognize the student immediately for responding to your cues.

3. **It may be necessary to add a more tangible reinforcer to the social reinforcer to compete with the rewards derived from peer-group approval.** Initially, students who are easily led by peers may need to be given tokens, points, star, etc., for avoiding trouble. The tangible reinforcers can be exchanged for something the student values.

Code: S-SR-EB-0008-L2-Ic

TEACHING STRATEGY

Objective: When a peer encourages the student to do something questionable, the student will avoid the wrong-doing.

Contingency Management

1. **Present the task in specific observable terms.** Explain to the students exactly what you expect them to do. If your friend or other students ask you to do something that you know is wrong, for example, something that is against the law or against the rules, something which will damage property or hurt someone:

(a) Tell them that you think it is wrong, why you think it is wrong and that you will not do it.

(b) Get away from them as soon as you can.

2. **Plan reinforcement.**

3. **State the contingency.** "If you avoid doing something wrong, even though your friends try to talk you into it, you will be rewarded." Since it may not always be possible to observe and reward the avoidance of wrong-doing, an aversive contingency may also be stated. For example, "If you allow yourself to be talked into doing something wrong by a classmate, you will be punished." Be specific about the terms of the reward or punishment. The behavior of allowing oneself to be led into wrong-doing by peers is often maintained by peer friendship and approval and the threat of loss of that approval for not going along with the peers. Therefore, rewards need to be strong in order to compete. Sometimes rewards for avoiding wrong-doing that can be shared with the peers are effective if they are valued by the peers.

4. **After the behavior has been presented to the student(s) and the contingency established, observe the naturally occurring behavior.** Reward those who successfully avoid wrong-doing, or deliver punishment for going along with wrong-doing peers.

5. **Example.** Terry was part of a mischievous little clique in Mr. Daniel's class. When questioned about her pranks, she usually said, "Well, Pam and Patty told me to," or something to that effect. Mr. Daniel knew that Terry was the youngest, the smallest, and the most impressionable of the "group" and was, indeed, often used by the other girls to carry out the pranks. He decided that if he could get Terry to stop cooperating with the others, the pranks would stop. He made a contract with her that when she refused to do something she knew was wrong, even though encouraged by her best friends, she would receive a reward she could share with her friends. Mr. Daniel went over with her the kinds of misbehavior she needed to avoid and helped her practice ways of saying, "No, I can't do it," and getting away from her friends if they still wanted to go ahead with doing wrong things. The contingency was that for each day Terry avoided being in trouble with her friends she would earn a gold star on her "Good Citizen" chart. When she had earned 10 gold stars, Mr. Daniel would take her out for ice cream and she could invite her friends. Mr. Daniel suggested that she tell her friends what she was working for, and he gave her praise and encouragement along with the gold star.

Expressing Feelings

S-SR-EF-0002-L2-S   To describe one's own feelings or moods verbally.
S-SR-EF-0004-L2-S   To recognize and label moods of others.

Skill: To describe one's own feelings and moods verbally.
        S-SR-EF-0002-L2

Objective: Student, when asked how he or she feels, can give an adequate verbal description of his or her feelings or moods.

Assessment: Assess from previous knowledge of student or through direct observation using the <u>Social Behavior Assessment Inventory</u>.

Code: S-SR-EF-0002-L2-Im

TEACHING STRATEGY

Objective: Student, when asked how he or she feels, gives an adequate verbal description of his or her feelings or moods.

Social Modeling

1. **Identify a need for verbalizing feelings through a discussion, a role-playing session, a simulation, a movie, tape, filmstrip, story, or whatever sources are available to you.** Discuss what feelings are, how it feels to be happy, sad, angry, etc., and how we tell what our feelings are. Discuss reasons for developing the ability to report feelings and why it is good to be able to tell someone how you feel. Write key points on the board.

2. **Identify specific behaviors to be modeled.** For example, when asked how he or she feels, the student will reply that he or she feels happy, sad, angry, etc.

3. **Model the described behavior for the class.** You may choose one or two students to help role-play a situation involving expressing feelings. Pretend to be angry and act angry by stamping your foot and frowning. Direct one of the students to ask, "What's wrong?" or something to that effect, and you may reply, "I feel angry." You can then role-play other emotions and report how you feel. Ask the students to identify the elements of the modeled behavior. Recognize all those students who make good responses.

4. **Provide an opportunity for all of the children to practice the behavior.** Have students role-play situations. Identify what feelings would be associated with the situations and how they would be expressed. Suggested role-playing situations:
   (a) Student feels left out by others.
   (b) Student wants to be included in "group" but is afraid to ask.
   (c) Student is angry because he or she thinks teacher likes the other students better.
   (d) Student wants to participate in discussion but is afraid of being laughed at.

(e) Student is new at school and withdraws from others, afraid of being rejected.

(f) Student opens presents for his or her birthday.

(g) Student feels angry because he or she has been punished unjustly.

(h) Student feels afraid of going home alone.

(i) Student responds to teacher's announcing a field trip.

(j) Use situation appropriate to the class and age group.

5. **Recognize students who verbally report feelings appropriate to the role-playing situation.**

6. **Maintain the behavior through consistent reinforcement.**

Code: S-SR-EF-0002-L2-Ir

TEACHING STRATEGY

Objective: Student, when asked how he or she feels, gives an adequate verbal description of his or her feelings or moods.

Social Reinforcement

1. **Identify target student by name when observed verbalizing his or her mood and feelings.** Praise the student, and call attention to the specific elements of his or her behavior, e.g., "I'm glad you told me how you felt, August. Now that you've told me that you're angry, we can do something about it." "Mary, you are good at telling other people how you feel." "John, I like the way you can express your feelings."

2. **Recognize students who appropriately verbalize their feelings.** Cue target student by praising others in close proximity.

3. **If social reinforcement alone does not facilitate a noticeable change in behavior, try pairing a token, or some other tangible reinforcer with the social reinforcement.**

Code: S-SR-EF-0002-L2-Ic

TEACHING STRATEGY

Objective: Student, when asked how he or she feels, gives an adequate verbal description of his or her feelings or moods.

Contingency Management

1. **State the task in observable terms.** When someone asks you how you feel:
   (a) Think about how you feel.
   (b) Then, report your feelings.

2. **Plan a reinforcement strategy after consulting the reinforcement menu.**

3. **State the contingency.** When someone asks you how you feel, if you:
   (a) Think about your feelings.
   (b) Then, tell us how you feel.
   (c) You will receive the reward we agree on.

   Remember to specify the type and amount of reinforcement.

4. **During normal activities be aware of how the children deal with their feelings.** Identify and reward those who attempt to identify and verbalize their feelings, rather than "act out."

5. **Example.** Hilde is an exceptionally moody child in Mr. Brown's class. Hilde's moods fluctuate often, for no apparent reason. Sometimes she is withdrawn; sometimes she is aggressive and hostile, sometimes negative; and sometimes she physically attacks others. Her behavior runs the gamut of "Acting-Out Behaviors." However, when questioned about her feelings, she usually shrugs or doesn't respond. Mr. Brown tries not to attend to Hilde's moody behavior in order not to reinforce it. He sets up a contract with Hilde that if, when he asks her how she feels, she thinks about it and then tells him, they will talk it over together. Hilde is fond of Mr. Brown, and any attention from him served as reinforcement to Hilde. Mr. Brown watches for signs of happy moods and was particularly careful to ask Hilde how she feels at these times.

Skill:	To recognize and label moods of others. **S-SR-EF-0004-L2**
Objective:	When presented with someone showing obvious signs of an emotion or "mood," the student provides a word or words to describe the emotion or mood.
Assessment:	Assess from previous knowledge of student or through direct observation using the <u>Social Behavior Assessment Inventory</u>.

Code: S-SR-EF-0004-L2-Im

TEACHING STRATEGY

Objective: When presented with someone showing obvious signs of an emotion or "mood," the student provides a word or words to describe the emotion or mood.

Social Modeling

1. **Identify a need for the behavior through a classroom discussion.** Structure the discussion by asking questions, and encouraging the children to formulate ideas. Have children identify different kinds of feelings and how we can tell how other people feel. Ask why it is important to have some idea how others are feeling. Additional media—such as a movie or story—may be very helpful in establishing a concept.

2. **Identify the specific behaviors to be modeled.** When someone is obviously upset, angry, or excited:

   (a) Think about what he or she might be feeling.

   (b) Think of a word you could use to talk about these feelings.

3. **Model the behavior for the class.** Assume various poses to suggest emotions, e.g., anger, sadness, happiness, puzzlement, etc., telling students what mood you are displaying and how they might be able to tell.

4. **Have each student practice describing moods of others.** Have students role-play moods or emotions while other students identify the moods. Suggestions:

   (a) Student runs into classroom smiling and clapping hands.

   (b) While working math lesson, student slams book shut and tears up paper.

   (c) After not being chosen as a "partner," student lays head down on desk.

   (d) After playing a competitive game, student bursts into tears.

   (e) Student comes into room and yells at another, "Just wait 'till recess; I'll get even with you then."

   (f) Student sits quietly, not talking or interacting with anyone.

   (g) After tests are graded and given back to students, one student starts to cry.

   (h) After talking to best friend, student gets up and runs out of the room.

5. **Recognize students who respond correctly.**

6. **Maintain the behavior through reinforcement.**

Code: S-SR-EF-0004-L2-Ir

TEACHING STRATEGY

Objective: When presented with someone showing obvious signs of an emotion or "mood," the student provides a word or words to describe the emotion or mood.

Social Reinforcement

1. **Identify and recognize by name target student when he or she demonstrates ability to name an emotion or mood.** The behavior may be demonstrated in connection with a discussion or a story, a movie, a role-playing situation, etc. "That's right, Mike. The boy in the story looks sad." "Good answer, Mary. When someone is smiling, it usually means he is happy." "You guessed it, John. When I look like this, it means I am angry."

2. **Cue the behavior in target student by identifying and praising others who are demonstrating understanding of other's moods.**

3. **Pair a more tangible reinforcer with the social reinforcer if necessary.**

Code: S-SR-EF-0004-L2-Ic

TEACHING STRATEGY

Objective: When presented with someone showing obvious signs of an emotion or "mood," the student provides a word or words to describe the emotion or mood.

Contingency Management

1. **State the task in observable terms.** From the expression on a person's face or the things he or she does or says, try to guess what feelings he or she has, and say whether he or she is happy, sad, angry.

229

2. **Choose a reward to use.**

3. **State the contingency.** If you can try to guess and make a statement about what mood a person is in from the way he or she looks or what he or she ways, you will receive the agreed-upon reward.

4. **In a situation where it is appropriate for the student(s) to make a statement about the mood or feelings of others, reward according to the contract for making a reasonable attempt to do so based on how the person looks or acts.**

5. **Example.** Robert and Ken are best friends. Robert has a health handicap that causes him to be moody; and frequently throughout the day, he gets angry or frustrated and wants to be left alone. Ken does not seem to understand why Robert wants to be left alone and becomes angry in turn or feels rejected; this leads to a fight between them. The teacher, Ms. DuPuy, took Ken aside and talked to him about Robert's moods and described some of the ways he looked and acted when it was better to leave him alone. She made a contract with Ken that when he saw one of these signs he was to leave Robert alone and come and report to her what he thought Robert's mood was. Ms. DuPuy worked out a plan with Ken's mother for a reward that would be given at home. She told Ken that for every day he could go without a fight with Robert, he would get a star on a chart. When he got 10 stars, he could invite Robert to go with him and his mother to an amusement park.

POSITIVE ATTITUDE TOWARD SELF

S-SR-PA-0002-L1-S	To say "thank you" when complimented or praised.
S-SR-PA-0004-L1-S	To be willing to have one's work displayed.
S-SR-PA-0006-L1-S	To make positive statements when asked about one-self.
S-SR-PA-0008-L2-S	To undertake a new task with a positive attitude.

Skill: To say "thank you" when complimented or praised.
S-SR-PA-0002-L1

Objective: Student says "thank you" when complimented and praised.

Assessment: Assess from previous knowledge of student or through direct observation using the <u>Social Behavior Assessment Inventory</u>.

Code: S-SR-PA-0002-L1-Im

TEACHING STRATEGY

Objective: Student says "thank you" when complimented and praised.

Social Modeling

1. **Identify a need for the behavior through a classroom discussion.** Use stories, films, or other aids where available. Have students contribute ideas to the discussion of how one should respond if someone gives praise and why one should thank others for praise or compliments. Write key phrases on the board as reminders.

2. **Identify specific behavior to be modeled.** For example, when praised or complimented say, "Thank you, _____."

3. **Model the behavior for the class.** Present a short puppet show. Have puppets compliment each other and respond with the appropriate thanking behavior. Ask students to identify elements of the modeled behavior. Reinforce students who make good responses.

4. **Have class practice the behavior, with each student given an opportunity to compliment or praise and verbalize the appropriate thanking behavior.** Write complimenting phrases on paper, e.g., "_____, that is a smart outfit you have;" "_____, I like that color on you." Have students select four phrases randomly. Students will be in pairs. One student will compliment. The other will respond with the appropriate thanking behavior. Reinforce students for acting appropriately in the modeling situation.

5. **Recognize those students who make the appropriate responses in the modeling situation.**
   Note: Students may feel self-conscious and react with silly responses in this activity. You can control this by ignoring silly responses and praising those who are taking the task seriously and trying to do a good job.

6. **Maintain appropriate thanking behavior in the classroom through reinforcement.**

Code: S-SR-PA-0002-L1-Ir

TEACHING STRATEGY

Objective: Student says "thank you" when complimented and praised.

Social Reinforcement

1. **Identify and praise by name target student when observed responding with "thank you" when he or she is complimented or praised.** Call attention to his or her specific verbal action, e.g., "Peggy, you remembered to say 'thank you'. Beautiful." "Sammy, I liked the way you thanked Tom for the compliment." "Charlie, you thanked Mr. Jones very politely when he praised your work."

2. **Cue appropriate behavior in target student by praising others who verbalize "thank you" when complimented or praised.** Watch for times when the target child says "thank you," and reinforce the thanking behavior.

   Note: If social reinforcement in the form of praise, attention, hand shakes, smiles, etc., is not sufficient to increase the desired behavior, it may be necessary to accompany social reinforcement with tangible reinforcement, i.e., coupons, trading stamps, stars, check marks, etc., to be exchanged for something the child wants.

Code: S-SR-PA-0002-L1-Ic

TEACHING STRATEGY

Objective: Student says "thank you" when complimented and praised.

Contingency Management

1. **Present task to student in specific terms.** When complimented or praised by someone, respond by saying, "Thank you, _____." Pictures in cartoon form depicting appropriate thanking behavior might be provided.

2. **Define a consequence valued by the student that will be given following demonstration of the desired behavior.** (Plan reinforcement strategy selected from reinforcement menu.)

3. **State the contingency.** If student demonstrates the appropriate verbal response, i.e., saying "thank you" to the individual complimenting or praising him or her, the student will receive the agreed-upon positive consequence.

4. **Watch for the behavior to occur naturally and reinforce it when it occurs according to the established contingency.** You may also set the occasion for the behavior to occur. During a given time period, you will praise or compliment the student, e.g., "Eric, your math paper is very neat. Beautiful work! Eric, great job of following directions!" The student may earn points by saying "thank you" when praised; these may be exchanged for minutes of free reading.

5. **Example.** Sally was an excellent artist. Other students and teachers were always praising her and complimenting her work. Sally's teacher observed

that Sally seldom thanked those who complimented her work or praised her and instead made responses such as, "It's not good." Sally and her teacher agreed upon a contract: If Sally said "thank you" and eliminated self-critical comments in response to praise from others, she would earn check marks. When 50 check marks had been accumulated, Sally could exchange check marks for a set of water colors.

Skill:	To be willing to have one's work displayed. **S-SR-PA-0004-L1**
Objective:	When teacher asks to display the student's work, the student agrees readily.
Assessment:	Assess from previous knowledge of student or through direct observation using the <u>Social Behavior Assessment Inventory</u>.

Code: S-SR-PA-0004-L1-Im

TEACHING STRATEGY

Objective: When teacher asks to display the student's work, the student agrees readily.

Social Modeling

1. **Identify a need for the behavior through a classroom discussion.** Use stories, films, or other aids when available. Have students contribute ideas to the discussion of why agree readily to have work displayed. For example, "Why does the teacher ask to display work? How should you respond to the teacher?" Provide an opportunity for students to express negative opinions about having work displayed, but steer discussion toward positive aspects of the behavior.

   Note: This behavior is important as an indicator of how a student evaluates his or her work in relation to that of others. Care should be taken never to display a student's work to the student's disadvantage. Displaying work would always be done in a positive context.

2. **Identify specific behavior to be modeled.** When the teacher asks to display work, you will agree readily saying, "Yes, _____, you may display my work," or some other response appropriate to the situation.

3. **Model the behavior for the class.** Select student to be the teacher. You will be completing task. Student will ask teacher to display work. You will agree readily by responding, "Yes, _____, you may display my work." Reinforce students who make good responses.

4. **Have students practice the behavior, with each student given an opportunity to be the teacher, asking to display work, and the other student agreeing readily to having work displayed.** "Yes, _____, you may display my work."

5. **Recognize those students who agree readily to having work displayed in modeling situation.**

6. **Maintain desired behavior in the classroom through reinforcement.**

Code: S-SR-PA-0004-L1-Ir

TEACHING STRATEGY

Objective: When teacher asks to display the student's work, the student agrees readily.

Social Reinforcement

1. **Identify, recognizing by name, target student when he or she agrees readily to have his or her work displayed.** Call attention to specific actions, e.g., "Ruth, thank you for letting me display your picture. It makes the bulletin board nicer to look at." "Robert, beautiful paper! I appreciate your letting me display your work."

2. **Cue appropriate behavior in target student by recognizing others who agree readily to having their work displayed.** Watch for the desired behavior, (i.e., agreeing readily to have work displayed) in the target child, and reinforce the behavior.

   Note: If social reinforcement in the form of attention, praise, smiles, etc., is not sufficient to increase the desired behavior, it may be necessary to accompany social reinforcement with tangible reinforcement, something the child wants.

Code: S-SR-PA-0004-L1-Ic

TEACHING STRATEGY

Objective: When teacher asks to display the student's work, the student agrees readily.

Contingency Management

1. **Present task to student in specific terms.** When teacher asks to display the student's work, the student will agree readily.

2. **Plan reinforcement strategy selected from reinforcement menu.** Define a consequence valued by the student that will be given following demonstration of the desired behavior.

3. **State the contingency.** If student agrees readily to the displaying of his or her work, he or she will receive the agreed-upon positive consequence.

4. **Watch for the behavior to occur naturally and reward it when it occurs according to established contingency,** or, set an occasion for the behavior to occur. Design a bulletin board to display student's work, e.g., "Work to Hoot About;" "Proud Place." If a student is asked to display his work and agrees readily, then he or she may select one activity to be taken off the classes' homework schedule.

5. **Example.** Although Billy, Charlie, and Kenny did good work, they did not agree readily to have their work displayed. When their teacher asked to display their work, they would laugh and hide their papers. Their teacher made three thermometers labeled Billy, Charlie, and Kenny. For each paper displayed by the student, the appropriate thermometer level was marked. The teacher and three boys agreed that the student with the highest

234

thermometer reading for work displayed would care for the hamster during the following week.

Skill:	To make positive statements when asked about oneself. **S-SR-PA-0006-L1**
Objective:	Student makes positive statements when asked about him or herself.
Assessment:	Assess from previous knowledge of student or through direct observation using the <u>Social Behavior Assessment Inventory</u>.

Code: S-SR-PA-0006-L1-Im

TEACHING STRATEGY

Objective: Student makes positive statements when asked about him or herself.

Social Modeling

1. **Identify a need for the behavior through a classroom discussion.** Use stories, film strips, or other aids where available. Bring up such points as the fact that everyone has good qualities and does some things well, even though no one is perfect. Have the class identify reasons why it's good to know about your own good qualities and recognize the things you do well. Have the class try to distinguish between behavior that could be considered "bragging" or inappropriately building oneself up at the expense of another and behavior that involves appropriately saying positive things about oneself and what one has done. Generate with the class some positive sentences one might use to describe one's accomplishments. For example, "I like my picture." "That was a good hit I made." "I'm happy that I got 100 on spelling."

2. **Identify specific behavior to be modeled.** When someone asks you to tell about yourself or about something good you've done, try to think of something positive to say. (Stress that one need not be perfect or do everything perfectly in order to find good things to say about oneself.)

3. **Model the behavior for the class.** Describe to the class some realistic positive traits you possess and skills you have. For contrast, you might insert some negative comments and have students distinguish between the two.

4. **Give each student an opportunity to practice.** Make up a list of positive statements as prompts. Give each student a copy of the list. Go around the class and have each student find a statement that could apply to himself or herself and read it in response to a prompting question from the teacher. Go around the class again and have each student think of another statement that is not on the list. Provide prompts wherever necessary. Reward students who make appropriate responses.

5. **Maintain through reinforcement the behavior of making positive statements about oneself or one's accomplishments.**

Code: S-SR-PA-0006-L1-Ir

TEACHING STRATEGY

Objective: Student makes positive statements when asked about him or herself.

Social Reinforcement

1. **Identify and praise by name target student when observed making positive statements about self.** Call attention to specific verbal actions. "Yes, George, I will display your math paper. I agree with you. It's a super job;" "I like the way Pam could think of good things to say about herself when I asked each person to tell about himself."

2. **Cue appropriate behaviors in target student by praising others who make positive statements about themselves.**

3. **Provide opportunities for students to tell good things about themselves,** or, after a student has done something positive, prompt the student's recognition of his or her accomplishment by asking how he or she feels about it. Reinforce when he or she can say, "I like it," "I'm proud of it, " "I'm happy about it," or words to that effect.

Code: S-SR-PA-0006-L1-Ic

TEACHING STRATEGY

Objective: Student makes positive statements when asked about him or herself.

Contingency Management

1. **Present the task to the student in specific terms.** When someone asks you to tell about yourself or about your work, think of some good things to say.

2. **Define a consequence valued by the student that will be given following demonstration of the desired verbalization about him or herself.** (Plan reinforcement strategy from reinforcement menu.)

3. **State the contingency.** If student says positive things when asked about him or herself, he or she will receive the agreed-upon desirable consequences.

4. **Listen for the behavior to occur naturally, and reinforce it when it occurs according to established contingency,** or, set up a situation in which the behavior can occur. Give the student an activity at which he or she does well. Ask the student questions about him or herself and his or her work. If he or she responds to questions about him or herself with positive statements, he or she will receive the established reward.

5. **Example.** Todd is a bright, well-behaved student in Mr. Down's class. In spite of Todd's assets, Mr. Downs suspects that he has a poor "self-concept," because Todd, when asked about his work, usually makes some negative response, such as, "It's no good," or "I could have done better." He is critical not only of himself but of others as well, and he is quick to find fault with what other students do. Mr. Downs feels that possibly some of Todd's negative statements are perpetuated by the reactions they get when he

"runs down" himself or his work. For example, somebody always responds by saying something like, "Oh no, Todd, it's **good**." Mr. Downs sets up a conference with Todd and discusses with him his observations - that Todd has many good qualities and accomplishments, but that he continually looks for negative things to say about himself and others. He describes to Todd and rehearses with him some positive statements he would like him to make instead. He helps Todd understand the difference between "bragging" and being realistically proud of one's accomplishments and acknowledging them when asked.

Mr. Downs contracts with Todd. For every positive statement Todd makes about himself or someone else when he is asked, Mr. Downs will give Todd two trading stamps. He will provide a bonus of five stamps if Todd can come and point out to him something good he or someone else has done which Mr. Downs is unaware of. Mr. Downs puts Todd in charge of a bulletin board labeled "Blowing Our Horn," on which are put positive observations that Todd and the others supply about members of the class.

Skill:	To undertake a new task with a positive attitude. **S-SR-PA-0008-L2**
Objective:	When required, student begins a new task willingly without complaining or hesitating.
Assessment:	Assess from previous knowledge of student or through direct observation using the <u>Social Behavior Assessment Inventory</u>.

Code: S-SR-PA-0008-L2-Im

TEACHING STRATEGY

Objective: When required, student begins a new task willingly without complaining or hesitating.

Social Modeling

1. **Identify a need for the behavior through a classroom discussion.** Use stories, films, or other aids where available. Have students contribute ideas to the discussion of what constitutes beginning a new task willingly without complaining or hesitating. For example, "How can we get ready to start doing a new task? What are some problems which might keep us from starting right in and doing the job? What are the advantages of beginning a new task quickly?" Discuss attitudes toward new tasks, e.g., saying "I can" instead of "I can't" to yourself. Write key words on the board.

2. **Identify specific behaviors to be modeled.**

   (a) Ready materials or equipment.

   (b) Make sure you understand the directions for doing the task.

   (c) Start doing the task without complaining.

3. **Model the behavior for the class.** Sit at your desk completing a task, cross task off schedule when completed, get materials or equipment for new task, read directions for the new task, and begin new task willingly, e.g.,

verbalizing positive statements about attempting the new task. Ask students to identify elements of modeled behavior. Praise students who make good responses.

4. **Have class practice the behavior.** Give each student an opportunity to demonstrate the appropriate behavior of beginning a new task willingly without complaining or hesitating.

5. **Recognize those students who demonstrated the appropriate behavior of beginning a new task willingly without complaining or hesitating.**

6. **Maintain through reinforcement, the appropriate behavior of beginning a new task willingly without complaining or hesitating.** Select several students who have demonstrated good work habits. Arrange seating so these students can serve as models for the other students.

Code: S-SR-PA-0008-L2-Ir

TEACHING STRATEGY

Objective: When required, student begins a new task willingly without complaining or hesitating.

Social Reinforcement

1. **Identify and recognize by name target student when observed beginning a new task willingly without complaining or hesitating.** Call attention to specific actions, e.g., "Larry, You got right to work on your new assignment!" "Stephanie, I appreciate the way you went on to your new task. Beautiful!" (Make sure the required task is within the student's ability to handle successfully.)

2. **Cue appropriate behavior in target student by praising others who begin a new task willingly without complaining or hesitating.** Watch for the appropriate behavior from the target student—beginning a new task willingly, without complaining or hesitating—and provide reinforcement when this occurs.

   Note: If social reinforcement in the form of praise, attention, smiles, handshakes, etc., is not sufficient to increase the desired behavior, it may be necessary to accompany social reinforcement with tangible reinforcement, e.g., chips, tokens, trading stamps, etc., to be exchanged for something the child wants.

Code: S-SR-PA-0008-L2-Ic

TEACHING STRATEGY

Objective: When required, student begins a new task willingly without complaining or hesitating.

Contingency Management

1. **Present task to student in specific terms.** When given a new task the student begins without complaining or hesitating.

238

2. **Define a consequence valued by the student** that will be given when he or she begins a new task willingly without complaining or hesitating.

3. **State the contingency.** If student begins a new task willingly without complaining or hesitating, he or she will receive the agreed-upon positive consequence.

4. **Watch for the behavior to occur naturally.** Reinforce if when it occurs according to established contingency, or set a situation for the behavior to occur. Present a lesson based on new material the student has not previously learned. Give student a worksheet based on the lesson, and observe student for beginning the task willingly.

5. **Example.** Shirley receives any new task with whining comments such as, "I can't do it; it's too hard." Then she sits and doodles, talks to her neighbor, or otherwise wastes time. Ms. George, her teacher, wants to increase the appropriate behavior of willingly beginning a new task. Ms. George and Shirley agree on a contract. When Ms. George gives Shirley a new assignment she explains it and makes sure Shirley understands. Then, Ms. George sets a timer. If Shirley is working without complaining when the timer goes off, Shirley will receive an index card. By the end of the week, she will earn a movie for the class. Ms. George first sets the timer for four minutes, then gradually shortens the time so the timer rings within a minute after Shirley is given a new task.

RESPONSIBLE BEHAVIOR

S-SR-RB-0002-L1-S	To be regular in school attendance.
S-SR-RB-0004-L1-S	To arrive at school on time.
S-SR-RB-0006-L1-S	To hang up one's clothes in required place.
S-SR-RB-0008-L1-S	To keep one's desk in order.
S-SR-RB-0010-L1-S	To take care of one's own possessions .
S-SR-RB-0012-L2-S	To carry messages for the teacher.
S-SR-RB-0014-L2-S	To bring required materials to school.

Skill:	To be regular in school attendance. **S-SR-RB-0002-L1**
Objective:	Student attends school daily, unless ill.
Assessment:	Assess from previous knowledge of student or through direct observation using the <u>Social Behavior Assessment Inventory</u>.

Code: S-SR-RB-0002-L1-Im

TEACHING STRATEGY

Objective: Student attends school daily, unless ill.

Social Modeling

1. **Explain the need for regular attendance at school.** Discuss with the class how a student who misses a day of school misses a day's work and needs to work very hard to catch up. A student might miss an important lesson and not be able to understand what follows. He or she might miss out on some "fun" activities. Students may be asked to contribute ideas to the discussion with questions, such as, "Why do we need to come to school every day?" "What might happen if we don't?" Students may also need to be informed of legal requirements involved in school attendance, truancy laws, minimum attendance needed for promotion to the next grade, and other relevant school rules.

2. **Identify specific behavior to be modeled.** Come to school every day, unless you are ill.

3. **Model the behavior.** Point out to the students that you come to school every day unless you are sick.

4. **Provide opportunity for practice.** Make an attendance chart and have students put a check, a star, etc. next to their names when they come in each day.

5. **Maintain regular attendance through reinforcement.**

Code: S-SR-RB-0002-L1-Ir

TEACHING STRATEGY

Objective: Student attends school daily, unless ill.

Social Reinforcement

1. **Recognize, by name, students who attend school regularly.** Tell the student what he or she is being praised for, e.g., "Cal, it's Friday and you've been here every day this week. I think that's terrific!" "Cynthia, you haven't missed a day of school in three weeks, good work!"
2. **Cue appropriate behavior in the target student.**
   (a) Praise, in the target student's presence, other students for attending school regularly.
   (b) Provide a written reminder for the student in the form of a sign or bulletin board display about the importance of daily attendance.
3. **If social reinforcement alone is not sufficient to increase school attendance, you may try pairing it with a more tangible form of reinforcement.**

Code: S-SR-RB-0002-L1-Ic

TEACHING STRATEGY

Objective: Student attends school daily, unless ill.

Contingency Management

1. **Explain to the student that you want him or her to come to school every day, unless he or she is ill.** Explain the importance of regular attendance to the student and that this is required.
2. **Plan reinforcement.**
3. **State the contingency.** Explain to the student that he or she will be rewarded for attendance at school. Specify type, amount, and schedule of reinforcement. Schedule should depend on the student's previous attendance record, building up from smaller requirements to total attendance. Also, explain that reward will not be withheld if the absence from school was excused by a note from home or a doctor saying that the student was ill that day.
4. **Keep the student's attendance record, perhaps on a classroom chart that the student can see.** Reward the student after the specified number of days of attendance or excused absences.
5. **Example.** Claude has been chronically absent for no apparent reason. Ms. Cobb discusses this problem with Claude and tells him that if he comes to school every day for an entire week, on Friday he will be allowed to select a table game to play with a friend. Interim reinforcement was provided by having Claude place a gold star next to his name on the attendance chart every morning he came to school. This contingency was kept for three months until Claude's attendance reached an acceptable 95% level–at which time it was replaced by social reinforcement.

Note: If a contingency management strategy with a meaningful reward is not effective, look for other reasons for absence that compete with the reward. Is there something about school that is aversive to the student that he is avoiding by staying home? Is he or she being required by parents to stay home to care for siblings? Are the parents too disorganized to get him or her to school each day? In some cases, it may be necessary to intervene with the parents.

Skill:	To arrive at school on time.
	S-SR-RB-0004-L1
Objective:	Student arrives at school on time.
Assessment:	Assess from previous knowledge of student or through direct observation using the <u>Social Behavior Assessment Inventory</u>.

Code: S-SR-RB-0004-L1-Im

TEACHING STRATEGY

Objective: Student arrives at school on time.

Social Modeling

1. **Present reasons for each member of the class to arrive at school on time.** Include reasons, such as the possibility of missing something important, as well as school requirements and penalties for arriving late. Also include the idea that a late arrival interrupts the class activity already in progress. Have students discuss how the class would be if everyone showed up at school at different times.

2. **Identify specific behaviors to be modeled.**
   (a) Tell class as a whole what time they are required to be in class.
   (b) Discuss with each student what time he or she needs to leave home to arrive at school on time.

   Post these times at the students' desks, or have them write them in the front of their notebooks as reminders.

3. **Model the behavior.** Arrive at school on time the next day and describe to the class the steps you took to get there, e.g., when you left home, how you came directly to school, etc. Ask students to describe what they do or can do to get to school on time. Recognize those who give appropriate responses.

4. **Provide opportunity for practice.** Keep a chart for the next few days recording the times each member of the class has arrived in class. Reward promptness with stars on the chart, praise, etc.

5. **Maintain the behavior through reinforcement.**

Code: S-SR-RB-0004-L1-Ir

TEACHING STRATEGY

Objective: Student arrives at school on time.

Social Reinforcement

1. **Reinforce the student with smiles, praise, nods, for arriving at school on time.** Inform the student that he or she is being praised for his promptness. "Danny, you got here at exactly 8:30. That's very good!" "David, thank you for getting to school on time. You are a very responsible boy."

2. **Cue appropriate behavior in the target by:**
   (a) Reminding the student verbally at dismissal that he or she should be on time the next morning.
   (b) Posting a reminder to the whole class stating the time they are expected in school in the morning.
   (c) Giving the target student a note at the end of the day reminding him or her of what time to be at school the next morning.

   Be sure to praise the student when on time.

3. **Provide tangible reinforcement along with social reinforcement where necessary to get the student to come to school on time.**

Code: S-SR-RB-0004-L1-Ic

TEACHING STRATEGY

Objective: Student arrives at school on time.

Contingency Management

1. **Present the task to the student in specific observable terms.** "You are required to be at school at 8:30," or "I want you to be in this room every morning by 9:00."

2. **Plan reinforcement.**

3. **State the contingency.** Explain to the student that he or she will be rewarded when arriving at school on time. Specify type, amount, and schedule of reinforcement. Schedule of reinforcement (how many times he or she needs to arrive on time before he or she receives the reinforcement) will depend on current percentage of lateness.

4. **Record the time the student arrives each morning.** This may be done on a chart displayed in the classroom to serve as a reminder to the student and help keep track of performance. Reward the student for promptness according to the prearranged schedule.

5. **Example.** Eddie is often late to school. Ms. Ellsworth decides to use a contingency management strategy to deal with his lateness. She discusses with Eddie the time he is due at school and the time he needs to leave home to get there. She informs him that if he can get to school on time for five mornings in a row, he will be sent to the art room for 30 minutes on Friday afternoon, something Eddie gets very excited about. The contingency is

kept for one month, or until Eddie seems to be in the habit of coming to school on time. The contingency is then dropped and social reinforcement is used to maintain prompt behavior.

Note: If a contingency management strategy with a meaningful reinforcer is not sufficient, look for some reasons for tardiness that are beyond the child's control, e.g., disorganization in the home or health problems. It may be necessary to teach the child ways to compensate for problems or to provide additional prompts, e.g., a "wake up" service, an alarm clock, an escort to school. It may also be necessary to intervene directly with the parents.

Skill:	To hang up one's clothes in required place.
	S-SR-RB-0006-L1
Objective:	After entering the room, student removes outer clothes, hangs coat or jacket properly, and leaves boots and umbrella in designated place.
Assessment:	Assess from previous knowledge of student or through direct observation using the <u>Social Behavior Assessment Inventory</u>.

Code: S-SR-RB-0006-L1-Im

TEACHING STRATEGY

Objective: After entering the room, student removes outer clothes, hangs coat or jacket properly, and leaves boots and umbrella in designated place.

Social Modeling

1. **Discuss with the class the necessity for hanging clothes up in the closet when coming into the classroom.** Include ideas, such as, clothes on the floor make the room look messy and get in the way; clothes on the floor get stepped on and ruined; if you keep your outer clothing on you get overheated. Discuss with the class (or role-play with them) what would happen if everyone put clothing everywhere.

2. **Identify specific behaviors to be modeled.** The student comes into the room and:

   (a) Removes outer clothing—jacket, sweater, boots, hat, gloves, scarf.

   (b) Hangs these items in the closet on the hook or hanger assigned.

   (c) Puts boots and umbrellas on the floor of the closet or in a box for that purpose.

   (d) Puts gloves in coat pockets or sleeve so they don't get lost.

   Show students the places in your classroom referred to in these steps.

3. **Model the behavior.** Take your coat and other garments along with boots, umbrellas, etc., and pretend you just came into the room. Go to the closet and store your garments as a student should. Have the students describe your actions and praise those who give accurate responses.

4. **Provide opportunity for practice by having students dress and go out in the hall and then come in and store their clothes in the closet.** Reinforce correct responses.

5. **Maintain the behavior through reinforcement.**

Code: S-SR-RB-0006-L1-Ir

TEACHING STRATEGY

Objective: After entering the room, student removes outer clothes, hangs coat or jacket properly, and leaves boots and umbrella in designated place.

Social Reinforcement

1. **Identify and praise a student for properly storing outer clothes when entering the classroom.** Praise specific behaviors, e.g., "Felix, thank you for hanging up your jacket on your hook;" "Fannie, it was very nice of you to put your boots in the boot box. That's how we keep our classroom looking neat."

2. **Provide cues for target student.**
   (a) Post written reminders, perhaps on the closet door. These can be in the form of words, such as "Hang up coats," or pictures, such as a picture of a coat.
   (b) Point to the closet as the child comes in if he or she looks in your direction.
   (c) Praise another student for hanging up his or her clothes. Be sure the target student can hear this.

3. **It may be necessary to pair tangible reinforcements with social reinforcement to maintain the behavior.** These additional reinforcers should be dropped as soon as possible, however.

Code: S-SR-RB-0006-L1-Ic

TEACHING STRATEGY

Objective: After entering the room, student removes outer clothes, hangs coat or jacket properly, and leaves boots and umbrella in designated place.

Contingency Management

1. **Meet with the student to explain how he or she is expected to store outer clothing.** Specify exactly where each item is to be hung or placed, when he or she is expected to take outer clothes off and hang them up, etc. Be sure the student knows what is expected.

2. **Plan reinforcement.**

3. **State the contingency.** The student will receive an agreed-upon reward for storing outer clothes in the proper manner as explained. Specify type and amount of reward and how many correct responses the student must make to receive it.

4. **Observe student as he or she comes into the classroom with outer clothing.** If he or she stores garments properly, deliver the reinforcement.

5. **Example.** Garth often drops his coat on the floor when he comes into the room in the morning. Ms. Gaines would like him to hang his things up, so she discusses with him how to do it. "Garth, your jacket should be hung in the closet. When you leave it on the floor it gets in other people's way, and it gets stepped on and dirty. I would like you to take it off when you come in and hang it in the closet on the hook with your name over it. Any boots, umbrellas, or other things like that should be put in the box underneath your hook."

She then states the contingency and/or reinforcement to him. "Each time you hang up your outer things like this when you come in, I will give you a token that you can exchange for something in the class store." She then observes him coming in and rewards him when he hangs up his clothing. After two weeks, she alters the contingency to two correct responses for each token. After several more weeks the contingency is dropped altogether in favor of maintenance through social reinforcement.

Skill:	To keep one's desk in order. **S-SR-RB-0008-L1**
Objective:	Student keeps own desk in order, i.e., books and papers organized inside the desk and the top of the desk clear to work on.
Assessment:	Assess from previous knowledge of student or through direct observation using the <u>Social Behavior Assessment Inventory</u>.

Code: S-SR-RB-0008-L1-Im

TEACHING STRATEGY

Objective: Student keeps own desk in order, i.e., books and papers organized inside the desk and the top of the desk clear to work on.

Social Modeling

1. **Meet with student or class to explain the need for keeping desks in order.** Ask questions, such as, "What can happen to your papers if they are allowed to fall out of your desk?" "How does the room look when everyone's desk is cluttered?" "If pencils, pens, or papers fall off your desk, what may happen?"

2. **Identify specific behaviors to be modeled.**
   (a) Keep papers and books neatly stacked inside your desk.
   (b) Keep pens and pencils inside your desk or in a bag or box if possible.
   (c) Keep top of desk clear to work on.

3. **Model the behavior.** Sit at your desk and have students gather around so they can see you. Take everything out of the desk and replace it in a neat, organized manner. Ask students to describe your actions, and praise appropriate responses.

4. **Provide opportunity for practice.** Give students a few minutes to clean up their desks. Have an inspection of desks and reward those students who have desks in order.

5. **Maintain the behavior through reinforcement.**

Code: S-SR-RB-0008-L1-Ir

TEACHING STRATEGY

Objective: Student keeps own desk in order, i.e., books and papers organized inside the desk and the top of the desk clear to work on.

Social Reinforcement

1. **Recognize the student for keeping desk neat and orderly.** Be specific in praising, e.g., "Holly, your desk is very neat. The top is nice and clear." "Harvey, your papers are neatly put inside your desk. Thank you for helping us keep the room looking nice."

2. **Provide cues for target student.**
   (a) Recognize another student, whose desk is near target student, for keeping desk neat.
   (b) Leave a note on the target student's desk as a reminder to straighten out the desk.
   (c) Verbally remind the whole class to put their desks in order.

3. **It may sometimes be necessary to provide a tangible reinforcement along with praise to motivate a student to keep the desk in order.**

Code: S-SR-RB-0008-L1-Ic

TEACHING STRATEGY

Objective: Student keeps own desk in order, i.e., books and papers organized inside the desk and the top of the desk clear to work on.

Contingency Management

1. **Present the task to the student in specific terms.** Keep your desk in order by neatly stacking books and papers and other items inside your desk, and leave the desk top clear to work on.

2. **Plan reinforcement.**

3. **State the contingency.** "I am going to check your desk twice a day. You won't know when I'll check it. If your desk is in order when I check it, you will receive a reward."

   Specify type and amount of reward.

4. **Check the student's desk during the course of the day. If the desk is in order, deliver the promised reinforcer.**

5. **Example.** Isabel's desk is usually very messy. Mr. Lane contracts with her to keep it neater. "Isabel, I would like you to learn to keep your desk neater. Your books and papers should be neatly stacked inside your desk. Pens and pencils should be kept in your pencil bag when you aren't using them. I'm

going to check your desk twice a day, once in the morning and once during the afternoon. If your desk is neat when I check it, I will give you a star on out Good Classroom Citizen chart" (which Isabel finds very rewarding).

Note: Students may earn the job of "desk inspector," relieving the teacher of the task and dispersing the notion of orderly desks.

Skill:	To take care of one's own possessions. **S-SR-RB-0010-L1**
Objective:	Student takes care of own possessions—keeps own books, clothing, and other possessions in reasonably good condition and does not regularly lose books, clothing, and other possessions.
Assessment:	Assess from previous knowledge of student or through direct observation using the <u>Social Behavior Assessment Inventory</u>.

Code: S-SR-RB-0010-L1-Im

TEACHING STRATEGY

Objective: Student takes care of own possessions—keeps own books, clothing, and other possessions in reasonably good condition and does not regularly lose books, clothing, and other possessions.

Social Modeling

1. **Discuss with the class the need to keep possessions in good condition and avoid losing them.** Ask students to contribute to the discussion of why we need to do these things. Ask questions, such as, "What happens to your toys, clothes, books, etc., if you aren't careful with them? If they get lost or broken, can you still use them or get another one? What could we do to keep from losing things that belong to us? How can we go about being careful with toys and with school materials?" Use stories, films, or other media to stimulate conversation.

2. **Identify specific behaviors to be modeled.** Identify a specific item or items with which more care needs to be taken. Identify the specific actions which go into the behaviors of taking better care of the items and describe them to the class. For example, to avoid losing your coat, have a particular, safe place to put it when you aren't wearing it. When you leave the area to go somewhere else, stop and think where you left it. Try to get in the habit of stopping to think, "Did I leave something behind?" Write key words on the board.

3. **Model the behavior.** Use possession in question as props and role-play appropriate ways to use them or avoid losing them. Show, for example, how to handle a book properly. Show what a book looks like when it is misused. Show proper and improper ways to take care of clothing. Ask students to describe your actions, and praise accurate responses.

4. **Provide opportunities for practice by assigning an activity in which the possession in question must be used.** Observe the student's handling of the possession and reward taking good care of his possessions.

5. **Maintain the behavior through reinforcement.**

Code: S-SR-RB-0010-L1-Ir

TEACHING STRATEGY

Objective: Student takes care of own possessions—keeps own books, clothing, and other possessions in reasonably good condition and does not regularly lose books, clothing, and other possessions.

Social Reinforcement

1. **Use social reinforcement to reward target student for taking care of possessions.** Let the student know specifically what actions are being rewarded. "Jason, you keep your books in good condition. You are very responsible." "Jill, you keep track of your clothing very well." "Jenny, you didn't lose your gloves all week. Very good."

2. **Provide cues for target student.**

    (a) In the presence of the target student, recognize another student who has taken specific action to care for his or her possessions.

3. **Social reinforcement may sometimes be insufficient alone to elicit the behavior.** In this case, add a tangible reinforcement to social reinforcement.

Code: S-SR-RB-0010-L1-Ic

TEACHING STRATEGY

Objective: Student takes care of own possessions: keeps own books, clothing and other possessions in reasonably good condition, and does not regularly lose books, clothing and other possessions.

Contingency Management

1. **Present task to the student in specific terms related to the possessions the student has a problem taking care of.** Demonstrate or describe the proper way to care for the items, e.g., "When reading a book, do not fold or crumple the pages; do not mark in the book. Keep a cover on the book, and turn the pages carefully." "Keep your clothing clean and neat by not marking on it or ripping or tearing it." "When you go from one place to another, check frequently to see whether you have your coat/boots/hat, etc. If you put them down, think about where you are leaving them."

2. **Plan reinforcement.**

3. **State the contingency.** If the student complies with the requirements of the task as set down in Step 1, the student will be rewarded. Specify type and amount of reward.

4. **Observe the student's handling of the possessions in question and reward the student for proper care.**

5. **Example.** Kyle messes up his books regularly by crumpling up the pages as he turns them and by drawing on the cover. Mr. Kit contracts with him to keep his books in better shape. He explains to Kyle that he must keep his books neat by not marking in them, by keeping a cover on them, and by turning the pages carefully, without crumpling them. If he manages this, he will be allowed to take home a library book of his choice, something Kyle enjoys very much. Mr. Kit arranges to examine Kyle's books at the end of each week; and if they remain in good condition, Kyle is given a library book to take home over the weekend. In order to continue receiving this privilege, Kyle must also return the library book on Monday in good condition.

Skill:	To carry messages for the teacher. **S-SR-RB-0012-L2**
Objective:	Student carries messages for the teacher when asked by taking message from teacher, delivering it to the appropriate person, and returning directly to the classroom.
Assessment:	Assess from previous knowledge of student or through direct observation using the Social Behavior Assessment Inventory.

Code: S-SR-RB-0012-L2-Im

TEACHING STRATEGY

Objective: Student carries messages for the teacher when asked by taking message from teacher, delivering it to the appropriate person, and returning directly to the classroom.

Social Modeling

1. **Discuss a need for the behavior with the class.** Discuss ways to help the teacher. Have the students contribute ideas to the conversation. Ask students to describe how they think the task of delivering messages for the teacher should be carried out.
2. **Identify specific behaviors to be modeled.**
   (a) Take the message from the teacher.
   (b) Go to the person for whom the message is intended.
   (c) Give the message to the person.
   (d) Find out if there is an answer to be brought back.
   (e) Return directly to the classroom.
3. **Model the behavior.** Have a student who knows how to carry messages model the behavior. Give the student a message and have him or her take it from you. Have the class line up and follow the message bearer to the recipient of the message (who has been told in advance of the activity) and then back to the classroom. Ask the students to describe the model's actions. Reward accurate and relevant responses.

250

4. **Have the class practice the behavior.** Send each student in turn to carry a message for you to a specified person in the building. Get feedback from the other person and reinforce correct responses.

5. **Maintain the behavior through reinforcement.**

Code: S-SR-RB-0012-L2-Ir

TEACHING STRATEGY

Objective: Student carries messages for the teacher when asked by taking message from teacher, delivering it to the appropriate person, and returning directly to the classroom.

Social Reinforcement

1. **Recognize a student by name for carrying a message for the teacher in an acceptable fashion.** Be descriptive in praise. "Kyle, thank you for taking the message to the secretary for me. I like the way you came right back to our room." "Kenny, it was very nice of you to take that message to Ms. Kite for me. You did it very well and came back quickly. That was very responsible."

2. **Provide cues for the target student.** Ask the student to carry a message for you. Remind the student where to take it and to come back immediately when he or she is done. Praise the student upon returning if accomplished properly.

3. **Tangible reinforcement may be paired with social reinforcement to maintain the behavior if necessary.**

Code: S-SR-RB-0012-L2-Ic

TEACHING STRATEGY

Objective: Student carries messages for the teacher when asked by taking message from teacher, delivering it to the appropriate person, and returning directly to the classroom.

Contingency Management

1. **Discuss the desired behavior with the student in specific terms.** The student will carry messages for the teacher by taking the message, in the form of a note or verbal message, going to the person the message is for, delivering it, and coming right back to the classroom.

2. **Plan reinforcement.**

3. **State the contingency.** The student will be rewarded if he or she carries a message for the teacher when asked by taking the message from the teacher, delivering it, and returning directly to the classroom. Specify type and amount of reinforcement.

4. **Ask the student to take a message for you.** Reward the student if he or she takes the message from you, delivers it to the proper person, and returns to the classroom quickly.

5. **Example.** Larry cannot be relied on to run errands for the teacher without getting sidetracked and failing to return to the classroom promptly. The teacher contracts with Larry to take messages, explaining the steps involved in carrying messages. The teacher states the contingency such that each time Larry carries a message, coming back to class immediately, he will be given 15 minutes at the interest center of his choice. The teacher keeps the contingency in effect long enough for Larry to demonstrate the behavior several times and then drops it in favor of social reinforcement.

Skill:	To bring required materials to school. **S-SR-RB-0014-L2**
Objective:	Student brings to school the required materials from home, e.g., books, paper, pens, pencils.
Assessment:	Assess from previous knowledge of student or through direct observation using the <u>Social Behavior Assessment Inventory</u>.

Code: S-SR-RB-0014-L2-Im

TEACHING STRATEGY

Objective: Student brings to school the required materials from home, e.g., books, paper, pens, pencils.

Social Modeling

1. **Identify a need for the behavior through a classroom discussion.** Ask students to discuss what happens when we do not bring in what we need for the class. If available, use a story to illustrate this point.
2. **Identify specific behaviors to be modeled.**
   (a) At home the student should collect everything needed to take to school and leave it all together in a convenience place—a table near the front door, the dresser, the kitchen table. (Have students discuss various places in their homes where they can leave their school materials.)

   Write the key words on the board.
3. **Model the behavior for the class.** Ask the students to pretend you are a student at home preparing for school in the morning.
   Act I: Collect what you need and leave it somewhere to be brought to school the next morning. (As you role-play, describe what you're doing.)

   Act II: Next morning, take the materials from where you left them and leave for school.

   Act III: Arrive at school with your materials and take your seat. Point out that you are now ready to work because you have the materials you need.
4. **Provide opportunity for practice.** Check the student's materials every day for a week, awarding a star or check on a chart for bringing everything that is required to school.

5. **Maintain the behavior through reinforcement.**

Code: S-SR-RB-0014-L2-Ir

TEACHING STRATEGY

Objective: Student brings to school the required materials from home, e.g., books, paper, pens, pencils.

Social Reinforcement

1. **Use social reinforcement to reward a student for bringing required materials to school.** Use descriptive praise. "Matt, I'm happy that you brought your paper and pencil today." "Mamie, thank you for bringing in your math book." "Maggie, you brought your pen today. That was very smart."

2. **Provide cues for target student.**
   (a) Praise another student near target student for bringing required materials from home.
   (b) Leave notes for the target student as reminders of what to bring to school the next day.
   (c) Verbally remind class before being dismissed for the day to bring required materials to school the next morning. Specify materials.
   (d) Send a note home to parents specifying what materials the student should bring each day.

Note: It may be necessary at first to pair tangible reinforcement with social reinforcement to elicit the behavior.

Code: S-SR-RB-0014-L2-Ic

TEACHING STRATEGY

Objective: Student brings to school the required materials from home, e.g., books, paper, pens, pencils.

Contingency Management

1. **Present the task to the student in specific terms.** "Bring everything you need for the school day to school with you in the morning, including the books you need, paper, pens, pencils, rulers, or other materials."

2. **Plan reinforcement.**

3. **State the contingency.** If the student brings all required materials to school, the student will be rewarded. Specify type and amount of reward.

4. **Check materials in the morning and reward student if he or she has remembered to bring everything required.**

5. **Example.** Nancy forgets her pencil regularly. Ms. Natches discusses this problem with her, explaining that just as a carpenter needs hammer, saw, and nails to work with, so does a student need pencils, books, etc., in order to do work. She states the contingency: "Each time you remember to bring your pencil to school with you in the morning, I will give you a star on our

'Responsible Classroom Citizen' chart. Ms. Natches chooses this reinforcement for its relevancy and its appeal to Nancy. A minimum number of stars per month on the chart entitles Nancy to a "Responsible Citizen Certificate."

Note: The natural consequences of failing to bring needed materials to school can be used. That is no loans to the student except at recess. At that time, he or she can do the school work missed because of the lapse in bringing the necessary material to school. In all cases, be certain that the student has access to the needed materials at home.

Self-Care

S-SR-SC-0002-L1-S   To use toilet facilities properly.
S-SR-SC-0004-L1-S   To put on clothing without assistance.
S-SR-SC-0006-L1-S   To keep face and hands clean.

Skill:	To use toilet facilities properly. **S-SR-SC-0002-L1**
Objective:	Student uses the toilet facilities when necessary, neatly, putting paper in bowl and remembering to flush the toilet.
Assessment:	Assess from previous knowledge of student or through direct observation using the <u>Social Behavior Assessment Inventory</u>.

Code: S-SR-SC-0002-L1-Im

TEACHING STRATEGY

Objective: Student uses the toilet facilities when necessary, neatly, putting paper in bowl, and flushing the toilet.

Social Modeling

1. **Most children when they reach elementary school will have learned to use the toilet properly.** Some children, however, have difficulty transferring behaviors learned at home to a group toilet facility such as that found in schools and thinking in terms of consideration of others in the use of school toilets. This skill may be introduced through a class discussion. Direct the students to develop rules for using the bathroom facilities properly by asking them questions, such as, "How do you feel when you use a bathroom that someone else has left messy? If you leave a mess, someone else will have to clean it up. Do you think that's fair? What can you do to help keep our bathrooms neat and clean?" In addition to use of the toilet, talk about washing hands and placing paper towels in the appropriate container. Help the children develop a list of rules to follow, and make a chart of those rules. Post the chart in the bathroom as a reminder.

2. **Identify specific behaviors to be modeled.** Depending on the competency of your class you may either want to simply describe the proper bathroom behavior or actually take students to the bathroom and show them exactly what to do. If necessary, have another teacher of a different sex assist you so boys and girls can be taken to their own bathrooms. Specify rules, such as, when you use the bathroom:
   (a) Try to be neat.
   (b) Put toilet papers into the toilet bowl.
   (c) Flush toilet when you're through.
   (d) Wash your hands.
   (e) Place paper towels in the container.

3. **Model the behavior.** If necessary, take the children to the bathroom and show them what to do.

4. **Provide opportunity for practice.** During the normal school day the children will have scheduled bathroom breaks. At those times observe their behavior and immediately reinforce those who remember to be neat according to the specified rules.

5. **Maintain the behavior through reinforcement.**

Code: S-SR-SC-0002-L1-Ir

TEACHING STRATEGY

Objective: Student uses the toilet facilities when necessary, neatly, putting paper in bowl, and flushing the toilet.

Social Reinforcement

1. **Identify and recognize by name student observed using the bathroom neatly.** Direct attention to the specific behavior. "Derrell remembered to use the bathroom properly. He didn't leave any papers lying around;" "Rollin, I noticed that you remembered to use the bathroom neatly;" "Mary, I like the way you picked up your paper towel and put it in the container."

2. **Provide cues for target student.** Remind the student of the proper way to use the bathroom by putting up signs or a list of rules or giving verbal reminders. Remember to reinforce all other students who behave properly. Immediately reinforce the target student for responding to the cues provided.

3. **If social praise does not produce a change in behavior it may be necessary to provide tangible reinforcers along with the social reinforcement.** Try pairing verbal praise, smiles, and pats on the back with a token or stars on a chart which the student can exchange for something he values.

Code: S-SR-SC-0002-L1-Ic

TEACHING STRATEGY

Objective: Student uses the toilet facilities when necessary, neatly, putting paper in bowl and flushing the toilet.

Contingency Management

1. **Explain the task to the children in specific terms.** When you use the bathroom, remember to:
   (a) Put toilet papers in the bowl.
   (b) Flush the toilet when you are through.
   (c) Wash your hands and put towels in the trash container.
   (d) Leave the area neat and clean for the next person to use it.

2. **Plan reinforcement.**

3. **State the contingency.** You will be rewarded when you remember to use the bathroom neatly.

4. **Observe the children's behavior in the bathroom.** Use a checklist if necessary, and reinforce those who are neat according to the established

contract. Since students often use the bathroom in a group, using student monitors with a checklist may be helpful, as well as establishing group contingencies where all have to cooperate in order to receive the reward. Scheduling bathroom breaks immediately preceding a desirable activity and not going on to the desirable activity unless the bathroom is left neat should help increase appropriate use of bathroom facilities.

5. **Example.** Archie sometimes gets silly on bathroom breaks. He throws papers on the floor and in the sink, or fills the toilet full of paper and walks out without flushing. Archie knows better, but he likes to be silly because of the attention it gets him. Ms. Jensen, his teacher, decides to contract with Archie to improve his behavior. She develops a chart that includes various grooming and hygiene behaviors. Bathroom behavior is included on the chart. Each day Ms. Jensen observes the students and puts stars on the chart for practicing good health habits. She explains to Archie that he can help earn a party for the class by behaving properly in the bathroom and receiving a star on his chart. When each child's chart is filled, the class is promised a party. Archie is also told that he could lose stars if he forgets and leaves the bathroom in a mess after he uses it.

Skill:	To put on clothing without assistance. **S-SR-SC-0004-L1**
Objective:	Student puts on outer clothing without assistance.
Assessment:	Assess from previous knowledge of student or through direct observation using the <u>Social Behavior Assessment Inventory</u>.

Code: S-SR-SC-0004-L1-Im

TEACHING STRATEGY

Objective: Student puts on outer clothing without assistance.

Social Modeling

1. **Identify a need for the behavior through a classroom discussion.** Use stories, films, manipulative material, or other aids where available. Have students contribute ideas to the discussion on why putting on outer clothing without assistance is important. For example, "Why should you put on your outer clothing without teacher's help or Mom's help? Why is it important to be able to put on your own outer clothing?" Have display board near coatroom that has manipulative materials to assist children in zipping zippers, tying, buttoning, snapping, etc.

2. **Identify specific behavior to be modeled.** When getting ready for recess or home, you put on your outer clothing without assistance.

3. **Model the behavior for the class.** Put outer clothing on by yourself, describing in detail what you are doing. Ask students to identify elements of the modeled behavior. Reinforce students who make good responses.

4. **Have class practice the behavior.** Give each student an opportunity to put on outer clothing, without assistance. Have students practice with difficult

items until they've mastered them. A chart could be provided listing names of clothing items to be checked off as each child demonstrates ability to put on the clothing independently.

5. **Recognize those students who correctly put on outer clothing without assistance in the modeling situation.**

6. **Maintain desired behavior by recognizing students who put on outer clothing independently.**

Code: S-SR-SC-0004-L1-Ir

TEACHING STRATEGY

Objective: Student puts on outer clothing without assistance.

Social Reinforcement

1. **Identify and recognize by name target student when observed putting on outer clothing without assistance.** Call attention to specific actions, e.g., "Tracy, you did a super job of putting your coat, hat, and mittens on by yourself." "Jim, I liked the way you put your coat on by yourself. Great!"

2. **Provide cues to the target student by praising others around the student who are appropriately putting on their outer clothing without assistance.** Then watch for the behavior in the target child and reinforce it.

Note: If social reinforcement in the form of winks, smiles, hugs, praise, etc., is not sufficient to increase the desired behavior, it may be necessary to accompany social reinforcement with tangible reinforcement, e.g., check marks, stars, tokens, etc., to be exchanged for something the child wants.

Code: S-SR-SC-0004-L1-Ic

TEACHING STRATEGY

Objective: Student puts on outer clothing without assistance.

Contingency Management

1. **Present task to student in specific terms.** Outer clothing (coats, sweaters, jackets, mittens) are to be put on without teacher assistance. (Check and make sure student learns how to put on each outer garment unassisted.)

2. **Plan reinforcement strategy selected from reinforcement menu.** Define a consequence valued by the student that will be given following demonstration of desired behavior of putting on outer clothing without assistance.

3. **State the contingency.** If student puts on outer clothing without assistance, he or she will receive the agreed-upon positive consequence.

4. **Watch for the behavior to occur naturally and reinforce it when it occurs according to established contingency,** or set up a situation in which the behavior will occur. For example, in a given time interval, the students are to put on outer clothing without assistance before going out to recess. If students beat the timer, they will receive extra recess time.

5. **Example.** Ms. Mitchell observed that Tami was very slow in putting on her outer clothing and often asked for help, even though Ms. Mitchell has observed that at times Tami could get completely dressed by herself. Ms. Mitchell set up a contract whereby Tami would earn a star for each occasion where she could put on her coat, hat, mittens, boots, etc., by herself without asking for help. When she earned a given number of stars, she could eat lunch with Ms. Mitchell. After the terms of this contract were met, Ms. Mitchell changed the contingency to requiring that Tami put on her clothing independently within a certain time limit before earning a star.

Skill:	To keep face and hands clean. **S-SR-SC-0006-L1**
Objective:	Student washes face and hands as needed.
Assessment:	Assess from previous knowledge of student or through direct observation using the <u>Social Behavior Assessment Inventory</u>.

Code: S-SR-SC-0006-L1-Im

TEACHING STRATEGY

Objective: Student washes face and hands as needed.

Social Modeling

1. **Identify a need for the behavior through a classroom discussion.** Use stories, films, or other aids where available. Have students contribute ideas to the discussion of why we wash face and hands. For example, "When should you wash your face and hands? Why is it important to have clean face and hands? Who can tell the best way to wash face and hands?" Write key phrases on the board.

2. **Identify specific behaviors to be modeled.** When face and hands are dirty, wash them.

3. **Model the behavior for the class either by having teacher model or by selecting a student.** Have the student go to the sink. As other students watch, explain why student is washing face and hands and point out what he or she is doing. Return to seats. Ask students to identify elements of the modeled behavior. Reinforce students who make good responses.

4. **Have class practice the behavior.** Give each student opportunity to demonstrate the appropriate behavior by going to the sink and washing face and hands.

5. **Praise those students who wash face and hands appropriately during the modeling situation.**

6. **Maintain appropriate behavior of washing face and hands through reinforcement.**

Code: S-SR-SC-0006-L1-Ir

TEACHING STRATEGY

Objective: Student washes face and hands as needed.

Social Reinforcement

1. **Identify and recognize by name target student when observed washing face and hands when needed.** Call attention to specific actions, e.g., "Billy, what a handsome, clean face;" "Sharon, I liked the way you came in and washed your hands and face after recess."

2. **Cue, in target student, appropriate behavior of washing face and hands when dirty by praising others who are washing their faces and hands when appropriate.** Then watch for the behavior in the target child and reinforce it.

   Note: If social reinforcement in the form of praise, attention, winks, smiles, etc., is not sufficient to increase the desired behavior, it may be necessary to accompany social reinforcement with tangible reinforcement, e.g., points, trading stamps, stars, coupons, etc., to be exchanged for something the child wants.

Code: S-SR-SC-0006-L1-Ic

TEACHING STRATEGY

Objective: Student washes face and hands as needed.

Contingency Management

1. **Present task to student in specific terms.** When your face and hands are dirty, wash them. If needed, provide pictures depicting students washing dirty faces and hands or put up reminder signs.

2. **Plan reinforcement strategy selected from reinforcement menu.** Define a consequence valued by the student that will be given following demonstration of acceptable behavior of washing face and hands.

3. **State the contingency.** If student remembers to wash face and hands when they are dirty, he or she will receive the agreed-upon consequence.

4. **Watch for behavior to occur naturally and reinforce it according to the established contingency,** or set up a situation for the behavior to occur. Arrange times before lunch, after recess, etc., for students to visit washroom; then check students for clean faces and hands. Students who have not washed hands and face adequately may be asked to return to the washroom again.

5. **Example.** Ms. Cornelius had several children who did not wash their faces and hands. Ms. Cornelius designed an area by the sink with a mirror, paper towels, and individual boxes containing soap. She explained to her students that they were to wash faces and hands when dirty, e.g., after recess, after physical education, after and before lunch, etc. She would check faces and hands three or four times daily. If hands and face were clean, the student would receive a star on a chart. On Friday, stars would be exchanged for special privileges.

260

6

TASK-RELATED BEHAVIORS

ASKING AND ANSWERING QUESTIONS

S-TR-AQ-0002-L1-S — To answer or attempt to answer a question when called on by teacher.

S-TR-AQ-0004-L1-S — To acknowledge when one does not know the answer to a question.

S-TR-AQ-0006-L1-S — To volunteer an answer to teacher's question.

S-TR-AQ-0008-L2-S — To ask a question appropriate to the information needed.

Skill:	To answer or attempt to answer a question when called on by teacher. **S-TR-AQ-0002-L1**
Objective:	Student answers or attempts to answer questions when called on by the teacher.
Assessment:	Assess from previous knowledge of student or through direct observation using the <u>Social Behavior Assessment Inventory</u>.

Code: S-TR-AQ-0002-L1-Im

TEACHING STRATEGY

Objective: Student answers or attempts to answer questions when called on by the teacher.

Social Modeling

1. **Set the stage.** Teacher tells the following story. Jimmy was on a TV game show last Thursday night. The winning prize was a free trip to Disneyland! All that Jimmy needed to do to win the great trip was to answer a question.

   The man asked Jimmy, "What holiday do we celebrate on December 25th?" Jimmy thought, "I think the answer is Christmas, but I'm not sure. I might be wrong, and then I will lose for sure! Christmas is probably the right answer, but I could be wrong."

The man said, "You only have 15 more seconds to answer."

Jimmy was so afraid he would be wrong, and the time was quickly ticking away. . ."What would you do?"

2. **Identify the specific steps.**

    (a) Children offer ideas on what they would do in Jimmy's situation.

    (1) "A good guess is better than not saying anything."
    (2) "Keep thinking about it until he's sure."

    (b) Discuss Jimmy's feelings if he didn't answer the big question, lost the prize, and then found out he was right after all. Relate this to answering questions in the classroom by asking:

    (1) "What would you do if a teacher asked you a question and you weren't sure of the answer?" (Student response.) "Why?"
    (2) "What would you think if you were the teacher, and a student didn't answer your question?" (Student response.)

3. **Model the behavior.** "Let's imagine this is a TV game show. I'll be the M.C., and Susie, you be the first contestant." (Arrange with a student who has demonstrated this skill to role-play with you. Have the selected student join you and your instructional group at the appropriate time.)

    "Welcome to the fantastic new big game show—'Take a Guess.' Here is our first contestant, Susie Cue. Susie Cue, you have the chance of a lifetime. By answering three questions, you will win a fantastic around-the-school cruise. Here's your first question: 'Who discovered America?'" (Student response.) "Very good, Susie, you through about the question and gave me a correct answer. Now, your second question: 'Why are criminals locked up?'" (Student response.) When student hesitates, encourage him or her by saying, "Take a guess."

    "Great, you took a guess at the answer." (If correct, give praise for correctness. If incorrect, go on to the next one.) "Now, your final question: 'Why should we keep our thermometers set on 68 degrees in the winter?'" (Student response.) Handle student response in fashion similar to that previously outlined.

    "You answered all three questions. When you were not sure of the answer, you took a guess. You have won that fantastic around-the-school cruise. I hope you enjoy the trip." (The idea of the game show can be played up or down depending on your preference. Repeat the game with one or more of the students in the class using your own questions. Be sure to recognize attempts at answering the questions.)

4. **Practice the behavior.** Teach a lesson that is normally scheduled and that requires students to volunteer answers in class. Ask questions of varying degrees of difficulty. Recognize correct answers and attempts. Be cautious not to punish incorrect answers, but reinforce child for attempting. For example, "Thank you for volunteering an answer;" "John, I'm pleased you answered my question;" "Sally, you have done an outstanding job of participating in our discussion."

5. **Maintenance.** Use one or more of the following:
   (a) Continue to reinforce students in classroom situations with verbal praise for attempting to answer questions.
   (b) Ask students at end of morning or end of reading group to tell you whom they observed volunteering answers to the teacher's questions.
   (c) Have one or two children record the number volunteering responses of designated pupils during a discussion period. Make a wall chart with each pupil's name across the bottom and numbers in the left-hand column. Record cumulatively, the number of volunteering responses for each pupil for a week. At the end of a week, determine if the wall chart needs to be continued.
6. **Additional suggestions.**
   (a) Students may offer inappropriate answers. Ignore this behavior and comment on well-thought-out answers by saying, "John, you really thought about that question. Good job."
   (b) Pass out "I Volunteered" buttons to students volunteering good answers in class.
   (c) If a student attempts to answer a question and is ridiculed by the others, say, "Susie, you did a good job because you tried. It's very important to try. I like that."
   (d) If social reinforcement is not adequate to establish and maintain the "answering behavior," attach backup reinforcers to the wall chart described above.

Code: S-TR-AQ-0002-L1-Ir

TEACHING STRATEGY

Objective: Student answers or attempts to answer questions when called on by the teacher.

Social Reinforcement

1. **Recognize students when they answer or attempt to answer a question when called on.** Recognize specific behavior. "Cynthia, you answered the question very well." "Jonathan, you made a good effort to answer the question." "Kevin, I'm glad you tried to answer the question."
2. **Provide cues by recognizing other students who answer questions.** Also cue answers by calling on student for an answer and providing prompts or restating the question if he or she has difficulty giving an answer.

Code: S-TR-AQ-0002-L1-Ic

TEACHING STRATEGY

Objective: Student answers or attempts to answer questions when called on by the teacher.

Contingency Management

1. **State the task in observable terms.** When you are called on to answer a question, make an effort to answer, even when you are not sure your answer is correct.

2. **Plan reinforcement.**

3. **State the contingency.** If the student answers or attempts to answer a question, he will be rewarded. Specify the amount of reinforcement.

4. **Set up a situation, a class discussion, or example in which students are asked to answer questions.** Observe the answering behavior and reward those who answer or attempt to answer questions according to the contingency set-up.

5. **Example.** Dujuan is shy and seldom volunteers to answer questions. When called on, his typical response is to lower his eyes to the floor, shrug his shoulders, and mumble, "I don't know." Ms. Daniels suspects that Dujuan really does know the answer to some of the questions she asks him and decides to contract with Dujuan. "When I ask you a question, if you answer or try to answer, I'll give you a point in my book. As soon as you have 10 points, you may be the person to get the gym equipment at recess." Ms. Daniels makes sure that the questions she asks are simple, and she gives hints to help him answer to make sure it is easy for him to earn the reward. She gradually increases the difficulty of the questions and discontinues the prompts. She rewards him for making a conscientious effort to answer rather than having a completely correct answer, and she accompanies the points with verbal praise.

Skill:	To acknowledge when one does not know the answer to a question. **S-TR-AQ-0004-L1**
Objective:	When asked a question to which the student does not know the answer, the student will reply that he or she doesn't know.
Assessment:	Assess from previous knowledge of student or through direct observation using the <u>Social Behavior Assessment Inventory</u>.

Code: S-TR-AQ-0004-L1-Im

TEACHING STRATEGY

Objective: When asked a question to which the student does not know the answer, the student will reply that he or she doesn't know.

Social Modeling

1. **Set the stage.** Play the game of "20 Questions." Before playing the game, prepare 3 x 5 cards for each pupil. On one card print "I know," and on the other card print "I don't know." Tell the students that in this game there are two ways to answer:

   (a) If you know the answer hold up the card that says "I know," wait to be called on, and give the answer.

(b) If you don't have any idea about the correct answer hold up the card that says "I don't know" and say, "I don't know" when called on.

Teacher can then ask questions that the children will know and questions they will not know. Below are some sample questions:

(1) What is your name?

(2) What is big, red, and used by firefighters?

(3) How many planets are in our solar system?

(4) What is my name?

(5) How many people are in the world?

(6) What shines in the sky at night?

(7) What is 1.265 times 6,024?

(8) How old are you?

(9) What are the seasons of the year?

(10) Who is President of the United States?

(11) Who is our Governor?

(12) How many miles is it to Miami, Florida?

(13) How many days in a year?

(14) What is Disneyland?

(15) Who is _____(principal's name)?

(16) What can you do with an umbrella?

(17) What is the capital of California?

(18) Please count to 10.

(19) How many birds are there in the world?

(20) What is 10 + 30?

After each question during the game, respond by saying, "Very good, Jim. You knew the answer and you said it;" "Bob, you didn't know the answer, and you said you didn't. That's the way to answer when you don't know." When the game is completed, collect the cards. Discuss the students' responses, review the two ways of answering questions and relate this to class discussions. You can ask "Why is it good to say 'I don't know' when you are sure you don't know the answer?" If the following reasons are not offered, mention them to the class:

(a) Wild guesses are time-consuming.

(b) Wild guesses are confusing to other class members and the teacher.

(c) Saying "I don't know" tells the teacher what he or she needs to teach and saves a lot of class time.

2. **Identify specific behaviors.** Say, "Josh, what will you do in class when you're called on and do not know the answer to the teacher's question?" (Student response.) "That's excellent, Josh. When you don't know the answer, the thing to do is to say, 'I don't know.' However, when you think you know the answer but are not absolutely sure, say, "I am not sure." (See S-TR-AQ-0002 for suggestions on how to encourage answering questions.)

3. **Model the behavior.**

(a) Ask one student to be the teacher and select two others who have previously demonstrated this skill, to be students. This should be arranged prior to the time of doing this activity. Begin by having "teacher" ask questions similar to game questions. Encourage the "teacher" to verbally reinforce students that respond, "I don't know," as well as those who give correct responses.

(b) Give other students opportunities to be teacher in role-playing situations.

4. Practice the behavior.

(a) Conduct a discussion over a previously completed assignment. Explain to the group that you want them to practice what they have learned and respond by saying, "I don't know," when you call on them to answer a question to which they do not know the correct answer. Verbally reinforce students who demonstrate appropriate behavior.

(b) During the remainder of the day "pop a question" every 15 minutes or so and then reinforce students' appropriate answers. Again, there could be questions the child definitely knows along with questions the student wouldn't know.

(c) During reading discussions, or in any academic area, respond to students' answers by reinforcing answers that are appropriate and by praising students for saying, "I don't know."

5. Reinforcement.

(a) Prepare 200 raffle tickets. Pass out a raffle ticket to pupils each time they respond to questions by giving correct answer, and/or saying "I don't know." At the end of the day collect all the raffle tickets and hold a drawing. Award two or three prizes.

(b) Recognize a student for answering the question or saying, "I don't know."

6. Additional suggestions.

(a) In playing "20 Questions," you may wish to add a third option. This would be, "I'm not sure, but I think the answer is. . ." Some questions to add to the game may be:

(1) What holiday comes on July 4th?

(2) What is our Vice-President's name?

(3) What are the days of the week?

(4) How do you spell "wonderful?"

(5) How many days in a year?

Give feedback on these questions by saying, "Nice try, Susie. You weren't sure, but you made a good try."

(b) You should gear "20 Questions" to appropriate grade level.

Code: S-TR-AQ-0004-L1-Ir

TEACHING STRATEGY

Objective: When asked a question to which the student does not know the answer, the student will reply that he or she doesn't know.

Social Reinforcement

1. **Identify by name and recognize the target student when he or she says, "I don't know," to a question whose answer he or she doesn't know.** Praise the behavior in specific terms. "Lenny, I'm glad you said you didn't know when I asked you that question rather than try to guess;" "Margaret, I'm glad you told us you didn't know where Pakistan is rather than guessing. It helps me teach you when I know what you don't know."

2. **Provide cues to the target student.**
   (a) Remind students before asking questions that they should say, "I don't know," if they can't answer the question.
   (b) Praise other students who say, "I don't know," to a question whose answer they do not know.

   Note: This objective is designed primarily for students who attempt to bluff or make wild guesses rather than admit they don't know. Students should still be encouraged to try to answer questions if they think they know the answer (TR-AQ-0002).

Code: S-TR-AQ-0004-L1-Ic

TEACHING STRATEGY

Objective: When asked a question to which the student does not know the answer, the student will reply that he or she doesn't know.

Contingency Management

1. **Describe in specific terms the desired behavior.** When you do not know the answer to a question, say, "I don't know," or something similar.

2. **Plan reinforcement.**

3. **Establish a contingency.** If you say, "I don't know," when you don't know the answer to a question, you will receive the reward we agreed on.

   Note: In order not to extinguish the behavior developed in Skill TR-AQ-0002, i.e., in answering or attempting to answer a question, it is best to emphasize the skill mainly for students who are reluctant to admit they don't know something and instead engage in wild guessing.

4. **Watch for the behavior to occur naturally.** Reward it when it occurs, or set up a situation for the behavior to occur by asking questions of the student.

5. **Example.** Roy had developed a pattern of bluffing and guessing when he was asked questions in class. It appeared to his teacher, Ms. Spring, that he might be embarrassed to admit he did not know something. She noted also that his classmates often laughed at his wild answers, and she suspected that he was being reinforced by their attention. Ms. Spring took him aside and talked to him about the behavior she would prefer, i.e., that he would say, "I don't know," rather than guess when he didn't know an answer. She told him she wanted him to try to answer questions when he really knew the answer. She set up a contingency that would be a secret contract between the two of them. She would keep track of times he either said, "I don't know," or gave a good answer to a question. A good answer

would be worth two points, saying, "I don't know," would be worth one point, and a wild answer would cause him to lose a point. Roy agreed to work on the contract and decided that he would like to exchange his points for special privilege coupons.

Skill:	To volunteer an answer to teacher's question. **S-TR-AQ-0006-L1**
Objective:	Student volunteers the answer to the teacher's question in a way appropriate to the situation.
Assessment:	Assess from previous knowledge of student or through direct observation using the <u>Social Behavior Assessment Inventory</u>.

Code: S-TR-AQ-0006-L1-Im

TEACHING STRATEGY

Objective: Student volunteers the answer to the teacher's question in a way appropriate to the situation.

Social Modeling

1. **Set the stage.** Begin by telling this story. "I need some help from you. This story is a mystery. It is called 'The Magic Show Mystery,' and you will need to solve it. Listen carefully."

   "There was a wonderful magic show in our city with a magician that could do every mysterious trick there is. Many children went to see this magic man because he was so good. One night during the show, Mr. Magic asked for someone from the audience to come up on stage and help him with his very best trick. All the children wanted to be the helper, and each boy and girl wanted to be chosen. Bret was a quiet little boy and kind of shy. He wanted very badly to be Mr. Magic's helper, but he was afraid to raise his hand. So Bret just sat and stared at Mr. Magic and didn't move a muscle. Brenda was sitting next to Bret, and she wasn't afraid to move at all. In fact, Brenda waved her hand so much she nearly fell out of her chair. She waved and yelled, 'Pick me, Mr. Magic. Pick me!' Mr. Magic looked at Brenda for a few minutes and then looked at the next girl—it was Maggie. There sat Maggie in her chair. She had a big smile on her face, and her hand was raised. Maggie wasn't moving, just smiling at Mr. Magic and raising her hand. Guess what? Mr. Magic chose Maggie for his helper!"

   (a) Say, "The mystery is why did Mr. Magic choose Maggie?" Discuss reasons why Mr. Magic chose Maggie.

   (1) She raised her hand.

   (2) She smiled at Mr. Magic.

   (3) She sat still.

   (4) She was quiet.

   (b) "Bret wanted very much to be chosen and so did Brenda, but they were not chosen. Why were Bret and Brenda probably not chosen?" Discuss reasons why they were not chosen:

268

(1) Bret did not volunteer; Mr. Magic had no way of knowing he wanted to be on stage.

(2) Brenda made too much noise and did not stay in her seat.

(3) Summarize by saying, "Maggie volunteered in a way appropriate to the situation."

(c) Say, "Just like Mr. Magic in the 'Magic Show Mystery,' I sometimes need pupils to volunteer to do certain jobs and to participate in group discussions. What would happen if I asked a question and no one volunteered an answer?" (Since it may happen following this question, be prepared to use the silence as an example.) (Student response.) "That's exactly right, Mindy. Nothing would happen until I say or do something else. If no one volunteers then there is no discussion."

2. **Identify the steps.** Say, "How do you volunteer in a class discussion?" (Student responses may include "Raise your hand and wait to be called on," "Stand up and wait your turn," or "Start talking as soon as no one else is talking.") List the responses on the board. Next, point out what is appropriate in your classroom. For example, "During class discussion where all of us are participating, the correct way to volunteer is to raise your hand, remain quiet, and speak when called on." Prepare a poster depicting these steps.

3. **Model the behavior.** Have a student play the teacher's role. He or she will ask questions of the group. Questions provided in a reading text or other regular material the class is working on could be used. In the role of student, volunteer to answer by raising your hand and providing answers. Be sure to model all three of the listed behaviors. After you model the behaviors, ask pupils to demonstrate the behaviors.

4. **Practice the behavior.** Have class practice the behavior asking each student to volunteer answers to simple questions in a structured situation requiring hand raising.

5. **Additional suggestions.**

(a) In this skill a distinction should be made between situations where the student answers when called on and those where the student volunteers the answer without initial prompting.

(b) Teach pupils the correct way to volunteer in situations where hand raising is not required in order to volunteer. (See IP-MC-0006-L1-S.)

Code: S-TR-AQ-0006-L1-Ir

TEACHING STRATEGY

Objective: Student volunteers the answer to the teacher's question in a way appropriate to the situation.

Social Reinforcement

1. **Recognize student who volunteers answers in a manner appropriate to the situation.** Be specific. "George, you answered that question very well. I liked the way you raised your hand."

2. **Use social reinforcement when you observe the target student volunteering the answer to yours question.** Call attention to specific actions.

"Williamea, you raised your hand and waited to be called on to answer my question;" "Darien, I'm glad you answered my question. It was a good point to mention;" "Nimrod waited to answer when no one else was talking."

3. **Cue target student to volunteer answers by praising others who volunteer answers to your questions.** For a student who very seldom volunteers, it might be necessary to provide an additional incentive by pairing social reinforcement with a tangible reinforcer.

4. **Often the best reinforcer for volunteering is to be called on to give the answer.** Try to call on those students who seldom volunteer as soon as they are seen volunteering.

Code: S-TR-AQ-0006-L1-Ic

TEACHING STRATEGY

Objective: Student volunteers the answer to the teacher's question in a way appropriate to the situation.

Contingency Management

1. **State the task to the student in observable terms.** When the teacher asks a question and you think you know the answer, or even part of the answer, raise your hand. When the teacher calls on you, give the answer.

2. **Plan reinforcement strategy selected from the reinforcement menu.**

3. **State the contingency.** If the student volunteers answers to your questions in a way that is appropriate to the situation, he or she will be rewarded. Criteria for reward for this skill should vary according to the needs of the student. A student who seldom volunteers should be rewarded for any attempt to volunteer an answer, regardless of the content. Students who volunteer frequently with irrelevant content will need to be reinforced only when the content is appropriate. Students who volunteer frequently with appropriate content but in inappropriate ways will need to be reinforced only when they follow the guidelines that have been established, such as raising hands and waiting to be called on.

4. **Set up a situation to necessitate students' volunteering answers to your questions.** For example, have a discussion, structured or free. Ask questions without calling on anyone by name. Wait for volunteers and reward those who emit appropriate behavior.

5. **Example.** Very few students in Ms. Cartledge's class volunteer answers to questions in class discussion, even though many of them know the answers. She suspects that at least some of the students are afraid of ridicule from some of the more aggressive members of the class. She establishes a contingency with the class. With a grocery store counter, she will keep track of the number of volunteered answers to questions in class discussions. The answer will have to be relevant to be counted, but it does not have to be completely correct. If it shows the person has been listening to the discussion, it will be counted. Each person who volunteers will be counted only once during any one discussion period to keep the same few people from volunteering all the answers. For every volunteered answer that is counted, the class earns a minute of extra recess. Ms. Cartledge also

talks to the class about polite ways to listen to others' answers and establishes that students could also lose extra recess minutes for making fun of anyone's answers.

Skill:	To ask a question appropriate to the information needed. **S-TR-AQ-0008-L2**
Objective:	Student asks a question appropriate to the information needed by using appropriate interrogative (who, what, why how, when) and phrasing a sentence so needed information is asked for.
Assessment:	Assess from previous knowledge of student or through direct observation using the <u>Social Behavior Assessment Inventory</u>.

Code: S-TR-AQ-0008-L2-Im

TEACHING STRATEGY

Objective: Student asks a question appropriate to the information needed by using appropriate interrogative (who, what why how, when) and phrasing sentence so needed information is asked for.

Social Modeling

1. **Set the stage.** Prepare enough invitations to pass out one to each pupil. Say, "Imagine you got this invitation in the mail. The only information on the card is the fact that there is going to be a party with a telephone number in the corner. What would you do?" (Student response.) If pupils do not indicate that they would ask questions, you can ask a second question which may produce a response, e.g., "What are some questions you can ask when you call the telephone number?" Questions to ask include who, what, when, where, and why.

Ask one volunteer to use imaginary telephone and find out about the party. Answer questions of student on the "telephone." You may also be the first caller in order to more clearly demonstrate appropriate questions. Dialogue may flow like this:

Caller: Hello, I got your note in the mail. Who is having the party?

Response:

Caller: What kind of party is it?

Response:

Caller: Where is the party?

Response:

Caller: When is the party?

Response:

Caller: Why is the party being held?

2. **Identify the specific steps.** The teacher should encourage discussion by asking:
   (a) Did the invitation tell us the important things?
       (1) What did it leave out?
       (2) How would you find out more about the party?
   (b) What words help us ask a question? (Answer: who, what, why, where, when.)
   (c) Are the words good enough by themselves or do we need a good sentence? (e.g., What? What did you ask me to do?) Have children give examples.
   (d) Summarize the discussion by saying, "Sometimes, as in the case of this party invitation, we need to have more information. We find out what we need to know by asking questions. To ask a question:
       (1) Use an interrogative: 'who, what, why, how, when, where.'
       (2) Use a complete sentence that tells exactly what you want to know.

   "Someone give me an example of a question that we used to find out more about the party." (Student response.) Recognize appropriate responses.

3. **Model and practice the behavior.** A version of "What's My Line?" will serve the purpose of modeling and practicing very well. Begin by asking for a volunteer who knows his or her father's or mother's occupation and will answer questions. Ask questions of the pupil until you can guess the occupation or you have used 20 questions. After you have modeled the behavior, another pupil volunteer can be used while the class members (one at a time) ask questions.

   As an alternative you could assign one student a job, and have the others ask appropriate questions to find out the assigned job. Whisper a job to another student (e.g., doctor, plumber, mailman, minister, teacher, etc.). Other students who raise hands, are called on by student, and ask appropriate questions.

4. **Reinforcement.**
   (a) At the beginning of the school day, you may elicit questions from students about the day's activities. For example, you can say, "You may ask some questions about what we will be doing today." Recognize good questioning techniques by the students. Say such specific things as, "That was a good question, Carol. You used a complete sentence to ask for information."
   (b) Keep a tally on a chart about the number of good questions asked by each student. The student with the most appropriately asked questions could be chosen as "teacher" for morning questions. Beforehand, relate daily activities so "teacher" will be able to answer students' questions.

5. **Additional suggestions.**
   (a) Adapt games such as "20 Questions" or "I've Got a Secret" as practice exercises.
   (b) During class discussions or reading groups, reward students for asking appropriate questions. Be specific in praising the child.

Code: S-TR-AQ-0008-L2-Ir

TEACHING STRATEGY

Objective: Student asks a question appropriate to the information needed by using appropriate interrogative (who, what why how, when) and phrasing sentence so needed information is asked for.

Social Reinforcement

1. **Identify target student and recognize by name when observed asking a question properly.** Call attention to specific actions. "Ashley, you remembered to use a question word. You asked, 'who.'" "Art, you started your question very well." "Devon asked his question properly by using words that told me exactly what he wanted to know."
2. **Cue appropriate questioning behavior in target student by recognizing others who are asking questions in an appropriate way.** If the target student follows the cue, reward him or her.
3. **Provide additional cues with a posted list of question words.**

Code: S-TR-AQ-0008-L2-Ic

TEACHING STRATEGY

Objective: Student asks a question appropriate to the information needed by using appropriate interrogative (who, what why how, when) and phrasing sentence so needed information is asked for.

Contingency Management

1. **State task in observable terms.**
    (a) Use interrogative words, such as who, what, why, how, when, where.
    (b) Use a complete sentence.
    (c) Tell exactly what it is you want to know.

    If needed, post a list of question words.
2. **Plan reinforcement strategy selected from reinforcement menu.**
3. **State the contingency.** If student asks a necessary question properly, he or she will be rewarded. Specify amount of reinforcement.
4. **Watch for behavior to occur naturally and reinforce it when it occurs according to established contingency,** or, set up a situation to necessitate asking questions. For example, give incomplete assignment, assign group discussion, play "I've Got a Secret." Observe questioning behavior and reward those who follow it correctly.
5. **Example.** Mr. Beagle has one student, Gretchen, who does not ask questions properly. She does not use interrogatives and phrases her sentences poorly. Mr. Beagle puts a list of question words on her desk: who, what, where, why, when, how. He tells her to use one of these words when she wants to ask a question. He has her demonstrate that she understands by having her ask a question using "what" in a complete sentence. He tells her that when she asks questions using one of these words in a complete

sentence, she will receive a star. When she has 10 stars, she can take a favorite book home overnight. Mr. Beagle watches her closely, at first rewarding her with a star for each good question, and praising her verbally. After her questions are consistently asked in the correct manner, he begins to reward for every two questions, then every five, gradually eliminating all but recognition.

ATTENDING BEHAVIOR

S-TR-AT-0002-L1-S   To look at the teacher when a lesson is being presented.

S-TR-AT-0004-L1-S   To watch an audiovisual presentation quietly.

S-TR-AT-0006-L1-S   To listen to someone speaking to the class.

Skill:	To look at the teacher when a lesson is being presented. **S-TR-AT-0002-L1**
Objective:	Student looks at the teacher when he or she is presenting a lesson.
Assessment:	Assess from previous knowledge of student or through direct observation using the <u>Social Behavior Assessment Inventory</u>.

Code: S-TR-AT-0002-L1-Im

TEACHING STRATEGY

Objective: Student looks at the teacher when he or she is presenting a lesson.

Social Modeling

1. **Set the stage.** Introduce the following game by saying, "Today we're going to play 'Look and Tell.' This game requires looking and telling about what you see. Who wants to play first?" (Student response.) "Thanks for raising your hand, Jake. You may be first. Please come to the front of the room." (Student response.) "Jake, please take a good look at me." (Give child maximum of 10 seconds to look.) "Now, turn around and face the class." (Stands directly behind pupil.) "All right, tell the class what I'm wearing." (When student response is general, e.g., "dress," ask questions to help him describe what you're wearing, e.g., "Tell me more about my dress.") (Student response.) (Have student describe at least four aspects of your wearing apparel.) "Wow, that was fantastic! Jake, you really are a good observer. You may return to your seat."

   "Who wants to be next?" (Student response.) "Sandra and Tim, come to the front of the room." (Student response.) "Sandra, take a good look at Tim." (Give student maximum of 10 seconds to look.) "All right, Tim, you stand here and Sandra you here." (Position Tim a few feet behind Sandra and about three feet to her left or right. Have both students face forward.) "Now, Sandra describe what Tim is wearing." (Praise other members of the class for not helping Sandra, e.g., "I'm glad the class is quiet and listening.") (Student response.) "Wow! That's a good description. What else can you say?" (Student response.) Again have pupil describe at least four different aspects of the other pupil. Repeat this procedure with two other pupils as needed.

   (After you have finished game, begin a discussion.) Ask, "What were Jake, Sandra...just doing?" (Student response.) Shape responses by adding cues if necessary. Possible cues include pointing to your eye and making looking motion with your head, saying,"What do we do with our eyes?" "Wow! Jackie you were doing it too; you were watching (or observing) Jake, Sandra...as they observed and then described what they saw."

Ask, "When do we need to be good watchers (or lookers or observers) in school?" (Student response.) "Right, Jim. When is another time?" (Student response.) "Yes, very good! Why do we need to be good observers?" (Student response.) Praise appropriate responses and solicit more ideas until list seems to be exhausted, i.e., until there is a long silence, 15 seconds or more.

2. **Identify the specific steps.** This step may be delayed until another session or may follow immediately. "What specific behaviors make up 'looking at the teacher?'" Give example if there is a lull. Examples: sitting in seat or standing with face in the direction of the teacher; eyes are directed at the teacher; eyes and/or head moves and follows teacher as she moves; when teacher points, we look in the direction she has pointed. Try to draw these from the class. Mention the behaviors if you are not able to bring them out in discussion. List the behaviors on the blackboard. Have students paraphrase the specific steps of the behavior.

3. **Model the behavior.** Assign one student to "play teacher" and to pretend he or she is teaching a lesson to the class. Sit in the student's chair, or where the rest of the class can see you easily, and model appropriate looking at the teacher. Ask students to describe your behavior. Reward appropriate responses with praise. For contrast, you might combine appropriate looking with looking out the windows, under the desk, at other students. Ask students to indicate which is correct "looking" behavior by raising their hands when they see a correct behavior. **Caution:** Don't overplay the incorrect behavior. You want the pupils to remember the correct behaviors, not the incorrect ones.

4. **Practice activity.** Say, "Now let's practice this behavior." Teach a lesson that you and the children will enjoy. A lesson that requires a demonstration by you is preferable to one where you just talk. As you teach the lesson, move around as much as possible. Observe for the specific behaviors listed as steps of "looking at the teacher." Give descriptive praise **often,** e.g., "Jake, you are looking right at me. Great. All of you are sitting in your chairs with your faces in my direction. Wonderful!"

5. **Maintenance.** To maintain the behavior, continue to give descriptive praise for "looking at the teacher." At first it may be necessary to use a symbolic form of reinforcement. Following is a description of an appropriate technique.

You may construct a large thermometer on tag board. It should be constructed on tag board approximately 20" x 30" and posted in a prominent location in the room. Make small name plates for each pupil.

You will also need to make thermometers for the pupils to use. A thermometer could be drawn on a ditto master and reproduced in quantity needed.

Pass out the individual thermometers to pupils and say, "These sheets have a thermometer on them that will go up when you look at me as I'm teaching a lesson. Here's how it works. I will set the timer for one minute. When the timer rings, I will tell everyone who was looking at me to color five degrees of his or her thermometer beginning at the bottom. At the end of the lesson, everyone will come to the front of the room and place his or her name plate on the big thermometer opposite the number of degrees on his or her own thermometer." (Practice for three minutes to be sure the pupils understand the thermometer's operation.) Praise looking behavior. As the children progress, increase the amount of time required to raise thermometer five degrees; also include more of the day in the system on a gradual basis.

6. **Additional suggestions.**

   (a) If the placing of the name tags on the big thermometer gets to be a problem, you may assume responsibility for moving the children's name tags the appropriate number of degrees.

   (b) As an alternative, choose the following procedure: Set a timer for two to five minutes (time varies depending on student). When the timer goes off, students who are looking at you will be reinforced with extra free time—one to five minutes. Walk to each of these students and give him or her a card that says, "You are a good looker. Take _____ extra minutes during free time." The reinforcer may be modified to meet the student's needs by writing any reinforcer that the pupil has earned on the card. For example, "For looking at the teacher, you have earned _____."

   Materials: 3 x 5 index cards with the information shown above printed on them.

   Note: Establish what the students would like to do most.

   (c) If a student is not learning this skill, check your expectations. You may have to begin with one of the steps of the skill and shape the desired behavior of looking at you when you are presenting a lesson.

Code: S-TR-AT-0002-L1-Ir

TEACHING STRATEGY

Objective: Student looks at the teacher when he or she is presenting a lesson.

Social Reinforcement

1. **Identify by name and recognize the target student when he or she is observed looking at you while a lesson is being presented.** Tell the child what he or she is being praised for. "Tony, thank you for watching me while I talk;" "Marie, I like the way you're looking at me;" "John's eyes are on me."

2. **Remind the target student to look at you by praising others nearby for looking at you.** Praise the target student immediately when he or she starts to look at you.

Code: S-TR-AT-0002-L1-Ic

TEACHING STRATEGY

Objective: Student looks at the teacher when he or she is presenting a lesson.

Contingency Management

1. **State the task in observable terms.** The student looks in the direction of the teacher or the materials the teacher is presenting for the major portion of the teacher's lesson presentation.
2. **Plan reinforcement from reinforcement menu.**
3. **State the contingencies.** If the student looks at you or the materials you are presenting continuously during a lesson, the student will be rewarded. If the student's rate of looking has been extremely low, begin contingency by specifying a short time during which he or she must watch you. As he or she meets with success, gradually increase watching time required for reward, until the student can "look" through an entire lesson.
4. **Present a lesson and observe the student looking at you as you speak.** When you are presenting materials, direct students' attention to the relevant things by saying, "Look at this," "Look here," or the equivalent, and pointing to the picture, words, figure, etc., to which you want the students to attend. Reward the target student after he or she fulfills his contract by looking the required amount of time. (He or she may not look 100% of the time, but reward if the student generally looked at you the major portion of the time.)

Skill:	To watch an audiovisual presentation quietly. S-TR-AT-0004-L1
Objective:	Student watches an audiovisual presentation, sitting relatively still and without speaking aloud.
Assessment:	Assess from previous knowledge of student or through direct observation using the <u>Social Behavior Assessment Inventory</u>.

Code: S-TR-AT-0004-L1-Im

TEACHING STRATEGY

Objective: Student watches an audiovisual presentation, sitting relatively still and without speaking aloud.

Social Modeling

1. **Set the stage and identify specific steps.** Ask, "Who knows how we are supposed to behave when we go to a religious service?" (Student response.) "Lou, tell us how to behave." (Student response.) "Wow, that was great! Now, who can show us how to behave?" (Student response.) Recognize students for appropriate behaviors. Say, "Name other instances where you would speak softly or sit very still." Have the students name five or six

places or instances. Reinforce verbally each student's appropriate answers. Say, "That's a very good example, Sue. You have all given me some excellent examples of times when we must sit still and speak very softly if we speak at all." Ask, "Why do we sit still and not speak in these situations?" (Student response.) As an alternative, you teacher could ask sample questions from the following list. When we are watching a (movie):

(a) Why should we sit quietly?

(b) Why should we talk softly?

(c) What should we do if we have to get up and leave?

(d) What happens if someone talks loudly?

(e) What happens if someone is wiggling in his or her seat?

2. **Audibly recognize correct answers by reflecting the various student responses.**

   Student's answer: You should talk quietly and sit still during a movie because other people may not be able to hear if you speak loudly. If you wiggle in your seat, it will cause people to look at you and miss the movie.

   Teacher: Very good. You feel that one should speak softly and sit still because this shows that you are considerate of others and do not want to distract those who are watching the movie.

   List the following behaviors on the chalkboard or prepare a poster:

   (a) Sitting with hands, feet, and body still.

   (b) Looking at the screen.

   (c) Keeping voice silent.

   For younger children, prepare a visual aid showing the scenes.

3. **Model the behavior for the class.** Show a movie or turn on the television. Take a seat among the students and show them the proper way to watch a presentation. Be sure to model each of the specific behaviors discussed above. Ask students to describe your behaviors. Recognize those students whose responses include the elements identified. Example: "Great, Jack. You said I was sitting still and looking at the screen."

4. **Practice activity.** Show a movie or television show. Ask the class to practice watching properly. (This practice activity may be delayed until the next day; however, if this is done you should review by repeating Step 3.) Inform the class that each minute they all sit quietly, keep voice silent and look at the screen you will flash a beam of light on the screen. (You will need a flashlight. Simply turn it on and off quickly when it's directed at the screen. Demonstrate the procedure for the children.) Arrange seating so that you will be able to walk behind each pupil without passing in front of another one. Give verbal praise to individual children by whispering.

5. **Maintain behavior through reinforcement.** For the first audiovisual presentation after the practice session, utilize the same reinforcement procedure and pass out special tickets when you give praise. Print tickets that have a miniature of the visual aid that was used in Step 2. Inform the pupils that the tickets they are earning can be used to buy popcorn at the end of the movie. One ticket buys 1/4 cup of popcorn. (Substitute another backup reinforcer if this one is not reinforcing for your class.)

Begin lengthening the time required for appropriate behavior before the reinforcers are given. The flashlight and verbal praise should be eliminated by the third audiovisual presentation since they will likely be distracting. Be sure to give praise after the audiovisual is finished, however. When you no longer pass out the tickets during a presentation, you will also begin to use the backup reinforcer only on an intermittent basis and eventually eliminate it except for special occasions.

6. **Additional suggestions.** To insure that the students can sit still quietly, play a game. "I'm going to count to three. Then I will begin to time you to see if we can sit still quietly for 15 seconds. . .Very good. Now let's see if we can do it for 30 seconds." Continue extending the time until target level is achieved. Reinforce the students with verbal praise. The class may be divided into teams competing against each other to see who watches the longest time in an appropriate way. Reinforce the winner by lining up first for lunch, bathroom, playground, or having first choice of playground equipment.

Code: S-TR-AT-0004-L1-Ir

TEACHING STRATEGY

Objective: Student watches an audiovisual presentation, sitting relatively still and without speaking aloud.

Social Reinforcement

1. **Identify by name and recognize aloud the target student when observed watching an audiovisual presentation quietly.** Tell the student what he or she is being praised for. "Nancy, you are watching very quietly. Thank you." "Jamie, you did a good job of sitting still during the movie." In order not to disrupt the ongoing program, immediate social reinforcement may need to be limited to nods, smiles, pats on the back.

2. **Cue the appropriate behavior in the target student if he or she isn't watching by reinforcing another student sitting nearby for watching carefully and quietly.** Reinforce target student immediately when he or she begins to watch the TV, movie, or other presentation quietly.

3. **Sometimes accompanying social reinforcement with a tangible reinforcer such as a token will help to increase sitting still and watching quietly.** This is particularly useful in a situation where the use of verbal praise may be disruptive.

Code: S-TR-AT-0004-L1-Ic

TEACHING STRATEGY

Objective: Student watches an audiovisual presentation, sitting relatively still and without speaking aloud.

Contingency Management

1. **State the task in observable terms.** The student will look at and listen to an audiovisual presentation such as a television show, movie, play, slide presentation, by sitting relatively still and without speaking aloud.

2. **Choose a reinforcement from reinforcement menu.**

3. **State the contingency.** If the student watches an audiovisual presentation, by sitting still and being quiet for a specified length of time, he or she will receive the specified reinforcement. The time should be set low in the beginning and gradually raised to include an entire presentation.

4. **When the student is given the opportunity to watch a movie or similar event with the class, reward him or her according to the established contingency for sitting still and being quiet for the specified time.**

5. **Example.** When the class goes to the auditorium for a movie, Brad creates problems for everyone around him by wiggling continuously and talking to other children. After talking with Brad and having him practice proper behavior, Ms. Downing contracts with him. She will give him a token when she sees him sitting quietly and not talking. If he can earn 10 of these during the movie, she will let him push the buttons to rewind the film and help her return the movie to the audiovisual room. Ms. Downing observes Brad and hands him a token with a pat on the back when she sees him behaving appropriately. She makes sure that she rewards him frequently enough that he earns the privilege. Occasionally she has to remind him by shaking her head and holding up the token when he starts to wiggle or talk. As soon as he settles down she hands it to him. After several periods of this approach she exchanges the privilege for a more general level of acceptable behavior.

Skill:	To listen to someone speaking to the class. **S-TR-AT-0006-L1**
Objective:	Student demonstrates that he or she has listened to the speaker by repeating some of what the person said.
Assessment:	Assess from previous knowledge of student or through direct observation using the <u>Social Behavior Assessment Inventory</u>.

Code: S-TR-AT-0006-L1-Im

TEACHING STRATEGY

Objective: Student demonstrates that he or she has listened to the speaker by repeating some of what the person said.

Social Modeling

1. **Set the stage.** Say, "Class, we're going to play a game. It's called 'How Well Do We Listen?'" Explain how the game is to be played. "I will tell the first student something, and he or she will in turn whisper what I said to the next person. You may whisper to the next person only once. Speak at your usual rate." Then whisper to the first person. The length and/or difficulty of the

message will vary according to the class level. All or part of the following example could be used, depending on the functioning level of the students.

"Yesterday, I went shopping at _____ Shopping Center after school. While I was shopping, I saw Jamie Wilcox and Louise Burton. We talked for a few minutes, and then I continued with my shopping. I was looking for wall paint to use in my living room. I found just what I wanted, bought it, and went home." Call one pupil to front of room away from the rest of the class. Whisper the message to him or her with the pupil looking directly at you. Call the next pupil to front. Have the first pupil report what you said to the next one. Repeat this procedure until every pupil has had a turn. After the last pupil has received the message, the teacher shall ask him or her to say aloud what was stated to him or her.

(Ask first pupil to repeat what he was told by you.) Say, "Are the messages of (name of first pupil) and (name of last pupil) the same?" (Student response.) "Why are their messages different?" (Student response.) Spend about three minutes maximum discussing student responses.

2. **Identify specific behaviors.** "What can you do to be sure that you report accurately what someone has said?" (Student response.) Try to draw out the following specific behaviors:

   (a) Look directly at speaker.

   (b) Listen to the person speaking.

   (c) Silently repeat to yourself what the speaker has said.

   (d) Repeat aloud, on request, what the speaker has said.

   Be sure to recognize appropriate verbal responses. List the above specific behaviors on the board.

3. **Model the behavior for the class.** Assign a "talkative" student to speak to the class about his or her favorite subject. Sit at one of the student's desks and listen to the speaker. Have the speaker ask questions to which you can respond. Ask the students to describe your listening behavior. Be sure to model all of the behaviors listed on the board. Recognize students who describe your behavior accurately.

4. **Have class practice the behavior.** Speak to the class and have them listen to you. Teach a lesson that you would normally be doing at this time. Recognize those students who respond accurately. Give descriptive praise. Example: "Pam, you did an excellent job of repeating what I said." "All of you are looking directly at me while I'm talking, that's great."

5. **Maintenance.** Utilize appropriate social reinforcers on a continuous basis initially. Reinforce children when they exhibit looking at the speaker and when they demonstrate that they have listened by paraphrasing or repeating some of what the speaker has said. Example: "Jack, you have done a good job of looking directly at me as I have been talking." "Your summary of what I said showed you were really listening, Mike. That's great."

6. **Additional suggestions.**

   (a) If pupil has a particular problem with this skill, assess S-TR-AT-0002 and/or S-IP-MC-0002.

   (b) Cue a student who does not appear to be listening while someone is speaking by remarking how nicely another student in his close proximity is listening to the speaker. Then reinforce the student immediately upon his or her assuming the appearance of listening.

(c) Accompany social reinforcement with more tangible reinforcement (like watering class plants) if social reinforcement is not sufficient to maintain listening behavior. Consult reinforcement menu.

Code: S-TR-AT-0006-L1-Ir

TEACHING STRATEGY

Objective: Student demonstrates that he or she has listened to the speaker by repeating some of what the person said.

Social Reinforcement

1. **Identify by name and recognize aloud target student when he or she has demonstrated listening to a person speaking to the class by repeating some of what the person has said when asked, by asking knowledgeable questions about what the person has said, or by discussing what was said.** Recognize specific behaviors, i.e., "Thank you for listening, Jane."

2. **Cue a student who does not appear to be listening while someone is speaking by remarking how nicely a nearby student is listening to the speaker.** Then reinforce the student immediately upon his or her assuming the appearance of listening. Accompany social reinforcement with more tangible reinforcement if social reinforcement is not sufficient to maintain listening behavior.

Code: S-TR-AT-0006-L1-Ic

TEACHING STRATEGY

Objective: Student demonstrates that he or she has listened to the speaker by repeating some of what the person said.

Contingency Management

1. **State the task in observable terms.** The student will demonstrate that he or she has listened to the person speaking to the class by repeating some of what was said; for example, giving the main idea.

2. **Choose reinforcement from reinforcement menu.**

3. **State the contingency.** If, after someone has addressed the class, the student demonstrates he or she has listened to the speaker by repeating the main idea(s) of what was said, the student will be rewarded according to the terms agreed upon. Specify type and amount of reinforcement.

4. **After you have said something to the class, ask the target student to tell you what was just said.** Reward the student for repeating or paraphrasing what you said. You may have to begin by having the student repeat very short statements only, and then gradually increase the amount he or she must listen to receive reinforcement.

5. **Example.** Andrew doesn't seem to listen. Mr. Carr contracts with him that each time he can repeat what was said to him when asked, he will receive

a token. After each short statement he makes to the class, Mr. Carr asks Andrew what he has just said. Andrew responds correctly only a small percentage of time even though the reinforcer is a highly potent one (one token for use at the class store). Mr. Carr increases Andrew's responses by adding an extra cue. Before Mr. Carr says something he wants Andrew to repeat, he says, "Andrew, listen." The cue increases the response to an acceptable level. Then he fades it to just "listen," and then drops it. Andrew continues to respond to the contract repeating longer statements without the cue. At this point, Mr. Carr gradually lowers the reinforcement level— one token for two responses, then three, four, five, etc.—until it is dropped without decreasing Andrew's listening behavior. Mr. Carr continues to praise Andrew for good listening.

CLASSROOM DISCUSSION

S-TR-CD-0002-L1-S	To use tone of voice in classroom discussion appropriate to the situation.
S-TR-CD-0004-L2-S	To make relevant remarks in a classroom discussion.
S-TR-CD-0006-L2-S	To participate in a classroom discussion initiated by teacher.
S-TR-CD-0008-L2-S	To bring things to class which are relevant to classroom discussion.
S-TR-CD-0010-L2-S	To express opinion in classroom discussion even when contrary to opinions of others.
S-TR-CD-0012-L2-S	To provide reasons for opinions expressed in group discussion.

Skill:	To use tone of voice in classroom discussion appropriate to the situation. **S-TR-CD-0002-L1**
Objective:	Student, when speaking to the class in a classroom discussion, speaks with an appropriate volume loud enough to be heard by everyone in class, and soft enough so as not to disturb those in other classrooms.
Assessment:	Assess from previous knowledge of student or through direct observation using the <u>Social Behavior Assessment Inventory</u>.

Code: S-TR-CD-0002-L1-Im

TEACHING STRATEGY

Objective: Student, when speaking to the class in a classroom discussion, speaks with an appropriate volume loud enough to be heard by everyone in class, and soft enough so as not to disturb those in other classrooms.

Social Modeling

1. **Set the stage.**
   (a) Through a discussion, have the students list places where it is appropriate to use loud voices. Ask, "When should we talk in a loud voice or yell?" (Student responses.) Examples:
      (1) Football game.
      (2) Playground.
      (3) Baseball game.
      (4) Hockey.
   (b) Then discuss and list on the board places where it is appropriate to use soft voices. Ask, "When should we speak in a very soft voice?" (Student response.) Examples:
      (1) Church.
      (2) Golf tournament.

(3) In the lunchroom.

(4) When working in small groups.

2. **Identify specific behaviors.** Ask, "What type of voice do we use during our class discussion?" (Student response.) "Correct, Jim! We speak in a normal or medium voice." (Incorrect student response.) "Do we speak at the same volume as when we are at a football game?" (Student response.) "In church?" (Student response.) "Right, we speak at a different volume. In class discussions, we should speak loudly enough for everyone in the room to hear but softly enough so that we are not heard in other classrooms."

3. **Model the behavior.** Through the discussion, speak in a voice of appropriate volume. Say, "I'm speaking and have been speaking in a voice that is loud enough to be heard but soft enough so that it is not heard in other classrooms."

Say, "Now, let's have someone else demonstrate for us." Select a pupil who is able to read well orally, knows a nursery rhyme; or speaks often about his or her experiences. Ask this pupil to go to the front of the room and begin reading, reciting, or talking in a whisper and gradually raise his or her voice as you raise your hand. When you stop raising your hand, he or she should stop increasing the volume but continue reading, reciting, or talking at the same level, until you say stop. Say, "That was great. You raised your voice to the correct level and kept it there as you continued talking. You spoke loudly enough to be heard in this room but softly enough so that you were not heard in other classrooms."

4. **Practice the behavior.** Repeat the procedure described in the preceding section in which each pupil gradually raises his or her voice. This activity can be done in conjunction with an academic task, e.g., reading from assigned reading material, show and tell, etc. Be sure to recognize appropriate volume.

5. **Reinforcement.** During a class discussion, have a list of all the students. Tell them they can earn points for every time they raise their hands and speak using the appropriate volume (voice level). The two children who earn the most checks will be the judge and recorder during the next discussion session. Praise students throughout the discussion who are using appropriate volume; for example, "Harold, you spoke very clearly and loudly enough for everyone to hear. Very good."

After discussion, review the number of points the students have earned—first the winners and then other students. For example, "George, you earned three points, that's great!" Use this procedure only until each child demonstrates mastery of the skill.

6. **Additional suggestions.**

(a) Provide cues for the target student by:

(1) Naming a student who has just spoken in an appropriate volume and recognizing him or her.

(2) Giving verbal "softer" or "louder" cues to the target student as he or she speaks, to aid him or her in modulating his or her own voice.

(3) Giving hand gestures to cue child when he or she is speaking, such as raising hand for louder or lowering hand for softer or putting hand up to ear for louder.

(b) Put up a bulletin board.

(1) Discuss the bulletin board with the students. Decide as a class where to list the activities according to appropriate voice volume for each.

(2) Bulletin board consists of a thermometer headed "Voice Volume" with categories such as "Football Game Cheering," "Class Discussion," "Lunchroom," and "Church." On the right side is the heading, "The Following Students Use Appropriate Voice Volume: (students' names)." Post students' names when they have earned enough points to be the voice judges and recorders.

(c) You may want to reverse the procedure used in the "Modeling and Practice" steps by having a pupil start out in a loud voice and gradually lower the volume until cued to stop and maintain that volume.

(d) The teacher may model the behavior as described in the "Modeling" section.

Code: S-TR-CD-0002-L1-Ir

TEACHING STRATEGY

Objective: Student, when speaking to the class in a classroom discussion, speaks with an appropriate volume loud enough to be heard by everyone in class, and soft enough so as not to disturb those in other classrooms.

Social Reinforcement

1. **Use praise to reinforce the student when he or she speaks in an appropriate volume in the course of a classroom discussion.** Specifically praise the volume of his or her voice. "Kate, you spoke loudly enough to be heard everywhere in the room. Very good." "Marcia, thank you for speaking softly so we do not disturb the other classes but loudly enough for us all to hear. Good speaking voice." "I like the tone of voice Joyce used when she gave her talk."

2. **Provide cues for the target student.**

   (a) Point out and praise a student who has just spoken in an appropriate volume and praising.

   (b) Give verbal or gestural "softer" and "louder" cues to the target student as he or she speaks, to aid him or her in modulating his or her own voice.

3. **Social reinforcement may sometimes prove inadequate.** In this case, tangible reinforcement may be paired with praise to increase motivation.

Code: S-TR-CD-0002-L1-Ic

TEACHING STRATEGY

Objective: Student, when speaking to the class in a classroom discussion, speaks with an appropriate volume loud enough to be heard by everyone in class, and soft enough so as not to disturb those in other classrooms.

Contingency Management

1. **State the task to the student in objective terms.** When the student speaks in a class discussion, he will keep his voice low enough so that other classes can not hear, but loud enough so that everyone in his own class can hear.
2. Plan reinforcement.
3. **Explain the contingency to the student.** "Each time you speak during our class discussions in a volume loud enough to be heard in our class but not loud enough to be heard in other classrooms, you will receive a reward." Specify type and amount of reinforcement.
4. **Have a classroom discussion in which the target student is given an opportunity to speak several times.** Reward each time he or she speaks in appropriate volume. Discussion could be structured around current class topics, hobbies, families, vacations, or school activities.
5. **Example.** Trina often speaks too softly to be heard in the class. Ms. Kaye tells Trina that she must speak more loudly in class so that everyone can hear her. She explains to Trina that if during class discussion she speaks in a loud clear voice, she will be given points toward time in the free reading corner. Ms. Kaye has Trina practice various tones of voice until she develops one that is loud enough, but not too loud.

   Ms. Kaye organized at least two classroom discussions each day. During these she sat across the room from Trina. When Trina spoke, if Ms. Kaye heard her across the room, she gave her a signal that she had earned a point. This contingency was kept in force for three weeks, at which time Ms. Kaye decided that Trina had adequately developed the habit of speaking loudly. Mrs. Kaye dropped the contingency in favor of social reinforcement for the behavior. She occasionally had to continue signaling Trina to remind her to raise her voice.

Skill:	To make relevant remarks in a classroom discussion. **S-TR-CD-0004-L2**
Objective:	In a classroom discussion, the student makes remarks relevant to the topic of conversation.
Assessment:	Assess from previous knowledge of student or through direct observation using the <u>Social Behavior Assessment Inventory</u>.

Code: S-TR-CD-0004-L2-Im

TEACHING STRATEGY

Objective: In a classroom discussion, the student makes remarks relevant to the topic of conversation.

Social Modeling

1. **Setting the stage and identifying the steps.** Begin by showing the pupils "What Doesn't Belong?" pictures. You may make transparencies of the pictures or just hold them up for a small group. While showing each picture

to the pupils, ask, "What doesn't belong in this picture?" (Student response.) "Is the (irrelevant object) necessary to make the picture complete?" (Student response.) "Why?"

After discussing each of the pictures, explain that during a discussion, unrelated comments to the main topic are just as out of place as the igloo on the tropical island. Then say, "Now let's see if you can tell when I say something unrelated to the topic as we discuss some of your favorite things. When I say something unrelated, raise your hand. First let's discuss our favorite TV shows. What is yours, Tommy?" (Student response.) "Boy, I wish it would rain." (Students raise their hands.) "Good, you caught me. I made an unrelated comment." Continue the discussion and repeatedly make irrelevant comments for the pupils to catch.

Praise pupils for making relevant comments and for identifying unrelated comments. Review the need for participants in a class discussion to make relevant remarks. Point out that a discussion is a group of people speaking on a topic; and if people don't stick to the topic, there can be no discussion. Explain that there are many different ways to make relevant remarks. The following are considered acceptable methods for making relevant remarks:

(a) A question about something already said.
(b) An opinion about something the group is talking about (define opinion).
(c) An explanation or addition to something already said.
(d) A story relating to what has already been said.

3. **Model the behavior.**
    (a) Stage a discussion with several students who already possess this skill to some extent. Periodically, stop and go back over what somebody said in the discussion. Ask students which remarks were relevant and what made them so. Praise correct responses.
    (b) During the discussion, stop and ask the class if a comment that was just made was a relevant remark. "Does it fit our definition?"

4. **Practice the behavior.** Have the class practice the behavior through a series of organized discussions on a selected topic, e.g., TV programs, vacations, etc. Make a "Stick to the Point" poster. Write the topic on the board; place the poster up where everyone can see it. Reinforce a student who makes relevant remarks during a discussion by giving the student a star and permitting him or her to go up to the poster and place the star by his or her name. Be sure to praise the child. "Wow, Susie, that was a very relevant remark. Nice job of sticking to the point."

5. **Reinforcement.**
    (a) Recognize by name a student who makes a relevant remark during a classroom discussion. Recognize the behavior in specific terms. "Jaimee, thank you for your comment about the bluebird you saw. It fit in very well with our discussion about birds." "Marcy, thank you for telling us what you heard on the news this morning. That adds a great deal to our current events discussion." "Good contribution, Chris."

Code: S-TR-CD-0004-L2-Ir

TEACHING STRATEGY

Objective: In a classroom discussion, the student makes remarks relevant to the topic of conversation.

Social Reinforcement

1. **Praise by name a student who makes a relevant remark during a classroom discussion.** Recognize the behavior in specific terms. "Jaimee, thank you for your comment about the bluebird you saw. It fit in very well with our discussion about birds." "Marcy, thank you for telling us what you heard on the news this morning; that adds a great deal to our current events discussion." "Good contribution, Chris."
2. **Cue the behavior in target child by recognizing a student for making a relevant remark within the target student's hearing, remembering to be specific in praise.** Immediately praise target student when he or she makes a relevant remark. You may need to provide additional cues by occasionally reminding students what the topic of discussion is.
3. **It may be necessary at first to pair a tangible reinforcer with social reinforcement in order to elicit the behavior.** For example, hand out a token or give a checkmark to a student when he or she makes a relevant comment. Drop this additional reinforcement as soon as possible.

Code: S-TR-CD-0004-L2-Ic

TEACHING STRATEGY

Objective: In a classroom discussion, the student makes remarks relevant to the topic of conversation.

Contingency Management

1. **Explain to the student that during a class discussion he or she is required to say something relevant to the topic of the conversation.** For example, ask a question about something already said, tell a story relating to what has already been said, give an opinion about something the group is talking about, or explain or add to something already said.
2. **Plan reinforcement.**
3. **Discuss the contingency with the student.** For each relevant remark the student makes in a class discussion, he or she will be rewarded, or the student will be rewarded after each classroom discussion to which he or she has contributed a given number of relevant comments. Choice of contingency should be based on how much control the teacher wishes to exert upon the situation. The second contingency gives him or her more control over how many times the student will speak. Specify type and amount of reinforcement.
4. **Arrange to have several classroom discussions.** Reward the student when he or she makes a comment or remark relevant to the topic under discussion, according to the terms of the stated contingency.

5. **Example.** What Bonnie says during class discussions is generally not related to the topic. Mr. Bart explains to her that she should say things during the conversation which are relevant. "Talk about the things the other people are talking about." He encourages her to ask questions, tell stories, or tell how she feels about the topic which other class members are discussing. He also tells her that for each relevant comment she makes during these discussions, she will get two points. (In some situations, the teacher might also want to take points off for irrelevant comments.) When she gets 20 points, she will be eligible to select a privilege. Bonnie complies with this, and three weeks later the contingency is altered to one point per remark. This is also met, and then the contingency is dropped in favor of social reinforcement.

Skill:	To participate in a classroom discussion initiated by the teacher. **S-TR-CD-0006-L2**
Objective:	When a classroom discussion is initiated by the teacher, the student participates by listening to what is said, raising hand and waiting to be recognized, and making remarks or asking questions relevant to the topic.
Assessment:	Assess from previous knowledge of student or through direct observation using the <u>Social Behavior Assessment Inventory</u>.

Code: S-TR-CD-0006-L2-Im

TEACHING STRATEGY

Objective: When a classroom discussion is initiated by the teacher, the student participates by listening to what is said, raising hand and waiting to be recognized, and making remarks or asking questions relevant to the topic.

Social Modeling

1. **Set the stage.**
    (a) Pick three or four students who have demonstrated this skill, and set up a model discussion. You may need to use older students from another class for this initial presentation.
    (b) Let the chosen students pick a topic with which they are familiar.
    (c) To ensure that each student participates, require that cash have at least two statements that he or she will present in the discussion written down on a piece of paper and placed in front of him or her.
    (d) Also write down the following statements on note cards to be placed in front of each student during the discussion:

        (1) Listen to what is said.

        (2) Raise your hand and wait to be recognized.

        (3) Make remarks that relate to the topic under discussion.

This should aid the students in modeling the task appropriately.

(e) To ensure that the participants provide a valid model, arrange for a practice session and coach the pupils in the target skill to be sure their behaviors are readily observable. (This session should take approximately 10 minutes.)

2. **Identify the specific steps.**

   (a) Have students with whom you have practiced demonstrate the skill for your class. (Dismiss these pupils when they have completed their role-playing duties.)

   (b) Discuss with the class how the students modeled the desired skill. Ask, "What did you observe these pupils doing?" (Student response.)

      (1) "Very good observation, Tim. They were listening to the statements of the other group members. What else did you observe?" (Student response.)

      (2) "Right, Cindy, they raised their hands and waited to be called on before they spoke. Anything else?" (Student response.)

      (3) "All right, they were all talking about the same thing." If the pupils have difficulty identifying these component behaviors, try asking questions, e.g., "What did you see them do?" "What did you hear them saying?" "What were some things that you saw several of them do?" You may ask for input from the pupils doing the role-playing.

   (c) Discuss why it is important to discuss topics in the above manner. Ask, "Why is it important when other group members talk?" (Student response.) "That's a good reason, Jan." (Repeat question for raising hands and making relevant statements.) Some possible answers include:

      (1) If students don't listen, they won't know what's being discussed.

      (2) If all the group members talked at the same time, without raising their hands and waiting to be recognized, we wouldn't be able to understand what anyone was saying.

      (3) If the members ask questions unrelated to the discussion topic, it will hinder the group.

   (d) Explain how these same discussion techniques can be used in classroom discussions initiated by the teacher, i.e., classroom discussion can be conducted more effectively if:

      (1) Students listen to what is said.

      (2) Students raise their hands and wait to be recognized before speaking.

      (3) Students make remarks that relate to the topic under discussion.

3. **Model the behavior.**

   (a) Repeat the activity described in Step 1. Set the stage with pupils from your classroom. Begin with Step 1 (b).

   (b) Periodically stop the discussion to ask class members to describe what behaviors they have observed. Have the three key component behaviors listed on the chalkboard:

      (1) Listen to what is said.

      (2) Raise hand and wait to be called before speaking.

(3) Make statements or ask questions relevant to the topic of the discussion.

(c) Praise correct responses.

4. **Practice the behavior.**

   (a) Provide practice through a series of classroom discussions to which the students can readily address themselves.

   (1) "How should the class celebrate Halloween?"

   (2) "Should students be permitted to make more of the class rules?"

   (b) Reinforce students who fulfill the requirements of participation during the practice activity by giving descriptive verbal praise; for example, "Bill, you raised your hand and waited until called upon. Thank you!"

Code: S-TR-CD-0006-L2-Ir

TEACHING STRATEGY

Objective: When a classroom discussion is initiated by the teacher, the student participates by listening to what is said, raising hand and waiting to be recognized, and making remarks or asking questions relevant to the topic.

Social Reinforcement

1. **Reinforce students with praise for either listening to what is said during a class discussion, raising their hand and waiting to be recognized, making remarks or asking questions relevant to the topic, or any combination of these.** Recognize specific behaviors. "Janie, thank you for waiting for me to call on you. That was a good comment you made." "Mark, you listened well to our conversation, and your story added a lot to the discussion." "Class, I like the considerate way you responded to each other in the discussion we had."

2. **Cue appropriate behavior in the target student by:**

   (a) Praising another student for participating in the discussion appropriately, within hearing of the target student.

   (b) Leaving a chart posted listing the appropriate behavior involved in participating in a discussion.

3. **It may be necessary at first to pair tangible reinforcement with social reinforcement, giving points, checkmarks, tokens, etc., for students who participate appropriately.**

4. **Additional suggestions.**

   (a) If students have a particular problem with this skill, check the following prerequisites: S-TR-AT-0006, S-TR-CP-0002, S-TR-CD-0004.

   (b) Since many students are hesitant to make contributions to a classroom discussion for fear of ridicule or embarrassment, emphasis should also be placed on courtesy to others; for example, avoid making fun or punishing in some way the student whose remark is not relevant. Ignore irrelevant remarks. Students who avoid making contributions because they feel they have nothing worthwhile to say may be taught that asking for clarification, i.e., "I don't understand what Mary said," or making a statement of agreement or dissent, i.e., "I agree with what John said," are legitimate ways to be part of a discussion.

Code: S-TR-CD-0006-L2-Ic

TEACHING STRATEGY

Objective: When a classroom discussion is initiated by the teacher, the student participates by listening to what is said, raising hand and waiting to be recognized, and making remarks or asking questions relevant to the topic.

Contingency Management

1. **State the task in observable terms.** Explain to the student that he or she is required to participate in classroom discussion by:
   (a) Listening to what is said, being considerate of others who make contributions.
   (b) Raising hand and waiting to be called on.
   (c) Making relevant remarks (or talking about what everyone else is talking about).
2. **Plan reinforcement.**
3. **State the contingency.** Explain to the student that he or she will receive a reward each time he or she participates in the classroom discussion in an appropriate way, or if you prefer, that he or she will be rewarded after each discussion in which he or she has participated a given number of times. The contingency should be chosen on the basis of student's previous frequency of participation and the frequency of participation desired. For example, a student who very seldom participates might be required to make only one or two contributions in order to be rewarded. Specify type and amount of reinforcement.
4. **Set up a series of classroom discussions on topics about which the students can readily speak.** Reward the students according to the terms of the contingency for participation.
5. **Example.** Colleen speaks out in class discussions, but does not wait to be recognized and often does not listen to what is being said. Consequently, her contributions are often irrelevant. She also sometimes laughs and makes fun of other students for what they say in the discussion. Ms. Carr discusses with her the things she needs to do to participate appropriately; she contracts with Colleen that for each discussion in which she makes two remarks that are relevant, waiting to be called on before speaking and listening to what is said, she will be given 10 minutes at the interest center of her choice. In addition, she will lose minutes at the interest center for inappropriate participation, such as calling out, irrelevant remarks showing she hasn't listened, or any inconsiderate behavior toward others' contributions. This contract is complied with and after Colleen receives her reward for 8 days of the 10 it is in force, the contingency is increased to three appropriate participations per discussion. The contingency is kept for 10 more days and then dropped in favor of praise for appropriate behavior in the classroom discussions.

Code: S-TR-CD-0008-L2-Im

TEACHING STRATEGY

Objective: Student brings things to class that are relevant to the class discussion.

Social Modeling

1. **Set the stage.**
   (a) Briefly explain to the class the difference between a basketball, volleyball, football, baseball, and golf ball.
   (b) Verbalize simple statements such as:
      (1) A basketball is big and round.
      (2) A volleyball is smaller, but it is also round.
      (3) A baseball is even smaller than a volleyball and is round.
      (4) A golf ball is round and smaller than a basketball, volleyball, or baseball.
      (5) A football is about the size of a volleyball, but it isn't round and has pointed ends.
   (c) Show the class a basketball, volleyball, football, baseball, and golf ball from the Physical Education Department and describe them in greater detail.
   (d) Indicate how much easier it is to describe the objects to the class when the students can actually see them.
   (e) Explain that bringing objects to class that relate to the class discussion is a good idea. However, only things that relate to the topic being discussed should be brought to class. Objects that relate to the discussion help us to learn because we can see, touch, smell, hear, and taste the real things that we are discussing.

2. **Identify the specific steps.**
   (a) Continue the discussion by asking, "What things should you bring to school?" (Student response.) "Exactly, Jennifer. It is a good idea to bring in those things that relate to our class discussions. When bringing something to class for discussion you need to:
      (1) Decide what you can bring to school.
      (2) Decide why it would be good to bring it to school.
      (3) Ask permission and explain why you want to bring it to school."

(b) After giving these directions to the class, ask: "What do you need to do when you want to bring something to class for discussion purposes?" (Student response.) Give praise for correct answer and proceed to get all three items paraphrased. Write these on chalkboard for older pupils in an abbreviated form:

(1) What to bring.
(2) Why to bring it.
(3) Ask permission.

3. **Model the behavior.** Explain to the class that you will demonstrate what needs to be done in order to bring something to school. Arrange with an older pupil, aid, or another teacher to be available in your classroom at a designated time to role-play the following. Assume the role of a student and take a student's seat. Have the other person be the teacher and begin to talk for a minute or so about the balls that were used in the "setting the stage" step. Have the "teacher" terminate his or her speech by saying, "That's the bell, we will continue this discussion tomorrow."

As the pupil, you will now go to the "teacher" and say, "Since we will be discussing the variety of balls that are used in games, I wonder if I could bring in some balls I have at home. They are different from the ones you have and should be interesting to talk about." "Teacher" responds by giving permission. Begin a discussion of the role-playing episode by asking, "What did I do as the student?" (Student response.) Recognize correct responses.

4. **Practice the behavior.**

(a) Provide practice by instituting a "show and tell period." Repeat this period weekly on a variety of topics that relate to your planned instruction.

(b) Inform students of the topic in advance and reinforce them when they bring in relevant materials.

(c) Consider students' interests when selecting the topics. (Ask for suggestions from pupils.)

(d) Make topics sufficiently general that each child would make a contribution. For example, ask students to bring in interesting items, e.g., rocks, leaves, newspaper articles, or pictures from magazines.

Code: S-TR-CD-0008-L2-Ir

TEACHING STRATEGY

Objective: Student brings things to class that are relevant to the class discussion.

Social Reinforcement

1. **Reinforce student with praise for bringing things to class that are relevant to what the class discussion is about.** Recognize specific actions, e.g., "Kate, thank you for bringing in your book about horses. It fits very well with our discussions about animals." "Lucy brought in a beautiful mounted butterfly. We can use it in our lesson about insects. Thank you, Lucy." "George, that was a good newspaper clipping you brought for our current events bulletin board."

2. **Provide cues for target student.**
    (a) Verbally remind students before dismissing class for the day that they may bring things in for "Show and Tell;" suggest kinds of things they might bring. (Emphasize items that any child might have available.)
    (b) Post topics for the week in a prominent place, with a reminder that students may bring in things relating to any of these topics.
    (c) Recognize other students who bring things.
    (d) Set aside the final five minutes of class for pupils to obtain permission to bring something to class.
3. **Tangible reinforcement may sometimes be necessary to stimulate this behavior. The additional reinforcement should be paired with social reinforcement and dropped as soon as possible.**
4. **Additional suggestions.**
    (a) Set the stage by using pictures rather than the real objects.
    (b) When setting the stage discuss any topic provided it will interest the students and provided that you have access to a plethora of demonstration items.
    (c) When the pupils have demonstrated that they can make appropriate decisions regarding what they may bring to school, you may drop the requirement for obtaining permission.
    (d) You may want to use the following guidelines. They provide additional structure for the pupil who has obtained permission to bring something to school.
        (1) Bring the object to teacher before school. Teacher will keep the object until it is needed.
        (2) Use object at appropriate time.
        (3) Take object home immediately after school, or make arrangements with teacher to leave it at school overnight.

Code: S-TR-CD-0008-L2-Ic

TEACHING STRATEGY

Objective: Student brings things to class that are relevant to the class discussion.

Contingency Management

1. **Describe the task to the student.** Explain that you would like him or her to bring something to class that relates to what is being studied in class. Make sure the contribution is something the child can easily provide.
2. **Plan reinforcement.**
3. **Explain the contingency to the student.** Explain that each time the student brings something to class that relates to the topic, he or she will receive a reward. Specify type and amount of reinforcement.
4. **Inform the student in advance of the topics the class will be covering.** Before or during a class discussion, ask if anyone has anything to show the class. If the student volunteers something he or she has brought, and if it is relevant to the topic, reward him or her.

5. **Example.** Mr. Ford liked to have a "show and tell" period, because he felt it provided the students with an opportunity to learn to speak in front of the class and to receive recognition for what they could contribute to class discussion. A few students never made a contribution, mainly because of shyness or a feeling that they had nothing worthwhile to bring. Mr. Ford divided the group into teams for "show and tell" and gave each team a topic for which it would be easy to find things to bring to school. One team was asked to bring flowers to show the class; another team brought leaves; another brought rocks. Team members were allowed to help each other find things to bring. Teams were given points for each member who brought something and described it to the class. The winning team was allowed an extra gym period on Friday. Since Mr. Ford made it easy for team members to help each other, it was possible for every team to earn the reward.

Skill:	To express opinion in classroom discussion even when contrary to opinions of others. **S-TR-CD-0010-L2**
Objective:	Student expresses his or her opinions during a classroom discussion even when contrary to opinions of others.
Assessment:	Assess from previous knowledge of student or through direct observation using the <u>Social Behavior Assessment Inventory</u>.

Code: S-TR-CD-0010-L2-Im

TEACHING STRATEGY

Objective: Student expresses his or her opinions during a classroom discussion even when contrary to opinions of others.

Social Modeling

1. **Set the stage.**
   (a) Initiate a class discussion. Choose a topic on which most students strongly agree. For example, "Why we like recess."
   (b) After a few minutes take an opposing stance in the discussion (i.e., "Why I don't like recess").
   (c) Then ask the students to describe what you did.
      (1) "What did I do in this discussion which was different from the rest of the class?"
      (2) "Did I express a different opinion from what most of you were saying?"
2. **Identify the specific steps.**
   (a) Discuss why and how individuals should express their opinions even when the possibility exists that others will disagree with them.
      (1) Let people know your true feelings (for example, some kids really don't like recess) so that the matter may be discussed. If a child said he or she didn't like recess, the teacher or class might be able to

find something else for him or her to do during this time. If you didn't like recess but you never expressed your opinion, you would always have to go to recess simply because no one knew your true feelings.

   (2) Never expressing your real opinion may cause other people to distrust you or think you have no opinions of your own.

   (b) Discuss the importance of free speech and the value of liking people even if their opinions differ from yours.

3. **Possible questions to ask class.**

   (a) Who is the best professional football player and why?

   (b) What do you think we should do to save energy?

   (c) Should everyone have to go to school all year round? Why?

   (d) Why should people care about the environment?

When discussing the observations, be sure to give positive feedback to the pupils who identify the specific behaviors listed.

4. **Practice the behavior.**

   (a) Divide students into equal teams—A and B—with two or four students on each team.

   (b) Each student on Team A should be paired with a corresponding student on Team B.

   (c) Team A will then **positively** discuss a topic which most students disagree with. For example, "School should be in session, and there shouldn't be a summer vacation." Team B will listen and take notes on what is being said, paying particular attention to the corresponding Team A students they are paired with.

   (d) Each member of Team A is required to state at least one opinion, supportive of the discussion topic, during the course of the discussion. Monitor the discussion to ensure that the criteria are met.

   (1) To be safe, students could have "canned" supportive statements prepared before the discussion begins. These should be written down and placed in front of them for easy access at any time.

   (2) The teacher should attempt to record each opinion stated.

   (e) At the conclusion of the discussion, each student on Team B will restate the opinions of the corresponding Team A member. During this time the Team B member will also verbalize his or her disagreement with what the Team A member said. Refer to your record of all the comments to tell the Team B member what was said in case he or she has forgotten.

   (f) Act as a coach to be sure all the pupils exhibit the five specific behaviors that comprise this skill.

Code: S-TR-CD-0010-L2-Ir

TEACHING STRATEGY

Objective: Student expresses his or her opinions during a classroom discussion even when contrary to opinions of others.

Social Reinforcement

1. **Recognize, by name, a student who has expressed a divergent opinion during a classroom discussion.**
2. **Cue appropriate behavior in the target student(s).**
   (a) Encourage students to express divergent opinions.
   (b) Praise another student in the discussion for expressing a divergent opinion.
   (c) Point out to students occasions when there may be different points of view.
   (d) Present arguments that are both pro and con on a given topic.
3. **Immediately recognize target students when they express a divergent opinion.**
4. **Tangible reinforcement, paired with social reinforcement, may be given to elicit appropriate behavior.**
   (a) Tokens.
   (b) Checkmarks.
   (c) Stars.
5. **Once the target behavior, stating divergent opinions, is firmly established, begin to reinforce those differing opinions that you determine are acceptable.**
6. **Additional suggestions.**
   (a) Set the stage by taking a divergent position in a discussion with a single student.
   (b) Set the stage by inviting an outside speaker to come into the class and present a topic with which you disagree. Ask the students to describe what they observed.

Code: S-TR-CD-0010-L2-Ic

TEACHING STRATEGY

Objective: Student expresses his or her opinions during a classroom discussion even when contrary to opinions of others.

Contingency Management

1. **Explain to the student that he or she should express his or her opinions or tell what he or she thinks about things, even when others disagree.** Explain that the others may want to hear his or her opinions and that they may welcome his or her different viewpoint. (At the same time, other students may need to learn ways of responding politely to opinions with which they do not agree.)

2. **Plan reinforcement.**

3. **State the contingency as follows:** If I (teacher) observe you expressing your opinion in a classroom discussion in spite of disagreement from other students, you will receive a reward. Specify type and amount of reward.

4. **Watch for the student to express opinions in the course of regular class discussions or make it necessary for him or her to express his or her opinion by placing him or her in a debate situation.** Set this up so the student may choose his or her topic and his or her side of the argument. The student may be given a list of topics to choose from, in line with his or her level of functioning. Sample topics may include political questions such as candidates or legislation, school issues or policies, classroom issues or policies (including the selection of class officers or monitors), relative merits of movies, TV shows, books, cartoons, etc. If the student expresses opinions that are different from the other students' opinions, deliver the agreed-upon reward.

5. **Example.** Jeremy is a chronic follower; he never expresses his own opinion in discussions but tends simply to go along with whatever his classmates say, even sometimes to the point of acquiescing to both sides of an argument and contradicting himself. Ms. Eagen decides to set up a debate between Jeremy and another student to give him an opportunity to practice expressing his own opinion. She explains first to Jeremy that she would like to see him say what he thinks more often rather than simply agreeing to everything anyone else says. She tells him that he is going to debate on a topic of his own choice in front of the class and that if he speaks in defense of his chosen viewpoint he will earn a box of crayons from the class store. Jeremy agrees to the contingency and chooses to debate whether or not school should be closed on a famous person's birthday. Jeremy says it should, and Louisa agrees to debate the opposite side.

The debate is successfully carried out on the following day, with Jeremy expressing his viewpoint adequately, though not really articulately. The teacher rewards him with the crayons. Ms. Eagen arranges several more debates of this type during the next month for Jeremy and for others having this difficulty. Each time, the students choose their own topics and are rewarded for expressing their opinions. In addition, Ms. Eagen uses social reinforcement to maintain the expression of individual opinion whenever she observes it occurring in regular classroom discussions.

Code: S-TR-CD-0012-L2-Im

TEACHING STRATEGY

Objective: Student, when asked, will give reasons for opinions he or she has expressed in group discussion.

Social Modeling

1. **Set the stage.** Tell the following story:

THE ANNOUNCEMENT

Once when I was in school, the principal walked into my class and said, "Today there will be no outside recess, no gym, no drinks from the water fountain." After saying this, the principal left our room. A lot of the kids in the class were angry and confused about what the principal had just said.

(a) Interrupt the story at this point and ask the following questions:

　(1) "How would you feel if the principal walked in and gave you those rules without telling the reasons behind them?" Possible responses:

　　(A) Upset.

　　(B) Disappointed.

　　(C) Angry.

　　(D) That the principal doesn't care about the students' feelings.

　(2) "Why would you feel that way?"

　(3) "What should the principal have done when he or she first told the class of the new rules?" Possible responses:

　　(A) Could have encouraged the students to ask questions about the new rules.

　　(B) Should have given the reasons for the rules when he or she first presented them to the class.

(b) Say, "The principal must have realized his or her mistake because he or she returned very shortly to our class."

Suddenly, the principal walked back into the room and said, "I just remembered that I forgot to tell you the reasons for these new rules. First, there are men working with heavy equipment on the playground so we can't have recess today. Second, we have to wax the gym floor this morning for the program tonight. It won't be dry until after school so we can't have gym today. Also, we just found out that the water pipes are dirty, and we are cleaning them right now. We should be finished by tomorrow morning, so you should be able to get drinks from the water fountain then."

    (c) Say: "Now, what would you think about these new rules?" Possible responses:

        (1) Not so bad.

        (2) Different.

        (3) O.K.

        (4) They are necessary.

    (d) "Why would you feel that way?" Possible responses:

        (1) Know why he or she made the rules.

        (2) Know he or she has a good reason.

        (3) Know what his or her feelings are and that he or she wasn't doing it just to be mean.

        (4) Makes more sense. Does not seem unfair now.

2. Identify the specific steps.

    (a) Say, "Sometimes when we state our opinion about something, we do what the principal in the story did initially; that is, we do not give reasons for our opinions. While it is not always necessary to give reasons, we should always be prepared to do so if asked. When giving reasons for opinions we need to:

        (1) State the facts that support our opinion.

        (2) Make statements brief.

        (3) Use appropriate tone of voice (see TR-CA-0002-L2-S).

        (4) Give opportunity for any other questions.

    (b) When asked for reasons to support your opinions there are four steps that make up the proper way to respond. What are they?" (Student response.)

    (c) Recognize appropriate responses and be sure to bring out each of the steps. Review the steps until they are paraphrased by one or more class members.

3. Model the behavior.

    (a) Explain to the class that you will be stating your opinion on various topics, and you want them to ask you to give reasons.

    (b) Instruct the class to listen to your responses to their questions and judge the responses according to the four criteria listed earlier. Review the four criteria:

        (1) State the facts that support the opinion.

        (2) Make statements brief.

        (3) Use appropriate tone of voice.

        (4) Give opportunity for any other questions.

    These can be abbreviated and listed on the board as follows:

        (1) Facts stated.

        (2) Brief (or short).

        (3) Proper voice.

        (4) More questions.

(c) After stating your opinion and giving reasons, have pupils evaluate your responses. Give praise for correct observations, e.g., "Excellent, Phil. You pointed out that I was brief and spoke loudly enough for everyone to hear."

(d) Possible topics:

(1) Amount of homework.

(2) Recess.

(3) Energy conservation.

(4) TV programs.

(5) Snacks.

(e) Be sure to get a response from each target pupil.

4. Practice the behavior.

(a) Set up a small discussion group (two or three students) in which members are required to give opinions. Suggested topics are:

(1) "I like summer vacation."

(2) "Recess and gym are fun."

(b) Students chosen for the first discussion should be those who have given the best feedback in the previous discussions under Steps 1, 2, and 3.

(c) When students in the discussion group state an opinion, you or another student should ask why he or she believes what he or she has stated.

(d) Praise students for telling the reasons for their statements. For example, "Johnny, I really like the way you tell me the reasons behind your opinions."

(e) Give each target pupil an opportunity to practice.

Code: S-TR-CD-0012-L2-Ir

TEACHING STRATEGY

Objective: Student, when asked, will give reasons for opinions he or she has expressed in group discussion.

Social Reinforcement

1. When student expresses an opinion, ask him or her to give reasons for the opinions. If the student gives acceptable reasons for them, recognize him or her by name. Praise specific actions. "Jessie, thank you for telling us why you think Carla should be class president. That was very clear thinking." "Maria, the reasons you gave for thinking the class should go to the principal's presentation were very sound." "Larry, I can see that you gave a lot of thought to what you said." It may be necessary to praise less-than-adequate attempts to give reasons for opinions in order to shape the behavior.

2. Cue appropriate behavior in target student.

(a) Ask the student to give reasons for an expressed opinion.

(b) Praise another student who has given good reasons for an expressed opinion.

3. **Be sure to praise target student immediately when he or she gives acceptable reasons for his or her opinion.** Tangible reinforcement may be used in addition to social reinforcement to elicit the behavior.

4. **Additional suggestions.**

    (a) Set the stage by making a statement to the class, such as, "People should not eat ice cream," and then asking the students what they think about such a statement. Then say, "The reason I don't like ice cream is that the coldness hurts my teeth so much that I get an upset stomach." Then begin a discussion with the class concerning the difference between the two statements.

    (b) "Setting the stage" step could be done through a debate format, i.e., pupils from another class could be invited in to debate an issue in front of the class. These pupils would, of course, need to have demonstrated this skill. You will need to stop the debate at times and point out specific behaviors to the class. The points that are outlined on the first page of this strategy sould be covered.

Code: S-TR-CD-0012-L2-Ic

TEACHING STRATEGY

Objective: Student, when asked, will give reasons for opinions he or she has expressed in group discussion.

Contingency Management

1. **Present the task to the student.** When you are asked why you have the opinion you have just expressed, you will be able to give the reasons.

2. **Plan reinforcement.**

3. **State the contingency to the student.** If, when asked, you give reasons for an opinion that you expressed, you will receive a reward. Specify type and amount of reward.

4. **Lead a discussion on a topic about which different opinions may be expressed, for example, politics, current events, personal preferences.** When target student expresses an opinion, ask him or her to give the reasons for this opinion. If he or she can give reasons for it, reward. You should exercise judgment and establish individual criteria in determining whether the student's reasons merit the agreed-upon reward. Students who make few contributions to discussions may become discouraged from contributing at all by being required to give good reasons for any opinion they express. In order to teach this behavior, you may need to use an approximation technique and, at first, reward attempts to give reasons even though they are not particularly clear or rational.

5. **Example.** Peggy, in Ms. Page's room, offers opinions freely during class discussions, but they are often impulsive and given without any thought behind them. Ms. Page discusses this with Peggy, emphasizing that she wants Peggy to continue expressing opinions, but she would like her also to be able to give reasons for the statements she makes. She contracts with Peggy that she will give Peggy points for being able to give reasons for her opinions. The points can be exchanged for jobs from the job board. Peggy

particularly likes to be in charge of feeding the gerbil. Thereafter, during discussions Ms. Page periodically asks Peggy for reasons and awards her points for being able to make some attempt to justify her opinions. As Peggy becomes better at giving reasons, Ms. Page eliminates the points and continues to recognize Peggy for thoughtful contributions.

COMPLETING TASKS

S-TR-CT-0002-L1-S	To complete assigned academic work.
S-TR-CT-0004-L1-S	To complete assigned academic work within the required time.
S-TR-CT-0006-L2-S	To continue working on a difficult task until it is completed.
S-TR-CT-0008-L2-S	To complete and return homework assignments.

Skill:	To complete assigned academic work. **S-TR-CT-0002-L1**
Objective:	When assigned an academic task at mastery level, the student works on it until it is completed.
Assessment:	Assess from previous knowledge of student or through direct observation using the <u>Social Behavior Assessment Inventory</u>.

Code: S-TR-CT-0002-L1-Im

TEACHING STRATEGY

Objective: When assigned an academic task at mastery level, the student works on it until it is completed.

Social Modeling

1. **Set the stage.** Tell students a story such as the following. Make sure the story is age appropriate.

THE UNFINISHED ROCKET

Two boys, Wally Want and Chuck Complete, were sharing a telescope and looking at the planet Mars one calm, clear night. Chuck Complete said, "Mars looks like a beautiful place to live! There's a red spot on it that looks like a sea of strawberry jam."

"Wow! Just think if we were on Mars, we could make toast every morning by the edge of the sea and have pounds of strawberry jam," said Wally Want. Strawberry jam happened to be both the boys' favorite sweet. "Why don't we build sky rockets and go to Mars?" Wally suggested.

Chuck replied, "Yeah! That's a great idea!"

Both boys went to their own backyards and began building their rockets. They knew their rockets had to be large enough to carry one boy and at least 20 loaves of bread for toast and jam. Chuck worked on his rocket every day, even when it rained or was very hot. One day it even hailed, but he still worked on the inside of his rocket. Wally worked on his rocket for several days, but then some friends asked him to play baseball. Since he was tired of working on the rocket, he went to play baseball even though he was almost finished with his rocket. The next day, Chuck, who had been working steadily, finished his rocket and was ready to go. He went to

307

Wally's house and said, "My rocket is ready to blast off. I have 20 loaves of bread, and I even have a toaster! Are you ready to go?" Wally knew his rocket was not finished, but he thought he could make it to Mars anyway.

He said, "I'm ready, let's go!" Both boys got into their rockets and started the countdown: 10-9-8-7-6-5-4-3-2-1-BLAST OFF! Chuck, who had steadily worked on his rocket, felt the rocket lift off. In a few minutes he was looking back at Earth growing smaller and smaller. Then he looked forward to Mars and its sea of strawberry jam growing larger and larger.

Wally felt his rocket sputter, and then he saw a billow of black smoke. Wally jumped out of his rocket and ran around the corner of his house. Just as he looked back, he saw his rocket topple over in a big heap. CRASH! Wally now realized that he was not going to fly to Mars and the great sea of strawberry jam. Wally frowned, looked up at the trail of smoke left by Chuck's rocket, and said, "Why does Chuck always have more fun?"

(a) Ask,

    (1) "Whose fault was it that Wally did not make it to Mars?"

    (2) "What could Wally have done differently so that he could have gone to Mars?"

    (3) "What did Chuck do that Wally did not?"

(b) Bring out these major points through discussion:

    (1) Completed work is rewarded.

    (2) Incomplete work is not rewarded.

(c) Ask, "Who should we be like in school, Wally or Chuck?" (Student response.) "That's right, Donald. Why should we be like Chuck?" (Student response.) "Exactly! When we finish our work, we will be rewarded with personal satisfaction, with a good grade, with recognition from our parents and teachers, and (insert whatever rewards you are using in your classroom)."

2. **Identify specific behavior to be modified.** Ask, "What does it mean to finish your assignment?" (Student response.) "That's right, George. You do everything you were asked to do. Give examples:

(a) When given a reading assignment, you read all of the assigned pages.

(b) When given a math assignment of 20 problems, you worked all 20 math problems.

(c) When given 10 science questions to answer, you answered all 10 questions."

3. **Model the behavior.** Show the students two examples of work, one that is finished and one that is obviously not finished. "Which is completed?" (Student response.) "Why?" (Student response.) "Excellent answer, John."

    Show the students two worksheets that they will hang in class, one that is finished and one that is not finished. Ask, "Which paper would you rather hand in to the teacher?" (Student response.) "Why?" (Student response.) "Very good explanation, Susie."

4. **Practice the behavior.** Have the class practice the behavior with regular academic work. Provide assignments that are at the students' mastery level (on which they can work independently) and ask them to work on them until they are finished. Give them assignments that are very short (two

minutes). Recognize completing behaviors: "Cindy, you finished all five of the assigned math problems. Great!" "Wow! Everyone has completed the three sentences I assigned."

5. **Reinforcement.** Put all **finished work** (correct or incorrect) on the bulletin board with a star or some other symbol of approval on it. Give verbal recognition to students immediately upon completion of an assignment.

6. **Additional suggestions.**

    (a) As students react positively to completing work, begin to stress correctness.

    (b) If some students consistently do not turn in finished work, reassess those students on the academic skills required for the assigned tasks. They may be at instructional or frustration level. If the skill, reassessed, is definitely at mastery level for the student, shorten the task until a finished product is returned. Reinforce verbally and begin to lengthen task slowly. Stop if unfinished work begins again.

    (c) A contingency management system may need to be set up for some students. For example, "Steven, when you finish this paper and give it to me, you may choose any game you like and play with it until we begin our next lesson." (It may be necessary to follow the procedure described in b above.) As pupil is able to complete an assignment, you may gradually increase the number of completed assignments required before the reinforcer is earned.

Code: S-TR-CT-0002-L1-Ir

TEACHING STRATEGY

Objective: When assigned an academic task at mastery level, the student works on it until it is completed.

Social Reinforcement

1. **Identify and recognize in specific terms students who complete assigned academic work.** "Marilyn, I noticed that you have finished your reading assignment. I am very proud of you." "Kevin, I see that you have completed your math problems. That's excellent." "Ruth Ann, you really kept working at that spelling paper, and you're all finished. Good work!"

2. **Provide cues by recognizing other students who turn in completed work and by providing reminders in relation to specific assignments of what has to be done in order to complete the work.** For students who consistently have problems completing work, you might consider reducing the amount or difficulty of work required. In addition, you might provide additional incentives in the form of tangible reinforcers for completed work that could be exchanged for a free-time activity.

Code: S-TR-CT-0002-L1-Ic

TEACHING STRATEGY

Objective: When assigned an academic task at mastery level, the student works on it until it is completed.

Contingency Management

1. **Present the task to the student in specific terms.** For example, "When I give you an assignment, continue working on it until it is finished, or until I ask you to stop."

2. **Plan reinforcement.**

3. **Explain the contingency to the student.** Each time I give you an assignment to do, if you continue working on it until it is complete or until I ask you to stop, you will receive a reward. Specify the type and amount of reward.

4. **Assign the student academic tasks at mastery level, that is, at the level where the student can experience at least 90% success.** If the student continues working on a task until completed, or until you interrupt him or her, deliver the promised reinforcement.

5. **Example.** Laurie skips from one assignment to another without completing any. Ms. Harvey explains to her that she should complete one assignment before going on to something else. Ms. Harvey tells Laurie that for each assignment she can complete before starting another, she will receive a token. The tokens are needed to purchase a privilege.

Skill:	To complete assigned academic work within the required time. **S-TR-CT-0004-L1**
Objective:	When assigned an academic task to complete in a reasonable time period, the student finishes it on time.
Assessment:	Assess from previous knowledge of student or through direct observation using the <u>Social Behavior Assessment Inventory</u>.

Code: S-TR-CT-0004-L1-Im

TEACHING STRATEGY

Objective: When assigned an academic task to complete in a reasonable time period, the student finishes on time.

Social Modeling

1. **Set the stage.** (Be sure to allot enough time to complete Steps 1 and 2 in one session—approximately 30 minutes for eight pupils.)

   Play the game "Beat the Clock" with the target pupils. In this game you will need to pair pupils and have them compete as a team against the clock. Select some appropriate rewards to use as prizes, e.g., table games, small toys, certificates for food at local hamburger stands, soft drinks, etc. Explain the game to the pupils. Give the following directions:

   "This game is called 'Beat the Clock.' You will work in pairs to complete a task in the allotted time. I have written enough tasks so that each of you will get a turn. I have written the tasks on a slip of paper and put the papers in this box. On each slip I have also indicated the amount of time you will have to complete the task. Jennifer and Sam, you will be the first contestants. Come to the front of the room and pick a task." (Students respond.) "You have chosen the following task: 'Write six three-letter words that rhyme with **man**. You will have 45 seconds.' If you beat the clock, each of you will earn a token. I will tell you the time in 10-second intervals." (If this task is too hard for your pupils, select one appropriate to their skill level.) "Write the words on the chalkboard. Are you ready?" (Student response.) "Begin!" (Teacher will call out the seconds: 10, 20, 30, 40, time.) "Wow! You did that in just 24 seconds. That's great! You beat the clock, so you have earned a token. Now, return to your seats and let's have the next team." Repeat the procedure for each pair of pupils.

The task cards and any materials required for the tasks will need to be prepared ahead of time and placed in a box for the pupils tor draw. Possible tasks include:

(a) Write the first names of all your classmates on the board. (60 seconds)

(b) Match 10 picture cards with their corresponding pictures. (40 seconds)

(c) Match the 26 upper-case letter cards with their corresponding lower-case letter cards. (50 seconds)

(d) Match 10 number cards with the cards depicting the correct number of objects. (35 seconds)

Select tasks that are at the mastery level of the pupils and set the time limits so that the pupils will be successful.

2. **Identify the specific steps.** After the "Beat the Clock" game is completed, begin a discussion by saying, "In this game everyone was able to beat the clock. They were able to finish their tasks before time was up. What were some of the things you did that helped you to beat the clock?" (Student response.) If the following behaviors are not mentioned by the pupils, be sure to insert them in the discussion:

(a) You asked questions about things not understood before time started.

(b) You got all necessary materials together and ready before starting.

(c) You started on the task immediately.

(d) You worked steadily on task until completed.

List these four behaviors on the chalkboard. Explain to the class that completing school work correctly in the time required is just like the "Beat the Clock" game, i.e., when pupils exhibit the four behaviors listed on the board, they are able to finish their school work on time and beat the clock.

3. **Model the behavior.** To model the behavior you may take the role of a pupil who has been given an assignment to complete in five minutes. Before beginning, review the four components of the skill and list them on the chalkboard. The four components are:

(a) Ask questions if unsure of assignment.

(b) Get necessary materials ready.

(c) Start on task immediately.

(d) Work steadily.

To role-play the situation, you will need to have another person play the role of teacher or tape record the following directions: "You will have five minutes to complete this worksheet." The worksheet should consist of a task appropriate to the level of pupils in your class. Rather than working five minutes, you should complete the task in approximately one minute.

Before you begin modeling the behavior, inform the pupils that they are to observe your behavior carefully so they can discuss the role-playing episode when it is completed. After the role-playing is completed, ask: "What behaviors did you observe?" When role-playing, be sure to exhibit all four of the component behaviors.

4. **Practice the behavior.** Leave the list of component behaviors that comprise the skill of finishing in the allotted time on the board or on a poster tacked on the bulletin board in view of the students. Give the students a short assignment to complete in 10 minutes and tell them to practice this skill. For the next several days, tell the students exactly how long they have to finish each assignment. You might write the time they are to be finished on the board. Tell them that they must hand in their work at that time. Use a timer to be sure the time is accurate. Whenever you see a student exhibiting a behavior according to the guidelines you have posted (i.e., going directly to the pencil sharpener and back to seat to begin work), recognize him or her. For example; "Joe, I know you are trying to get your work done in the time you are allowed. Thank you. You are a good worker." When the students hand in their work, tell them when you will return it. For example, "I will have this paper graded for you by 3:00." Be sure to return the papers within the time you allotted for yourself.

5. **Reinforcement.** Continue to praise those students who work and complete assignments by the time the timer rings. One of the best ways to reinforce students who complete work on time is to provide a desirable activity for those who complete work ahead of time, for example, a sheet to color, a puzzle to work, table games to play, a book to read, etc. This procedure is effective for all age groups. It is, however, necessary that at least five extra minutes be allotted for the reinforcing consequence.

6. **Additional suggestions.**
   (a) In shaping this behavior, strike a balance between correctness of work and completion on time. If the work is done on time but is largely incorrect, allot more time or adjust the level of difficulty of the work.
   (b) You may need to assess related skills: S-TR-OT-0002 through S-TR-OT-0008.
   (c) Provide cues to students for completing academic assignments within specified time by recognizing others who are exhibiting appropriate behavior in the proximity of target student. Watch for the behavior in the target student and be sure to reinforce it. Other cues can be provided by drawing a clock face on the board indicating when the work is to be done or by providing verbal cues, such as, "You have 20 minutes left to finish your paper." Make sure that time demands are reasonable and difficulty level of the work is appropriate for the student.
   (d) S-TR-CT-0002-L1-S is a prerequisite skill. After the student is able to complete assigned tasks, the time required should be modified.

312

Code: S-TR-CT-0004-L1-Ir

TEACHING STRATEGY

Objective: When assigned an academic task to complete in a reasonable time period, the student finishes on time.

Social Reinforcement

1. **Identify by name and recognize target student when he or she completes an academic assignment within the specified time.** Call attention to student's completion of assignments: "Margaret, you finished your spelling paper on time. That is excellent." "Lawrence, you are getting your work done before the period is over. Good work!"

2. **Provide cues to students for completing academic assignments within specified time by recognizing others who are exhibiting appropriate behavior in the proximity of target student.** Watch for the behavior in the target student and be sure to reinforce it. Other cues can be provided by drawing a clock face on the board indicating when the work is to be done or providing verbal cues, such as, "You have 20 minutes left to finish your paper." Make sure that time demands are reasonable and difficulty level of the work is appropriate for the student.

3. **If social reinforcement alone is not sufficient to motivate students to complete work within the required time, give a tangible reinforcer, such as points or tokens, for work that has been completed on time.**

Code: S-TR-CT-0004-L1-Ic

TEACHING STRATEGY

Objective: When assigned an academic task to complete in a reasonable time period, the student finishes on time.

Contingency Management

1. **Describe in specific terms the desired behavior.** When a time limit is given for completing an assignment, work steadily and complete the assignment on time.

2. **Plan reinforcement.**

3. **Establish a contingency.** For example, if you complete this paper by the time the bell rings, you may be line leader for recess. It may be well also to build in a requirement related to correctness of work; for example, if you complete this paper by the time the bell rings with not more than two errors...

4. **Watch for the behavior to occur.** If the student completes the work on time, provide the agreed-upon reward.

5. **Example.** Mr. Kabler wanted to create incentives to encourage his class to finish their work within the time allotted. He set up a free-time corner with a number of activities that could be used for short periods of time; for example, a jigsaw puzzle set up on a table, games, such as, checkers, card games, "Spill and Spell," magic markers, and construction activities, such as, erector sets. He contracted with the class that if they completed their

assigned work on time and had at least 75% correct, they could borrow materials from the free-time corner for 15 minutes. Those who finished the work sooner could spend more time in the free-time corner and be among the first to choose activities.

Skill:	To continue working on a difficult task until it is completed. **S-TR-CT-0006-L2**
Objective:	When assigned a difficult task (below the student's mastery level), the student will continue working until it is completed, asking for help when necessary.
Assessment:	Assess from previous knowledge of student or through direct observation using the <u>Social Behavior Assessment Inventory</u>.

Code: S-TR-CT-0006-L2-Im

TEACHING STRATEGY

Objective: When assigned a difficult task (below the student's mastery level), the student will continue working until it is completed, asking for help when necessary.

Introduction: The task assigned to pupils should be one within their instructional range (70%-90% correct). This may require that the pupil make efforts to get help from the teacher and/or a classmate. S-TR-CT-0002 should be mastered as a prerequisite skill to this one.

Social Modeling

1. **Set the stage.** Tell the students a story about a youngster, similar to them in age, who entered a competition and needed some instruction. He or she was insightful and sought the needed help. As a result, the youngster did quite well in the competition. Another youngster, also in the same competition, needed instruction but chose not to seek help. That youngster did poorly in the competition.

2. **Identify the specific steps.** Explain to the target pupils that just as in the story, we sometimes face a difficult task in school. Say, "When we are confronted with a difficult task, we have two choices. We can give up or continue working on it. I think that doing as the first youngster did and continuing to work is the best thing. Sometimes the task will require something we do not understand. In these cases we look for help by reading or by asking someone for help."

Inform the pupils of the steps in this behavior:

(a) Try to complete the task without help initially.

(b) Seek help by asking someone for help or by reading.

(c) Keep working until it is completed.

3. **Model the behavior.** Take the role of a student working on a difficult arithmetic paper. Ask a student to take the part of the teacher or a helping peer. Talk out loud as if to yourself as you work on the paper, describing your actions; for example, "I finished this problem, but now there is one I

can't get. I'll have to get help." Raise your hand and demonstrate getting help; then resume the monologue. "Now I'll try the next problem. I think I can do it because it looks like the last one." Continue in this manner until the paper is complete. Ask students to identify your actions.

4. **Practice the behavior.** Give each student a task that is below his or her mastery level, i.e., one that he or she can't work on completely independently. Ask students to work at the task until it is finished. Make yourself and other students available to provide assistance. Provide reinforcement to students who continue working. Recognize students both for working and for completing the paper. Inform the pupils that when they complete the task they will earn the privilege of selecting a job from the job board (or some other appropriate reward). As each person completes the task, he or she will make his or her choice of reward. Be sure to include enough desirable rewards so that the last child to finish will have a choice.

Code: S-TR-CT-0006-L2-Ir

TEACHING STRATEGY

Objective: When assigned a difficult task (below the student's mastery level), the student will continue working until it is completed, asking for help when necessary.

Social Reinforcement

1. **Identify and recognize the target student when he or she is working persistently on a difficult task.** Use praise that describes his or her behavior. For example, "Anne, I like the way you are working on that difficult task. You are trying very hard." "Neil, I am pleased that you kept on working on that assignment until it was done."

2. **Provide cues for target student by recognizing other students who are working persistently on difficult tasks.** If necessary to develop a high level of persistent on-task behavior, accompany social reinforcement with a tangible reinforcer such as points or checkmarks for continuing to work.

Note: Be aware that if a task is too difficult for a student a high level of reinforcement alone will not maintain on-task behavior.

3. **Additional suggestions.**
   (a) Construct a bulletin board with the theme "The Crate Car Derby." Inform the pupils that for each activity period they work on a difficult task, they will earn the opportunity to advance their "car" one space and that when they cross the finish line, they will earn (a reward that you have determined is appropriate through a discussion with the pupil).
   (b) S-TR-AQ-0008, S-TR-IW-0002, and S-TR-OT-0010 are related skills that may prevent the pupil from mastering S-TR-CT-0006. If the target pupil has particular difficulty learning S-TR-CT-0006, you should assess the pupil's level of functioning on these three skills and teach them, if necessary.
   (c) In the modeling portion of this strategy, the monologue portions could be put on tape and played as your thoughts. Explain this procedure to the pupils before beginning the modeling episode.

(d) Remember that if a task is too difficult for a student, even a frequent rate of reinforcement will not maintain on-task behavior.

Code: S-TR-CT-0006-L2-Ic

TEACHING STRATEGY

Objective: When assigned a difficult task (below the student's mastery level), the student will continue working until it is completed, asking for help when necessary.

Contingency Management

1. **Present task to the student in specific terms.** When you are given a difficult task, keep working on the task until it is completed. Ask for help if necessary.

2. **Plan reinforcement.**

3. **State the contingency.** If the student continues to work on a difficult task, asking for help when necessary, he or she will receive the agreed-upon reward.

4. **Watch for the behavior to occur in the classroom and reinforce when it occurs according to the established contingency,** or set up a situation in which the behavior can occur. For example, give the student a short assignment that is difficult for him or her. Reinforce the student according to the agreed-upon contingency if he or she completes the task. Make sure that help is available if needed.

5. **Example.** Mr. Carl worked with Pete and several other students for 15 minutes daily on two-digit subtraction with borrowing. At the end of the instruction period, Mr. Carl would give the students 10 problems of two-digit subtraction with borrowing for practice. Pete would not do the problems but would sit and look out the window instead. Mr. Carl talked to Pete about doing the problems and made sure he understood how to do them. Then Mr. Carl contracted with Pete. If he would keep working in class and finish his practice papers, he would earn a privilege. Mr. Carl reminded Pete that he could ask for help if he wanted, and he assigned another student to be available to help Pete if Mr. Carl was busy. For every problem completed, Pete was given two tokens toward earning a privilege. Mr. Carl also worked on building Pete's on-task behavior by going by when he was working and making a positive comment or giving him a pat on the back.

Skill:	To complete and return homework assignments.
	S-TR-CT-0008-L2
Objective:	When assigned homework, the student completes and returns the assignment at the required time.
Assessment:	Assess from previous knowledge of student or through direct observation using the <u>Social Behavior Assessment Inventory</u>.

Code: S-TR-CT-0008-L2-Im

TEACHING STRATEGY

Objective: When assigned homework, the student completes and returns the assignment at the required time.

Social Modeling

1. **Set the stage.** Begin a discussion by asking the class, "Who can tell me about (name of a well-known athlete)?" After students' responses, ask about a few other famous athletes. After discussing three or four famous athletes ask, "How did these athletes learn to play their sports at such an outstanding level?" (Student response.) If practice is not mentioned during the discussion, you will need to bring it out. You should also say, "Athletes must practice to make the team and be good at their sport. Dancers must practice to become good dancers. Artists must practice to become good artists."

   Tell all the students to take out a sheet of paper to work some math problems. Put three math problems on the chalkboard that are above the instructional level of the pupils. Next, ask if anyone can do the problems. (Try to have problems that are difficult enough that you are reasonably sure none of the students can answer them.) The teacher should then ask the students why they would have trouble doing the problems. Some possible answers: "It's too hard," or "I don't know how to do it."

   Then say, "To do these problems you need to learn more about how to do certain types of math. We all have a lot of new things to learn this year. We will need practice to become good at what we are going to be learning. We must practice to become good at math and English and all our subjects. Practice takes a lot of time. Dancers and athletes practice many hours each day. We don't have enough time for practice at school because we have many things to do during the day. If we spend the same amount of time in school, can you think of any way we might get the time we need for practice?" If no one mentions doing practice work at home, you may mention it and explain to the class that the need for practice is the reason for homework.

2. **Identify the specific steps.** Begin a discussion by saying, "Doing school work at home involves several steps. What are some of the things you must do in order to do homework?" Students responses may include:

   (a) Get homework assignment from the teacher, the chalkboard, the wall chart, or whatever is used in your classroom.

317

(b) Write homework assignment down.

(c) Locate materials needed to complete homework assignment: books, paper, pencil, etc.

(d) Take necessary materials home.

(e) Find a quiet place to work.

(f) Begin to work on assignment.

(g) Ask for help from parents, as needed.

(h) Work steadily on assignment until completed.

(i) Put completed work in location where you will remember to bring it to school.

(j) Bring completed homework to school.

List the student responses on the board as they are offered. Add any that they leave out. Arrange the steps in the proper sequence and review with the pupils.

3. **Model the behavior.** Play the role of a student looking at the chart to locate the homework assignment, taking books or papers home, finding a quiet place to work, asking for help from parents or older sibling or telephoning a friend for help if necessary, putting the work where he or she can easily remember it in the morning, bringing it to school, and getting a star on the chart. Give a monologue as you role-play describing your actions; for example, "I'm not going to study in the living room because the TV is on in there. I'm going to move to the kitchen table." Elicit a discussion when you have completed the role-playing by asking questions, such as, "What did I do when it was too noisy in the living room to work?" "What did I do when I got stuck and needed help?" "What did I do to help remember to take my work to school?" Recognize students who give appropriate answers.

   Ask each student to write on a piece of paper his or her name, the time he or she could do homework, and the room of the house in which he or she could work. Read these slips and discuss how people do homework at different times and in different places. Discuss who, if anyone, the student could ask for help with the homework. Have each pupil work out the specific steps he or she is going to follow to do the homework. If students write, have them write the steps out.

4. **Practice the behavior.** Assign to each student homework that is at mastery level. Homework is to be completed and returned the following morning. Establish a reward contingency to be used. When students complete homework, have them describe in front of the class what they did to complete their assignment and reinforce according to the agreed-upon contingency. The first homework assignments should be short and easy for the pupils to complete. Gradually the length and difficulty can be increased but should be within the mastery level of the pupil.

5. **Reinforcement.** For the first several weeks, have a chart on the wall to show the homework assignments of each child. Place a star or some other symbol on the chart when the student's homework is completed on time. Use verbal praise to all who turn in their assignments completed and on time.

6. **Additional suggestions.**

   (a) Be sure the material in the students' homework is at mastery level.

   (b) Periodically, provide a time for the students to do some of their homework in class.

   (c) Stars on the wall chart could be used as secondary reinforcers to buy backup reinforcers.

Code: S-TR-CT-0008-L2-Ir

TEACHING STRATEGY

Objective: When assigned homework, the student completes and returns the assignment at the required time.

Social Reinforcement

1. **Use social reinforcement when the student completes and returns assigned homework on time.** Be specific in praising. For example, "Good work, Jim. You got your homework in on time." "Kathy, you really worked hard to get this homework done."

2. **Provide cues for the target student.** Recognize other students who complete homework and return it on time. Give the student cues by writing a note telling the student what the task is and when it is to be completed. Post homework assignments on the board. If necessary, provide parents with information about what homework is required and when it is due so parents can provide cues at home.

3. **If necessary, provide tangible reinforcement along with social reinforcement for completing and returning homework.**

Code: S-TR-CT-0008-L2-Ic

TEACHING STRATEGY

Objective: When assigned homework, the student completes and returns the assignment at the required time.

Contingency Management

1. **Present task to student in specific terms.** When you are assigned homework, complete the assignment and return it on the specified day.

2. **Plan reinforcement.**

3. **State the contingency.** If the student completes the homework assignment and returns it on time, he or she will receive the agreed-upon consequences. Depending on the situation, the teacher may also want to set up contingencies related to the quality of the homework.

4. **Set up a situation in which the student is given a homework assignment on a skill mastered.** Go over the assignment with the student to make sure he or she understands the nature of the assignment and when it is due. If the student completes the task and returns it on time, the student receives the agreed-upon reinforcement.

5. **Example.** Mr. Cromwell gave homework assignments to provide students with additional drill on skills they have received instruction on in class. He was careful not to assign homework that students could not do independently. Several students had difficulty getting their homework completed and returned. Mr. Cromwell went over the assignments with them to make sure they knew how to do them. He then set up a contingency that for every day they returned their homework on time and completed, they would each receive a point to be applied to additional gym time for the whole class on Friday. He found that one student did not respond to the contingency and determined that conditions in that student's home made it very hard for the student to do homework. He, therefore, set up a time during school when the student could complete the homework and receive points.

FOLLOWING DIRECTIONS

S-TR-FD-0002-L1-S   To follow teacher's verbal directions.

S-TR-FD-0004-L2-S   To follow written directions.

S-TR-FD-0006-L2-S   To follow directions in taking a test.

Skill:	To follow teacher's verbal directions. **S-TR-FD-0002-L1**
Objective:	Student follows the teacher's verbal directions.
Assessment:	Assess from previous knowledge of student or through direct observation using the <u>Social Behavior Assessment Inventory</u>.

Code: S-TR-FD-0002-L1-Im

TEACHING STRATEGY

Objective: Student follows the teacher's verbal directions.

Social Modeling

1. **Set the stage.** Tell the following story:

SAMMY, THE SINGING SNAKE

Sammy was a snake who sang all the time. His song went like this: "S-S-S-Sammy, beautiful Sammy, you're the only singing snake that I know." (To the tune of K-K-K-Katy.)

Sammy's fondest dream was to some day sing in a carnival show. One day Sammy heard that a carnival show was coming to town for two days. Sammy called the owner of the carnival show, Mr. Listen, to ask if he could join the show. Mr. Listen told Sammy that he would have to audition for the show. They set up an appointment for Sammy to come to Mr. Listen's office the next day at 5:00 to audition for the show. Mr. Listen told Sammy to make sure he was on time because the carnival was leaving at 6:00 to move on to the next town. Sammy said he would be there.

Sammy practiced his singing all night and all the next day. At 3:00 Sammy began to get ready to leave for his audition, and he remembered he didn't know where Mr. Listen's office was. So Sammy asked his mother. His mother said, "Now listen, Sammy, and I will tell you how to get to Mr. Listen's office. Go down Main Street till you come to the railroad tracks and turn left. Go two blocks, and you will see a big red trailer. That trailer is Mr. Listen's office." Sammy thanked his mother, gave her a good-bye kiss, and left for Mr. Listen's office.

Sammy started down Main Street to the railroad tracks, but he decided to take a shortcut so he could get to Mr. Listen's trailer more quickly. He went one mile but didn't see a red trailer! He went two miles but didn't see a red trailer; he went three miles and didn't see a red trailer. He looked at his watch, and it was 15 minutes 'til 5:00. "Oh no," he said, "I'm going to be late." Sammy thought of his mother's directions and said, "I didn't follow my mother's directions." He decided to go back. Sammy tried to hurry, but snakes do move slowly. He went back one mile, he went back two miles, he went back three miles. Once again he was at Main Street. He looked at his watch; it was 5:45. "Oh no!" he thought, "I'm late. Well, I'll just hurry." This time he went down Main Street to the railroad tracks and turned left. He looked at his watch, and it was five minutes 'til 6:00. He went two blocks and saw the big red trailer driving off with the carnival show following right behind. Sammy began to cry. "Oh!" he sobbed, "The carnival show won't be back for another year. If only I had followed my mother's directions. Well, I will from now on."

2. **Identify the specific steps.**

   (a) Ask, "Why was Sammy crying?"

   (b) Ask, "Why did he get lost?"

   (c) List reasons why it is important to follow directions.

   (d) Ask, "What would happen if no one followed directions?"

   (e) Explain the steps necessary in order to follow teacher's directions:

      (1) Listen carefully to the teacher (prerequisite skill S-TR-AT-0006).

      (2) Repeat the directions audibly or silently.

      (3) Do as directed.

3. **Model the behavior.** Tape record the following series of directions. Leave approximately 10 seconds of blank tape between each.

   (a) "Take out your math book and open it to page 104."

   (b) "Take out a sheet of paper and print your name in the top right hand corner."

   (c) "Go to the blackboard." (Pause 15 seconds.) "Write the following sentence. Today is _____ (fill in the correct information)."

   Play these tape recorded directions in class and model "following the directions." After you have modeled the behaviors, have a pupil model them.

4. **Practice the behavior.** Choose one or more of the following:

   (a) Play the game "Move Out Front." Students line up behind a line. Teacher stands behind the finish line and calls out directions, "Take three giant steps. Touch your nose. Take one baby step and turn all the way around." The students who do not follow the directions go back and start again. The person who crosses the finish line first earns the job of being caller.

   (b) Give a verbal direction and call on a student to carry it out. For example, open the door, put your math paper on the teacher's desk, put your head down on your desk, or shake hands with the teacher. Allow each student to have an opportunity to follow directions. Vary the complexity of the directions according to the abilities of the students. Reinforce correct responses with verbal praise, e.g., "Tim, you followed my directions exactly."

   (c) Have the students stand and simulate driving a car. Drive forward, turn left, stop. Start again, drive in reverse, drive forward, turn right, etc. Set up a Good Driver's Club. Allow students to earn points for following directions during the simulated driving, and with the points they may earn a membership in the Good Driver's Club. Make a driver's license to pass out where points can be earned. Fill in the space until the pupil earns 50 points. When 50 points are earned, put the pupil's name on a special bulletin board.

5. **Social Reinforcement.** Recognize students for following your direction: "Stanley, you did a super job of following my directions when you came in from recess."

6. **Additional suggestions.** Practice activity: Give all students one piece of paper and have them take out their crayons. Teacher says:

Number 1. Fold your paper in half.

Number 2. Now fold it in half again.

Number 3. Open it up.

Number 4. Draw a triangle in the upper left block.

Number 5. Draw a circle in the upper right block.

Number 6. Draw a square in the lower left block.

Number 7. Draw a rectangle in the lower right block.

Number 8. Turn paper over, print your name in the upper left block.

Collect the papers and repeat with your own set of directions. If these directions are too easy or difficult, make the necessary adjustments for your group.

Code: S-TR-FD-0002-L1-Ir

TEACHING STRATEGY

Objective: Student follows the teacher's verbal directions.

Social Reinforcement

1. **Identify and praise aloud target student when observed following the teacher's verbal direction.** Be specific in praising. For example, "Harold, thank you for following my directions. You did a beautiful job of carrying them through;" "Carl, you did just what I told you. Thank you."

2. **Provide cues for the target student.** Recognize another student who has carried out the directions. You may also remind the student. For example, "Harold, thank you for following my directions;" "Let's see how good a listener you are today." Provide written or pictorial cues for the directions that are to be followed.

3. **If needed, provide tangible reinforcers such as tokens, coupons, or stars, along with social reinforcement.** The tangible reinforcers should be phased out as soon as possible and the behavior maintained with praise, smiles, and attention.

Code: S-TR-FD-0002-L1-Ic

TEACHING STRATEGY

Objective: Student follows the teacher's verbal directions.

Contingency Management

1. **Present task to student in specific terms.** When I give a verbal direction, listen and do what I say. Explain to the student why he or she should follow a verbal direction you give.

2. **Plan reinforcement.**

3. **State the contingency.** If the student, when given a verbal direction by the teacher, follows the direction, he or she will receive the agreed-upon reinforcement. Specify type and amount of reinforcement.

4. **Watch for the behavior to occur naturally or set a situation for the behavior to occur.** For example, give the student a direction. If the student follows the verbal direction stated by the teacher, the student receives the agreed-upon reinforcement.

5. **Example.** Joey seldom followed directions given by Ms. Cartwright. Joey would ignore the directions and do as he pleased. Ms. Cartwright talked with Joey about following directions. She and Joey practiced the behavior. Ms. Cartwright played a game of "Simon Says" with Joey, giving him directions to perform, such as, "Simon Says, 'Go and sit in your seat;' Simon Says, 'Walk quietly to the door;' Simon says, 'Write your name on the top of this paper.'" She used social reinforcement if Joey followed the directions in the game. Ms. Cartwright then set up a contract with Joey. She told Joey that each time he followed the teacher's verbal directions, he would receive one star. When Joey had earned 20 stars, he would be a student visitor in Ms. Elbott's room. Joey was eager to do this because his brother was in Ms. Elbott's room. After Joey had earned the privilege, Ms. Cartwright repeated the contingency requiring a larger number of points for the reward.

Skill:	To follow written directions. **S-TR-FD-0004-L2**
Objective:	Student follows written directions.
Assessment:	Assess from previous knowledge of student or through direct observation using the <u>Social Behavior Assessment Inventory</u>.

Code: S-TR-FD-0004-L2-Im

TEACHING STRATEGY

Objective: Student follows written directions.

Introduction: When asking a student to follow written directions, consider the student's reading vocabulary. It may be necessary to introduce and/or practice "direction" words prior to introducing this strategy. If it is necessary to teach "direction" words, be sure to proceed in small steps. That is, introduce no more that two new words at a time and code the student's seatwork to these words. Primary children need to begin with very simple written coded directions such as "O the red Bb's."

There are many words and phrases which must be read and understood as prerequisites to following written directions. For example: first, second, after, underline, next to, over, under, on left, right, etc. Be sure the words and concepts to be used can be read and understood before proceeding with this strategy. Vary the presentation as needed to meet the reading levels of your students.

Social Modeling

1. **Set the stage.** Have several props prepared ahead of time, such as, a game, a ditto, a workbook. Hold up one item at a time and ask students questions, such as the following: "Here is a new game. I've never played it. How could I find out how to play?" (Student response.) "Exactly right, I could read the directions!"

   "I'm supposed to do this workbook page. How can I find out how to do it?" (If response is, "Ask teacher," continue with, "Is there any other way?") "Very good, we know there are many times that we need to read directions. We named two just now. Are there any other times or places that you can think of where we need to read directions?"

   (a) Street signs.

   (b) Buildings and store directions.

   (c) Applications (for older age groups).

   (d) To send in for products from magazines, cereal boxes, etc.

   Have students name several occasions such as the above in which we can't depend on someone else to tell us what to do verbally.

2. **Identify the specific steps.** Say to students, "Let's see. Can anyone tell me how we follow directions when they are not told to us?" Accept reasonable answers and summarize essential steps on the board.

   (a) Read the directions carefully before beginning to work.

   (b) Do exactly what the directions say.

3. **Model the behavior.** Prepare five 3 x 5 cards with written directions. The level of difficulty must be in accord with the pupils' reading skills at mastery level. Explain to students, "I have some cards here that give directions. I am going to pick one and do what it says." Pick a card, read it, but before following the directions, say, "Read my card and see if I follow the directions correctly!"

   Ask another student to choose a card and do as it says. Repeat as needed. Suggested directions for 3 x 5 cards:

   (a) Write your name on the chalkboard in script.

   (b) Take out one sheet of paper and fold it in half.

   (c) Stand up and clap your hands three times.

   (d) Get your math book out and open it to page 17.

   (e) Walk to the front of the room and face the class.

4. **Practice activity.**

   (a) Make a worksheet with nine squares that are 2" x 2." Below the box, on the ditto, have the following directions:

      (1) In the first box, put an "X."

      (2) In the next box, write your name.

      (3) In the last box in the first row, draw an apple.

(4) In the first box in the second row, write the letter "Z."

(5) In the middle box, draw a flower.

(6) In the next box, draw a tree.

(7) In the first box in the last row, make the letter "T."

(8) In the next box, draw a ball.

(9) In the last box, draw a snowman.

(Depending on your group, you may wish to have fewer boxes and easier directions.)

Code: S-TR-FD-0004-L2-Ir

TEACHING STRATEGY

Objective: Student follows written directions.

Social Reinforcement

1. **Identify and praise by name, aloud, target student when observed following written directions.** Call attention to specific actions, e.g., "Milt, I see you colored the pictures just as the directions said." "Tonia, how beautifully you followed those directions by underlining the correct word and crossing out the wrong words." Remember to praise following the directions even if other aspects of the words are incorrect.

2. **Hold up papers that have been handed in and recognize the pupils for following directions.** For each paper that is handed in with all directions followed correctly, award one raffle ticket. At the end of the day (or week), hold a drawing and award three prizes that are appropriate reinforcers for your class.

3. **Additional suggestions.**

   (a) The following game could be an alternative practice activity. Say, "We are going to play a game. You will read the directions very carefully. Then do as the card tells you. If you follow the directions correctly, you may stay in the game. If not, you must be out until the next time." Have large cards prepared with directions written in Magic Marker, for example:

   (1) Jump up and down three times.

   (2) Walk around your desk.

   (3) If you are a girl, sit down.

   (4) Make a big smile.

   (5) Kneel on the floor and then sit down in your seat.

   (6) Hop three times if you are a boy.

   (7) Put both hands on your head.

   (b) In setting the stage with older children, you might give them the following worksheet: "Read and follow all the directions carefully."

   (1) Put your name on this paper.

   (2) Read all the directions before you continue.

   (3) Laugh out loud.

(4) Put an "X" on the bottom of the page.

(5) Jump up three times.

(6) Draw a circle around your name.

(7) Shout out your name.

(8) Draw a man on the back.

(9) Now that you have read the directions, go back and do only number one.

Many of the students will not read all the directions before they continue, and they will find out how important it is to read carefully and follow directions.

Code: S-TR-FD-0004-L2-Ic

TEACHING STRATEGY

Objective: Student follows written directions.

Contingency Management

1. **State the task in observable terms.**
   (a) Read the directions before beginning your work.
   (b) Do as the directions say—underline, circle, color, cut-out, write word.
   (c) Read directions, if any, at end of work and do as they say.
2. **Plan reinforcement strategy selected from reinforcement menu.**
3. **State the contingency.** If the student follows written directions correctly, he or she will be rewarded according to the agreed-upon terms. Specify amount and type of reinforcement.
4. **Set situation to necessitate students following written directions.** Write several sets of directions on the board and give each student a specific one to follow or give each a worksheet with written directions. Observe if they follow the directions, and reward those who follow them correctly.
5. **Example.** Ms. Polk had been having trouble with five of her students following any kind of written directions. Although they could read the directions, they often skipped over them and consequently ended up doing many papers incorrectly. Ms. Polk discussed with these five students why it was important to read the directions. She set up the contingency that each time one of these students followed directions properly she would hang his paper on the bulletin board. As soon as the board was filled up with at least five papers for each of these students, the class would have a party. She gradually increased this to 8, 10, 12 papers required and changed the reward to other things, such as, film, walk, or extra recess.

Skill:	To follow directions in taking a test.
	S-TR-FD-0006-L2
Objective:	Student follows directions in taking a test when the directions are given verbally by the teacher or when the directions are written on the test sheet itself.
Assessment:	Assess from previous knowledge of student or through direct observation using the <u>Social Behavior Assessment Inventory</u>.

Code: S-TR-FD-0006-L2-Im

TEACHING STRATEGY

Objective: Student follows directions in taking a test when the directions are given orally by the teacher or when the directions are written on the test sheet itself.

Social Modeling

1. **Set the stage.** Tell the following story:

TILLIE TEST TAKER

Tillie Test Taker had one thing she could do exceptionally well. Do you know what it was? That's right, she could take tests very well. One day, Millie Mistake Maker, who didn't do so well on tests (in fact, very often missed all the questions) asked Tillie Test Taker, "Tillie, why are you such a good test taker?"

What do you think Tillie answered? (If the students have difficulty with this question, ask the following ones.)

(a) Is it because she never reads directions?

(b) Does she listen carefully?

(c) Does she read directions on the tests?

(d) Is it because she always rushes through her work?

(e) Does she try very hard and work carefully?

2. **Identify the specific steps.** Tell the students the steps, showing cards with visual cues. "If you would like to be a Tillie Test Taker, what would you do? Would you:

(a) Listen carefully to the teacher?

(b) Read written directions carefully?

(c) Work carefully and follow the directions?"

"I have made up some tests that are just for fun. Who would like to be the teacher and read the directions for the first test to me?" Student reads directions: "Write your name on the paper." You follow directions. Hold up paper and ask, "Did I follow the directions? Yes, I did. What did I do to follow the directions?" (Student response: "Listened carefully as teacher gave directions.") On the next test, you don't have to give directions out loud; the student reads them. (Read and follow the directions.) Hold up

328

paper. "Did I follow the directions? You're right, I did. What did I do to follow the directions?" (Student response: "Read the directions carefully.")

Suggested test for modeling behavior:

(a) Use blank sheet of paper. Student reads, "Write your name." You model behavior by writing your name.

(b) Use page with written directions: "On your paper draw three balloons." You read directions and draw three balloons.

4. **Practice activity.** Say, "Now I am going to pass out a fun test to you. On this first test I will give the directions out loud, so what should you do?" (Student response.) "Listen very carefully. Let's begin." Walk around verbally praising those students following directions. "Good job, now let's try this next test. The directions are written at the top. What should we do?" (Student response: "Read directions very carefully.") Walk around verbally praising students who have followed the directions.

Suggested tests for practicing the behavior:

a) Oral directions: Give students a piece of 8 1/2 x 11 newsprint, and say:

(1) Print your name on the top of the page.

(2) Write your address under your name.

(3) Draw a happy face on the bottom of the page.

(4) Draw a house in the middle of your paper.

(b) Written directions. Give the student a mimeographed sheet with these directions on it:

(1) Put your name on this line.

(2) Do all your writing with a pencil.

(3) Draw a boy.

(4) Don't write in this box.

(5) Write your age here.

(6) How many people live in your house? Write that number here.

These tests may have to be altered, depending on the students' abilities.

Code: S-TR-FD-0006-L2-Ir

TEACHING STRATEGY

Objective: Student follows directions in taking a test when the directions are given orally by the teacher or when the directions are written on the test sheet itself.

Social Reinforcement

1. **On a bulletin board or blackboard have the title, "Can You Get a Bullseye?"** Each day, each student would get a worksheet with a bullseye shown on the paper surrounded by a number of rings. A drawing of an arrow should also be on the sheet. The number of rings in the target would depend on the number of assignments that require following directions. For example, if Tommy had four assignments on Tuesday that required direction following, his target would have four circles. When the student

completed the first assignment, he would cut out the arrow and place it in the outer ring. Every additional completed assignment would mean he would move in one more ring. When the student hits the bullseye, he hangs his target on the bulletin board or takes it home. This could be done one or two times a week (as necessary). Verbal praise should always be given for the target behavior.

2. **Additional suggestions.** For very young children you might substitute the following poem to set the stage:

> These are my ears (touch ears).
> I use them to listen.
> These are my eyes (touch eyes),
> I use them to see.

Have students do this with you several times, and then say, "Follow directions and make one happy face."

Code: S-TR-FD-0006-L2-Ic

TEACHING STRATEGY

Objective: Student follows directions in taking a test when the directions are given orally by the teacher or when the directions are written on the test sheet itself.

Contingency Management

1. **State the task in observable terms.**
   (a) When the teacher is giving directions for a test, look at him or her and listen to the directions.
   (b) Begin the test only when directed to do so.
   (c) When given a test with written directions, read the directions before beginning the test.
   (d) When given directions for taking a test, do exactly as the directions say, e.g., "underline, write, circle, cross out, color, or complete."
2. **Plan reinforcement strategy selected from reinforcement menu.**
3. **State the contingency.** If student follows test directions he or she will be rewarded. Specify amount and type of reinforcement.
4. **Set situation to necessitate students' following test directions.** Give students verbal and written directions for taking a test.
5. **Example.** Several students in Ms. Rivera's class had difficulties following directions on tests she administered to the class. There were always a few who would do the opposite of the directions. Ms. Rivera explained the problem to the class and said she had a new plan. She made a chart; and each time she gave a test, each member of the class would get an opportunity to earn a star. If everyone in the class followed directions on a test, they could vote an extra recess, movie, or nature walk. As the class improved, the requirements for reinforcement were increased, i.e., two test periods with correct following of instructions before earning the privilege to choose a reward for following directions.

GROUP ACTIVITIES

S-TR-GA-0002-L1-S	To share materials with others in a work situation.
S-TR-GA-0004-L2-S	To work cooperatively on a task with a partner.
S-TR-GA-0006-L2-S	To carry out plans or decisions formulated by the group.
S-TR-GA-0008-L2-S	To accept ideas presented in a group task situation which are different from one's own.
S-TR-GA-0010-L2-S	To initiate and help carry out a group activity.

Skill: To share materials with others in a work situation.
S-TR-GA-0002-L1

Objective: Student shares materials willingly with others in a work situation by letting other students use materials and using materials conjointly with others.

Assessment: Assess from previous knowledge of student or through direct observation using the <u>Social Behavior Assessment Inventory</u>.

Code: S-TR-GA-0002-L1-Im

TEACHING STRATEGY

Objective: Student shares materials willingly with others in a work situation by letting other students use materials and using materials conjointly with others.

Social Modeling

1. **Set the stage.** Develop the concept of sharing by telling the story of the Little Red Hen who couldn't find anyone to help with the work, so in turn did not share (at first) her freshly baked bread. After the story, discuss what sharing means.

   Continue with a situation such as the following. "Boys and girls, today I wanted to do an art project with you, but I don't have enough (scissors or special forms to trace) for everyone. I guess we can't do the project unless someone has an idea." (Lead into the idea of sharing the supplies so that all can do the project.)

   "I'm really glad you decided to share. I think there are many times we need to share our materials in school. Let's see how many we can list." Allow students to name specific instances where sharing materials is required, for example; listening center, seesaw, trampoline, balls, jump rope, etc.

2. **Identify specific steps.** Say, "There are certain rules we have to remember to share well. Let's see if we can list some rules for sharing on the board." Encourage students to make suggestions. Use directed questions to identify three rules similar to the following:

   (a) Take turns using the materials.

   (b) When not using the materials, keep them in a place available to all in the group.

331

(c) Choose something else to do while waiting for another to finish with the item you need.

3. **Model the behavior.** Say: "Let's see how well we know the rules of sharing. We're going to glue these pictures to make a bulletin board." (Prepare cartoons and captions of sharing to reinforce rules just decided upon.) "I'll be in the group. I need two helpers." (Select two students who have demonstrated mastery of the skill. Use pupils from another class if necessary.) "The rest of you watch and see if we follow the rules on the board."

Continue to complete the project in this contrived setting. Be specific and obvious in your comments and actions, e.g., "Here is the glue, Jon. I'll need it again when you're finished with it." "You may use the glue, Fred. I'll cut pictures while you're using the glue."

Prepare the captions on separate sheets of paper to be cut out and pasted on other strips of colored construction paper. Put the cartoons on separate sheets also, to be cut out and matted with construction paper. The finished product will be a bulletin board with each cartoon posted above the proper caption.

4. **Practice the behavior.** Have rules posted and review before initiating your practice session. Divide children into groups of three to five children each. Provide each group with one jar of glue, two pairs of scissors, magazines, and one piece of 12" x 15" construction paper. Instruct children to find pictures of food (or whatever is appropriate for your group) and make a collage. "You'll have ten minutes to complete your collage. Remember, we'll have to share to get our job done in time." Be sure to praise specific, appropriate behaviors, e.g., "Juan, I really like the way you kept busy while John was using the scissors that you needed."

Code: S-TR-GA-0002-L1-Ir

TEACHING STRATEGY

Objective: Student shares materials willingly with others in a work situation by letting other students use materials and using materials conjointly with others.

Social Reinforcement

1. **Recognize the target student by name, loudly enough so others can hear, when seen sharing materials with other students.** Call attention to the student's specific actions: "Sammy, thank you for sharing your book with George;" "Lawanda, you are very thoughtful to share your crayons with Lisa."

2. **Cue the target student to share materials by reinforcing others who share their materials.** Watch for behavior in the target child and reinforce it. When praise alone is not enough to encourage a student to share with others, praise for sharing behavior might be accompanied by a tangible reinforcer, or you might want to write names on the board of students who are "good sharers."

3. **Additional suggestions.** There should be ample opportunities for students to share materials. For students needing special help in developing the skill, be sure to cue them often, review rules for sharing, and specify when you expect them to share. You may provide added practice by contriving special projects that involve sharing, e.g., puppet shows, art projects, reports.

Code: S-TR-GA-0002-L1-Ic

TEACHING STRATEGY

Objective: Student shares materials willingly with others in a work situation by letting other students use materials and using materials conjointly with others.

Contingency Management

1. **Present the task to the student in specific terms.** When you are working, let other students share materials that you have when you are through with them, or let other students use them at the same time you are using them by taking turns.

2. **Define a consequence valued by the student that will be given after demonstrated appropriate sharing behavior.**

3. **State the contingency.** If student shares materials with other students, he or she will receive the agreed-upon positive consequence.

4. **Watch for the behavior to occur naturally and reinforce it when it occurs,** or set up a situation in which the behavior can occur. For example, divide the class into small groups. Assign tasks to the groups, such as art tasks or measurement tasks. Give a limited number of supplies to each group. If students demonstrate the appropriate behavior of sharing in their group, a reward could be earned for the group.

5. **Example.** Tim was not willing to share school art materials with the other students at his table. He liked certain items, for example, the black crayons; and he tended to grab for these and not let others use them. In order to encourage Tim to share, the teacher contracted with him. Tim and the rest of the class liked music during art. If the teacher saw Tim sharing the black crayons and other materials, he or she would let him pick out and put records on the record player during art. When a record was over, Tim would have to be sharing materials in order to put on another one.

Skill: To work cooperatively on a task with a partner.
S-TR-GA-0004-L2

Objective: When given a task to work on with someone, the student will cooperate with that partner by exhibiting some of the following behaviors: sharing materials, dividing responsibilities and completing assigned responsibility, exchanging opinion and information, and accommodating his or her viewpoint to that of the partner.

Assessment: Assess from previous knowledge of student or through direct observation using the <u>Social Behavior Assessment Inventory</u>.

Code: S-TR-GA-0004-L2-Im

TEACHING STRATEGY

Objective: When given a task to work on with someone, the student will cooperate with that partner by exhibiting some of the following behaviors: sharing materials, dividing responsibilities and completing assigned responsibility, exchanging opinion and information, and accommodating his or her viewpoint to that of the partner.

Social Modeling

1. **Set the stage.** Tell the students the following story:

WORKING TOGETHER

Joanne and Teddy were getting ready for the science fair at their school. Each student was assigned a partner to work on a project. Joanne was working with Glen on a project about the solar system. Teddy was working with Karen on a project about rocks and minerals. Teddy and Karen worked very hard together on their science project. They each wrote two reports about different kinds of rocks and minerals. They each collected rocks and minerals and shared them to make a giant display. They read books about rocks and reported the information to each other. Teddy and Karen did not agree about how their display should be set up, but they talked it over and came to an agreement.

Joanne and Glen did not work together on their project. Glen did not want to share his books with Joanne, and Joanne wanted Glen to write all the reports. Glen wanted to make a model of the solar system, but Joanne didn't like the idea, so she didn't help him.

On the day of the science fair, Ted and Karen were all ready to set up their display and answer questions. When the judge came to their project, they were able to answer all the questions perfectly. Joanne and Glen had a very small display because Joanne had left almost all the work to Glen. When the judges came to their display, Glen and Joanne could not answer the questions about the solar system because they had not discussed the reports or shared information about the project.

After the judging, all of the students were anxiously waiting in the auditorium to hear the results of the judging. Every student was hoping that his project had won first prize. The judges began the announcement. "First prize for the best project goes to Ted Williams and Karen Barnes." Ted and Karen were very happy when they received the trophy! Later Joanne and Glen congratulated them and said, "You both deserved the prize, since you worked so hard on it together. Next time, we'll work together and share the responsibilities the way you did!"

Begin discussion by asking the class, "Why do you think Karen and Ted won first prize?" (Student response.) Continue the discussion by asking the following questions:

(a) What does it mean to cooperate?

(b) When we share materials, are we cooperating?

(c) Why is it important to divide up responsibilities to get a job done?

(d) Why is it important to exchange opinions and information?

(e) If you disagree with your partner, what is the best way to handle this disagreement?

2. **Identify the specific steps.** What are some of the steps you should follow when you're working on a task with a partner? Refer to the story as the points are discussed, i.e., "How did Ted and Karen handle their disagreement?" For example, when working with a partner:

(a) Share materials

(b) Divide responsibilities equally.

(c) Exchange opinions and information.

(d) Work out your disagreements.

Instruct students to make a copy of these rules for their own use in a later activity.

3. **Model the behavior.** (You may want to delay this section until the next day. If it is delayed, be sure to review Step 2.) Model each of the following behaviors with another student.

(a) Sharing materials.

(b) Dividing responsibilities.

(c) Exchanging opinions and information.

(d) Accommodating his or her viewpoint to that of the partner.

Select a project that you plan to assign to the class as a project to be completed by pairs of students. Have a pupil from your class or another class who has mastered this skill role-play with you. Begin the role-playing episode by stating the project on which you will be working; then, make a list of all the materials needed and begin discussing what you have that you will share. Proceed to model each of the behaviors listed above.

4. **Practice the behavior.** Assign each student a partner for working on a project. For example, the project may be making a scrapbook, and each pair is responsible for contributing one page to the scrapbook. The theme of the scrapbook can be about their hobbies or may be related to an area they are studying in another project. Remind the students to follow the steps for working with someone. Refer to the copy of rules each student made about this behavior.

During the practice, be sure to reinforce cooperative behaviors by giving descriptive praise; e.g., "Millie and Todd, you did a super job of working out the disagreement you were having over how many pictures should be on one page of your scrapbook." When each pair has completed planning their project, they may discuss and evaluate their cooperative behavior.

5. **Reinforcement.** Assign different pairs of students to make displays on the bulletin board each day. Observe each pair as they work and praise when desired behaviors are exhibited, calling attention to specific actions; e.g., "Donna, I appreciate the way you are working with your partner;" "Sammy, you are doing a beautiful job of sharing materials with your partner. You are developing good ideas together."

6. **Additional suggestions.**

    (a) For those students who do not learn the behavior, you may wish to ask each student to work with you on a small project, such as, taking attendance, hanging pictures, etc. As the student exhibits the behavior or anything close to it, you should immediately praise him or her; e.g., "I appreciate your sharing the responsibilities of this task with me," etc.

    (b) A contingency contract may need to be set up for student(s) not responding to the praise.

    (c) Be sure the first project the pupils are assigned is something they will enjoy. Base your choice for the first project on what you have observed about your pupils' interests. The first project need not be academic in nature. Your primary goal should be to reinforce cooperative behaviors.

Code: S-TR-GA-0004-L2-Ir

TEACHING STRATEGY

Objective: When given a task to work on with someone, the student will cooperate with that partner by exhibiting some of the following behaviors: sharing materials, dividing responsibilities and completing assigned responsibility, exchanging opinion and information, and accommodating his or her viewpoint to that of the partner.

Social Reinforcement

1. **Identify and praise by name target student when observed cooperating with a partner by exhibiting some of the following behaviors:**

    (a) Sharing materials.

    (b) Dividing responsibilities and completing assigned responsibility.

    (c) Exchanging opinion and information.

    (d) Accommodating his or her viewpoint to that of the partner.

    Call attention to his or her specific actions, e.g., "Donna, I appreciate the way you are working with your partner;" "Sammy, you are doing a beautiful job of sharing materials with your partner. You two are developing good ideas together."

2. **Cue cooperatively working with partner in target student by praising others around him or her who are working well with a partner.** Then watch for the behavior in the target child and reinforce it.

336

3. If social reinforcement in the form of praise, attention, smiles, pats on the back, etc., is not sufficient to increase the desired behavior, it may be necessary to accompany social reinforcement with tangible reinforcement, e.g., tokens, chips, points, stars, etc., to be exchanged for something the child wants.

Code: S-TR-GA-0004-L2-Ic

TEACHING STRATEGY

Objective: When given a task to work on with someone, the student will cooperate with that partner by exhibiting some of the following behaviors: sharing materials, dividing responsibilities and completing assigned responsibility, exchanging opinion and information, and accommodating his or her viewpoint to that of the partner.

Contingency Management

1. **Present task to student in specific terms.** When working with a partner, student should:

   (a) Share materials.
   (b) Divide responsibilities and complete assigned responsibility.
   (c) Exchange opinions and information.
   (d) Accommodate his or her viewpoint to that of his or her partner.

   If needed, provide a list of appropriate behaviors which define cooperatively working with a partner.

2. **Plan reinforcement strategy selected from reinforcement menu.** Define a consequence valued by the student which will be given following demonstration of acceptable behaviors of cooperatively working with partner.

3. **State the contingency.** If student, when given a task to work on with someone, cooperates with the partner by sharing materials, dividing responsibilities and completing assigned responsibility, exchanging opinion and information, and accommodating his or her viewpoint to that of the partner, the student will receive the agreed-upon consequence. (You may wish to define "cooperating" to include additional behaviors.)

4. **Watch for behavior to occur naturally and reinforce it when it occurs according to established contingency,** or set up a situation for the behavior to occur in. Assign the target student to work with another student on a task, e.g., design bulletin board, plan field trip, etc. State the contingency to the student. Observe the target student. If he or she demonstrates the behaviors of cooperatively working with his or her partner, both will receive the agreed-upon consequence.

5. **Example.** Joey did not work well with other students. He refused to share materials, insisted that things be done his way, and often did not carry through on his part of a task. Mr. George and Joey discussed the behaviors which constitute cooperatively working with a partner. Joey and Mr. George agreed on a contract. Mr. George would observe Joey working with another student on a Social Studies project. If Joey exhibited behaviors of cooperatively working with his partner, Joey would receive the agreed-

upon consequence of running the visual-aid equipment for the class movies on Friday. Because there are a number of behaviors that make up "cooperative" behavior, and Joey had problems with several of them, Mr. George did not expect perfection right away from Joey, but rewarded him initially for effort in the right direction. As Joey improved, Mr. George gradually changed his criteria for rewarding Joey to expecting more cooperative behavior from him.

Skill:	To carry out plans or decisions formulated by the group. **S-TR-GA-0006-L2**
Objective:	When the group of which the student is a member makes a reasonable plan or decision, the student will take action to help carry out the plan or decision.
Assessment:	Assess from previous knowledge of student or through direct observation using the <u>Social Behavior Assessment Inventory</u>.

Code: S-TR-GA-0006-L2-Im

TEACHING STRATEGY

Objective: When the group of which the student is a member makes a reasonable plan or decision, the student will take action to help carry out the plan or decision.

Social Modeling

1. & 2 Set the stage and identify the specific steps. Read the following story to the class:

CAMPING OUT

Jenifer was unusually excited as the last bell of the school day rang.

Her teacher said, "Jenifer, you really seem excited about something today."

Jenifer responded, "I am! Susan, Maribeth, Libbie, and I are going camping tonight with our dads. We're going to Salt Lick Park. I have to hurry home because we're leaving today after school."

"Well, have a good time, " said the teacher. Jenifer said good-bye, met her sister, Susan, and Libbie and Maribeth in the hall. Together, they hurried home. When they arrived home, they found their fathers busily packing the station wagon. The supplies and equipment had been assembled the evening before according to the plan that the four girls and their fathers had decided upon. Each person was given responsibility for bringing his or her own clothing and other assigned supplies and equipment. All of these things were brought to Jenifer's and Susan's home in backpacks the evening before so that their fathers would be able to pack the car early. This way, they could leave in time to arrive at Salt Lake Park, make camp, and eat before dark.

By four o'clock, the car was packed, and they were on their way. Everyone was excitedly talking about all the things they were going to do while on their camp-out.

After nearly two hours of driving, they arrived at Salt Lick Park, located their campsite, and began making camp. Mr. George, Maribeth and Libbie's father, started to build a fire while Maribeth and Libbie carried firewood from the shelter to their campsite. Jenifer and Susan helped their father put up the two tents. One tent was ready, and they were working on the second when they were unable to find the tent stakes. According to the list of assigned equipment, Libbie was to have packed the George's tent and tent poles, lines and stakes. Mr. Lock called to Libbie. He explained that they were unable to find the tent stakes. Libbie turned white. She remembered leaving the stakes on her basement floor when she had stopped packing in order to watch a TV program. When her father asked her to take the tent over to Jenifer's, she had forgotten about the stakes. Libbie explained that she had left the tent stakes in her basement.

Mr. Lock then called everyone together. After a brief discussion, it was decided that Mr. George, Libbie, and Maribeth would sleep in the station wagon, and the next day they would go to the General Store and buy some more tent stakes. Libbie felt terrible about having to sleep in the car, but knew that this was because of her own behavior. Although Libbie was unhappy about her mistake and sleeping in the car for the first night, she and everyone else enjoyed camping out the second night. Libbie had learned a good lesson from her mistake and promised herself she would never make that mistake again.

After reading the story, hold a discussion by asking the following questions as they are appropriate:

(a) Why did Libbie sleep in the car?

(b) Why was it Libbie's responsibility to bring the tent stakes?

(c) Did Libbie's failure to do as she had agreed affect anyone else?

(d) What could Libbie have done differently and thereby avoided the problem?

(e) When you are part of a group that decides on a plan to accomplish a task by giving each person a specific job, why is it important for you to carry out your assignment?

(You may want to postpone the remainder of the lesson until the next session.)

3. **Model the behavior.** Set up a simulation of a group activity where teacher and a small group of pupils who have demonstrated that they have this skill (pupils may have to be from another class) carry out a plan for making the materials needed for a puppet show. Tasks to be completed include:

(a) Making paper hand puppets.

(b) Writing script.

(c) Making puppet costumes.

(d) Making proscenium arch.

(e) Making scenery.

All necessary materials should be made available within the classroom. Specific assignments should be decided ahead of time and repeated to the role-players at the time of the simulation for the benefit of the observing children. All the role-players should model the behavior of carrying out their tasks. (To make sure that the modeling activity is not too long, it is suggested that each of the tasks be completed ahead of time and that the role-players begin to duplicate their work. After two minutes of work, you can ask each to show his or her finished product.)

Ask the question, "What did _____ do to help the group?" This question should be repeated for each role-player. Be sure to praise appropriate verbal responses.

4. **Practice the activity.** Ask the class to develop a monthly bulletin board. Say, "What must we do first?" (Student response.) "Yes. We must decide what to put on the bulletin board. Do any of you have suggestions?" (Students give various responses.) "You all have excellent ideas. Now let's vote on which to use." (Students respond.) "Now that we've decided to make a mural of sport activities (or whatever students choose), what must we do?" (Students respond.) List responsibilities on board:

   (a) Find sports pictures.
   (b) Make a background.
   (c) Draw pictures.
   (d) Cut out letters.
   (e) Clean up.
   (f) Assemble bulletin board.

   Divide the class into committees to perform the tasks stated above. Each committee should assign further duties to individuals, such as, who looks through what magazine.

5. **Additional suggestions.**
   (a) Allow two or three days for class to carry out group project. This allows repeated practice of skill.
   (b) An older group could plan an open house for parents or a school display.
   (c) The group project could be incorporated into a Social Studies unit. For example, plan a state fair for the unit on a particular state. Display products of that state or states.
   (d) S-TR-GA-0002 and S-TR-GA-0004 are prerequisite skills that need to have been mastered. Assess these if pupils are having difficulty.

Code: S-TR-GA-0006-L2-Ir

TEACHING STRATEGY

Objective: When the group of which the student is a member makes a reasonable plan or decision, the student will take action to help carry out the plan or decision.

Social Reinforcement

1. **Praise the target student when he or she does his or her share to help carry out a group project.** Be specific in calling attention to his or her actions. "Carl, you did a terrific job on your part of the group assignment;" "Martha, you did a beautiful job of helping the group finish the mural."

2. **Provide cues to the target student by praising efforts of others who are helping to carry out a group plan.** Make sure that the group members know what their part of the group activity is and how to carry it out.

As part of asking a group to formulate a plan or make a decision about carrying out an activity, the teacher might want to ask the group members to report on how they plan to go about the task and who will be responsible for carrying out each part. You can then provide reinforcement for the students who are doing their part.

Code: S-TR-GA-0006-L2-Ic

TEACHING STRATEGY

Objective: When the group of which the student is a member makes a reasonable plan or decision, the student will take action to help carry out the plan or decision.

Contingency Management

1. **Present the task to student in specific terms.** When you are working in a group that has made a reasonable plan or decision, you will help the group to carry out the plan or decision. If needed, provide a list of appropriate behaviors to help carry out the group plan or decision or go over with the student what his specific responsibility is. Make sure that he or she understand what his or her part of the group activity is and how to go about it.

2. **Define a consequence valued by the student that will be given after he or she helps carry out the group activity.**

3. **State the contingency.** If the student helps carry out the plan or decision of the group, the student will receive the agreed-upon positive consequences.

4. **Watch for the behavior to occur naturally and reinforce it when it occurs, according to established contingency, or set up a situation in which the behavior can occur.** For example, divide the class into small groups or carry out a project related to a unit of study or to making plans for a holiday or special event. Observe target student(s) and reward them for carrying out their part of the activity.

5. **Example.** Ms. Kelly was aware that in her class some students usually did the "lion's share" of any group activity while other students did little or nothing. She felt that it was sometimes because the latter students did not know what to do or had fewer skills than the others. The class was invited to help carry out a community service project for the local children's hospital. The activity which the class agreed on was to make scrapbooks. Ms. Kelly divided the class into several groups and had the groups meet to decide on topics for their scrapbooks. She helped each group divide and

assign responsibilities, i.e., bringing magazines, finding relevant pictures, cutting out the pictures, pasting them on construction paper, writing a text for the scrapbook, and binding the book together. The teacher made a checklist for each group and had each student make a checkmark when he or she had completed his or her part. She also monitored the performance and gave an additional checkmark if she agreed, or she asked the student to do something additional. Students who had two checkmarks for doing their part of the project were invited to go on a field trip to present the scrapbooks to the hospital.

Skill:	To accept ideas presented in a group task situation which are different from one's own. **S-TR-GA-0008-L2**
Objective:	When the group is working on a task, and other members of the group present ideas which differ from his or hers, the student will listen to these ideas, weigh the advantages and disadvantages of the ideas, and help incorporate these ideas into the group task.
Assessment:	Assess from previous knowledge of student or through direct observation using the <u>Social Behavior Assessment Inventory</u>.

Code: S-TR-GA-0008-L2-Im

TEACHING STRATEGY

Objective: When the group is working on a task, and other members of the group present ideas which differ from his or hers, the student will listen to these ideas, weigh the advantages and disadvantages of the ideas, and help incorporate these ideas into the group task.

Social Modeling

1. **Set the stage.** Tell the following story:

PLANNING THE SPRING PARTY

It was a bright sunny morning when Andy woke up. He hurriedly got dressed and ate breakfast. Andy could hardly wait to get to school. Today his class was planning a spring party. When he arrived, everyone was already together chattering about the fun things they wanted to do. Andy joined them and started talking about playing football and having relay races. He wanted ice cream and cake. No one was paying attention to what he was saying.

Suddenly, Melissa broke in. "Wait," she said. "Andy has some ideas. We should listen to him also because he's part of our class."

Andy felt happy that Melissa was there. He told everyone what he wanted at the party and they all listened. Then Tom said, "Andy, I like your idea of playing relay races. Everyone can play these and win prizes. Football would take too long and not all the kids would like it." Everyone agreed with Tom.

Then, Linda said, "Andy's idea of having ice cream and cake sounds really good, too. Everyone likes those party foods." Andy was so happy that the group liked some of his ideas and would use them.

2. **Identify the specific steps.**

   (a) Discuss how Andy felt at various times in the story:

      (1) How did Andy feel when he got up and came to school?

      (2) How did Andy feel when no one listened to him?

      (3) How did Andy feel when his classmates listened to his ideas and liked them?

   (b) Say, "In the story, the pupils displayed four very important behaviors that all of us need to know and do when we work in groups. These behaviors are:

      (1) Listen to other's ideas.

      (2) Find and say positive things about others' ideas.

      (3) Agree to use the good ideas in the project.

      (4) Explain why some ideas are unacceptable.

3. **Model the behavior.** Set up a simulated committee meeting with all of the pupils being taught this skill to plan a mural for the school hall. The topic of the mural is "Sports in Action." Provide each student with a slip of paper containing a suggestion that the student is to present. (For pupils unable to read, give them the idea orally that they will volunteer later, or put the suggestions on tape and play the tape rather than having pupils give suggestions.) For example, "Put up magazine pictures, put up hand drawings and paintings, make paper maché people playing different sports games, use real sports equipment, divide mural into two parts (women's sports and men's sports), devote mural to local sporting events, key in on Olympic sports, just do football." Distribute one slip of paper with a suggestion to each of the pupils being taught this skill. Instruct the pupils that they are to pretend to be part of a committee that is planning a mural and that they will present the suggestions on their slips of paper when called on.

Demonstrate listening to each idea, make positive comments about it, tell politely why you agree or disagree, and explain how to incorporate it into the task, if possible. For example, in response to the suggestion of putting up magazine pictures, you may say, "John, that is an excellent idea. Magazine pictures are easy to find and easy to put up on the board. I think we should use that idea for our mural." In response to "just football" the teacher may say, "Tom, football is very popular, and it would be a good idea to include it in the mural. We could find many things to include in our mural about it. However, some people are interested in other sports and would like to see things about those sports. While we should definitely include football in our mural, we will also do other sports. Tom, you may be in charge of the football part."

Have students identify the specific elements of your behavior. Recognize proper responses.

4. **Practice the behavior.** Have the class plan a party. Give each student an opportunity to role-play the committee chairperson. Another student will suggest an idea for the party. The chairperson must demonstrate listening

to the ideas, making some positive response to them, explaining why some ideas are unacceptable and incorporating the good ideas into the group task. Explain to the class that when the chairperson does perform the desired behavior, he or she may choose his or her replacement. Each child should be given one turn. Give specific praise for proper behavior, e.g., "Jane, I'm glad you let Fred add corn chips to the food list after you listened to his reasons."

Code: S-TR-GA-0008-L2-Ir

TEACHING STRATEGY

Objective: When the group is working on a task, and other members of the group present ideas which differ from his or hers, the student will listen to these ideas, weigh the advantages and disadvantages of the ideas, and help incorporate these ideas into the group task.

Social Reinforcement

1. **Observe students when they are working on group tasks.** Recognize students who show signs of being able to adjust to ideas that are different from their own and incorporate them into group tasks. Be as specific as possible. "Mark, I'm glad you let Peter add Indians to the mural, even though you didn't want to at first." "Jane, thank you for working Gail's ideas into the report."

2. **Provide cues for target students by watching for students who are making efforts to listen to and make use of other's ideas, even though they differ from their own.**

3. **Additional suggestions.**
   (a) Provide real situations for practicing the behavior, e.g., if planning a party, use these ideas and really have a party.
   (b) Provide tasks appropriate to the age and ability level of the class.
   (c) The behaviors included in this task are complex ones that require a number of prior skills, for example, listening to another person, finding something positive about his or her ideas, accepting them if they are different from one's own, and finding some way to use another person's ideas. See S-IP-MC-0002-L1-S, S-IP-PA-0002-L1-S through S-IP-PA-0006-L2-S for prerequisite and related skills. If a pupil is having a particular problem with S-TR-GA-0008, one of these other skills may need to be taught.

Code: S-TR-GA-0008-L2-Ic

TEACHING STRATEGY

Objective: When the group is working on a task, and other members of the group present ideas which differ from his or hers, the student will listen to these ideas, weigh the advantages and disadvantages of the ideas, and help incorporate these ideas into the group task.

Contingency Management

1. **Present the task to the student in specific terms.** When you are working on a task in a group, listen to ideas of others, think of the advantages or disadvantages of these ideas, and help find ways of using other people's ideas in the group task.

2. **Define a consequence valued by the student that will be given after he or she demonstrates being able to accept and work with others' ideas.**

3. **State the contingency.** If the student listens to group ideas, considers advantages or disadvantages of these ideas, and helps incorporate them into the group task, he or she will receive the agreed-upon positive consequences.

4. **Watch for the behavior to occur naturally when the class is working on group tasks.** Reinforce it when it occurs according to the established contingency, or set up a situation in which the behavior can occur. For example, form a small committee. Include the target student and select him or her to chair the committee. Observe the student to see how he or she listens to and incorporates the ideas of others. If the student demonstrates the desired behavior, he or she will receive the agreed-upon reward.

5. **Example.** Ms. James had a student, Rhonda, who was aggressive and tended to dominate groups and insist on her own way. Because of this she was not well liked. Ms. James took Rhonda aside and discussed the problem with her, pointing out that Rhonda had some very good leadership qualities and that she wanted her to learn to be even more effective as a leader. She set up a contingency with Rhonda that if she would make an effort in a group task to listen to the ideas of others and find ways to incorporate them into the activity, she would let Rhonda have a turn being office monitor, running errands for the principal. Rhonda was eager to have this responsibility. The teacher did some role-playing with Rhonda so that she could learn to avoid some responses, for example, making negative comments about others' ideas, and instead listening and thinking about positive aspects of the others' ideas. Rhonda was put in charge of a committee to plan the Valentine party. Ms. James impressed on her that a committee is responsible for getting ideas and participation from the members. She monitored Rhonda's efforts and praised her for trying to listen to others, not insisting on her own ideas to the exclusion of those of others. The teacher met with the committee to hear their report. When she found that the ideas from the committee reflected those of all the students, she provided Rhonda with the agreed-upon reward.

Skill: To initiate and help carry out a group activity.
S-TR-GA-0010-L2
Objective: The student, when in a group situation, suggests an activity for the group.
Assessment: Assess from previous knowledge of student or through direct observation using the <u>Social Behavior Assessment Inventory</u>.

Code: S-TR-GA-0010-L2-Im

TEACHING STRATEGY

Objective: The student, when in a group situation, suggests an activity for the group.

Social Modeling

1. **Set the stage.** The emphasis in this skill is placed on taking the initiative to suggest an activity rather than carrying out ideas that others have suggested. You should tell the following story and display the illustrations that appear at the end of the strategy.

WHAT CAN WE DO?

George, Samantha, and Larry had gone over to Alisha's house to go swimming in her family's backyard pool—afterward, Alisha's mother told the children to come inside, which they did.

After the children were all inside and in dry clothes, Larry said, "Now, what can we do?" The children all looked at each other. No one spoke.

George was thinking to himself, "We could play table tennis or pool in the basement."

Samantha thought, "I would love to play 'Monopoly,' and I know Alisha has it."

Alisha was remembering how much fun this same group had had playing with some of her mother's clay, the last time they were trapped inside by the weather. No one was speaking. After ten minutes of silence, Ms. Lewis, Alisha's mother, came into the room. She saw everyone's long face and said, "What seems to be the problem?"

Alisha answered, "There's nothing to do."

Ms. Lewis said, "You've decided you don't want to play table tennis or pool, or work with some of my clay, or play table games, like 'Monopoly,' or watch TV?"

Alisha said, "Well, not really." The children then began discussing what they would like to do and decided to play table tennis. (Display the illustrations in Figure 27 as the story is read, pointing to the appropriate frames.)

Discuss the story. Following are some questions which may be helpful to stimulate discussion:

(a) Why did the children sit doing nothing for 10 minutes? (If no one offers an answer which indicates that the kids did not suggest anything to do, give this answer.)

If appropriate response is given ask, "What did the children not do when they were thinking of things to play? or what did Ms. Lewis do that the children did not do?"

(b) After Ms. Lewis came into the room and spoke to the children, what happened?

(c) What do you think would have happened if one of the children had made a suggestion as soon as they all were dressed in dry clothes?

2. **Identify the specific steps.** Say, "In the story, "What Can We Do?," the children sit around doing nothing until someone suggests an activity. This is a very important skill because when no one in a group offers a suggestion, nothing happens." There are several parts to this skill; they include:

(a) When working in a group situation, tell the group about an activity you think they should consider.

(b) Speak firmly and loudly so others can hear the suggestions.

(c) If group accepts your suggestion, help carry it out:

    (1) Assign duties, jobs, or roles.

    (2) Break activity down into smaller steps if necessary.

    (3) Suggest alternative ways of doing activity.

    (4) Plan desired outcome or final product. (Note: This aspect is a prerequisite skill, S-TR-GA-0006-L2-S.)

3. **Model the behavior.** Play the role of a student and demonstrate the effective ways of making suggestions to a group of students for something to play on the playground, something to do for a class project, etc. Be sure to model each of the component behaviors. Have the pupils describe what you did.

Note: S-TR-CD-0010-L2-S and S-TR-CD-0012-L2-S are skills that may have to be taught if pupil begins to offer suggestions and then ceases.

4. **Practice the behavior.** Begin by placing the target pupils in groups of two or three pupils each. Assign pupils to the group so that no one pupil will dominate the others. Instruct the pupils that they have ten minutes to decide upon an activity that would be appropriate for them as a group to do during "free time" or inside recess. Listen and give praise to pupils who offer suggestions.

Code: S-TR-GA-0010-L2-Ir

TEACHING STRATEGY

Objective: The student, when in a group situation, suggests an activity for the group.

Social Reinforcement

1. **Recognize students for suggesting activities in group situations.** Call attention to specific actions. "Mark, that is a terrific activity for the group to do;" "Shannon, your idea of a play is beautiful;" "Rose, thank you for your idea for the party."

2. Provide cues for students to suggest ideas for group activities by recognizing students who do make such suggestions, or elicit suggestions by asking students for their ideas.

   Note: The skill described here is an extension of skills TR-GA-0006 and TR-GA-0008. The stress in this skill is on the leadership displayed by the student. Praise and social reinforcement to build this behavior should be directed at indications of initiative taken by the student.

3. **Additional suggestions.**

   (a) For the practice activity, you may give the small group a task to accomplish, e.g., choosing a theme and constructing a bulletin board.

   (b) A poster could be placed in front of the room that states: "Did you make your suggestions today?"

   (c) To provide more opportunity to practice the skill and to give more social reinforcement, you could set aside five to ten minutes per day for one or two weeks prior to recess and have the total group decide on a group recess activity. Instruct pupils that they have ten minutes to decide on an activity that would be appropriate for them as a group to do during "free time" or inside recess. Listen and give praise to pupils who offer suggestions.

Code: S-TR-GA-0010-L2-Ic

TEACHING STRATEGY

Objective: The student, when in a group situation, suggests an activity for the group.

Contingency Management

1. **Present task in specific terms.** When in a group situation, suggest an activity for the group and help to carry it out.

2. **Define a consequence valued by the student which will be given when the student suggests an activity for the group and helps carry it out.**

3. **State the contingency.** If the student suggests an activity in a group situation, he or she will receive the agreed-upon positive consequences.

4. **Watch for situations when the student takes initiative and makes suggestions for the group, or set up a situation that requires the behavior.** For example, form a small group and include the target student in the group. Give the group a task to plan, such as, carrying out an academic assignment, planning a social service project, planning for a party or field trip. Assign a chairperson who will record points for each person who has made a suggestion about how to carry out this activity, and reward those who make suggestions.

5. **Example.** Sally was a shy student who followed the lead of others in group situations and seldom made a contribution of her own. Ms. Jones felt that Sally and some other students needed help being more assertive. She formed a small "assertiveness training" group with Sally and some other similar students and practiced with them how to get their ideas across to other students, stressing looking at others when they talked to them, talking in a loud, firm voice, and making gestures when appropriate. The

group role-played with each other such behaviors as greeting others, carrying on conversations, expressing opinions, and getting their ideas across when making suggestions about activities on the playground or in the classroom. In order to increase taking the initiative and suggesting group activities, Ms. Jones had each student record on a cumulative chart the times they made suggestions and the times their suggestions were accepted. They brought the charts to the weekly session with Ms. Jones and reported on their suggestions and the outcomes. They practiced those situations in which the outcomes were not successful. The students earned points on their charts for suggesting activities and for either having their suggestions accepted or being able to role-play how they might have been more successful. As soon as all the students reached a certain point on the chart, they went out to lunch with Ms. Jones.

INDEPENDENT WORK

S-TR-IW-0002-L1-S   To attempt to solve a problem with school work before asking for help.

S-TR-IW-0004-L2-S   To find productive use of time while waiting for teacher assistance.

S-TR-IW-0006-L2-S   To find acceptable ways of using free time when work is completed.

Skill:	To attempt to resolve a problem with school work before asking for help. **S-TR-IW-0002-L1**
Objective:	When given an academic assignment, the student will attempt to resolve problems with the assignment alone before asking for help.
Assessment:	Assess from previous knowledge of student or through direct observation using the <u>Social Behavior Assessment Inventory</u>.

Code: S-TR-IW-0002-L1-Im

TEACHING STRATEGY

Objective: When given an academic assignment, the student will attempt to resolve problems with the assignment alone before asking for help.

Social Modeling

1. **Set the stage.** To set the stage for a discussion of this skill, begin by telling the children they are going to be given some riddles that they are to try to solve. Examples:

   (a) What's black and white and read all over? (A. A newspaper.)
   (b) What does a duck do that flies upside down? (A. It quacks up.)
   (c) How can you say Elizabeth and Eliza with out E's? (A. Beth and Liz.)
   (d) What state is round on the ends and high in the middle? (A. Ohio.)

   Add riddles of your own. Additional riddles may also be found in *Highlights* magazine. You may also ask students to contribute riddles of their own. As students respond to the riddles, praise them for continuing to work on the riddle rather than asking for help.

   Regardless of which activity is used, the following procedures are recommended:

   (a) Give pupils maximum of four minutes for activity.
   (b) Write on the blackboard names of pupils who worked for entire four minutes and/or who finished the task.
   (c) Give correct answers to the activity after the time limit or when all pupils have finished.

350

(d) Point out the names on the blackboard and explain why the names are written there, i.e., these pupils attempted to solve the problem (complete the task) before asking for help.

(e) Explain that attempting to solve any problem before asking for help is a good idea. Say, "When we find we have a problem the first action we should take is to look at the task again and think about it. Often, we are able to solve our own problems by re-examining them before we ask for help."

2. **Identify the specific steps.** Say, "I'm going to list the specific behaviors that you should do before asking for help. These suggestions will help you solve many of your problems without asking for help." When the student is having difficulties with an assignment, he or she might:

(a) Look at the assignment again and think about it.

(b) Re-read the instructions, or try to remember instructions which were given verbally.

(c) Look for examples of similar work, and see how it was done.

(d) Go back and re-read earlier material and assignments that preceded the present one.

3. **Model the behavior.** Take the part of a student with a difficult assignment and demonstrate application of various problem-solving efforts, describing aloud to students the actions being taken. You may select a previous assignment that many of the class members found very difficult and often asked for help. If you prefer, use the assignment that is described and provided for the practice activity in the next step. Students should be asked to identify the problem-solving behaviors. Praise students who make appropriate responses.

4. **Practice the behavior.** Give the students an assignment that contains characteristics that will cause a problem. For example, say, "I have given each of you a math worksheet that may cause some problems for you. Before you ask for help, attempt to resolve your problem on your own. What are the things to do when trying to solve a problem with an assignment?" (Student response.) Be sure to draw out all four behaviors and list them on the chalkboard. "When you have a problem, raise your hand. I will come to your desk so you can tell me the problem, but I won't give you any help. I want you to try to solve it yourself."

Problems that may arise include:

(a) How do we know what operation to use?

(b) Do we have to write the answer?

(c) Where do we put the answers when we are finished?

After five to ten minutes, discuss some questions that the students had at first but later knew the answer. For example:

(a) What do we do with the top example?

(b) Why are some problems multiplication and some division?

Discuss the ways in which the students found the answers to those questions by themselves:

(a) Looked at the worksheet and re-read the directions given.

(b) Thought about previous, similar assignments that were set up the same way.

Code: S-TR-IW-0002-L1-Ir

TEACHING STRATEGY

Objective: When given an academic assignment, the student will attempt to resolve problems with the assignment alone before asking for help.

Social Reinforcement

1. **Identify and recognize aloud target student when observed attempting to resolve a problem with school work before asking for help.** Call attention to specific behavior, e.g., "Robin, you certainly did a nice job of trying to work out your math problem on your own, first. I see that you asked for help **after** you tried it by yourself;" "Fred, I noticed that you went back and re-read the directions before asking for help;" "Melissa, you are doing a wonderful job of trying to answer your reading questions on your own. I am happy to see you are trying to work problems out by yourself."

2. **Recognize others around the target student who appear to be trying to work independently before asking for help.**

3. **Additional suggestions.**
   (a) Distribute cards to students when they are observed solving their own problems. For example:
      (1) "Very good thinking, I have a surprise for you during recess."
      (2) "Good try. You have earned library time."
      (3) "I'm proud you solved your problem alone. You may move your desk to another spot for the rest of the day."
   (b) Construct chart entitled, "Practically Nothing Puzzles Me." At the end of each day, write the student's name who has received the most cards.
   (c) A crossword puzzle, simple magic trick, science demonstration, or any other activity that will not have immediately apparent answers can be used for setting the stage. Select an activity that you believe is appropriate for the group.

Code: S-TR-IW-0002-L1-Ic

TEACHING STRATEGY

Objective: When given an academic assignment, the student will attempt to resolve problems with the assignment alone before asking for help.

Contingency Management

1. **State the task to the student in observable terms.** When you have an assignment with which you have difficulty, try to do as much as you can by yourself before you ask for help. Suggest ways for the student to keep working, for example, going on, skipping the difficult part and coming back to it later, looking at earlier work for explanations or models.

2. **Plan reinforcement.**

3. **State the contingency.** If student attempts to resolve a problem with school work before asking for help, he or she will be rewarded.

4. **Watch for the behavior to occur naturally in the course of ongoing academic assignments and reward it according to the established contract.**

5. **Example.** Lonnie seemed to be very dependent on Ms. Alvarez for help, and it seemed to her that he seldom worked independently. First, she made sure that the work given to Lonnie was at least in his instructional range. She discussed with him some things he could do to try to figure out how to do the work before asking her for help. She started with a math worksheet on which the problems were very similar, so if Lonnie understood how to do the first one, he should understand how to do all of them. Ms. Alvarez set up a contract with Lonnie involving a point system—two points for each problem done correctly after asking for help, five points for each problem done correctly on his own, and three points for a problem attempted independently but with the wrong answer. (For this last, the problem had to be at least partially right.) The points were exchanged at the end of the day for play money which Lonnie saved toward a model airplane. Ms. Alvarez extended the contract to other kinds of math problems and to reading seatwork; and as Lonnie began to do more work on his own, she gradually increased the requirements, for example, two problems done correctly and independently for five points.

Skill:	To find productive use of time while waiting for teacher assistance. **S-TR-IW-0004-L2**
Objective:	Student finds something productive to do, such as continuing with school work, while waiting for the teacher's assistance.
Assessment:	Assess from previous knowledge of student or through direct observation using the <u>Social Behavior Assessment Inventory</u>.

<u>Code: S-TR-IW-0004-L2-Im</u>

TEACHING STRATEGY

Objective: Student finds something productive to do, such as continuing with school work, while waiting for the teacher's assistance.

Introduction: Before using this strategy, it is advisable to specify alternate activities that you want the students to engage in while waiting for help. If students do not know what things are allowed, they may choose activities that you consider inappropriate. Also, there must be sufficient motivation for keeping busy while waiting for help. If there is no consequence for finding something productive to do, students may find it equally reinforcing to disturb the class or to sit and wait unproductively.

If you have observed that problems with this skill in your class originate because students simply do not know what is expected, you may choose to present the skill by simply explaining what is acceptable behavior while waiting for help. List the activities on the board or on a chart for reference. You might have folder work or extra work (dittos, workbooks) for each child to go to if he or she needs to wait for assistance. Explain the situations when these activities are to be used and the procedures to be followed. Then provide practice and reinforcement as noted below.

Social Modeling

1. **Set the stage.** Dramatize the desired behavior by using a puppet or by playing the role of Brenda, or by telling the story as follows:

BUSY BRENDA

In the (insert your school) Elementary School there was a girl everyone called Busy Brenda. Brenda was given her nickname because she was always busy doing her work. Sometimes Brenda would need help from the teacher. While she waited for the teacher to come to her, she did work from her other subjects, read a book, or did bonus work. At the end of the day, Brenda had free time to use in the Listening Center or work at the Art Table. (Insert reinforcers appropriate in your management system.)

Say, "Now, let's see who were good listeners." Ask the following questions in a discussion session:

(a) "Why did Brenda get the nickname?"

(b) "What things did Brenda do if she needed to stop her assignment and wait for the teacher's help."

(c) What happened to Brenda at the end of the day since she was a good worker all day?"

2. **Identify the steps.** Ask the following questions:

(a) "What things could we do if we have to wait for the teacher?" (Take student suggestions of appropriate activities and list on board. Add activities if you have others you want them to choose.)

(b) "How should we let the teacher know that we need help?"

Note: If the pupils have not had a procedure outlined to accomplish this, do so at this time. Raising a hand and keeping it up until the teacher gets to the pupil is normally not a good procedure when more than 30 seconds elapse between the onset of handraising and teacher help.

(c) "When you decide that you need my help with school work, what is the first thing you will need to do?" (Student response: "Put our 'Help Please' flags on our desks," or "Write our names on a 'Request for Assistance' card and place it on your desk." The response should be in accordance with whatever procedure is appropriate in your classroom.)

(d) "After you have (insert the appropriate action for your class at this point in the sentence), what do you do next?" (Student response.) "Exactly, Billie. You would set your work to the side and choose an activity from our list of things to do while waiting for help."

(e) "And what next?" (Student response.) "Right. You would begin your chosen activity and stay with it until I came to you to give you help with your problem."

3. **Model the behavior.** You or a student who has demonstrated mastery of the skill should serve as the model student while another student plays the role

of teacher. (Brief the student who will be "teacher" ahead of time.) Role-play a situation in which a student needs help with a contrived assigned task and finds the teacher is busy with another student. Be sure to model the following three specific behaviors:

(a) Putting "Help Please" flag on desk (or whatever is appropriate in your classroom).

(b) Putting work aside and choosing activity from list.

(c) Beginning the chosen activity and continuing with it until the teacher gives help.

After modeling the behavior, have each pupil in the class do likewise. Say, "Now, let's see who would like to show us what we do when we need help but the teacher is busy." Choose volunteers.

(a) "What did _____ do when he or she needed help?"

(b) "Was the teacher busy?"

(c) "What did _____ do while he or she waited?"

4. **Practice the behavior.** Provide a contrived task for target students to practice the behavior to be sure they know the procedures to follow. Review procedures with class before beginning individual work periods for several days. The goal is to have individual assignments at mastery level. Do **not** assign work to cause difficulty.

5. **Additional suggestions.**

(a) S-TR-IW-0002-L1-S is a prerequisite skill. This skill should be mastered by the pupil prior to working on S-TR-IW-0004-L2-S.

(b) Since S-TR-IW-0004-L2-S may weaken S-TR-IW-0002-L1-S, the teacher must give more frequent reinforcement for S-TR-IW-0002-L1-S to maintain it at an acceptable level.

Code: S-TR-IW-0004-L2-Ir

TEACHING STRATEGY

Objective: Student finds something productive to do, such as continuing with school work, while waiting for the teacher's assistance.

Social Reinforcement

1. **Use social reinforcement of smiles and recognition when student is observed working on a constructive task while waiting for the teacher's assistance.** Tell the student exactly what he or she is doing. For example: "Diane, I liked the way you went on and tried the next math problem, even though you were having difficulty;" "Tess, I am glad to see that you went on to the next assignment and did not sit and wait for me to answer your question. You used your time wisely;" "Bruce, looking at your library book was a good thing to do while you were waiting for me to help you."

2. **Provide cues for target student.** Remind the student at the beginning of the task that if he or she has difficulty and needs assistance he or she should go to the next problem or find something productive to do until you come. You may suggest some specific alternatives for the students. You may also provide cues by praising another student who is demonstrating the

appropriate behavior and reinforcing target student when he or she responds correctly.

3. **If needed, you might provide tangible reinforcement, such as coupons or tokens, along with social reinforcement to encourage the desired behavior.**

Code: S-TR-IW-0004-L2-Ic

TEACHING STRATEGY

Objective: Student finds something productive to do, such as continuing with school work, while waiting for the teacher's assistance.

Contingency Management

1. **Discuss with student that when he or she has difficulty with a problem, and you are busy with another student, he or she should go to the next problem or find something productive to do until you can assist.** When necessary, suggest specific alternatives that would be considered productive.

2. **Plan reinforcement.**

3. **State the contingency.** Tell the student that if he or she goes to the next problem or task or finds something productive to do while waiting for your assistance, he or she will receive the agreed-upon positive consequences. Specify amount and type of reinforcement.

4. **Watch for the behavior to occur naturally or set up a situation in which the behavior can occur.** For example, give the student an assignment in which he or she will need your assistance. Note when he or she raises his or her hand and delay responding. If the student goes to the next problem or finds a productive alternative, reinforce the student.

5. **Example.** Kevin would raise his hand when he needed the teacher's assistance. If there was a delay before the teacher could get to him, Kevin would put his hand down and turn around to chat with his neighbor. Ms. Sanford suggested to Kevin that while waiting for assistance he could go on to the next problem or task or find some productive activity such as quietly reading. A contract was set up that if Kevin had difficulty or needed assistance, he would raise his hand until Ms. Sanford acknowledged it. If Ms. Sanford was unable at that moment to help Kevin, he would go on to the next problem or task. If Kevin demonstrated this behavior, he would receive one to four bingo numbers from Ms. Sanford when she came to help him. He could keep those numbers matching his bingo card and he would return those not matching to Ms. Sanford. When Kevin's card read "Bingo" he would get 10 minutes of a desired activity.

<table>
<tr><td>Skill:</td><td>To find acceptable ways of using free time when work is completed.
S-TR-IW-0006-L2</td></tr>
<tr><td>Objective:</td><td>During a period of time when nothing is scheduled for the student, he or she will find ways of using the unscheduled time that the teacher defines as acceptable or constructive.</td></tr>
<tr><td>Assessment:</td><td>Assess from previous knowledge of student or through direct observation using the <u>Social Behavior Assessment Inventory</u>.</td></tr>
</table>

Code: S-TR-IW-0006-L2-Im

TEACHING STRATEGY

Objective: During a period of time when nothing is scheduled for the student, he or she will find ways of using the unscheduled time that the teacher defines as acceptable or constructive.

Social Modeling

1. **Set the stage.** Give the pupils an assignment which can be completed in approximately five minutes. Tell them that they have 15 minutes to do the work, and they are to find something constructive to do if they finish before time is up. After 10 minutes, call time out; have the students stop what they are doing and sit near the spot where the activity was taking place. List on the board of what each student was doing. Make no evaluative comments about the students' use of free time. Have students continue with their activities. Shortly before the scheduled end of free time activities, stop the students again and add to the list any new activities that may have been going on. Repeat this procedure at least one more time during the school day.

2. **Identify the specific steps.**
   (a) Using the list on the board, divide the activities given into constructive and nonconstructive activities. Ask the pupils to add any activities they can recall that they have engaged in during free time. Once these lists have been developed, erase the nonconstructive column.
   (b) Discuss the positive consequences of the constructive activities listed:
      (1) Homework may be completed.
      (2) Getting extra help on subjects could increase grade.
      (3) By completing other school work you will have free time after school.
      (4) Teacher will be pleased.
      (5) Peers will appreciate your quiet behavior.
   (c) Ask, "When you finish an assigned task and have free time, what should you do?" (Student response.) "Very good, Heath. Reading a library book is an excellent activity. Beginning today, when you complete a task and have unscheduled time, you are to select an activity from those listed on the board. If you have some other activity that you prefer that is not listed, ask for permission to do it. If it is acceptable, it will be added to the list."

357

3. **Model the behavior.** Select a pupil from your class to play the role of the classroom teacher. Practice the role-playing with him or her ahead of time. In the role-playing you should complete the assigned task and then begin to do an activity from those listed on the board. The pupil playing the role of the teacher should give you an assignment, e.g., "Read page 110 in your Social Studies book. You have five minutes." This pupil should also be instructed to give praise for your selecting and beginning an activity from those listed after you have completed the assignment. After the role-playing episode is completed, ask your class to describe what happened. Be sure to recognize appropriate responses.

Next, select two or three pupils to serve as models. Give these pupils a very short assignment, e.g., four math problems and more than enough time to complete them. The pupils should be asked to demonstrate using "free time" according to the outlined procedure. After each role-play has selected and begun an activity, have the other pupils identify the appropriate choices.

4. **Practice activity.** Divide the class into small groups and give each group an assignment to be completed. The members of each group will show how they can use unscheduled time according to the guidelines that have been established. Provide more than adequate time for each member of the group to complete the assignment and have unscheduled time. Reinforce correct responses.

5. **Additional suggestions.**

   (a) Provide cues for the target student. Remind the student that when given free time, he or she is to use the time in an acceptable manner. Post a list of free time activities. Praise another student who is using unscheduled time as you define as acceptable or constructive. As the students discover new ways to use unscheduled time, they can add them to the chart.

   (b) Consider videotaping your pupils while they have unscheduled time. use the results for setting the stage in Step 1.

Code: S-TR-IW-0006-L2-Ir

TEACHING STRATEGY

Objective: During a period of time when nothing is scheduled for the student, he or she will find ways of using the unscheduled time that the teacher defines as acceptable or constructive.

Social Reinforcement

1. **Use social reinforcement when student is observed using free time in a way which is acceptable to the teacher.** Be specific in praising the student. For example, "Jean, I liked the way you chose to read a book. You used your free time wisely;" "Neil, thank you for using your free time catching up on your math work;" "Mike, I liked the way you and Pete were able to play a game quietly without disturbing the others who were working."

2. **Provide cues for the target student.** Remind the student that when given free time, he or she is to use the time in an acceptable manner. Suggest ways

to use free time or put up a list of free time activities. Praise another student who is using free time as you suggested.

3. **If necessary provide tangible reinforcement (i.e., tokens, coupons, stars) along with social reinforcement to provide additional incentive to the student to find constructive ways of using his or her free time.**

Code: S-TR-IW-0006-L2-Ic

TEACHING STRATEGY

Objective: During a period of time when nothing is scheduled for the student, he or she will find ways of using the unscheduled time that the teacher defines as acceptable or constructive.

Contingency Management

1. **Present the task to the student in specific terms.** When given unscheduled time, use that time in ways that are acceptable according to the guidelines that have been established for the class. Specify acceptable ways to use such time, for example, drawing, puzzles, talking quietly with a friend, listening to a record, looking at library books, etc.

2. **Plan reinforcement.**

3. **State the contingency.** If when given unscheduled time the student uses the time according to the defined rules, the student will be reinforced. State type and amount of reinforcement.

4. **Watch for the behavior to occur naturally or set up a situation for the behaviors to occur.** For example, allow for an unscheduled time period. If the student uses the time in an acceptable way, reinforce the student according to the contract.

5. **Example.** Ms. Southard observed that when Mark had unscheduled time, he did not use that time in an acceptable manner. Instead, he walked around the room bothering other students or did such annoying things as calling out the window or running up and down the hall. Ms. Southard talked with Mark about better ways of using his time. She suggested some more acceptable ways to use unscheduled time, for example, drawing, coloring, sitting quietly and talking with a friend, working puzzles, or playing a game with a friend. Ms. Southard had Mark think of some additional things to do during unscheduled time periods.

She then established a contract that for every unscheduled time period, if Mark chose one of the acceptable ways of spending his time, he could earn up to five chips. If he did one of the unacceptable things he could also lose chips. On Friday, Mark could exchange chips for something he wanted from the "store" in the classroom. Ms. Southard also praised Mark for good use of his time, and eventually phased out the chips in favor of social reinforcement alone.

On-Task Behavior

S-TR-OT-0002-L1-S	To sit straight at desk when required by teacher.
S-TR-OT-0004-L1-S	To do seatwork assignment quietly.
S-TR-OT-0006-L1-S	To work steadily for the required length of time.
S-TR-OT-0008-L1-S	To ignore distractions from peers when doing a seatwork assignment.
S-TR-OT-0010-L1-S	To discuss academic material with peers when appropriate.
S-TR-OT-0012-L1-S	To change from one activity to another when required by the teacher.

Skill:	To sit straight at desk when required. **S-TR-OT-0002-L1**
Objective:	When required to do so by the teacher, the student sits on chair at desk, upright and facing front, with chair legs on the floor, and with feet in front of him or her.
Assessment:	Assess from previous knowledge of student or through direct observation using the <u>Social Behavior Assessment Inventory</u>.
Note:	It is critical that the desk and chair properly fit students; otherwise, students will naturally adjust their bodies to fit the furniture.

Code: S-TR-OT-0002-L1-Im

TEACHING STRATEGY

Objective: When required to do so by the teacher, the student sits on chair at desk, upright and facing front, with chair legs on the floor, and with feet in front of him or her.

Social Modeling

1. **Set the stage.** Display two pictures, one of a boy sitting properly at his desk and the other of a girl sitting properly at her desk. "Here are two students who know how to sit at their desks at school in the proper way. Since they are seated properly, they are ready to work hard and do a good job on their lessons. It is easier for them to learn when they are sitting the right way. Sometimes, students need to sit upright and face front, with chair legs on the floor and feet in front of them. Why is it good to sit up straight?" (Student response.) "Very good, everyone!" (Reinforce any response such as, "It helps you study," "It's easier to see the teacher," "It's better for your posture, etc.) "Why is it good to keep the legs of the chair on the floor?" (Student response.) "That's right, Sue." (Reinforce any response such as, "It's harder to study because you can't reach the desk if the legs aren't on the floor," "The chair might break," "The student might get hurt," etc.) "Why should you be facing front?" (Student response.) "Very good, Glen." (Refer to pictures often during this discussion.) "When are some of the

360

times you might be required to sit up straight during school?" (Student response.) "Great."

Continue discussion, asking students to identify times outside school when sitting straight would be helpful or required. Give each student several opportunities to respond during discussion.

2. **Identify the specific steps.** Tape a large piece of paper or cardboard to the wall. "When we are required to sit on our chairs properly at our desks, what are some of the rules we should follow?" Students respond by stating rules for the above behavior, while you list them on the chalkboard. Rules to be included are:

   (a) Upright and facing front.
   (b) "Six Feet Rule"—four chair legs plus two of yours.
   (c) Feet in front of you.

   Then ask students to draw pictures demonstrating each rule. The pupils should copy the rules and draw their pictures beside each rule. If the children don't have adequate writing skills, have them make their drawings for each rule as you read them. (This drawing activity may be eliminated if the target students do not have adequate fine motor skills.) Ask the pupils to paste their rules on the wall of their carrel or on the bulletin board. After the pictures are completed, you should say, "Now, whenever we forget how to sit on our chairs correctly, we may look at our list of rules to remind us."

3. **Model the behavior.** Place a chair and desk in front of the classroom and sit in the chair to demonstrate sitting properly. "Look at the rules for sitting properly at your desk. Tell me if I am doing it the right way." If students fail to comment on one or more of the aspects of proper sitting behavior, question the students about this aspect. Give praise for correct responses.

   Next, let each student come to the front of the room, one at a time, to demonstrate sitting appropriately. Other students will then evaluate the student's sitting behavior according to the rules.

4. **Practice the behavior.** Students may play a variation of musical chairs. Students will be divided into two teams. First, Team No. 1 will play musical chairs by walking around their chairs and desks until the music stops or until you stop clapping. The students will then seat themselves appropriately as quickly as possible, and then Team No. 2 will begin to evaluate each student on Team No. 1 according to how he or she is seated. Each student who is seated correctly according to all three rules receives three points; if he or she is seated correctly according to only two rules, he or she receives two points, and so on. Next, Team No 2 will play musical chairs while Team No. 1 evaluates their sitting behavior. The team with the most points wins the game.

   Note: If this game seems inappropriate for the age group under instruction, the students may be divided into two teams, with one team evaluating the other during a seatwork assignment.

5. **Reinforcement.** Provide cues often by praising students and reminding them that you want to see them sitting properly, e.g., "Sandy, I like the way you are sitting upright and facing front;" "Good, Dan. You remembered the 'Six Feet Rule.' You are keeping your feet and the chair's feet on the floor;" "Tony, you study well when your feet are on the floor in front of you."

6. **Additional suggestions.**
   (a) Students may draw or paint pictures to display around the room showing people sitting properly on the chairs at their desks . Also, the students may enjoy making a collage by drawing or cutting out pictures of different people sitting properly in different situations.
   (b) Make a bulletin board to use for reinforcement. Beside each student's name on the bulletin board, place a star or checkmark whenever that student exhibits the proper sitting behavior.
   (c) This is often a problem for one or two students in particular. If this is the case:
      (1) Establish rules and demonstrate acceptable behavior.
      (2) Set up a contingency contract or monitoring system for the student(s) needing special help.
   (d) Make miniature pictures of the two demonstration pictures used in setting the stage. Pass these out as coupons to children who are seated properly. Backup reinforcers could be attached if desired.
   (e) Photograph pupils in your class to show the proper way to sit. This could also be used as a reward, e.g., pupils who sit properly for a designated period of time or who earn a designated number of coupons could be reinforced by having their pictures taken.

Code: S-TR-OT-0002-L1-Ir

TEACHING STRATEGY

Objective: When required to do so by the teacher, the student sits on chair at desk, upright and facing front, with chair legs on the floor, and with feet in front of him or her.

Social Reinforcement

1. **Use social reinforcement when student is observed sitting appropriately.** Be specific in praising. For example, "Margie, you're sitting up very straight. I like the way you are sitting, facing the front with your feet on the floor;" "Jim, thank you for sitting up so nicely. I appreciate your sitting with the chair legs on the floor."

2. **Provide cues for target student.** When students are required to sit as defined, the teacher will go over the correct way to sit and state the specific rules. Target student can be cued by praising others nearby who are sitting up straight. "Jim has his feet on the floor;" "Mary is sitting up straight and keeping her hands to herself;" "Jane is facing front."

3. **If necessary, provide tangible reinforcement such as tokens, chips or coupons along with social reinforcement for good sitting.** Tangible reinforcement can be exchanged for desirable items.

Code: S-TR-OT-0002-L1-Ic

TEACHING STRATEGY

Objective: When required to do so by the teacher, the student sits on chair at desk, upright and facing front, with chair legs on the floor, and with feet in front of him or her.

Contingency Management

1. **Discuss with student how to sit in his or her chair and the specific ways to sit appropriately.** Make sure students understand the conditions under which they are required to sit up straight.

2. **Plan reinforcement.**

3. **State the contingency.** If, when required to do so by the teacher, a the student sits on his or her chair, at his or her desk, upright and facing front, with chair legs on the floor and with feet in front, he or she will receive a specific reward.

4. **Watch for the behavior to occur as stated in the contingency.** Prompt the behavior by reminding the class that this is the time you would like to see good sitting by recognizing students who are sitting straight. Reinforce the students for correct behavior according to the agreed-upon contract.

5. **Example.** Mr. Terry liked to have students learn to sit straight in their chairs with their feet on the floor under their desks. He felt that it helped them to pay attention and that there were fewer problems if students did not have their feet stuck out, and were not tipping back in their chairs or leaning on other student's desks. One student, Ron, was continually turned around in his seat, sitting sprawled out with his feet in the aisle, or rocking back on the back legs of his chair.

   Mr. Terry discussed with Ron how he would like him to sit and defined some particular times when he wanted him to sit appropriately, e.g., during seatwork, during the presentation of a lesson or a movie. A contract was arranged with Ron that a 3 x 5 card could be put on Ron's desk. Mr. Terry would watch for Ron to be sitting appropriately and would punch a hole in the card when Ron was doing a good job. Each punched hole would earn Ron a minute of free time for playing games at the end of the day.

   Note: Conditions under which students are required to sit up straight in their seats will vary according to teacher and classroom situation.

Skill:	To do a seatwork assignment quietly.
	S-TR-OT-0004-L1
Objective:	When given an assignment to complete, the student works without speaking aloud.
Assessment:	Assess from previous knowledge of student or through direct observation using the <u>Social Behavior Assessment Inventory</u>.

Code: S-TR-OT-0004-L1-Im

TEACHING STRATEGY

Objective: When given an assignment to complete, the student works without speaking aloud.

Introduction: Working on seatwork assignments quietly is somewhat dependent on the assignment. When you expect this behavior, be certain that the assigned seatwork task is at the pupils' mastery level.

Social Modeling

1. Set the stage.

(a) Prepare an audio (video if available) tape of three situations as described below:

   (1) General procedure: Locate the tape recorder in an inconspicuous position in the classroom and inform the class that part of the class activities that day will be recorded. If the device is a unique experience for the pupils, give them several exposures to it before proceeding with the actual taping.

   (2) Tape three episodes of the teacher giving an assignment and the pupils working on it.

   (A) Tape 1: In this instance record yourself giving instructions and a group of noisy pupils (but not to the point of being ridiculous) working on the assignment. This situation could be taped in another classroom, or you could have pupils who have mastered S-TR-OT-0004 role-play the episode.

   (B) Tape 2: This time, record a quiet group of pupils. If there are no pupils in the class who have mastered S-TR-OT-0004-L1-S, record this situation in another classroom. Again, have a group of pupils role-play the situation. The same procedure of giving a normal assignment with typical directions should be followed.

   (C) Tape 3: When target pupils are given a seatwork assignment, begin recording. In this case, record a normal situation in the classroom. Give a normal assignment with typical directions.

   (3) In addition to the direction-giving segment, select approximately two minutes from each of the tapes for use in class. (If equipment is readily available to make the task simple, put the selected portions on one tape with a short segment of blank tape between them.)

364

(4) Plan when this strategy will be implemented in the class and set aside 30 minutes to complete all of the steps.

(b) Play Tapes 1 and 2 and ask:

(1) "What did the teacher do on the tapes?"

(2) "What did the pupils do on the tapes?"

(c) Say, "When given an assignment to work on in class, which group of pupils demonstrated the appropriate behavior?" (Student response.) "That's exactly right, Yolanda. Why did you pick Tape 2?" (Student response.) "Very good observation." (If pupils do not answer correctly, give them the answer.)

(d) Discuss why "working quietly" is desirable.

(e) Say, "Now, listen to this tape." (Play Tape 3.) "As you can tell from listening to the tape, our class sounds more like the class on Tape 1 than Tape 2. We are going to begin working to sound like the class on Tape 2."

2. **Identify the specific steps.** Inform the students that the observable behaviors that made up this skill include:

(a) Remaining in seat unless given permission to move.

(b) Beginning and continuing to work on the assignment.

(c) Speaking only with permission.

3. **Model the behavior.**

(a) Model the behavior by taping directions and then responding to them in the appropriate manner. Each of the elements described in "2" above should be modeled. Pupils should be asked to describe the modeled behaviors. Appropriate responses are, of course, recognized.

(b) Identify specific behaviors to be modeled—"When given an assignment to do at your seat, sit at your desk and work quietly without talking out loud." Choose a student to model this behavior for the others by giving a specific assignment to work on and asking him or her to show how a student would follow the rules about working quietly. Ask other students to describe the appropriate behavior. Students who make good responses should be praised.

(c) If a videotape is used to record the "quiet" group of pupils, this tape could be played again and used as a model. Pupils should be asked to describe target behaviors.

4. **Practice the behavior.** Practice should be accomplished by giving the pupils a typical assignment. Post the three component behaviors until they are mastered. Iinform target pupils that they should practice doing their seatwork quietly. Praise those students who exhibit the target behaviors, for example, "Gail, you worked for a full 10 minutes without talking. That's fantastic!"

5. **Reinforcement.** Using a stopwatch to time the pupils' working quietly is often effective in improving performance. Inform the pupils that you are timing them to determine how long they can work quietly. These times may be plotted on a large graph (see Figure 32) posted in the room. If necessary, backup reinforcers can be attached to the timing procedure by indicating that a specific reinforcer will be given when the class works quietly for a designated period of time.

6. **Additional suggestions.** If taping equipment is not available, use pupils who have mastered S-TR-OT-0004 to present a play where they act out the situations described for Tapes 1 and 2.

Code: S-TR-OT-0004-L1-Ir

TEACHING STRATEGY

Objective: When given an assignment to complete, the student works without speaking aloud.

Social Reinforcement

1. **When target student is observed working silently on an assignment, praise aloud by name.** Specific behaviors should be mentioned. "Stan, good quiet work;" "Audrey, you are wise to work so quietly;" "I like the way Greg is sitting quietly and working."
2. **Appropriate behavior may be cued in the target student by praising others in the class who are sitting and working quietly.** Watch for the behavior to occur in the target child and be sure to reinforce it.
3. **In addition to praise, some kind of tangible reinforcer such as points, tokens, or checkmarks might be given to students at first to increase sitting and working quietly.** A 3 x 5 card may be placed on the student's desk. You can give checkmarks or punch holes in the card when the student is working appropriately, giving praise at the same time. The checkmarks or punches can be exchanged for something the student wants.

Code: S-TR-OT-0004-L1-Ic

TEACHING STRATEGY

Objective: When given an assignment to complete, the student works without speaking aloud.

Contingency Management

1. **State the task in observable terms.** When given an assignment to complete at your seat, work on the assignment at your seat quietly without talking to others.
2. **Plan reinforcement strategy selected from reinforcement menu.**
3. **State the contingency.** When you complete your seatwork by working quietly at your seat without speaking aloud or moving around, you will be rewarded. (The student should be aware of the type and amount of reinforcement.)
4. **Watch for those who display good seatwork behavior, working quietly at their seats, and reward them.** Set up a situation requiring students to demonstrate seatwork behavior. For example, give an assignment that must be completed at students' seats.
5. **Example.** Mr. Cody had a difficult time doing any type of individual or group work with his class because the other students were too noisy. Although he had given students work they could do, the disruptions continued to be a problem. Mr. Cody explained the problem to his students

366

and told them he was going to set up a chart. The chart showed each student's name. Each time he had group or individual work, the other students could earn checkmarks if they worked quietly at their seats. Mr. Cody observed the students and made checkmarks periodically for those students who were working appropriately. He also used social reinforcement, calling out to students such remarks as, "Good work, Jim;" "Checkmark for Mary;" "Laurie is doing a good job." As soon as each student earned five checkmarks, the class would get an extra 10 minutes of recess. As this was successful, Mr. Cody increased his expectation to a larger number of checkmarks for the extra recess. He soon found the chart was not necessary but still remembered to praise good seatwork behavior and give the students intermittent rewards.

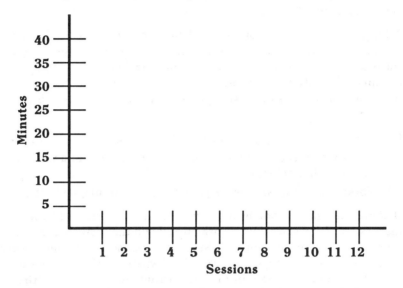

Figure 5. Amount of time spent working quietly during study lessons.

Skill:	To work steadily for the required length of time. **S-TR-OT-0006-L1**
Objective:	The student, when given an assignment to work on, will work steadily for the length of time required by the teacher.
Assessment:	Assess from previous knowledge of student or through direct observation using the <u>Social Behavior Assessment Inventory</u>.

Code: **S-TR-OT-0006-L1-Im**

TEACHING STRATEGY

Objective: The student, when given an assignment to work on, will work steadily for the length of time required by the teacher.

Social Modeling

1. **Set the stage.** Present the students with a fun worksheet containing a short game or puzzle like connect-the-dots, a secret message to decode, or a word scramble using a particular theme. The task should be no more than five minutes in length.

   Note: Make sure the task is appropriate for age level of the students and within the students' repertoire.

   When students are working on this task, recognize students who attend to the task steadily and students who complete the task by working on it continuously, i.e., "Good, Jenny, you're working steadily on your puzzle," or, "That's great, Mike, you worked on your paper continuously until you were all finished!"

   After all students have completed their worksheets, begin discussion of reasons for working steadily on a task for the length of time required by the teacher. Say, "Why did you work on the puzzle I gave you until you were all finished?" (Student response.) "Good!" Elicit from students reasons involving the benefits of finishing a task on time. Reasons offered should include:

   (a) By working steadily you will be able to accomplish more of the task.

   (b) By working steadily you will finish the task sooner and will then have time for other activities.

   (c) Working steadily will please your teacher, parents, and others.

   If these reasons are not brought out by the students, add them to the discussion. "Why should you work steadily on the assignments I give you for the length of time required?" (Student response.) "Excellent, everyone! What are some other times outside school when you should work on a task steadily for a certain amount of time?" (Student responses.) "Great!"

2. **Identify the specific steps.** When given an assignment to work on, what steps must we go through so that we can work steadily for the length of time required? As students offer suggestions, list the steps on the chalkboard. If students do not respond at first, prompt by giving clues about the necessary steps. Steps to be included are:

   (a) Decide what materials and equipment you need to do the assignment and obtain these materials.

   (b) Go to the area where you will be working (desk, listening booth, library, etc.).

   (c) Begin to work on the assignment.

   (d) Continue working on the assignment for the required time.

   (e) Work **only** on that assignment during the required time.

3. **Model the behavior.** Prepare a tape recording of directions for typical classroom assignments. For example, prepare short worksheet consisting of two or three sample math problems. Put the following instructions on tape and play it in the classroom while individual students come to the front of the room to model the desired behaviors. "Work the math problems on your worksheet. You will have three minutes to work." (Two minutes of blank tape during which specific behaviors are modeled.) "Put your math

work away and get ready for reading." Have the students observe and identify the desirable behaviors. Praise appropriate responses.

4. **Practice the behavior.** (This strategy may be completed over two or three different days or lessons.) On the next occasion, when you give the students an assignment to work on, remind them to work steadily for the length of time required. If this activity is implemented on a different day, review the lesson on this skill briefly. Say, "Let's see if you can all work steadily on this assignment for the next _____ minutes." Recognize students who are working steadily. After the required time is up, discuss briefly with students how the steps for this behavior were followed. Remember to begin with a shorter amount of time than the desired terminal behavior and gradually increase the time as pupils can handle it.

5. **Additional suggestions.**

   (a) While students are working on a given assignment, pass out happy faces to those students working steadily for the specified time. Also, you may wish to use these happy faces to establish where students may exchange happy faces for different privileges or activities.

   (b) Prepare a board entitled "The Great Time Race." Make a large racetrack and have pupils make a race car (or bring one from home). Each time a seatwork assignment is made, inform the pupils before they begin that by working steadily for the required length of time, they will be able to move their cars a designated number of spaces along the track. Explain that every pupil who finished the race by lunch (or by the end of the day) will earn five minutes of extra recess for the next recess period. When the desired terminal behavior is reached, begin to phase out the game by requiring the pupils to finish the race for two days, then three, four, and five. Then inform pupils that special privileges may be earned from time to time.

Code: S-TR-OT-0006-L1-Ir

TEACHING STRATEGY

Objective: The student, when given an assignment to work on, will work steadily for the length of time required by the teacher.

Social Reinforcement

1. **When the target student is observed working steadily on an assignment for a specified length of time, praise aloud and by name.** Attention should be directed to specific actions, e.g., "Hal, thank you for working on your math for the entire 20 minutes."

2. **Working steadily for a specified length of time can be used by praising others near the target student who are exhibiting the desired behavior.** Watch for steady working in the target student and reinforce it when it occurs.

3. **If social reinforcement is insufficient to elicit working on an assignment for a specified time, pair social reinforcement with tangible reinforcement such as points, checkmarks, tokens, etc., that may be exchanged for something desired by the student.**

Code: S-TR-OT-0006-L1-Ic

TEACHING STRATEGY

Objective: The student, when given an assignment to work on, will work steadily for the length of time required by the teacher.

Contingency Management

1. **State the task in observable terms.** When given an assignment by the teacher, the student will work on the assignment steadily for the length of time designated by the teacher.
2. **Plan reinforcement strategy selected from reinforcement menu.**
3. **State the contingency.** When you work steadily on an assignment for the length of time required, you will be rewarded. Specify amount and type of reinforcement to be provided to the student.
4. **Watch for those who work steadily for the required time and reward them.** Create a situation where pupils are required to work steadily on an assignment for a specified length of time. State the contingency for students.
5. **Example.** Ms. Hutch had problems with a few of her students working on assigned tasks for the time she had designated. She explained the problem to the students. She then told them that she would set a timer when she gave assignments, and each time the students worked on the assignments until the timer sounded, they would receive one token. When a student accumulated five tokens, he or she would earn five extra minutes in a play activity such as modeling with clay or playing a game. Ms. Hutch observed her pupils after stating the contingency and giving an assignment. She awarded tokens to those who worked steadily until the timer rang. She also used social reinforcement as she was awarding the tokens. For example, "Jonathan, you really stuck to it!" "Very good job, Tamara."

When a student had earned five tokens, Ms. Hutch added five extra minutes to the pupil's normal in-class free-time period. Initially, Ms. Hutch set the timer for short periods, e.g., five minutes, then gradually increased the length of time required until she reached her goal of 20 minutes. Ms. Hutch eventually found that the tokens were no longer needed; pupils worked steadily for the required time even when she stopped awarding tokens. However, she continued giving social reinforcement for working steadily, with an occasional intermittent reward of five minutes of extra free time.

Skill:	To ignore distractions from peers when doing a seatwork assignment.
	S-TR-OT-0008-L1
Objective:	When presented with potentially distracting actions or verbalizations from peers while doing a seatwork assignment, the student will ignore the distractions by not responding and by continuing with his or her work.
Assessment:	Assess from previous knowledge of student or through direct observation using the <u>Social Behavior Assessment Inventory</u>.

Code: S-TR-OT-0008-L1-Im

TEACHING STRATEGY

Objective: When presented with potentially distracting actions or verbalizations from peers while doing a seatwork assignment, the student will ignore the distractions by not responding and continuing with his or her work.

Social Modeling

1. **Set the stage.** Tell this story:

THE HERO

Mark was a hero of Tiffin Elementary School. He was going to compete on a TV show where he could win a minibike and 10 boxes of bubble gum. Also, the school would get a brand new swing set for the playgrounds. Mark and his classmates were very excited when the big day came. Mark had 10 minutes to answer 24 math problems. He started very fast, and the time kept ticking away. Finally, he had five problems left and two minutes remaining on the clock. Everyone started shouting, "Hurry, Mark, you only have two minutes left. Hurry! Hurry!" Mark kept hearing everyone's voice and turned each time to look. Finally, he thought, "I know I can do these problems, but everyone is bothering me. I'll just pretend they're not here and keep working." Mark kept working and did not look at the people shouting. Just as Mark finished the last problem, his time ran out. Mark had won!

2. **Identify the specific steps.** Discuss and list what helped Mark win the prize:

   (a) Ignored distracting voices, i.e., he did not listen and did not look at the people.

   (b) Continued with his work.

3. **Model the behavior.** Say, "Now we're going to role-play. I'm going to pretend that I'm a student working on an assignment." (Sit at student's desk with pencil and paper.) "Volunteers from the class (you may choose to use pupils from another class) are going to carry out some activities that could distract me from my work. Watch how I ignore them and keep on working." (Distractions could include knock at door or noise in hall.) Have the students identify elements of desired ignoring behavior when role-play is completed. Praise students contributing proper ideas.

4. **Practice the behavior.** Have the class take turns being the student doing work and the ones who do other acceptable activities that may distract them. Make sure each student has an opportunity to practice the appropriate ignoring behavior. Praise students exhibiting desired behavior. Praise aloud for others to hear and be specific, e.g., "Matt, I'm really glad to see you working and not paying attention to the noise around you."

   Note: Do **not** allow students to practice inappropriate behaviors, e.g., calling by name the person who is practicing ignoring, or poking him or her.

5. **Additional suggestions.**
   (a) Develop a puppet show displaying how to ignore distractions and continue working.
   (b) When the distracting behavior is an inappropriate behavior, be sure not to reinforce the student creating the disturbance by giving attention for misbehavior.
   (c) In order to have the desired behavior continue, reinforce it frequently when it occurs for at least one week. Later, reinforce it on an intermittent schedule.

Code: S-TR-OT-0008-L1-Ir

TEACHING STRATEGY

Objective: When presented with potentially distracting actions or verbalizations from peers while doing a seatwork assignment, the student will ignore the distractions by not responding and by continuing with his or her work.

Social Reinforcement

1. **When the target student is observed ignoring distracting stimuli by not responding and continuing with work, he or she should be praised.** Praise aloud or take the student aside depending on the student and the situation. Identify specific actions, e.g., "Matt, I'm really glad to see you working and not paying attention to the noises around you." Taking Brenda aside, "Brenda, I know John has been bothering you. You are doing so well continuing with your work and not paying attention to him."

   Note: Be careful not to reinforce student creating the disturbance by giving attention for misbehavior.

2. **Ignoring distracting stimuli can be cued in target student by praising others close to the target student who are successfully ignoring distracting events.** When the target student shows indications of appropriate behavior, reinforce him or her, also.

3. **If social reinforcement in the form of praise, attention, smiles, winks, etc., is not sufficient to increase the desired behavior, it may be necessary to pair social reinforcement with tangible reinforcement, e.g., chips, coupons, tokens, stars, etc., to be exchanged for something the child wants.**

Code: S-TR-OT-0008-L1-Ic

TEACHING STRATEGY

Objective: When presented with potentially distracting actions or verbalizations from peers while doing a seatwork assignment, the student will ignore the distractions by not responding and by continuing with his or her work.

Contingency Management

1. **State the task in observable terms.** Student will continue working and ignore other students who do or say things to distract him or her.

2. **Plan reinforcement strategy selected from reinforcement menu.** Define a consequence valued by the student that will be given following demonstration of the desired working behavior.

3. **State the contingency.** If student continues working and ignores distractions from other students, he or she will be rewarded. Specify amount and type of reinforcement to students.

4. **Watch for behavior to occur naturally or arrange the environment to require classmates to work and ignore distracting stimuli.** Give an assignment and announce to students that you will be watching for those who are able to work steadily without responding to interruptions. Reward students who show signs of successfully ignoring others.

5. **Example.** Alison was a good worker when she had her mind on her work, but she spent a great deal of time turned around in her seat looking at or listening to other children. She was easily drawn into arguments, responding to anyone who tried to tease her. Her teacher, Ms. Hanes, set up a private contract with her that she could earn extra recess for the class by keeping her eyes on her work and not responding to distractions. Ms. Hanes put a card on Alison's desk and told her that she would watch her and put tally marks on the card when she saw Alison working steadily and ignoring others. Each mark would represent a minute of extra recess. Before recess, Ms. Hanes would let the class know that Alison had earned extra recess for them by being a good worker.

Skill:	To discuss academic material with peers when appropriate. **S-TR-OT-0010-L1**
Objective:	The student talks about academic material to peers when appropriate, i.e., when directed to do so by teacher or when such a discussion would facilitate school work.
Assessment:	Assess from previous knowledge of student or through direct observation using the <u>Social Behavior Assessment Inventory</u>.

Code: S-TR-OT-0010-L1-Im

TEACHING STRATEGY

Objective: The student talks about academic material to peers when appropriate, i.e., when directed to do so by teacher or when such a discussion would facilitate school work.

Social Modeling

1. **Set the stage.** Read the following story to the group or, if their reading skills permit, duplicate and distribute it to the students for them to read.

THE TRYOUTS

John was a 10-year-old boy who wanted very much to be a pitcher on his neighborhood's Little League team. He practiced pitching every day with his neighbor, Bob, who wanted to be a catcher. Each day John and Bob practiced for one hour. John wondered to himself, "Can I do it? Can I make the team as a pitcher? Am I throwing the ball the way I should?" Each day John practiced, he wondered how he was doing, but he never discussed his pitching style with Bob.

Finally, the big day of the tryouts came. John was so excited that he left for the baseball field one-half hour earlier than usual so he would not be late. When he arrived at the field, he saw several other boys had already arrived and were busy playing catch. Very shortly, Bob arrived at the ball field. Bob and John began talking. John said, "Bob, look at Jerry. When he throws the ball, he really leans forward."

"Yeah, that's so he can throw it harder," Bob replied.

"Do I do that?" asked John.

"Kinda, but not as much as Jerry," said Bob.

John began to wonder if he should change his pitching style and wished he had talked with Bob about it before now. John was thinking that perhaps Bob could have judged his pitching, and the two of them could have compared ideas about what John might do to improve.

As John was thinking about it, the coach arrived and announced the start of the playing position tryouts. When the tryouts were completed, John was disappointed because he did not get a pitching position; however, he was pleased to be on the team and looked forward to playing his shortstop position.

Begin a discussion of the story and ask the following questions:

(a) "When John practiced, what else could he have done to improve his pitching style?" (Content of response: Discussed it with Bob.)

(b) "Why would discussing it with Bob help him to improve?" (Content of responses: Corrective feedback and, possibly, new ideas.)

(c) "Have you ever discussed your ball playing, piano playing, report writing, or anything else with one of your friends?"

(d) "Why did you discuss it?" (Possible student responses: "I liked talking about it." "Jim tells me what parts he likes and why he likes them. That helps me do a good job of report writing.")

Based on the student responses, lead the discussion to the question of when it is appropriate to discuss academic materials in school. Say, "As some of you have pointed out, talking with a friend about your performance on a task is often helpful to your learning. Would it be all right to talk about school work in class?" (Student response.) "That's very good, Tim. It is all right to talk about school work in class when it can help you learn. Give me some examples of when it would be good to talk about school work in class." (Possible answers: "When you're not sure of an answer." "When you finish an assignment and want to go over it with someone." "When I tell you to discuss a topic." "When you get stuck for an idea in a report," and so on.) "Very good idea, Jack."

2. **Identify specific steps.** List the following steps on the chalkboard and elaborate on them for the class:

   (a) Determine the reason for talking to classmate.

   (b) Raise hand or go to teacher's desk.

   (c) Explain why you need to talk to classmate, and ask for permission.

   (d) Go to classmate and ask him or her to talk to you.

   (e) Talk with classmate quietly.

   (f) Thank classmate and return to your seat.

   (Steps "b" and "c" should be eliminated when the student has demonstrated legitimate reasons for talking with peers.)

3. **Model the behavior.** Identify a pupil to play the role of teacher. This pupil may be from another class if necessary. Explain to the pupil that he or she will be playing the role of teacher and should give permission to the person asking to talk with his or her classmate. You should take a seat in a pupil's desk and proceed to model each of the behaviors listed above. After the behaviors are modeled, ask the pupils to identify the specific behaviors you exhibited. Recognition should be given for appropriate descriptions, such as:

   (a) "Jan, that is an excellent observation."

   (b) "Ted, you repeated some of the reasons I gave for asking to talk with Jennifer. That's great."

4. **Practice activity.** Each pupil shall be asked to role-play the specific behaviors that are outlined above. A procedure similar to the one discussed above should be followed. Recognize pupils for specific behaviors.

5. **Additional suggestions.**

   (a) Formal peer tutoring situations may be set up that require one student to discuss work with another.

   (b) IP-GA-0002 through IP-GA-0010 and IP-MC-0004 are related skills that may have to be taught. Assess each of these skills if the pupil is having problems with TR-OT-0010.

   (c) Since this behavior is one that can be easily overdone, you may want to set a time limit for each consultation and specific times of the day when consulting with a peer is permitted.

Code: S-TR-OT-0010-L1-Ir

TEACHING STRATEGY

Objective: The student talks about academic material to peers when appropriate, i.e., when directed to do so by teacher or when such a discussion would facilitate school work.

Social Reinforcement

1. **Identify and praise the student when talking about academic material to peers when appropriate.** Be specific with praise. "Marty, I'm glad you checked your answers with John." "Beth, I like the way you got together with Roger to talk about the reading assignment."

2. **Encourage the desired behavior in the target student by praising others who discuss academic work with classmates under appropriate conditions.** Provide cues by suggesting to students that they ask another student for help or by asking two students to study together. Formal peer tutoring situations may be set up that require one student to discuss his work with another.

Code: S-TR-OT-0010-L1-Ic

TEACHING STRATEGY

Objective: The student talks about academic material to peers when appropriate, i.e., when directed to do so by teacher or when such a discussion would facilitate school work.

Contingency Management

1. **Meet with the class and discuss when students should talk with peers about academic material.** Suggest times when it is appropriate, for example, when directed by teacher and when it would facilitate school work.

2. **Plan reinforcement strategy selected from reinforcement menu.**

3. **State the contingency.** When you discuss academic material with another student as a result of being directed to do so by the teacher or because such a discussion would help your school work, you will be rewarded. Be sure to specify amount and type of reinforcement.

4. **Watch for the behavior to occur naturally and reinforce it,** or set up a situation for the behavior to occur. For example, give the class an assignment, allowing the students to discuss it with another student to check answers. If the student talks with a peer about the academic tasks, reinforce according to the agreed-upon contingency.

5. **Example.** Mr. Albright observed that members of his class seldom spoke with each other about academic material. Mr. Albright talked with the class and told them that there are situations in which they may wish to discuss school work with another student. He gave examples of appropriate situations, such as, when directed by the teacher or when discussion would help school work. Mr. Albright stated to the class that during the morning schedule, an assignment would be given in which students discuss with each other. He told the class that students who discussed academic material with their peers would be rewarded. Reinforcement was defined as receiving two raffle tickets. At the end of the morning period, a raffle was held. The student who was holding the winning raffle ticket was awarded one special privilege card. Mr. Albright continued the contingency for three days, then every other day for two weeks. After two weeks, Mr. Albright dropped the contingency. Social reinforcement for discussing academic material in appropriate situations was continued.

Skill:	To change from one activity to another when required by the teacher.
	S-TR-OT-0012-L1
Objective:	When required by the teacher, the student changes from one activity to another promptly, without excessive hesitation or complaining.
Assessment:	Assess from previous knowledge of student or through direct observation using the <u>Social Behavior Assessment Inventory</u>.

Code: S-TR-OT-0012-L1-Im

TEACHING STRATEGY

Objective: When required by the teacher, the student changes from one activity to another promptly, without excessive hesitation or complaining.

Social Modeling

1. **Set the stage.** Stop the class during a work period and ask all students to get their chairs and make a circle in an open area of the room. Time their transition from the time you tell them to stop their work to the time that everyone is seated in a circle. Record the time taken for later use. When the children are seated, ask: "What did we just do?" (Student response.) "Very good, Roger. When we changed from _____ to this activity; it took us _____ minutes. I want us to make the change in _____ minutes or less." Discuss moving from one activity to another. Ask, "When changing from one activity to another, how quickly should we change?" (Student response.) "Exactly, George. Why?" (Student response.) Encourage student responses by asking questions and recognizing students who volunteer answers. Possible questions include:

    (a) When you change slowly, will we get more or less school work finished?

    (b) Will there be time later to finish the task you are asked to leave?

    (c) How will changing quickly help you and me?

    (d) How will changing slowly hurt you and me?

2. **Identify specific behaviors to be modeled.** List the specific behaviors on a wall chart or chalkboard. Adopt a routine procedure for changing from one activity to another. This will provide for faster learning of the desired behaviors. Pictorial representations of each of the specific behaviors may be helpful to younger children. This step should immediately follow the "setting the stage" step. Say, "When we change from one activity to another, we should do the following."

3. **Model the behavior.** To model this behavior, record the following directions. Have a pupil play teacher and give the directions to you or ask another adult to be teacher and give them to you. The directions are, "May I have your attention, please. Put your math work away. Take out your reading book and go to the reading center." Assume the role of a pupil. Model each of the specific behaviors outlined in Step 2. Exaggerate the behaviors somewhat to be sure they are observable. Caution: Don't overdo it because the students will imitate your behavior; this is the purpose of your modeling.

377

After modeling the behavior ask, "Will someone tell me what I did? That's right, Jamie. I stopped working on math as soon as the teacher began talking. What else did I do?" (Continue to give specific descriptive praise for each of the component behaviors. If students leave out one of the components, refer them to the wall chart and explain what was omitted.) "Now, who wants to try to follow the same directions?" (Student response.) "OK, Jennie." (Have pupil begin working math problems at his or her seat. Give the student the same directions that you just followed. Again, have the class identify the specific behaviors the student exhibits. Recognize correct responses.

4. **Practice the behavior.** "I'm very pleased with the way everyone has participated in this activity. Please pick up your chairs, return to your desks and be seated." (Student response.) "Now, that was fantastic. Everyone looked right at me as I gave directions, remained quiet, and then followed my directions immediately. Let's practice some more. Everyone begin to work on one of your seatwork assignments." (Wait three or four minutes.) "May I have your attention, please. Leave your pencils and papers on your table and go to the chalkboard." (Student response.) Recognize specific correct behaviors as before. Have students return to their seats. Continue to practice the behavior, if needed.

5. **Reinforcement.** Explain to the children that you have timed their changing from one activity to another during the past week. Report your findings. Explain that for the next two weeks, you will continue to record the time it takes them to change activities. Prepare a table similar to the one in Figure 6 for recording purposes. Record the total amount of time used each day in changing activities. Continue to recognize specific behaviors as described above. In addition, give immediate feedback after each activity change regarding the time taken; for example, "Wow, you just set a new record for changing activities. That change took only one minute and 30 seconds." Stop posting time after second week, but continue to give verbal feedback and praise.

	Week 1	Week 2	Week 3
M			
T			
W			
Th			
F			

Figure 6. Time to change activities.

6. **Additional suggestions.**
   (a) Attach backup reinforcers to "Time to Change Activities" table if necessary. One alternative is to give extra recess time equivalent to the amount of time saved, over the average time required during baseline,

on a daily basis. After one week, the amount of earned recess time can be reduced. The earned recess time should gradually be reduced and eliminated.

(b) If child has a particularly difficult time with this skill check prerequisites: S-TR-AT-0002, S-TR-AT-0006, S-TR-FD-0002.

Code: S-TR-OT-0012-L1-Ir

TEACHING STRATEGY

Objective: When required by the teacher, the student changes from one activity to another promptly, without excessive hesitation or complaining.

Social Reinforcement

1. **When a student is observed changing from one activity to another with little or no complaining or hesitating, reinforce the behavior with descriptive praise and a smile or a pat on the back.** For example, "Martha, thank you for putting away your math book and getting out your science book. I appreciated how quickly you got ready for your science lesson." "Carl, I liked the way you got ready to go to math class when I asked. You put your card game away quickly without complaining. Thank you."

2. **Provide cues for the target student.** Recognize another student, for the target student to hear, who is demonstrating the desired behavior. When the target student responds to the cue by modeling the behavior, be sure to reinforce with praise.

3. **If social reinforcement does not produce the desired behavior, provide tangible reinforcement (e.g., tokens, chips, coupons, etc.) paired with social reinforcement (smiles, praise, pats on the back, etc.).** The token reinforcers may be exchanged for desirable items and/or activities.

Code: S-TR-OT-0012-L1-Ic

TEACHING STRATEGY

Objective: When required by the teacher, the student changes from one activity to another promptly, without excessive hesitation or complaining.

Contingency Management

1. **Present the task to the student in specific terms.** For example, when directed to change activities the student will change quickly with little or no hesitation and no grumbling or complaining.

2. **Select and plan a reinforcement strategy from the reinforcement menu.**

3. **State the contingency.** When the student changes activities as directed by the teacher quickly, with little or no hesitation and no complaining, the student will be rewarded. Specify amount and type of reinforcement.

4. **Watch for the behavior to occur naturally or create a situation for the behavior to occur.** For example, ask target student to change activities. If the student follows through with the change quickly and without hesitation or complaining, he or she is provided the agreed-upon positive consequences.

5. **Example.** When Mr. Cartwright asked students in his gym class to change activities, Don did not. Don told Mr. Cartwright that he did not want to play "this silly old game." Mr. Cartwright repeatedly had such difficulties with Don who, when required, rarely changed activities quickly and without hesitation or complaining.

Mr. Cartwright told Don that activities would continue to change in gym class. He further stated to Don that at times those activities might not be desirable to Don, but might be desirable to his classmates. Mr. Cartwright explained to Don that by changing activities when required, without hesitation or complaining, he would earn two points. Mr. Cartwright continued, "The points you earn will be counted up weekly. Each week that you earn twelve or more points, you may reserve a basketball for yourself and some friends to use during the lunch break on Tuesday and Thursday of the next week." (Mr. Cartwright had observed that Don played basketball at every opportunity but frequently complained that he hardly ever got to the gym in time to get a ball for use during the lunch recess.)

Each time that Don changed activities quickly and without complaining, Mr. Cartwright awarded Don his two points paired with social reinforcement. For each of the next three weeks, Don earned twelve points and was granted his reserved basketball. The fourth week, Don earned 12 points but did not come to claim his reserved ball. During the next week, Mr. Cartwright continued recognizing Don for changing activities but did not award any points. Don has continued to change activities without difficulty. Mr. Cartwright still uses social reinforcement to maintain Don's behavior.

PERFORMING BEFORE OTHERS

S-TR-PF-0002-L1-S	To participate in a role-playing activity.
S-TR-PF-0004-L1-S	To read aloud in a small group.
S-TR-PF-0006-L1-S	To read aloud before a large group or the entire class.
S-TR-PF-0008-L2-S	To make a report before a small group.
S-TR-PF-0010-L2-S	To make a report before a large group or the entire class.

Skill:	To participate in a role-playing activity. **S-TR-PF-0002-L1**
Objective:	Student will participate in a role-playing activity by pretending he or she is the person whose role he or she is playing and acting as that person might act.
Assessment:	Assess from previous knowledge of student or through direct observation using the <u>Social Behavior Assessment Inventory</u>.

Code: S-TR-PF-0002-L1-Im

TEACHING STRATEGY

Objective: Student will participate in a role-playing activity by pretending he or she is the person whose role he or she is playing and acting as that person might act.

Social Modeling

1. **Set the stage.** Tell the following story:

CHO LIN, THE STORYTELLER

About 500 years ago, there was a man called Cho Lin. He lived in China, and some people thought he was the wisest man in the whole world. People came from all around to ask Cho Lin questions. They knew Cho Lin could help them find answers to their questions.

However, Cho never answered their questions right away. In fact, he never spoke at all. When people asked him for help, he only nodded. They told him their troubles and went away. That night Cho would write a play about the person's story and give the play to his grandson, Tau. His grandson and his grandson's friends would learn the parts of Cho's play. When they had learned their parts well, they invited the person with troubles to watch the play. As the person watched the play, he or she learned the answers to the question. This made the person happy.

When the play was over, the person who had a question now had an answer and would thank Cho and go home. Cho never said a word. His play did his talking for him.

Discuss the story immediately after you read it. Direct the discussion by asking questions such as the following:

(a) "Did Cho Lin answer people's questions directly?" (Response: "No.")

(b) "What did he do instead of talking about their troubles to them?" (Response: "Wrote a play.")

(c) "What happened after he wrote the play?" (Response: "His grandson and friends learned the parts and put on the play for the person having troubles.")

(d) "How did the person get the answer to his question?" (Response: "He or she learned it from the play.")

(e) "Do you think that making plays can help us learn things?" (Response: "Yes.")

(f) "What plays or movies have you seen that helped you learn something?" (Plays, TV specials, etc.)

(g) "Is it interesting to see a play about how a person solves a problem instead of just talking about the problem?"

(h) Say, "I think role-playing is a good way to learn things, too. It is important, though, to play a role in the right way so that the play will tell the story it is supposed to."

At this point, you may need to specify what "the right way" means. You can mimic some basic imitation through facial gestures to make your point. You might also ask for volunteers to demonstrate. For example, ask, "How would someone look if he or she were happy, scared, excited, sad, angry, etc.?"

2. **Identify specific steps.** The specific steps involved in role-playing should be identified. Outline the specific steps for the students.

(a) Identify your part, i.e., who are you supposed to be and what is the story about?

(b) Identify how the person you will be playing thinks and feels in this pretend situation.

(c) Pretend and act out that person's part by using gestures, actions, words, and expressions.

After presenting this information ask, "When you role-play, what must you do?" (Go to various pupils for elaboration on the initial response.)

3. **Model the behavior.** Role-play one of the situations described below or one of your own. First, read it to the class, then do it. Next, choose a willing student who has good role-playing skills and ask him or her to role-play one of the following:

(a) Student who is coming into class bursting with excitement because his cat just had three baby kittens.

(b) Student who is coming to school on the day of a big spelling bee and is nervous.

(c) Student who is working quietly and hears the fire bell ringing.

Before the child begins to role-play, reemphasize the steps to follow when role-playing. After he or she finishes, ask students to identify the steps again.

4. **Practice the behavior.** Have each student work with a partner or in small groups to practice role-playing. Encourage the students to use their imaginations. You may begin with a small step, such as acting out specific

382

emotions through gestures and expressions, or you may suggest some simple situations. Keep in mind that the skill to be practiced is how to role-play. Students should not be required to act out situations involving additional social behaviors that are not mastered at the time. Have the pupils do steps one and two (identify their part and identify how the person they will be playing feels) aloud so that you may give corrective feedback and praise.

Situations:

(a) Two boys, John and Bob, are playing a game. Bob is upset because he loses.

(b) A group of students are playing a game. A new student comes up and is shy. The others ask the student to join them.

(c) Sandy just got an "A" on her spelling paper. She is telling her friend Terri.

5. **Additional suggestions.**

(a) As a follow-up activity, you may have students observe and list behaviors in and around the classroom that need improvement. (Example: Lining up for lunch.) Small groups could work out a skit and role-play for the class (with your help if needed).

(b) If students need more practice to be comfortable about role-playing, small groups could role-play and/or use puppets to role-play familiar situations (eating in cafeteria, working at math time, etc.) or familiar stories ("Three Billy Goats Gruff,"etc.).

(c) With primary groups, additional discussions and/or demonstrations (puppet skit) may be needed initially. The children may not have seen many "plays" and may need help to understand what is meant by pretending. Using hand puppets to begin with may be necessary. Thus, you may wish to substitute a short, paper-bag-puppet skit that relates to their level for the Cho Lin story. You could also use a nursery rhyme or a fairy tale.

(d) For students who are unwilling to participate in a role-playing activity, begin by bringing cassettes of songs to class and have the children act out the songs.

(e) Have reluctant role-players begin by playing charades with actions words, e.g., jump, run, walk, crawl, etc.

Code: S-TR-PF-0002-L1-Ir

TEACHING STRATEGY

Objective: Student will participate in a role-playing activity by pretending he or she is the person whose role he or she is playing and acting as that person might act.

Social Reinforcement

1. **In introducing new social skills, role-playing is often a very effective means of instruction.** Most children seem to enjoy this technique and will readily "get into role." However, more shy or timid children may have

difficulty performing in this manner and may need some additional encouragement. Provide praise when the student is observed participating in the assigned role. Be specific in praising behavior, so the student knows what was done right. "Sandy, you did a really good job playing teacher!" "Nancy, you acted as if you enjoyed that role. That makes me happy." "Good role-playing, Everett."

2. **Provide cues for target student.** In role-playing sessions, encourage the target student with gestures, nods, smiles, and facial expressions. Also praise aloud other students who are doing a good job. When the target student responds appropriately, remember to reinforce immediately.

3. **If, initially, social reinforcement alone does not provide sufficient encouragement, when the student makes an effort to role-play, pair the social reinforcement with something tangible that the student likes and would be willing to work for.**

Code: S-TR-PF-0002-L1-Ic

TEACHING STRATEGY

Objective: Student will participate in a role-playing activity by pretending he or she is the person whose role he or she is playing and acting as that person might act.

Contingency Management

1. **If you use role-playing frequently as a teaching device and have a reluctant student, you will probably want to meet with the student alone to describe specifically what you want him or her to do.**
2. **Plan reinforcement.**
3. **State the contingency contract with shaping in mind.** Remember that "acting" in front of a group can be frightening for some students. In making a contingency contract with the reluctant student, don't demand a great deal initially; rather, plan to gradually shape the desired active participation. For example, "When you participate in the roles I assign you in a role-playing activity, you will be rewarded." Specify amount and type of reinforcement.
4. **During regularly scheduled role-playing situations, observe the behavior of the target child and reward when he or she participates.**
5. **Example.** Mr. Phelps often uses role-playing in his classroom, to introduce new concepts, to work through difficulties, and to practice social skills. The technique is very effective, and most of the students have fun while learning. However, one child in his class, Rollin, is very shy and refuses to participate in any of the roles. If prompted at all, Rollin ends up crying and running out of the room. Mr. Phelps talked to Rolling privately one day during a "free time" period when Rollin seemed to be happy and amicable. Mr. Phelps explained that he felt bad that Rollin didn't enjoy the activities. They made the following agreement, according to the stated contingency. "When you go willingly to the group to which you have been assigned, then you will be given a 'Happy Face' and you know that 'Happy Faces' help you earn extra free time."

Note that no requirement for participation is demanded at this point. After two weeks, Rollin was going to the role-playing situation with no problem. Mr. Phelps' next step was to state the following contingency to Rollin. "When you participate in the role I assign you in a role-playing activity, you will earn an additional 'Happy Face.'" Mr. Phelps continued awarding one 'Happy Face' for going to the group and an additional one for participation. Initially, Mr. Phelps assigned nonverbal roles to Rollin, then roles with a minimal requirement for verbalization, then more verbal roles. After four more weeks, Rollin was participating in the role-playing activities at a satisfactory level.

Skill:	To read aloud in a small group.
	S-TR-PF-0004-L1
Objective:	When required, the student will willingly read aloud in a small group of three or four other students, without signs of excessive nervousness or fear.
Assessment:	Assess from previous knowledge of student or through direct observation using the <u>Social Behavior Assessment Inventory</u>.

Code: S-TR-PF-0004-L1-Im

TEACHING STRATEGY

Objective: When required, the student will willingly read aloud in a small group of three or four other students, without signs of excessive nervousness or fear.

Introduction: The pupil who is reluctant to read before a group of peers and/or adults, typically has poor reading skills. When beginning to work on this skill, the pupil should be requested to read aloud material at his or her mastery reading level. He or she should also be given the opportunity to read over the material before reading aloud in a group.

After the target pupil is comfortable reading aloud material at his or her mastery reading level, you may then begin to require oral reading of material at his or her instructional reading level. Under no circumstances should a pupil be required to read orally when the reading material is above his or her instructional level. Corrections should be made in a very matter-of-fact fashion without initial comments when pupils read orally at their instructional levels.

Social Modeling

1. **Set the stage.** Begin by reading a short story to the target pupils as a group. If the story is too long to be read in one 10-minute session (the session length depends on the group attention), it should be broken down into segments and read through completely. The story selected should be one of previously demonstrated high interest level. After the story is completed, a brief discussion about the story may be held before proceeding to a discussion of your reading behavior. When the discussion of the story content is completed, say:

(a) "Did you enjoy my reading the story to you?"

(b) "This is one reason why we read aloud to others. Sometimes pupils also read aloud in school because they are asked to do so by their teachers. Reading aloud in class when I ask you to helps me to learn about your reading skills and will also help you to learn."

2. **Identify the specific steps.** (To follow Step 1 immediately.) Say, "When asked to read aloud to a small group you should:

    (a) Read loud enough to be heard by all in the group.

    (b) Hold body still.

    (c) Pause according to punctuation.

    (d) Read aloud at normal speaking rate."

3. **Model the behavior.** Read a short passage to the group and model each of the four behaviors specified above. Pupils should be asked to make observations about your behavior. (If possible, the selected passage should be at the mastery level of all pupils and pupils should have a copy of the text.) Recognition should be given to appropriate pupil responses.

4. **Practice the behavior.** Provide reading material at each pupil's mastery level for the practice activity. Direct pupils to form groups of two or three (or assign partners) and take turns reading aloud. No more than three groups should be formed, since the activity of one group may interfere with another if the groups are too close together. Instruct the pupils to read the material over silently before reading the material aloud.

    If a pupil will not read aloud in these practice groups or evidences a severe difficulty with this skill, have the pupil begin by practicing alone with a tape recorder that only he or she will listen to initially. You might listen next, and then have a small group of pupils listen. After the pupil is comfortable with hearing himself or herself read aloud via a tape recording, begin to phase in live performances.

5. **Additional suggestions.** Consider using a shaping procedure with this skill. Listed below are several behaviors that would be used as a shaping sequence for this skill.

    (a) Reading aloud into a tape recorder while alone.

    (b) Reading silently as tape is played in presence of one person (parent, peer, teacher). (Tape could then be played for two or three persons before going to a live performance.)

    (c) Reading aloud for one person (peer, parent, teacher).

    (d) Reading aloud for two persons.

    (e) Reading aloud for three persons.

    (f) Reading aloud for three persons at normal rate of speech.

    (g) Reading aloud for three persons, loudly enough to be heard by all and at a normal rate.

    (h) Reading aloud for three persons, loudly enough to be heard, at a normal rate, and pausing for punctuation.

    (i) Reading aloud for three persons, loudly enough to be heard, at a normal rate, pausing for punctuation, and holding body still.

Code: S-TR-PF-0004-L1-Ir

TEACHING STRATEGY

Objective: When required, the student will willingly read aloud in a small group of three or four other students, without signs of excessive nervousness or fear.

Social Reinforcement

1. **Reinforce target student verbally when he or she willingly reads aloud when asked.** When praising the student, be specific enough that he or she understands why you are pleased, increasing the likelihood that the behavior will be repeated. "Martin, you read so well! Thank you." "Barbara, you seem to enjoy reading. That makes me happy." "Sidney, I like to hear you read." "Allison, you did a good job with that hard paragraph."

2. **Provide cues for target student.** Praise students who are willing to read. Also, gently coax target student and promptly reinforce for responding. Make sure the material is within his or her mastery level.

3. **If the desired behavior is not produced through social reinforcement, try pairing praise with a tangible reinforcer such as a token backed up with something you know is desirable and effective.** The tangible reinforcement should be temporary, used only until the behavior is firmly established.

Code: S-TR-PF-0004-L1-Ic

TEACHING STRATEGY

Objective: When required, the student will willingly read aloud in a small group of three or four other students, without signs of excessive nervousness or fear.

Contingency Management

1. **A contingency contract for a student who is hesitant or fearful of reading aloud may initially need to involve providing materials with which he or she can have some success, requiring that he or she read only small amounts aloud to the group, and providing time to practice alone or with a tape recorder.** Establish criteria such as:
    (a) The student reads willingly.
    (b) The student reads clearly at an appropriate voice level.
    (c) The student reads at an appropriate pace.

2. **Plan reinforcement.**

3. **State the contingency.** If you agree to read to a small group when asked, you will be rewarded. Establish criteria to fit the student involved.

4. **During reading sessions observe those students who willingly agree to take their turn to read aloud, and reward them accordingly.**

5. **Example.** Ariel was a good student in Mr. Land's third grade class. She read quickly, accurately, and with comprehension. She would eagerly read to the teacher when asked. However, when asked to read aloud in her small

reading group, she would often refuse or at least hesitate excessively and have to be coaxed. When she finally did agree to read, she did not read with the fluency she demonstrated when reading to the teacher. Mr. Land felt that Ariel had some fear of being criticized by the group for her reading, partly because she had very high standards for herself. He suspected that she also enjoyed the process of being coaxed. Mr. Land decided to contract with Ariel that when Ariel read aloud willingly when asked, she would be permitted to assist in grading the reading worksheets and placing the stars on the class chart. He gave the reward initially for reading without being coaxed. Later, he built in requirements having to do with the quality of the reading.

Skill:	To read aloud before a large group or the entire class. **S-TR-PF-0006-L1**
Objective:	When required, the student willingly reads aloud in a large group (seven or more) or before the entire class, without signs of excessive nervousness or fear.
Assessment:	Assess from previous knowledge of student or through direct observation using the <u>Social Behavior Assessment Inventory</u>.

Code: S-TR-PF-0006-L1-Im

TEACHING STRATEGY

Objective: When required, the student willingly reads aloud in a large group (seven or more) or before the entire class, without signs of excessive nervousness or fear.

Introduction: In many classes, reading aloud before a large group or the entire class may not be a requirement. When it is, the teacher should make sure that reading material provided is within the student's mastery level. The teacher should also be sure that the student has mastered S-TR-PF-0004 before proceeding with teaching this skill.

Social Modeling

1. **Set the stage.** Begin by reading a short story to the entire class (seven or more pupils). The story selected should be of interest to all pupils. It need not be short enough to be read in one period. The story may be broken down into several segments to be read over a period of days. The reading sessions should be of a duration commensurate with the attention span of the class. After the story is completed, lead a short discussion of the story content. Then discuss the reasons for reading before a large group. Some possible reasons include:

   (a) To share themes, stories, and reports written by the student himself.

   (b) To act out a play that has been assigned in class.

   (c) To gain confidence in speaking before a group of one's peers.

   (d) To share specific material with the whole group at the same time for discussion purposes.

There undoubtedly are other reasons why a teacher may want pupils to read aloud. Each teacher should state his or her specific reasons to the class.

2. **Identify the specific steps.** When asked to read orally to your teacher and classmates, remember to:
   (a) Speak loudly enough to be heard by all in the room.
   (b) Remain still so your movements won't distract the listeners.
   (c) Read at a normal rate of speed.
   (d) Use tone of voice in sentences according to punctuation.
   (e) Occasionally look up from reading material in the direction of the audience .
   (f) Pause appropriately according to punctuation.

3. **Model the behavior.** Select a short passage of appropriate interest level for the class and read it orally to the class. For emphasis and clarity, you may want to demonstrate correct oral reading and incorrect oral reading. Ask the students to identify the elements of the correctly modeled behavior. This can be done by dividing the passage into sections and pausing after each section to ask, "What behaviors did you observe that were appropriate oral reading behaviors?"

   Note: Items 2(d) and 2(f) above require a tone of voice and pauses appropriate to punctuation. These cannot be observed unless copies of the reading passage are provided to the pupils.

4. **Practice the behavior.** Reading materials at each pupil's mastery level of reading skills will need to be provided for the practice activity. Each pupil should be given an opportunity to read the passage silently and to practice reading aloud in small groups before he or she is required to read to the class. When the students have practiced in small groups, they may be directed to demonstrate their new skills by reading the same material to the whole class. The length of the reading passage should be short initially, and gradually increased. Remember to reinforce the student for specific oral reading behaviors.

5. **Additional suggestions.**
   (a) A shaping procedure may be helpful for specific individuals. (See S-TR-PF-0004-L1-lm, No. 5-a.)
   (b) Some pupils may be able to begin by reading passages over the public address system and then be phased into reading before the class.

Code: S-TR-PF-0006-L1-lr

TEACHING STRATEGY

Objective: When required, the student willingly reads aloud in a large group (seven or more) or before the entire class, without signs of excessive nervousness or fear.

Social Reinforcement

1. **Reinforce the target student verbally with smiles, gestures, and facial expressions when he or she willingly reads to a large group.** Direct

attention to the specific behavior. "August, we all enjoyed your reading to us. Thank you." "Otto, you really did a good job! I like to hear you read." "Marie, thank you for volunteering to read to the class. I like that."

2. **Provide cues for target student.** Praise other students who read to the class.

3. **If the student is exceptionally reluctant to participate, try pairing the social reinforcement with something tangible that the student likes and will willingly work for.** Once the behavior becomes more firmly established the tangible reinforcer can be phased out, and the social reinforcement alone should sustain the desired behavior.

Code: S-TR-PF-0006-L1-Ic

TEACHING STRATEGY

Objective: When required, the student willingly reads aloud in a large group (seven or more) or before the entire class, without signs of excessive nervousness or fear.

Contingency Management

1. **It is essential that the reading material a reluctant student is required to read orally before a large group be within his or her mastery level.** Initially, small amounts of reading should be required and opportunities for practice before a small group should be provided. The task should be presented to the student in specific observable terms. For example, "When reading before the class, speak loudly and distinctly, read at a comfortable, smooth pace without long delays, stand erect and still, use a tone of voice appropriate to the punctuation, and look up from the reading material occasionally."

2. **Plan reinforcement.**

3. **State the contingency.** When you read the material that I designate aloud in a large group, you will be rewarded. State amount and type of reinforcement. Establish more specific criteria to fit the individual student.

4. **Watch for the target behaviors during oral reading sessions.** Reinforce specific behaviors when they occur using praise and the agreed-upon reward.

5. **Example.** Ms. Cook had a great deal of difficulty persuading Reggie to take his turn to read orally to the class. When Reggie did read, it was very difficult to understand him, since he mumbled, fidgeted around, and displayed overt signs of nervousness, e.g., shaking hands and quivering voice. Ordinarily, Reggie is not nervous or fidgety, so Ms. Cook concluded that the oral reading activity was precipitating Reggie's nervous behavior. Ms. Cook decided to make a contingency contract with Reggie. Together they decided that when Reggie read orally without hesitation and without complaining, he would be given a note to take home to his mother stating that he had performed well. By the end of one week, Reggie was reading without coaxing. In addition to the note, Ms. Cook was sure to praise Reggie's appropriate behavior when he read aloud.

She now met with Reggie and changed the contract to, "When you read orally in a loud voice and stand still, you will be given a note to take home." Ms. Cook asked Reggie to practice reading the specific material at home the night before it was to be ready in class. Initially, she asked Reggie to read only a few lines. Gradually, the amount to be read orally was increased until it was equivalent to the rest of the class. At this point, Ms. Cook explained to Reggie she would be sending notes home just once a week. Eventually, Ms. Cook no longer found the notes necessary. She maintained the behavior with social reinforcement in class.

Skill:	To make a report before a small group. **S-TR-PF-0008-L2**
Objective:	Student makes a report before a small group of three or four classmates, without signs of excessive nervousness or fear.
Assessment:	Assess from previous knowledge of student or through direct observation using the <u>Social Behavior Assessment Inventory</u>.

Code: S-TR-PF-0008-L2-Im

TEACHING STRATEGY

Objective: Student makes a report before a small group of three or four classmates, without signs of excessive nervousness or fear.

Social Modeling

1. **Meet with the class to talk about how to give reports in front of other people.** Involve the class in talking about whether they like to give oral reports or not and why some people feel nervous or afraid when they give a report. Talk about the fact that it is very common to feel nervous and that the nervousness is often related to a fear of saying or doing something wrong and then being criticized or laughed at. It may be necessary to stress that other people's opinions should not matter as much as they often do and that others often make mistakes, too. Talk about qualities of a good oral report. Recognize students who make good contributions to the discussion.

2. **Identify specific behaviors to be modeled.** When asked to make a report to a small group of classmates remember:

   (a) Stand up straight.

   (b) Speak directly to us.

   (c) Speak in a loud and clear voice.

3. **Model the behavior.** You may want to have an experienced, older student demonstrate the proper way to give an oral report. Ask the students to identify the elements of the modeled behavior. Recognize those who give good responses.

4. **Provide opportunity for practice.** Direct the students to form small groups and practice giving oral reports to each other. You may want to let them develop their own topics for reports or select a topic of particular interest

from their "Weekly Readers" or the newspaper, or a list of simple topics might be provided. The members of the group should be instructed to watch for things the speaker does well and provide comments only on good aspects of the report. Reinforce the speaker for standing straight, speaking clearly, appearing relaxed, or for making efforts in this direction. Reinforce the other group members who make positive observations. Students who have particular trouble with oral reports may need to start by presenting only one or two sentences in front of just one or two people, gradually increasing the size of the presentation and the size of the audience. Reinforcement for succeeding in small steps will encourage the student to make larger efforts. Making oral reports also involves, at times, the use of outlines, cue cards, and other props. Students should be helped to develop and use the devices.

5. **Maintain the behavior through reinforcement.**

Code: S-TR-PF-0008-L2-Ir

TEACHING STRATEGY

Objective: Student makes a report before a small group of three or four classmates, without signs of excessive nervousness or fear.

Social Reinforcement

1. **Praise the student verbally by name and with smiles and nods when he or she makes an oral report.** Make your praise specific. "Tammy, that was a very interesting report." "Joan, you remembered to stand up straight and speak clearly. You are getting good at speaking to a group." Make praise appropriate to the needs of the student. Some students may need praise and encouragement for very small efforts.

2. **Provide cues for target student.** Recognize aspects of reports other students give. Provide encouraging gestures, smiles, and nods to target student when it is his or her turn. Various kinds of prompts may be provided, such as, cue cards, outlines to follow, gestures suggesting a louder voice, cards with a smiling face held up when the student is making an effort in the right direction. If the student is fearful of negative feedback from other students, arrange in advance to have some students smile and nod in an approving way while the target student gives the report.

3. **If the student is shy or otherwise reluctant to report, it will probably be necessary to pair a more tangible reinforcer with the social reinforcement to increase the desired behavior.** You may want to pair the smiles, nods, etc., with a token, star, checkmark, etc. that may be exchanged for something valuable to the student.

Code: S-TR-PF-0008-L2-Ic

TEACHING STRATEGY

Objective: Student makes a report before a small group of three or four classmates, without signs of excessive nervousness or fear.

Contingency Management

1. **Present the task in observable terms.** When asked to make an oral report:
   - (a) Stand up straight.
   - (b) Speak directly to the group.
   - (c) Speak clearly in a voice that is appropriate.
2. **Plan reinforcement.**
3. **State the contingency.** When you make an oral report to a small group, you will be rewarded. Specify criteria for evaluating the report, as well as the type and amount of reward.
4. **When appropriate, in conjunction with regular group work or unit study, direct the students to prepare short reports on their study topic.** Provide opportunities for the students to practice their reports within small groups. Criteria for reward will vary according to the needs of the student. A student who is fearful of making oral reports may be rewarded initially for a report of one or two sentences delivered to a small group of close friends. The criterion may gradually be changed to a more lengthy report delivered to a larger audience. Some students may initially be allowed to read reports from their seats, gradually working toward giving reports standing up in front of the class with an outline or cue cards. Observe students when presenting reports in small groups and reward those who meet the individual criteria set up for them.
5. **Example.** Veikko is from Finland. He has only been in this country for one year. He speaks English very well and is able to participate in all activities in Ms. DuPuy's class. As a culminating activity in a unit study, Ms. DuPuy required each child to make an oral report on his project. Veikko told Ms. DuPuy that he would not make a report to his group because he was afraid. Ms. DuPuy decided to contract with Veikko to help him overcome his fear of speaking to a group. She told him that if he would agree to make the report, he would be permitted to practice his report beforehand with the teacher, and afterward he could stay in the room and eat lunch with her. Interaction with Ms. DuPuy is reinforcing to Veikko, and he readily agreed to those terms.

Skill:	To make a report before a large group or the entire class. **S-TR-PF-0010-L2**
Objective:	Student makes a report before a large group (seven or more) or the entire class, without signs of excessive nervousness or fear.
Assessment:	Assess from previous knowledge of student or through direct observation using the <u>Social Behavior Assessment Inventory</u>.

Code: S-TR-PF-0010-L2-Im

TEACHING STRATEGY

Objective: Student makes a report before a large group (seven or more) or the entire class, without signs of excessive nervousness or fear.

Social Modeling

1. **Set the stage.**
   (a) Begin a discussion by asking:
      (1) "Will someone tell me where they saw or heard someone make a report or speech?"
      (2) "Who watched TV last night? Who watched ____?" (Fill in the blank with an example of an oral report given on TV.)
   (b) Explain to the class that there are times when it is appropriate to give oral reports to the entire class; for example, when a pupil has just returned from a trip to an historical site, he or she could report to the class.

2. **Identify the specific steps.**
   (a) Prepare a report outline (written if pupils have the skills, taped if pupils who cannot write).
   (b) Speak slowly and clearly, following the outline.
   (c) Speak directly to the class.
   (d) Hold body still except when using gestures related to report content.
   (e) Speak loudly enough to be heard in the back of the room, but softly enough that it is not heard in the next room.

3. **Model the behavior.** You or an older student may model the behavior. If an older student is used, he or she should practice with you before speaking to the class. When the skill is modeled, have the class make verbal observations about the behaviors they observe. The model must be sure to demonstrate all of the correct behaviors. Student comments will indicate whether they perceive the specific behaviors for giving oral reports. Be sure to praise correct observations. For example, say, "Julius, your observation about my speaking slowly was excellent."

4. **Practice the behavior.** To give each child an opportunity to practice before the class, ask the pupils to prepare an oral report on a topic that is simple, general, and interesting to them, such as, pets, community helpers, classroom jobs, my favorite TV show, our class project. The topic will depend on the level of the class.

   Although it is easier to identify what a student is doing wrong and provide correction, it is important for you to emphasize positive aspects of the student's talk and prompt other students to do the same. If a portable videotape camera is available, videotape feedback where you and the student and can watch and critique performance can be effective. The student can identify behaviors he or she whould like to improve and can practice those behaviors. Similarly, audiotape feedback can be effective in helping a student determine when he or she is speaking clearly and in an appropriate tone of voice.

5. **Recruitment.**
   (a) You may prepare and present certificates for making an oral report.
   (b) The teacher should review each student's talk, reinforcing all positive behaviors.
   (c) Special bonus credit for grades could be given for making oral reports.

6. **Additional suggestions.**
   (a) If video and audio taping equipment is available, a portion of the classroom can be set aside for the student to review his or her oral report.
   (b) Practice in this skill can be accomplished by having students make reports on academic subjects.
   (c) For the pupil who can give an oral report to a small group, tape record (videotape is preferable, it if is available) the pupil giving an oral report to a small group. Play this tape in a large group with the target pupil present. If the target pupil does not want to be present when his or her tape is played, honor the request.

   After the tape has been played in the large group, request that the same report be given live. If the student will not do so, begin a shaping procedure to increase the size of the group for the target pupil to present.

Code: S-TR-PF-0010-L2-Ir

TEACHING STRATEGY

Objective: Student makes a report before a large group (seven or more) or the entire class, without signs of excessive nervousness or fear.

Social Reinforcement

1. **Use social reinforcement when student willingly makes an oral report to a large group or to the entire class.** Call attention to specific behaviors. "Andy, I really liked your report. You speak very well." "Michael, thank you for reporting to us. We all enjoy listening to you." "Jane, I could hear you at the back of the room very well."
2. **Provide cues for the target student.** Recognize aspects of reports given by other students who make oral reports. Encourage the target student verbally and with smiles, nods, gestures. Reinforce for responding to your cues.

Code: S-TR-PF-0010-L2-Ic

TEACHING STRATEGY

Objective: Student makes a report before a large group (seven or more) or the entire class, without signs of excessive nervousness or fear.

Contingency Management

1. **State the task for the students in specific, observable terms.** When asked to give an oral report, speak loudly and clearly, stand straight and tall, and look at the audience.
2. **Plan reinforcement.**
3. **State the contingency.** If the student meets the criteria established for giving an oral report, he or she will be rewarded. (Criteria will vary according to the performance level of the particular student. Some

students may need to be rewarded for any small effort. Others can be required to meet stringent criteria.)

4. **Provide an opportunity for oral presentations, for example, book reports or reports on projects.** Reinforce students who give oral reports, meeting the individual criteria that are appropriate for them. For those with difficulty, provide small group practice before they make presentations to the whole class.

5. **Example.** Honey was frightened to speak before her whole class. Mr. Reeves frequently required oral reporting in conjunction with his teaching units. As the year progressed, Honey's fear seemed to get more intense, until finally, during a report, she started to cry. Mr. Reeves decided it was time to intervene. One day before school started Mr. Reeves noticed that Honey was in an unusually good mood, and decided that would be a good time to talk to her about her fear of speaking to the group. He set up a time when Honey could meet with him and practice giving a report. He made it a pleasant occasion for her with cookies and milk. He was careful to be very positive about her efforts. He repeated the practice session, asking Honey to bring two or three friends and again provided milk and cookies. When she became comfortable in the practice sessions, he made a contract with her that if she would give the talk to the whole class, she could earn extra points in her grade book and a treat for the entire class. He prompted her friends to smile and nod encouragingly to her during her talk.

QUALITY OF WORK

S-TR-QW-0002-L1-S	To turn in neat papers.
S-TR-QW-0004-L2-S	To accept correction of school work.
S-TR-QW-0006-L2-S	To make use of teacher's corrections to improve work.
S-TR-QW-0008-L2-S	To go back over work to check for errors.

Skill:	To turn in neat papers. **S-TR-QW-0002-L1**
Objective:	Student's work is generally neat, papers are uncrumpled, papers have few stray marks, and writing is unsmudged.
Assessment:	Assess from previous knowledge of student or through direct observation using the <u>Social Behavior Assessment Inventory</u>.

Code: S-TR-QW-0002-L1-Im

TEACHING STRATEGY

Objective: Student's work is generally neat, papers are uncrumpled, papers have few stray marks, and writing is unsmudged.

Social Modeling

1. **Set the stage.** Prepare a bulletin board on which you will post "neat papers"—i.e., papers that are clean and flat and that only have writing and other marks that are essential to the assigned task. Explain the bulletin board to the class. Say, "Beginning today, we have a new neighborhood in class. It is called 'Neat Street.' Each morning, I will post neat papers from the day before on 'Neat Street.' A neat paper looks like this (hold up an example of a neat paper you have prepared or a paper of one of the pupils). This paper is clean, flat, and smooth and has only writing and marks that are part of the assignment." Ask, "Why is this a neat paper?" Hold up a second neat paper. (Student response.) "Excellent, because it has no stray marks, and it is flat and smooth."

2. **Identify the specific steps.** (This step follows Step 1 immediately.) Ask, "What do you do to have a neat paper?" The following steps should be brought out in discussion. If pupils do not mention these, point them out.

   (a) Place paper flat on desk top to avoid crumpling.

   (b) Hold paper in place with one hand to prevent it from moving when writing with the other hand.

   (c) To prevent smudging, do not rub hand or arm across the paper.

   (d) Cross out mistakes with a single line or erase carefully.

   (e) If a paper is too messy, ask for another sheet of paper and begin again.

3. **Model the behavior.** Begin to model the five specific steps for writing a neat paper. Sit at your desk or a large table where all the students can watch and comment. Review the steps outlined above by asking questions. For example:

(a) "Am I holding the paper correctly, Johnny?"

(b) "Did I smudge the paper, Emmy?"

(c) "Is that a neat erasure, Nancy?"

4. **Practice the behavior.** After discussing the model paper and making sure each student has given verbal feedback as to how a neat paper can be prepared, have the pupils do a regular class assignment. Walk around the room, stopping at each desk to praise (so that other students may hear) each student who follows or approximates the neat paper format. Example:

(a) "That's the correct way to hold the paper, Billy,"

(b) "My, that's a clean paper, Tommy. I don't see a smudge on it."

5. **Maintain the behavior through reinforcement.** Reinforce the student and hold up a paper to show the class. For example:

(a) "Class, see how neatly Billy did his paper? His paper goes on 'Neat Street.'"

(b) Other papers should be displayed on the board when they meet criteria.

6. **Additional suggestions.**

(a) Draw an illustration of a correct paper on the board and leave it there to remind students.

(b) Since some students may have trouble doing a neat paper correctly at first, reinforce successive approximations to the desired criteria.

(c) Contingency contracting (e.g., points for neat papers) may have to be arranged to maintain neat paperwork for some pupils over time.

Code: S-TR-QW-0002-L1-Ir

TEACHING STRATEGY

Objective: Student's work is generally neat, papers are uncrumpled, papers have few stray marks, and writing is unsmudged.

Social Reinforcement

1. **Identify by name and recognize the student when he or she has handed in a neat paper.** Be specific in praising. "Maggie, what a neat paper!" "Louisa, you kept your paper neat and clean." "Mark, I'm glad you were able to keep your paper from getting wrinkled."

2. **Provide cues for the target students by recognizing other students who have neat papers.** Display and talk about papers that are clean and neatly done so students can understand what is expected. If necessary, provide tangible reinforcement along with praise for papers that are neat.

Code: S-TR-QW-0002-L1-Ic

TEACHING STRATEGY

Objective: Student's work is generally neat, papers are uncrumpled, papers have few stray marks, and writing is unsmudged.

Contingency Management

1. **State the task in observable terms.** The student will turn in neat papers that are not crumpled and have few stray marks and smudges. (Show the students examples of neat papers.)

2. **Plan reinforcement.**

3. **State the contingencies of reinforcement.** Each time you hand in a neat paper (i.e., uncrumpled, unmarked, and unsmudged), you will receive the agreed-upon reward.

4. **Give the student regularly assigned work to do and have him or her hand the papers in when finished.** Reward if they are neat, uncrumpled, unmarked, and unsmudged.

5. **Example.** Tammy's papers were consistently messy, and Ms. Luckey decided to contract with her to do neater work. She told Tammy what she wanted her to do and that each time she turned in a neat paper, she would receive a gold star on the class performance chart. Ms. Luckey made up a check list for Tammy to do a paper over if necessary. In addition to praise and gold stars, Ms. Luckey wrote positive comments on the neat papers and put them on the bulletin board.

Skill:	To accept correction of school work. **S-TR-QW-0004-L2**
Objective:	When receiving correction of school work, student will respond with verbal affirmation when it is appropriate and/or will respond without signs of anger or dejection.
Assessment:	Assess from previous knowledge of student or through direct observation using the <u>Social Behavior Assessment Inventory</u>.

Code: S-TR-QW-0004-L2-Im

TEACHING STRATEGY

Objective: When receiving correction of school work, student will respond with verbal affirmation when it is appropriate and/or will respond without signs of anger or dejection.

Introduction: This skill is intended for individual students having a problem with accepting corrections. Although "setting the stage" can be done subtly with a small group, it is not advisable to discuss mistakes at length in a group situation. The following **teacher behavior** should be analyzed prior to indicating a strategy with an individual student.

(a) Demonstrate a matter-of-fact and polite reaction to mistakes. This should encourage students to take it in stride if their work needs to be checked over.

(b) It is an essential prerequisite that the teachers' verbal corrections are given in a calm, helpful tone and preceded by a positive comment. For example, "I'm glad you got this paper completed. Now I think we need to look at this problem again." "You did a nice job. You need to try again on just this one part." The student must **not** be made to feel threatened.

399

(c) When working on a one-to-one basis, the teacher may point out that the student needs to respond to his or her comments and corrections. This may enable her to re-explain the assignment.

(d) It must be taken into account that the number of correct responses needs to be greater than the number of errors. If frequent mistakes and corrections are encountered, the student may be too frustrated and may be reacting to work that is too difficult at this time.

Social Modeling

1. **Set the stage.**

   (a) Focus on appropriate ways to respond to criticism by setting up a situation in which you make an obvious error and then acknowledge the student's correction. For example, doing a lesson at the board, you may write and say, "2 + 2 = 3." When corrected, say, "Oops, I made a mistake," or "Thanks, I'd better fix that," or "Thank you for pointing that out; that gives me trouble sometimes."

   When using such a contrived situation, be sure to make an obvious error. This is not the time to be tricky. You may want to use this technique with the whole class on several occasions before using it as a referent to initiate a strategy with an individual child.

   (b) An alternative approach may be to have a poster or bulletin board which has caricatures with the caption, "Oops, I made a mistake!" Use the poster as a stimulus to discuss the fact that we all make mistakes and that no big deal should be made of it. Ask questions, e.g., "What do you see in the picture? Do you know what this says? What do you think the student will do now that he or she knows he or she made a mistake? Why is it good to admit that we make mistakes? Why is it important for our friends to admit to mistakes?"

2. **Identify the specific steps.** After setting the stage as in "a" or "b" above, help the child review and list the steps involved in accepting criticism.

   (a) Listen to the correction.

   (b) Question the person if the comments are not understood, or politely ask for a restatement.

   (c) Acknowledge his or her comment by "OK," "Thanks," or "Oops."

3. **Model the behavior.** Rather than focusing on individual mistakes of students, repeat at the board the contrived situation in which you will make an error. Cue a student by saying, "I'm going to put a number sentence on the board. (2 + 3 = 8) John, will you check it for me?" When the student corrects you, acknowledge his or her comment with "OK," "Thank you," "I'd better fix it," and correct your mistake. Review the steps you followed in response to John's comment: "Let's see, did I remember to:

   (a) Listen?

   (b) Ask questions if needed?

   (c) Let him know I heard and understood?"

Caution: Never set up a situation in which a student is made to demonstrate an error.

4. **Practice the behavior.** Practicing the behavior should be on a one-to-one basis. Give each student who needs this skill an opportunity to react to your corrections during the course of the day. Before beginning the correction, tell the student that he or she should practice the skill of accepting correction.

5. **Reinforcement.** Along with discussion and practicing the behavior on a one-to-one basis, set up a contract or token system for self-monitoring of the behavior. For example, "Johnny, you will keep this paper in your desk. When you follow all three steps in response to corrections I make on your work, you may fill in one happy face."

   This must be watched carefully. Use this as a monitoring device and pair it with positive comments, such as, "I like the way you admitted your mistake," or "Thank you for being polite about my comments." Discontinue the close counting of responses as soon as the frequency of behavior increases. Otherwise, you run the risk of **over focusing** on mistakes.

6. **Additional suggestions.** Provide cues for the target student:
   (a) Before correcting the target student's school work, praise aloud a student, within the target student's hearing, for accepting correction of work appropriately.
   (b) When correction of school work is done in writing, provide a written cue to the target student, e.g., "Respond appropriately to correction."

Code: S-TR-QW-0004-L2-Ir

TEACHING STRATEGY

Objective: When receiving correction of school work, student will respond with verbal affirmation when it is appropriate and/or will respond without signs of anger or dejection.

Social Reinforcement

1. **Identify a student who has responded to correction of school work with verbal affirmation when appropriate and/or without signs of anger or dejection.** Recognize specific behaviors, e.g., "Connie, I'm glad you accepted my correcting your work without getting mad or unhappy;" "Louise, I'm glad you didn't stop smiling when I corrected your spelling paper. That's very grown up of you."

2. **Provide cues for the target student.**
   (a) Before correcting the target student's school work, praise aloud a student, within the target student's hearing, for accepting correction of work appropriately.
   (b) When correction of school work is done in writing, provide a written cue to the target student, e.g., "Respond appropriately to correction."

3. **If necessary, pair tangible reinforcement with social reinforcement to elicit the appropriate response.**

Code: S-TR-QW-0004-L2-Ic

TEACHING STRATEGY

Objective: When receiving correction of school work, student will respond with verbal affirmation when it is appropriate and/or will respond without signs of anger or dejection.

Contingency Management

1. **Discuss the desired behavior with the student.** Outline the appropriate responses to correction, including saying yes or some other verbal affirmation to indicate that the student has heard, asking questions if the student does not understand the correction, and responding without anger or dejection.
2. **Plan reinforcement.**
3. **State the contingency.** Each time you accept correction of your work without getting angry and with appropriate verbal response, you will be rewarded. Specify type and amount of reinforcement.
4. **When correcting the student's work in the course of normal academic activity, observe the student's reaction.** If the student reacts in an appropriate fashion, deliver the agreed-upon reinforcement.
5. **Example.** Billy often cried when his work was corrected. Ms. Charles discussed with him the need to accept correction without becoming unhappy or mad. She explained that everyone makes mistakes and that she expects all of her students to make errors. She told Billy that each time he accepted correction of his work appropriately, he would receive five extra minutes of time at the interest center of his choice. This contingency was kept in force for three weeks. After three weeks, Billy was responding to correction of his school work without crying, by making needed changes, and/or by asking questions. At this point, Ms. Charles began using only social reinforcement to maintain the behavior.

Skill:	To make use of teacher's corrections to improve work. **S-TR-QW-0006-L2**
Objective:	When student receives a corrected piece of work from the teacher, he or she will redo the work, incorporating the teacher's corrections.
Assessment:	Assess from previous knowledge of student or through direct observation using the <u>Social Behavior Assessment Inventory</u>.

Code: S-TR-QW-0006-L2-Im

TEACHING STRATEGY

Objective: When student receives a corrected piece of work from the teacher, he or she will redo the work incorporating the teacher's corrections.

Social Modeling

1. **Set the stage.** Set aside 15 mintues for Steps 1 and 2. The rest of the strategy can be done a second day. (This strategy will be most meaningful if used immediately preceding the rewriting of corrected papers.) Make up two mock papers for each of two conditions: original student paper with teacher corrections (A1) and redone student paper with teacher comments (A2). Prepare the mock papers on "newsprint" so that all of the pupils may view them.

   After displaying samples A1 and A2, say, "These themes were handed in for corrections. The corrections were marked and passed back to the pupils so they could do the assignment again." Then say, "This is Chico's second paper." (Display sample B1 directly below A1, as you continue talking.) "Look at this paper and compare it with the first paper. Tell me what you see." (Student responses. Display sample B2.) "Did Martha do a good job of correcting her errors?" (Student response.) "Now look at Chico's paper. Tell me what you see." (Student response.) "Why is it a good idea to make corrections on your papers when the teacher marks your mistakes?" (Student responses may include: "You'll get a bad grade if you don't." "The teacher will think you are lazy." "You will learn more by correcting your mistakes." "So you can get a better grade.") "Very good reason, Lawanda."

2. **Identify the specific steps.** Say, "These are steps that we take when redoing work and using the teacher's corrections:

   (a) When teacher hands you your paper say, 'Thank you.'

   (b) Read over the paper completely.

   (c) Ask the teacher any necessary questions.

   (d) Redo the paper.

   (e) Hand in redone assignment with teacher corrections made."

   Have the pupils repeat and/or paraphrase these steps to be sure that they remember what you said. List the steps on the chalkboard as the pupils repeat them.

3. **Model the behavior.** Present a fictitious theme written and then corrected. (This need only be two or three sentences long, written in blue or black magic marker, with corrections done in red. Include a few misspellings, absent punctuation, and incorrect use of capitals. Modify as needed for your age group, being sure that corrections and skills are well within mastery level for modeling purposes.

   Say, "This is Jane's paper that was returned for her to copy over." (Be sure Jane is fictitious. Do **not** use a real student's paper to model corrections.) "I'm going to pretend that I'm Jane copying my paper. You watch carefully and tell me afterward what Jane did correctly. Be sure to look for the way Jane acts when the teacher gives her the paper, how quickly she gets to work, what she does while she's recopying the paper, what the paper looks like when she's finished, and what she does with the paper when it's finished."

   Ask a student to be the teacher, hand you the paper, and say, "Rewrite this paper and make the needed corrections." Follow the established proce-dure—either taking a clean piece of paper from desk or going to central location for this paper. Use chalkboard as desk so class can see corrections being made as you do so (use a magic marker—blue or black—as the writing implement). Do with the corrected paper what you want the students to do with theirs. For example, thank the teacher for the paper, return to seat, read over the paper. (Have tape recording of the paper which you can plan; tell the pupils that the tape is what you are thinking. The tape should contain statements, e.g., "Bill should have been capitalized because it is a proper name.") Rewrite the paper (on chalkboard), making corrections, and hand it in."

4. **Practice the behavior.** "I'm going to give each of you one of your papers that needs to be rewritten. I'm going to be on the lookout for students who are following the rules we've listed on the board."

5. **Reinforcement.** As students are working, move quietly around the room complimenting each on the rule being followed. For example, (in a whisper) "Good John, I'm glad to see you are reading through the assignment before starting to write."

6. **Additional suggestions.**
   (a) Hold a class discussion first, listing proper procedures; then have two children role-play the situation. Afterward, have the group name correct things that happened.
   (b) Class could make a wall chart listing proper behavior to be used.
   (c) Follow-up may be needed on an individual basis. That is, specific students may need help in going over papers while the entire group would not benefit from more time spent on this skill.
   (d) It should be noted that the number of "do over" papers should not exceed the number of acceptable papers. If this is the case, the student may be in need of prerequisite skills, such as completing work neatly and/or correctly the first time. See skill numbers S-TR-CT-0002 through S-TR-CT-0008 and S-TR-QW-0004.

Code: S-TR-QW-0006-L2-Ir

TEACHING STRATEGY

Objective: When student receives a corrected piece of work from the teacher, he or she will redo the work, incorporating the teacher's corrections.

Social Reinforcement

1. **When handing out students' corrected school work, look for the target student to redo his or her work incorporating the corrections.** Praise the target student aloud when he or she exhibits the correct behavior. Use specific phrases, such as, "Margie, I like the way you have redone your spelling paper with the corrections I've made. That is very conscientious." "Rhonda, I'm glad you redid the math assignment with the corrections I've made. You are a very good worker."

2. **Provide cues for the target student.**
   (a) Write "redo with corrections" or an equivalent statement on work handed back to the student.

(b) Praise a student near target student for redoing work incorporating your corrections.

3. **Sometimes a tangible reinforcer needs to be paired with social praise to elicit the desired behavior.** The tangible reinforcer should be phased out as quickly as possible.

Code: S-TR-QW-0006-L2-Ic

TEACHING STRATEGY

Objective: When student receives a corrected piece of work from the teacher, he or she will redo the work, incorporating the teacher's corrections.

Contingency Management

1. **Point out to the student that he or she is required to redo corrected work incorporating the corrections that were made.** Explain that this is a necessary part of learning and that it will help him or her learn the material. Specify the conditions under which the work is to be done.

2. **Plan reinforcement.**

3. **State the contingency to the student.** If you redo corrected work with the corrections made by the teacher, you will receive a reward. Specify type and amount of reinforcement as decided on in Step 2.

4. **During the course of everyday academic work, hand corrected papers back to the student.** If the student redoes the paper, making use of the corrections, reward the student as promised.

5. **Example.** Caroline often does not seem to pay attention to corrections made on her papers. She seems to make the same mistake again and again. Ms. Cole explains to her that she must redo her papers, making the corrections indicated by the teacher. She informs Caroline that for each correctly redone paper she hands back she will receive a gold star on her "Good Work" chart. Caroline has been very anxious to fill up her chart and is grateful for the opportunity to earn stars. Caroline begins to redo her papers and fulfills the requirements of the contingency for two weeks. After this, Ms. Cole increases the requirements to two redone papers for one star. Three weeks later, the contingency is dropped in favor of a social reinforcement strategy.

Code: S-TR-QW-0008-L2-Im

TEACHING STRATEGY

Objective: Student looks over his or her work to check for errors before he or she hands it in.

Social Modeling

1. **Set the stage.** Read students the following story:

WIN A TRIP TO THE MOON

Cape Countdown was having a launch, but this wasn't just any moon launch; it was a special one. There were three astronauts who would be aboard the spacecraft, but someone else would also be going with them. And that someone was the girl or boy who wrote the best essay on "Why I Want to Go to the Moon." Patty and Mark were good friends, and they both decided to write an essay.

The men at the Space Center read all the essays and decided Mark's and Patty's were the best. But only one of them could go to the moon. Finally, they announced the winner; it was Patty. The men at the Space Center said, "We chose Patty's essay as the best, because we could tell she took time to go over her work and correct any of the mistakes she made. She wrote a good essay that was very neat and had all the right spelling and punctuation." Everyone congratulated Patty and hoped her trip to the moon would be great!

2. **Identify the specific steps.** Say, "What things did Patty do to make her essay the winner?" (Student response: "She checked her work before sending it in.") "When she checked her work, what were some of the things she did?" (Student responses will vary considerably depending on skill level. Examples: "She made sure she used capital letters in the correct places." "She corrected all spelling errors." "She made sure she used periods and question marks correctly."

Make a list of specific items to check before handing in papers. The list will need to be appropriate to the mastery level of your students. (Type the list on a ditto and prepare checklists to distribute to your pupils.) Since a different set of standards is applied to math papers, you will need to follow a procedure similar to that outlined in this section for developing a checklist that the pupils may use with their math papers.

3. **Model the behavior.** (If this task is above the mastery level of your pupils, use the same procedure with a different task.) Say, "I have a letter here

(have it written on chart paper and taped on chalkboard so all students can see) which I want all of us to examine."

Suggested letter:

Mr. Johnson,   (This could be the principal or someone else in the building, and the letter would be about something that involved a student recently.)

i would like to thank you for leting me seee the magic show I liket it very much.

Say, "I have already written this letter, and now I need to go back and check for any mistakes I might have made." Go over your letter with the class and make all the necessary corrections. For example, "I forgot to capitalize the word 'I' so I will have to correct this." If corrections cannot be erased and redone neatly, you will have to explain. "My letter doesn't look very neat with everything crossed out, so I will have to write it over, and then I can give it to Mr. Johnson." If time permits, recopy letter and reread it when finished; explain that now you can give it to the principal because you have checked all your work.

4. **Practice the behavior.** Say, "I am going to give you a story that has already been written, and I would like you to check it. Make sure that all the spelling is correct, all the capital letters are correct, and all the periods are where they should be.

Suggested story: "i went to the stor with my mom she bought lots of good food? Tonight we are having my favorite meal. It is chicken and french fries"

The above practice task or a similar one based on student's mastery level can be contrived, or you can use the next regularly scheduled individual assignment as a practice session for this skill. In any case, reminders should be given before beginning subsequent independent work. For example, "Let's remember to check our work before we hand it in. Can anyone remind us of what things to look for?"

5. **Reinforcement.** Play the "Award Winning Work Game." Contract with each student. When the student fulfills the contract, he or she will get a work award. The student could either wear the award or hang it up on a chart. The number of papers would be determined for each student according to the particular work. If Sue has four papers to do and is really sloppy, you might start by having her complete and correct one paper and gradually increase the number.

6. **Additional suggestions.**

    (a) Write comments on their papers to maintain the behavior. For example, "Good work! I'm glad you checked this over."

    (b) Remember—suggestions given here for setting the stage and modeling the behavior must be adapted for the group and/or target student. Be sure examples and practice activities present academic skills at mastery level. Students cannot revise work they cannot do well initially.

    (c) Pupils who have not mastered the prerequisite skills listed below should not be expected to master this one: S-TR-CT-0002-L1-S through S-TR-CT-0008-L2-S and S-TR-QW-0002-L1-S.

Code: S-TR-QW-0008-L2-Ir

TEACHING STRATEGY

Objective: Student looks over his or her work to check for errors before he or she hands it in.

Social Reinforcement

1. **Name and recognize a student when you see him or her looking over his or her work and checking for errors before handing it in.** Recognize specific behavior: "Greg, very good. I see you are checking over your work before handing it in." "Thank you, Louise, for looking for errors before handing your paper in."

2. **Cue checking over work for errors before handing work in by praising aloud a student near the target student for exhibiting this behavior.** Immediately praise target student when he or she checks his or her work for errors before handing it in.

3. **Tangible rewards for papers that are handed in without errors may be necessary.** You may also ask students to check and initial each other's papers. If the work contains no errors, both students are rewarded. Provide a reminder by asking student to write "paper checked" on the bottom of the paper after the student has gone over it.

Code: S-TR-QW-0008-L2-Ic

TEACHING STRATEGY

Objective: Student looks over his or her work to check for errors before he or she hands it in.

Contingency Management

1. **State the task in observable terms.** Before you hand your work in, remember to look over your work and check it for errors.

2. **Plan reinforcement from reinforcement menu.**

3. **State the contingency for reinforcement.** If you look over your work to check for errors before you hand it in, you will be rewarded. Specify type and amount of reinforcement.

4. **In the course of regular academic work, observe the student before he or she hands in his or her assigned work.** If he or she looks over his or her work to check for errors, reward him or her. If you are not able to observe the behavior of checking and correcting the paper, you might reward for a decrease in careless errors in the papers that are handed in.

5. **Example.** Tommy always handed in carelessly done work. Ms. Lynne looked over his papers and showed him where he had made careless errors. She showed him how to check and correct the papers. She then contracted with him to check his work for mistakes before handing it in, with the following contingency: "Tommy, if you check over your work for errors before you hand it in so your papers have fewer errors, you will receive two points toward the class field trip." (One hundred points were needed.) Ms. Lynne observed him working and checked whether he was looking over his

work before handing it in. He received a reward if she observed him checking for errors or if the number of careless errors on his paper was less than before. She kept this contingency in effect until the field trip and then dropped it in favor of social reinforcement.

REFERENCES

Homme, L., Csanyi, A.P., Gonzales, M.A., & Recks, J.R. (1969). *How to use contingency contracting in the classroom.* Champaign, IL: Research Press.

Milburn, J.F. (1974). *Special education and regular class teacher attitudes regarding social behaviors of children: Steps toward the development of a social skills curriculum.* Unpublished doctoral dissertation. Columbus, OH: The Ohio State University.

Stephens, T.M. (1975). *Behavioral approaches in elementary and secondary schools.* Columbus, OH: Charles E. Merrill.

GLOSSARY

Key words and phrases used in this handbook are defined below. The definitions here reflect the meaning intended in this handbook.

Assessment Data: Results from evaluating students' responses in advance of instruction to determine what instruction is needed.

Behavior Rehearsal: Behaviors that are practiced by target students in order to improve their social skills in natural settings.

Consultants: Personnel who provide advice and suggestions to teachers, e.g., psychologists, counselors, supervisors, and building principals.

Contingency Management: An if...then method, where students are told which behaviors will be rewarded. Both the behavior and the reward are specified before the behavior occurs.

Directive Teaching: A system of teaching, consisting of assessing students' academic and social performance, planning instruction based upon the assessment information, implementing the instructional strategies within the plan, and evaluating the effects of instruction.

Evaluation: An assessment of behavior following instruction.

Instructional Strategy: A plan for teaching specific behaviors.

Positive Reinforcement: Any event that is satisfying to the student and increases his or her performance.

Punishment: Any event that reduces the student's performance or behavior.

Reinforcement Strategy: A plan for rewarding students for their performance.

Reinforcer: Any stimulus or event that, when presented, results in an increase in behavior; when withdrawn, it results in a decrease in behavior.

Reward: Any event that is satisfying to the student and increases the probability of the student's continuing or increasing performance.

Social Behavior: Performance that involves others, the self, and/or environmental activities. Social behavior is distinct from academic-type behaviors that are typically taught in schools.

Social Behavior Assessment Inventory: A rating scale used in conjunction with *Social Skills in the Classroom.*

Social Modeling: Ways of learning through observing and imitating others.

Social Reinforcement: Events that increase students' performance. These occur without prior contingencies or contracts but take place following the students' behavior.

Social Skills: Specific responses that are directly observable. These responses comprise the social skills curriculum as distinct from the academic skills curriculum.

Target Students: Pupils for whom observation and instruction are intended.

SOCIAL SKILLS INDEX

Skills are indexed both according to positive skills to be taught and problem behaviors which may be eliminated by teaching the incompatible positive behaviors. Each skill and/or problem has the code numbers of all related skills listed.

415

Criticism,
accepting
S-IP-CC-0012, S-TR-QW-0004, S-TR-QW-0006 . . . . 104, 399, 402
giving
(See Praise, giving)

Cruelty
(See Attitude, toward others; Anger; Consideration of others)

Cursing
(See Name calling)

Daydreaming
S-TR-CD-0006, S-TR-CT-0004, S-TR-OT-0006 (See also Attentiveness) . . . .
. . . . 291, 310, 367

Defeat, accepting
S-IP-OP-0008 175

Defiance
(See Authority)

Democratic behaviors
S-IP-AA-0010, S-IP-PL-0008, S-TR-GA-0006, S-TR-GA-0008 . . . . . . 82, 194, 338, 342

Dependence
(See Independence)

Depression
S-SR-PA-0006, S-SR-PA-0008 . . . . 235, 237

Destructiveness
S-ER-CE-0006, S-ER-CE-0008, S-IP-PR-0006, S-SR-AC-0002 through
S-SR-AC-0006 . . . . 40, 42, 203, 207–214

Directions, following
S-TR-FD-0002 through S-TR-FD-0006 321–330

Disobedience
(See Obedience)

Disorganization
(See Organization)

Disrespectful behavior
(See Respectful behavior)

Hypoactivity

(See Activity level, normal)

Hypersensitivity

S-IP-CC-0002, S-IP-CC-0012, S-TR-GA-0008, S-TR-QW-0004 . . . . . 87, 104, 342, 399

Impatience

(See Patience)

Impressionability

S-SR-EB-0008 223

Impulsivity

S-IP-GA-0004, S-IP-MC-0006, S-IP-OP-0004 (See also Directions, following) . . . . . .
. . . . 110, 156, 171

Inattentiveness

(See Attentiveness)

Inconsideration, of others

(See Consideration of others)

Independence

S-IP-AA-0010, S-SR-EB-0008, S-SR-RB-0010, S-SR-RB-0014, S-SR-SC-0004,
S-TR-CD-0010, S-TR-GA-0010, S-TR-IW-0002 through S-TR-IW-0006 . . . .
. . . . 82, 223, 248, 252, 257, 298, 346, 350–359

Industriousness

S-TR-CT-0006, S-TR-IW-0004, S-TR-OT-0006 . . . . 314, 353, 367

Initiative

S-IP-MC-0014, S-IP-MC-0016, S-IP-PL-0002, S-IP-PL-0004, S-IP-PL-0010,
S-TR-GA-0010, S-TR-IW-0002 . . . . 164, 166, 187, 189, 196, 346, 350

In-seat behavior

S-ER-MO-0004, S-TR-OT-0002 . . . . 62, 360

Insecurity

(See Self-image)

Insolence

(See Authority; Respectful behavior, Self-image)

Interrupting behaviors

(See Conversation; Group participation)

Intolerance

(See Tolerance)

ABOUT THE AUTHOR

Thomas M. Stephens is Professor and Associate Dean, College of Education, The Ohio State University, Columbus, Ohio. Dr. Stephens has been a classroom teacher, a school psychologist, and a teacher educator. An author of numerous journal articles and nine books, he received the 1986 Merrill Teacher Educator of the Year award from the Teacher Education Division of the Council for Exceptional Children. The first edition of *Social Skills in the Classroom* was published by Cedars Press in 1978.